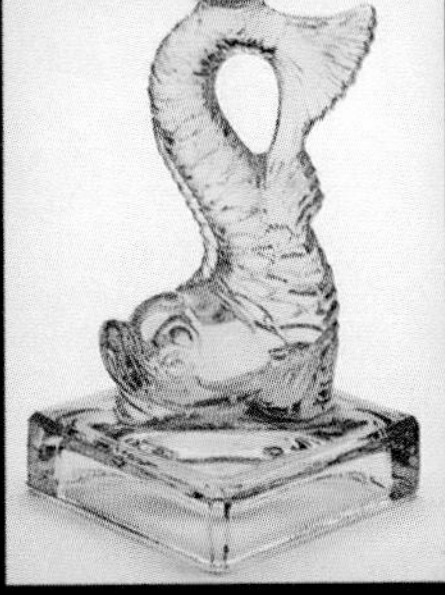

Glass Animals

including

ANIMAL & FIGURAL RELATED ITEMS IDENTIFICATION & VALUES

SECOND EDITION

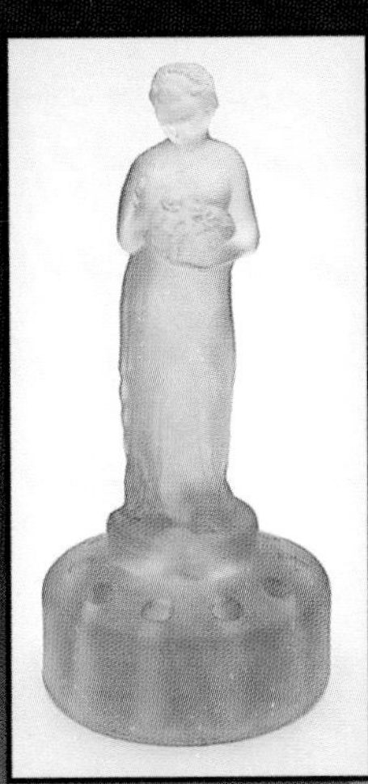

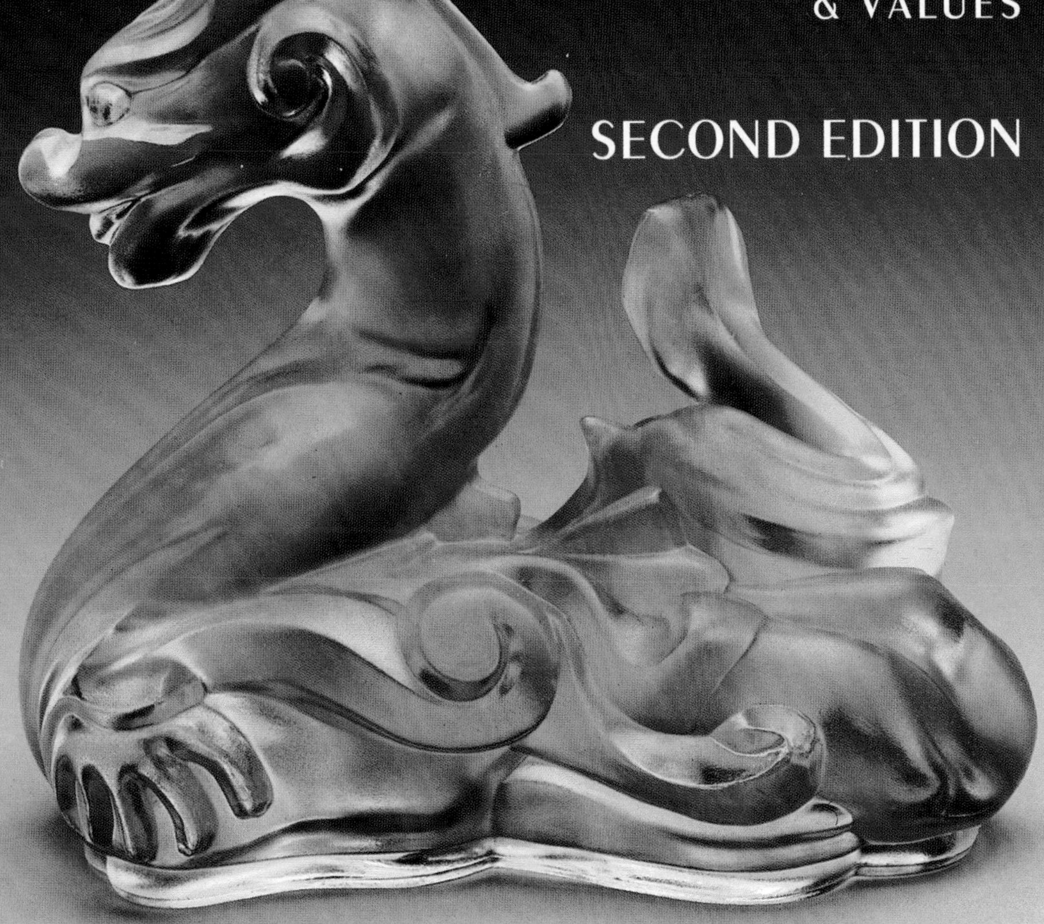

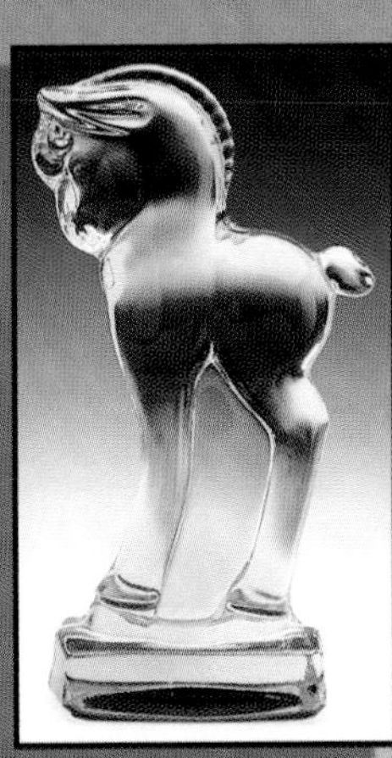

Dick & Pat Spencer

COLLECTOR BOOKS
A Division of Schroeder Publishing Co., Inc.

Front cover, center: Dragon Candleholder, see Plate 222. Left row: Dolphin Candlestick, see Plate 202; Chessie Candy Box, see Plate 88; Rose Lady, see Plate 555; Colt Standing, see Plate 440; Sea Horse Book End, see Plate 734. Bottom row: Bull, see Plate 84B; Dragon Swan, see Plate 226; #443-SJ Swan Janice Line, see Plate 866.

Back cover, top row: Dolphin Comport, see Plate 214; Long Stem Roses, see Plates 367 – 369; Wolfhound, see Plate 178; Swan Handled Pitcher, see Plate 838. Center: Federal Column Book Ends, see Plate 266.

Cover design by Beth Summers
Book design by Terri Hunter

COLLECTOR BOOKS
P.O. Box 3009
Paducah, Kentucky 42002-3009

Dick andPat Spencer
1203 N. Yale
O'Fallon, IL 62269

www.collectorbooks.com

The current values in this book should be used only as a guide. They are not intended to set prices, which vary from one section of the country to another. Auction prices as well as dealer prices vary greatly and are affected by condition as well as demand. Neither the authors nor the publisher assumes responsibility for any losses that might be incurred as a result of consulting this guide.

Contents

Acknowledgments

Our sincere thanks to those who gave of their time and effort, through loaning prized pieces for photography, supplying needed information, helping with pricing, and for just being there in a supportive role.

To Lee Garmon, co-author of the first edition, whose busy schedule prohibited her from co-authoring this edition, a big thanks for finding time to always be there for advice, support, and for just being "Lee."

To Neil and Eddie Unger, unpublished authors in their own right, for sharing their collection, vast knowledge, and their home, we will always be indebted.

To Finis and Lana Riggs who graciously shared their collection for photography, we humbly say "thank you."

Sonny and Maxine Larson
Gary and Sue Clark
Ernie and Shirley Launer
Chip and Diana Humbles
Art and Shirley Moore
Kelly O'Kane
Cindy Arent
Roni Sionakides
Dawn Minicozzi
Bud and Dorothy Hines
Fred and Mary Lou Bohl
Al Ray Zipfel
Brady Boudreaux
J.W. Courter

Tom Wieneman
Terri Farrell
Gene and Cathy Florence
Ken Nicol
Todd Harris
Jim and Beverly Harris
Lynn Welker
Kevin Kiley
Helen Wheely
Bill and Hazel Daniels
Lois Johannes
Norman Woodson
Robert and Mary Kreimer

Thanks to the staff at Collector Books, including the Schroeder family, Charles R. Lynch who took most of the photos, Beth Summers for an outstanding cover, Gail Ashburn, Lisa Stroup, Amy Sullivan, Donna Ballard, Terri Hunter, and Laurie Swick.

Because this is a second edition, and some items were carried forward from the first edition, we would like to reaffirm our "thanks" to those contributors in the first edition.

Neil and Eddie Unger, Fred Bickenheuser, P.J. Rosso, Jr., Lorraine Kovar, Bill and Phyllis Smith, Addie and Everett Miller, Milbra Long, Bob and Sharon Huxford, Dick Green, Gail Krause, Ferril J. Rice, Wanda Huffman, Mary Van Pelt, Frank Wollenhaupt, Louise Ream, Antique Publications, Verna and Emil Boucher, Jerry and Carrie Domitz, Rita Lesko, Jan Cimarossa, Pat and Paul Randolph, Willie Kulick, Linda Bogan, Verne Garrett, Floyd Craft, Doris Frizzel, Ed Pitts, Jewell Gowan, John and Judy Bine, Charles Larson, Beth Finkle, Harold and Mildred Willey, John Day, Jean Day, Ron Morgan, Dick Marsh, Chuck Bails, Boyd Art Glass, Bob and Myrna Garrison, Marilyn Kreutz, Tom Clouser of Curtis & Mays Studio.

Introduction

Our first book, published in 1993, consisted of mainly solid glass animals which were formatted by company. This book differs in that it is formatted by animal or figurine and has been expanded to include animal and figural related items. Animals and figurines first produced in an original mold do not change and we have therefore carried them forward to this edition. We have, however, updated the prices to meet current market demands.

Over the years, many glass companies closed their doors, the molds have been scattered and sometimes destroyed, especially during the war effort in the 1940s. We have tried to account for as many molds as possible, primarily through identification of companies making reissues from the original molds. When possible we have included production dates on reissues as well as on the original item. Technology has advanced to a point whereby a mold can be made very easily from a piece of glass, which is often done in foreign countries.

Measurements reflected for items shown in this publication are actual measurements made by the authors. One must remember that when dealing with handmade glass, especially items that have been finished by grinding and polishing, the measurements will vary.

The efforts and labor expanded in writing this book is an expression of our love for glass animals and animal and figural related items.

Pricing

Values reflected in this book should be used only as a guide. We are not attempting to establish prices on items shown. Prices are normally established by supply and demand; however, they will vary from dealer to dealer and especially from region to region throughout the country. The Internet, as well as the present state of the economy, has had a tremendous influence on current prices. Prices reflected in this publication are for items in mint condition. Some items shown are from private collections and the owners ask us not to reflect a price; therefore, one will see "Private Collection — Market" reflected. Some items are very scarce and are rapidly increasing in price, for these items we left a high-side value off and replaced it by "To Market." Then there are a few items, possibly one of a kind or at least one of a very few, and for these items we stated "Rarity Prohibits Pricing." One must remember the actual value of an item is the price just negotiated between buyer and seller.

BEARS

Plate 1
CO-OPERATIVE FLINT GLASS COMPANY
Bear and Cover. Amber, 1928, rare.
$450.00 – 500.00

Also came in crystal, transparent colors, and milk glass. Mold was scrapped during WWII.

Plate 2
FENTON GLASS COMPANY
#5151 Sitting Bear Cub. French opalescent, 3½" tall, circa 1986 – 87.
$20.00 – 25.00

Produced from 1984 to present in multiple colors and some with decorations.

Plate 3
SUMMIT ART GLASS COMPANY
Polar Bear. Blue frosted, 4½" high.
$45.00 – 55.00

Summit Art Glass, founded by Russell Vogelsong and wife Joann, produce lovely novelty ware and some new glass from old molds, purchased from defunct glass companies. This bear is like Fostoria's bear, but has a round instead of square base. See Plate 4.

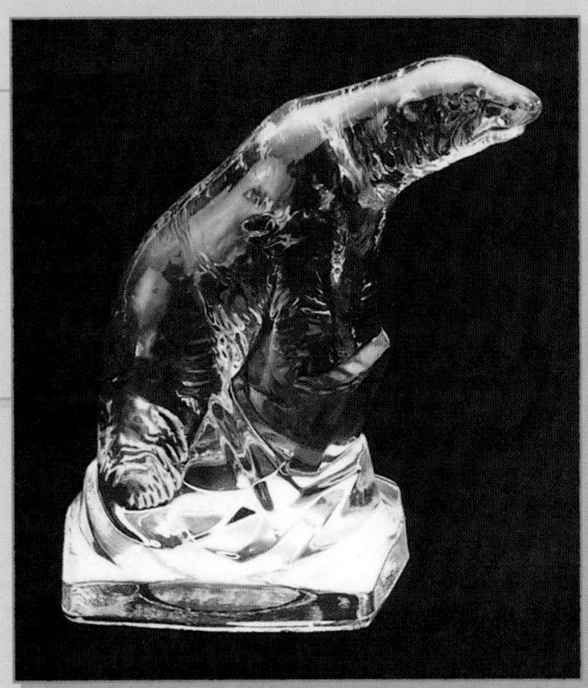

Plate 4
FOSTORIA GLASS COMPANY
#2531 Polar Bear. Crystal, 4⅝" high, 1935 – 44.
$55.00 – 65.00

Other colors: topaz, 1935 – 36; silver mist, 1936 – 43; and gold tint, 1937 – 39. (Topaz was changed to gold tint in 1937.)

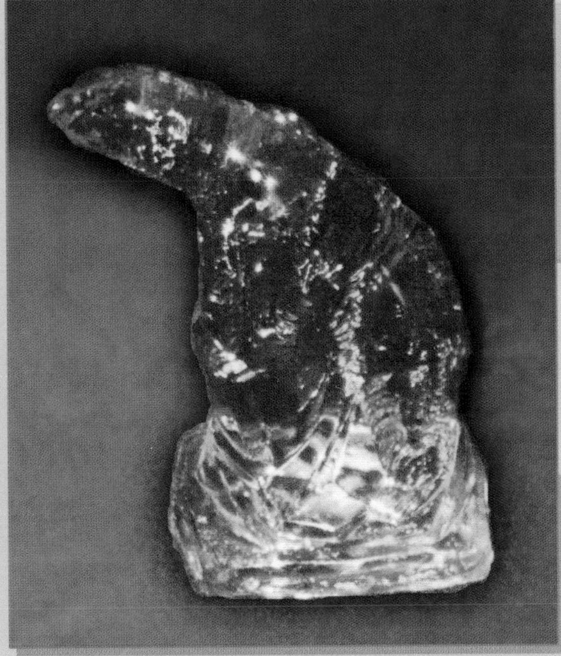

Plate 5
FOSTORIA GLASS COMPANY
#2531 Polar Bear. Topaz, 4⅝" high, 1935 – 36.
$125.00 – 150.00

Plate 6
FOSTORIA GLASS COMPANY
Bear, Sitting. Crystal, 2½" high, circa 1990s.
$10.00 – 14.00

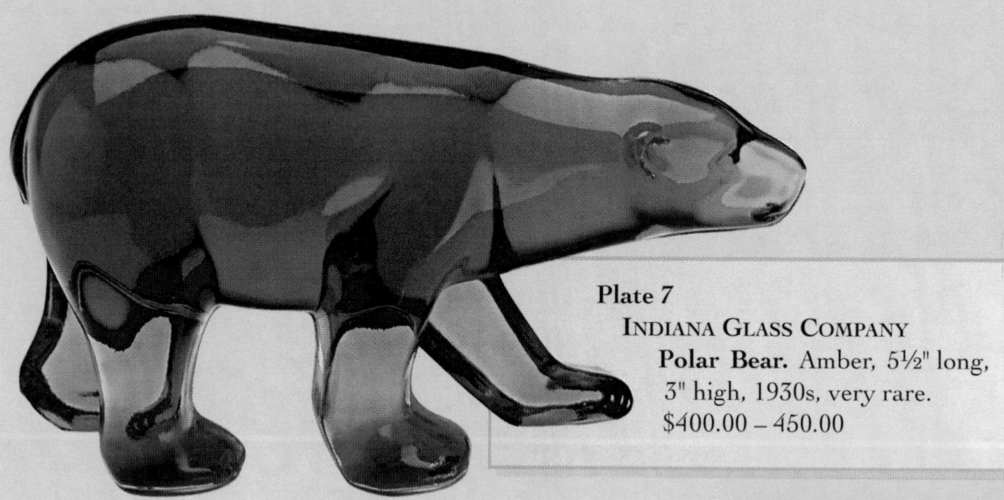

Plate 7
Indiana Glass Company
Polar Bear. Amber, 5½" long, 3" high, 1930s, very rare.
$400.00 – 450.00

Plate 8
Paden City Glass Company
#611 Polar Bear on Ice Floe.
Crystal, 4½" high.
$60.00 – 70.00

Bear has been seen without the ice floe. Reissues: Reissued by Dalzell-Viking in crystal, crystal frosted, black, and perhaps other colors (1990 – 1991).

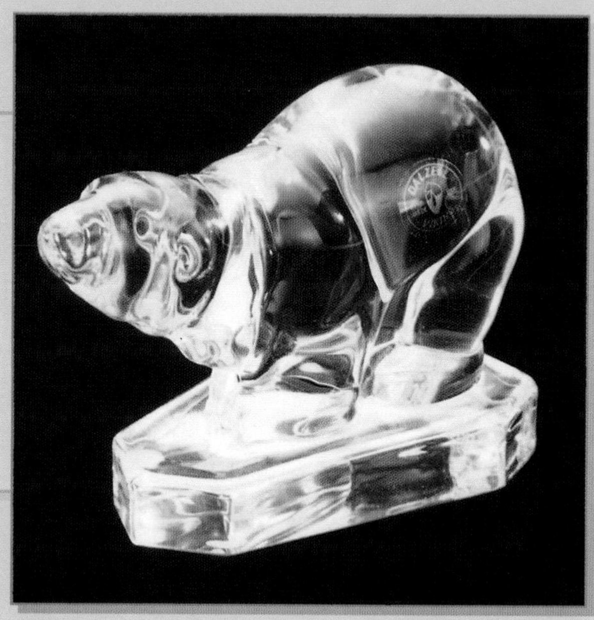

Plate 9
Dalzell-Viking Glass Company
(Original Paden City Mold see Plate 8.)
Polar Bear on Ice. Black, 4½" high.
$200.00 – 225.00.

Other colors: crystal, crystal frosted, and perhaps others.

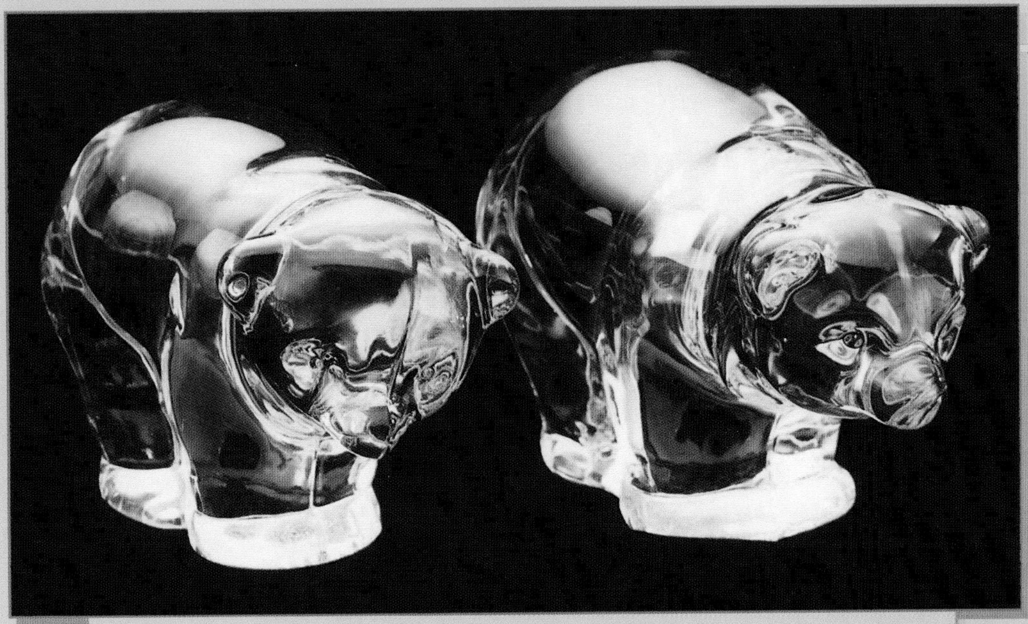

Plate 10
New Martinsville Glass Company
#488 Mama Bear. Crystal, solid, 4" high, 6" long, 1938 – 51.
$175.00 – 225.00
#489 Papa Bear. Crystal, solid, 4" high, 6½" long, 1938 – 51.
$200.00 – 250.00

Reissues: In 1985 Mama Bear was made by Viking for Mirror Images. First in a series of five, marked with a "V," in ruby, ruby satin, or ruby carnival. See Plates 13 and 14. 1988 – 90 Mama was reissued by Dalzell-Viking in crystal, and black in 1991. Papa Bear in ruby, for Mirror Images by Dalzell-Viking in 1999. Only 40 were made.

Mama Bear's head is slightly turned and Papa Bear has little rolls of fat under his chin. There is ½" difference in their length.

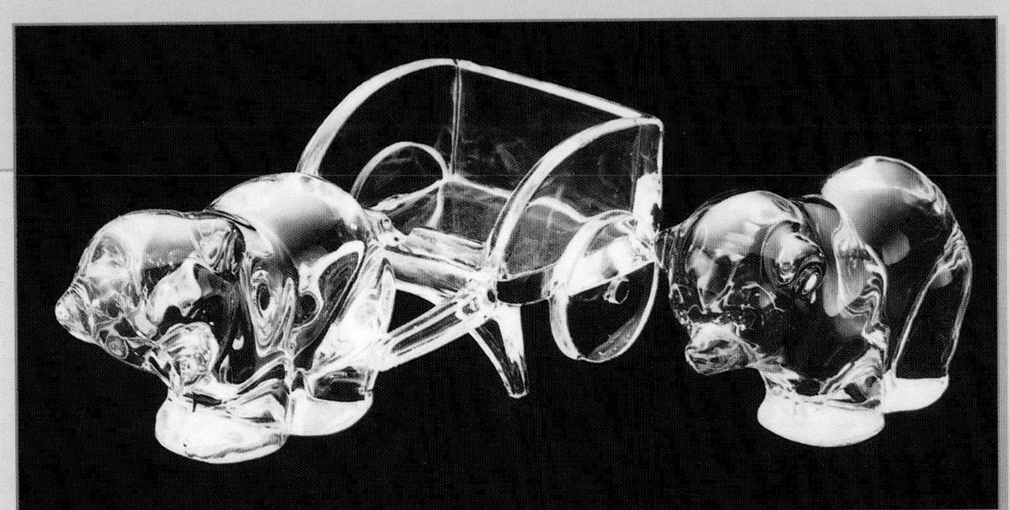

Plate 11
New Martinsville Glass Company
Baby Bear, Head Turned. Crystal, 3" high, until 1954.
$35.00 – 45.00
#508 Cigarette Cart. Crystal, 5" long, until 1954.
$20.00 – 25.00
#487 Baby Bear, Head Straight. Crystal, 3" high, until 1954.
$35.00 – 45.00

Other colors: Baby Bears also came in frosted crystal, a few in milk glass. Limited run in black with cart.

Reissues: Baby Bear, head straight, reissued for Mirror Images by Viking in mid-1980s, in ruby, ruby satin, and ruby carnival. Fourth in a series of five, limited edition of 500. Marked with a "V" (see Plates 13 and 14). #487 Baby Bear, head straight, reissued by Dalzell-Viking, 1988, crystal; 1990, crystal; and 1990 – 91 black (see Plate 16).

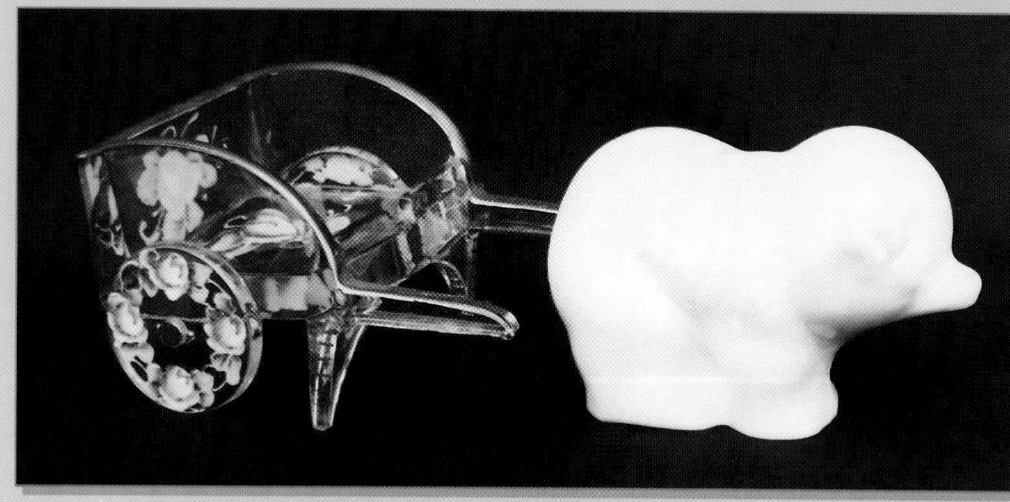

Plate 12
NEW MARTINSVILLE GLASS COMPANY
Baby Bear, Head Straight. Milk glass, 3" high, with cigarette cart, crystal with Charleton hand-painted flowers, 5" long.
Baby Bear, $175.00 – 200.00
Cart, $40.00 – 50.00

Plate 13
VIKING GLASS COMPANY (New Martinsville mold)
Made for Mirror Images
Mama Bear. Ruby, solid, 4" high, 6" long.
$100.00 – 150.00
Baby Bear, Head Straight. Ruby, solid, 3" high.
$75.00 – 125.00

Made by Viking for Mirror Images, first in a series of five, limited edition of 500. Marked with a "V."

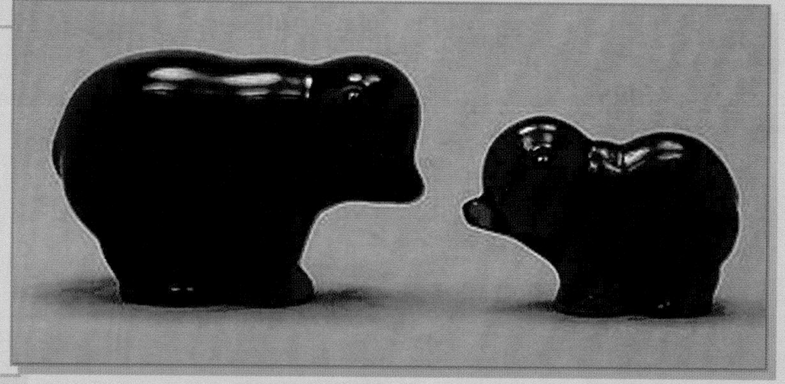

Plate 14
VIKING GLASS COMPANY
(New Martinsville mold)
Made for Mirror Images
Mama Bear. Ruby carnival, solid, 4" high, 6" long.
$100.00 – 150.00.
Baby Bear, Head Straight. Ruby, solid, 3" high.
$75.00 – 100.00.

Made by Viking for Mirror Images, limited edition, marked with a "V."

Plate 15
VIKING GLASS COMPANY
(New Martinsville mold)
Baby Bear, Head Straight. Black, solid, 3" high, 1990 – 91.
$175.00 – 200.00

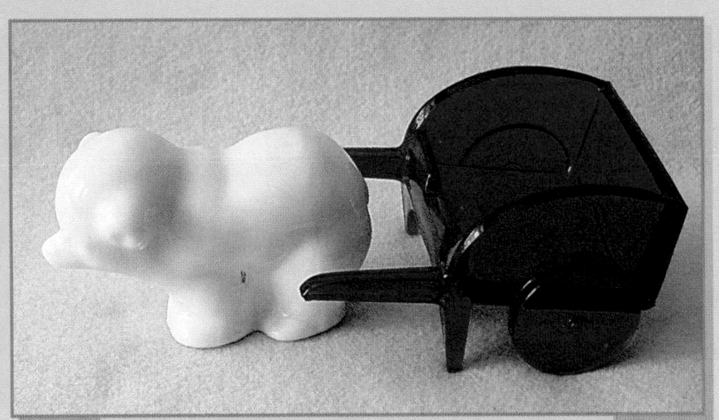

Plate 16
VIKING GLASS COMPANY
(New Martinsville mold)
Baby Bear, Head Straight. Milk glass, 3" high with cobalt cigarette cart.
Bear and cart set, $275.00 – 325.00

Set has Viking paper labels.

Glass Cart Comparison — Duncan Vs. New Martinsville/Viking

Basically there were two unattached carts produced which sometimes causes confusion. Other than Duncan and New Martinsville/Viking, the other carts had a figure attached. The two plates below are a side-by-side comparison.

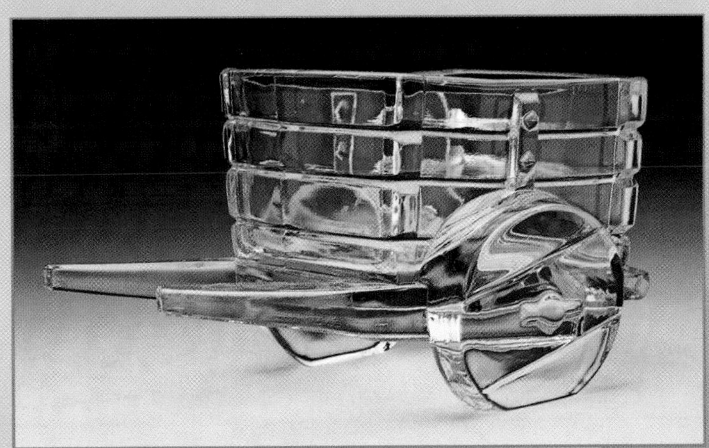

Plate 16A
DUNCAN GLASS COMPANY
Glass Cart. Crystal, 5¼" long, 3" high (front of box), 4" wide (wheel to wheel).
The Duncan cart has a complete "box" and shows the outline of the boards in the box. This cart is very scarce. See Plate 215.

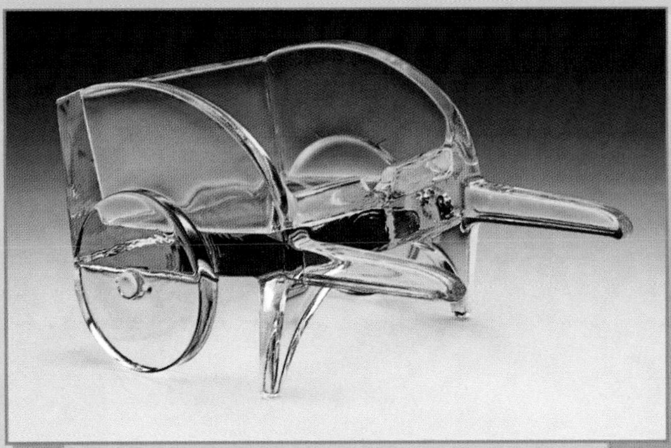

Plate 16B
NEW MARTINSVILLE GLASS COMPANY
Glass Cart. Crystal, 5¼" long, 3" high, and 4" wide.
This cart does not have a complete "box" as there are no front boards. It also has supports on both sides of the front under the box which makes it sit upright. There are no outlines of boards. It was reissued by Viking and is seen quite often. See Plate 12.

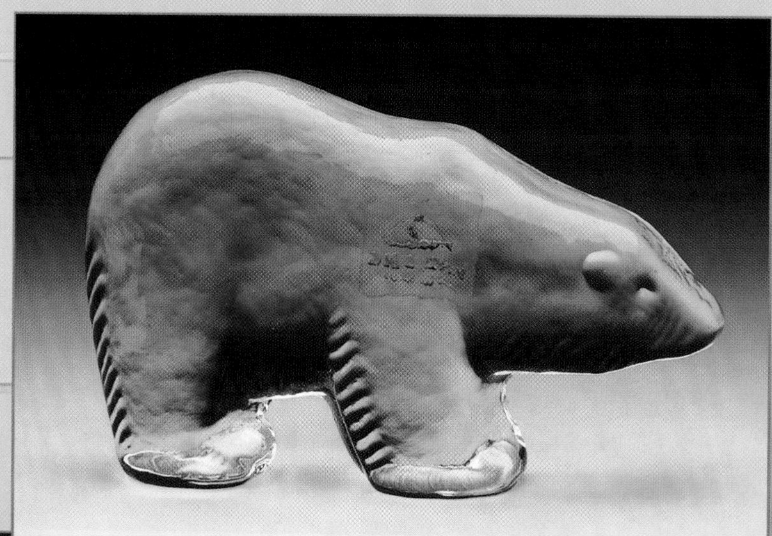

Plate 17
VIKING GLASS COMPANY
Bear, Standing. Crystal frosted, 3" high, 5" long.
$12.00 – 16.00

Plate 18
RODIFER GLASS COMPANY
Bear on Cake of Ice. Crystal, 9½" high, made for Imperial Glass Festival in Bellaire, Ohio.
Rarity prohibits pricing.

Rodifer Glass Company was mostly noted for its commercial opalware gearshift knobs for automobiles, silicon shields for gas wells, and opalware blanks for Wavecrest.

Plate 19
UNKNOWN MANUFACTURER
Polar Bear on Ice Floe. Crystal floe, crystal frosted bear, 4¼" high, 7½" long, ground and polished bottom, excellent glass.
Has been seen in $45.00 – 55.00 range.

Plate 20
WESTMORELAND GLASS COMPANY
Bee. Green, 1½" long, rare.
$275.00 – 300.00

Other colors: marigold carnival, black and yellow decorated, milk glass, and probably other colors.

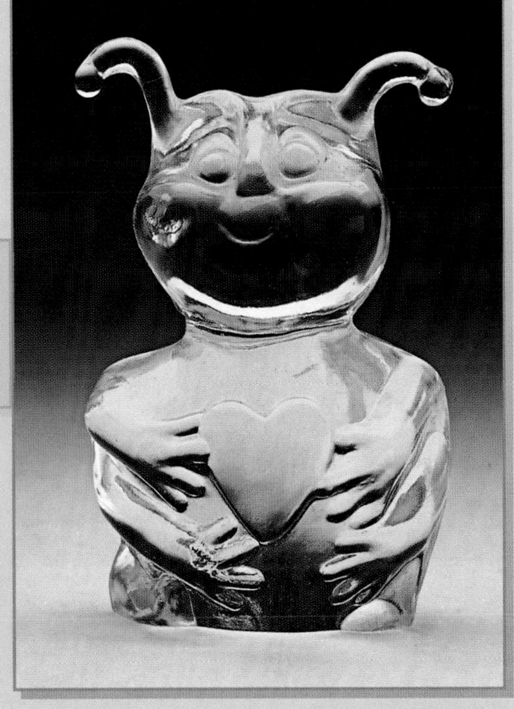

Plate 21
FENTON ART GLASS COMPANY
#5149 Luv Bug. Crystal, 2¾" high.
$25.00 – 30.00

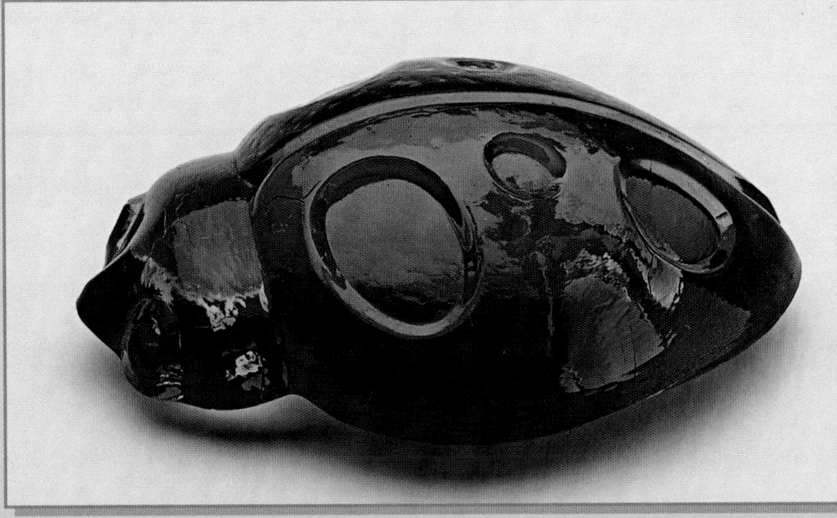

Plate 22
FOSTORIA GLASS COMPANY
Lady Bug. Olive green, 1¼" tall, 3¼" long.
$25.00 – 35.00

Other colors: crystal, crystal frosted, and lemon.

Plate 23
Cambridge Glass Company
Moth. Crystal satin, 2¼" wide, circa 1930.
$25.00 – 30.00

Other colors: peach blo.

Plate 24, Bottom
Cambridge Glass Company
#2 Butterfly. Crystal satin, circa 1930.
$25.00 – 30.00
Top
Mosser Glass Company (reissues)
Opalescent, pink (left), and green (right).
$15.00 – 20.00 each

Reprinted courtesy of Antique Publications

Plate 25
Fenton Art Glass Company
#511 Butterfly. White carnival, circa 1928.
#512 Butterfly. Light blue carnival, circa 1928.
Rarity prohibits pricing.

These very rare butterfly ornaments were originally given away as premiums, along with a larger glass purchase. Documentation states they were not commercially produced. Also, they were, in some instances, attached to the handle of glass baskets with a dab of putty. The butterfly is the official symbol of the Fenton Art Glass Collectors of America.

Plate 26
Fenton Art Glass Company
1989 Fenton Souvenir Issue
Butterfly candleholder. Ruby carnival, 7½" long, with 5" body containing three candle sockets.
$75.00 – 85.00
Frosted ruby carnival issued in 1992
$75.00 – 85.00

Plate 27
Fenton Art Glass Company
Butterfly on Stand. 5" high.
Left: Tinted fuchsia and crystal base.
Used as 1979 F.A.G.C.A. banquet souvenir.
$35.00 – 40.00
Center: Gold, circa 1990.
$35.00 – 40.00
Right: Ruby carnival, circa 1990.
$40.00 – 45.00

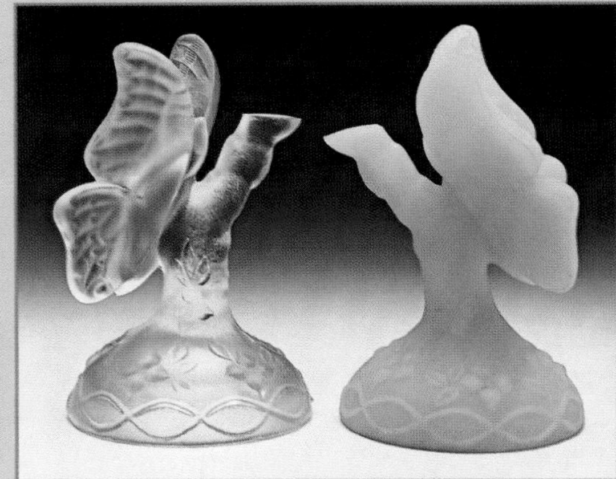

Plate 28
Fenton Art Glass Company
Butterfly on Stand. 5" tall.
Left: Crystal velvet, 1978 – 88.
$25.00 – 30.00
Right: Lime sherbet, 1979 – 80.
$35.00 – 40.00

Other colors: custard satin, blue satin, velva blue, carnival, candle glow yellow, heritage green, amethyst, dusty rose, ruby marble, periwinkle blue, and topaz opalescent.

Plate 29
Fenton Art Glass Company
#5170 Butterfly. Colonial green, 4¼" wide, 3½" long, circa 1970.
$35.00 – 40.00

No pattern on wings. Other colors: colonial blue, colonial amber orange, ruby, crystal, and amethyst carnival.

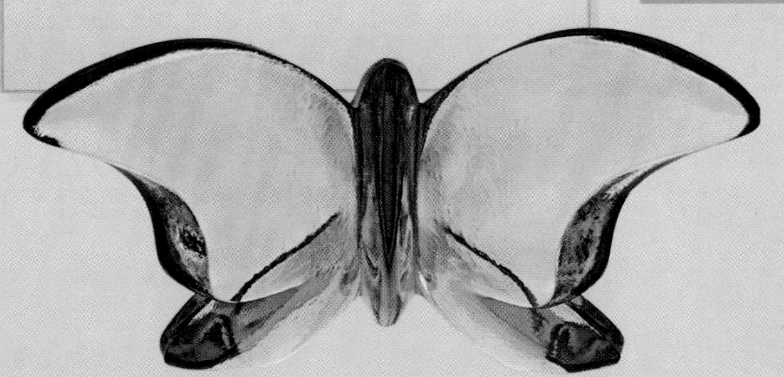

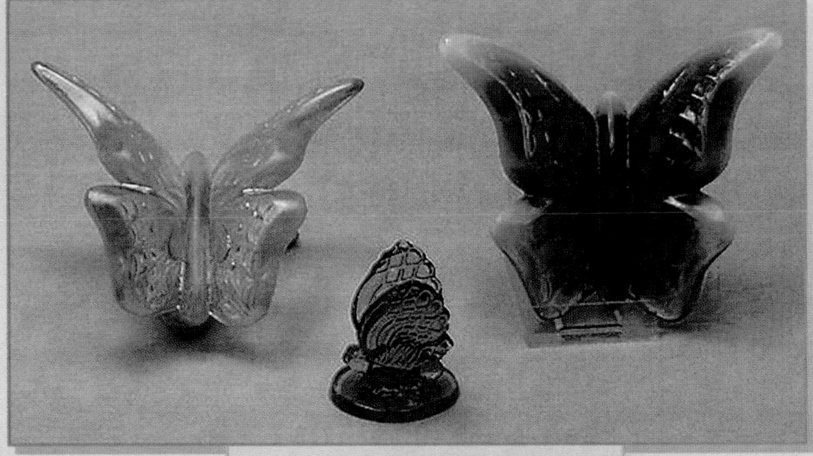

Plate 30
Fenton Art Glass Company
Butterfly.
Left: Pink carnival.
$40.00 – 45.00
Center: Charcoal gray, whimsey.
Used as finial on rose candy box.
$25.00 – 30.00
Right: Plum opalescent.
$50.00 – 55.00

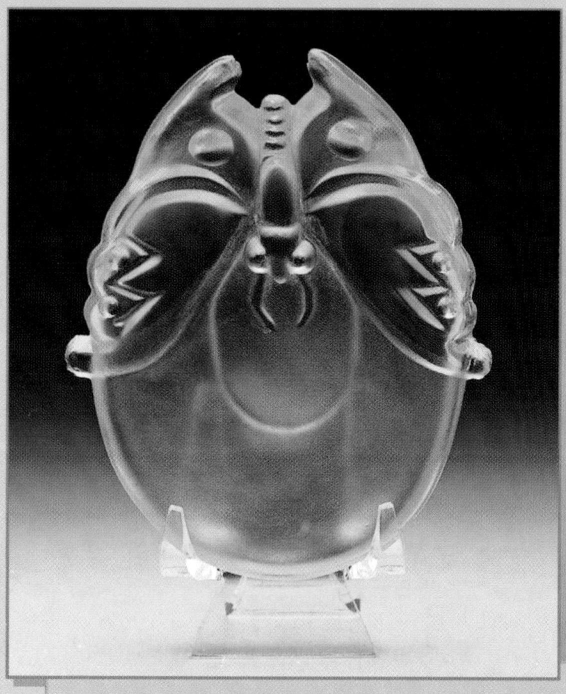

Plate 31
Imperial Glass Company
#5006 Butterfly Ashtray. Crystal frosted, circa 1949 – 57.
$45.00 – 55.00

Script signature of designer, Virginia B. Evans.

Part Imperial's Cathay Crystal line. Butterfly is Chinese cupid. Symbol of long life and happiness. See Plate 224.

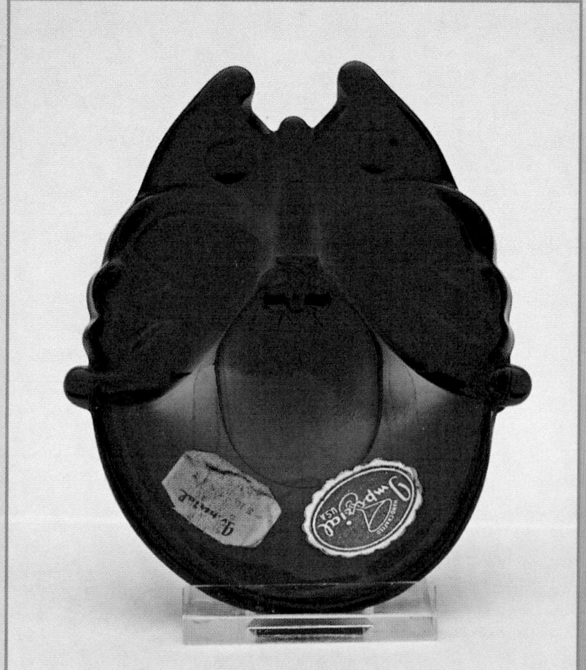

Plate 32
Imperial Glass Company
#5006 Butterfly Ashtray.
Ruby, circa 1969.
$50.00 – 60.00

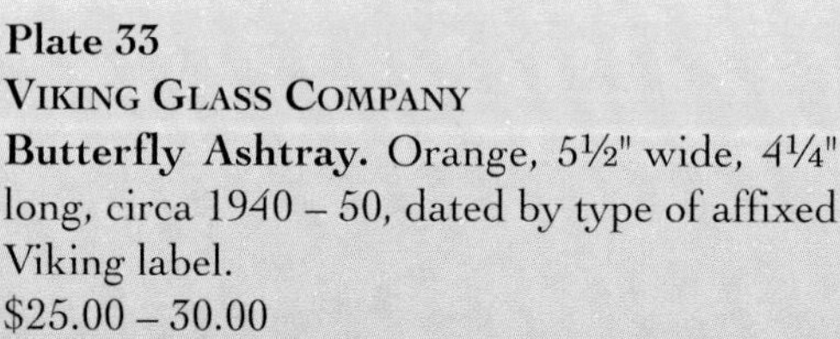

Plate 33
Viking Glass Company
Butterfly Ashtray. Orange, 5½" wide, 4¼" long, circa 1940 – 50, dated by type of affixed Viking label.
$25.00 – 30.00

Other colors seen: blue.

Plate 34
Unknown manufacturer
Butterfly. Crystal frosted, 2¾" tall.
Seen at $10.00 – 14.00

Plate 35
WESTMORELAND GLASS COMPANY
#2 Small Butterfly. Green mist, 2½" wide.
$20.00 – 25.00
#2 Small Butterfly. Blue mist, 2½" wide.
$20.00 – 25.00
#3 Large Butterfly. Crystal, 4½" wide.
$25.00 – 30.00

Other colors, #2 Butterfly: crystal, mint green, light and dark blue, pink, apricot and yellow mist, pink opaque carnival, yellow opaque, purple carnival, almond, cobalt carnival, smoke gray, pink mist, and possibly others. Other colors, #3 Butterfly: pink, yellow, antique blue and brown mist, purple marble, brown marble, antique blue, almond, mint green, and vaseline. Carnival and marble colors are more expensive.

Reissues: 1977 limited edition in purple carnival for the Historical Glass Museum Foundation.

Large Butterfly #3 also came with a peg to fit into tree stump base.

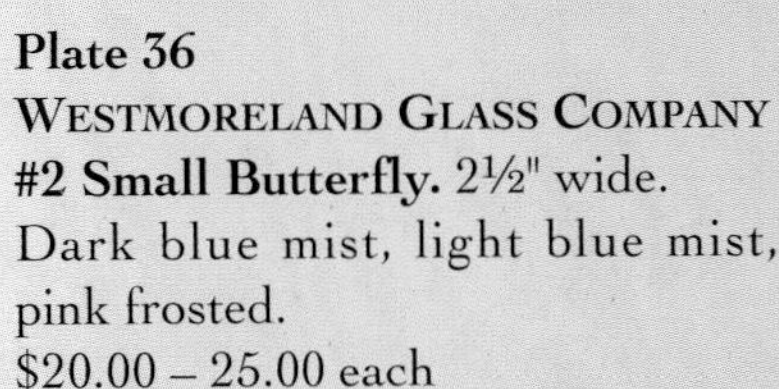

Plate 36
WESTMORELAND GLASS COMPANY
#2 Small Butterfly. 2½" wide.
Dark blue mist, light blue mist, pink frosted.
$20.00 – 25.00 each

Plate 37
WESTMORELAND GLASS COMPANY
#3 Butterfly. 4½" wide.
Pink mist, dark blue mist, blue opaque.
$25.00 – 30.00 each

Birds

Plate 38
Cambridge Glass Company
Sea Gull Flower Holder. Crystal, 8" high.
$65.00 – 75.00

Other colors: crystal frosted.

Production of this item started in the late 1930s and probably continued until Cambridge closed. The Sea Gull is seen quite frequently. It was reissued by Imperial Glass Co. in the early 1960s and reportedly has a ribbed base whereas the base on the Cambridge production was smooth.

Plate 39
Cambridge Glass Company
Blue Jay Flower Holder. Crystal, 5½" high.
$135.00 – 150.00
Peg only: crystal, 4½" high.
$135.00 – 150.00

Other colors: crystal satin, moonlight blue, emerald, mandarin gold, and possibly other colors.

Reissues: none.

The Blue Jay was also made without the base. It is 4½" high and has a peg bottom that fits into a candle socket.

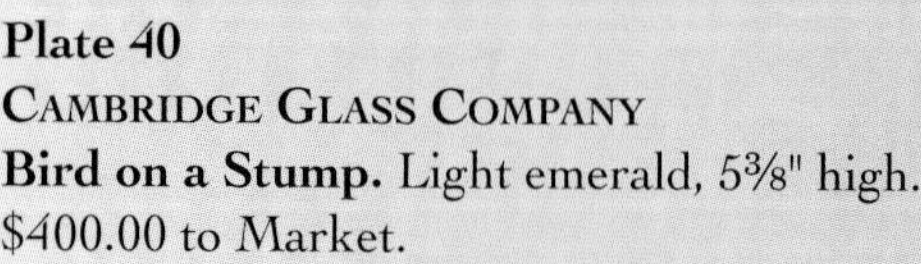

Plate 40
Cambridge Glass Company
Bird on a Stump. Light emerald, 5⅜" high.
$400.00 to Market.

Although Cambridge records have not been found that will support this flower holder being produced by them, the colors is right and the dimensions of the base are the same as the Eagle. We will simply refer to it as Bird on a Stump. It has only been seen in light emerald.

Plate 41
CAMBRIDGE GLASS COMPANY
No. 3 Bird. Crystal, 2½" long, or crystal frosted.
$28.00 – 32.00
Left: **MOSSER GLASS CO.**
No. 3 Bird. Pink, 2½" long.
$10.00 – 12.00

Mosser produced these birds in multiple colors.

Plate 42
MANTLE LAMP COMPANY OF AMERICA
G234 Golden Pheasant. Alacite glass, circa 1941.
$175.00 – 200.00

The Mantle Lamp Company of America began operations in 1908 with kerosene burning lamps being their main production until the 1940s (even with electric lamps in the picture). Aladdin Lamps became their trade name, and the collectible lamps of today were made in Alexandria, Indiana. In 1949, they moved operations to Nashville, Tennessee. "Alacite" was introduced in 1939.

Plate 43
DUNCAN GLASS COMPANY
Dove on Base.
Dove: Crystal, 11½" long.
$175.00 – 200.00
Base: $200.00 – 225.00

Other colors: crystal satin.

Reissues: none.

The base for the dove is very difficult to find. Perhaps they were sold with or without the base or perhaps they got separated from the dove or broken.

Plate 44
DUNCAN GLASS COMPANY
Dove, Head Down. Crystal, 11½" long.
$175.00 – 200.00
Dove on Bust-Off. Crystal, 11½" long.
$175.00 – 200.00

When the dove was taken out of the mold, it was on a round "bust-off" (as pictured). This was then removed and the bottom ground and polished. The bottom was ground at different angles thus changing the height of the head. At least four different angles have been seen.

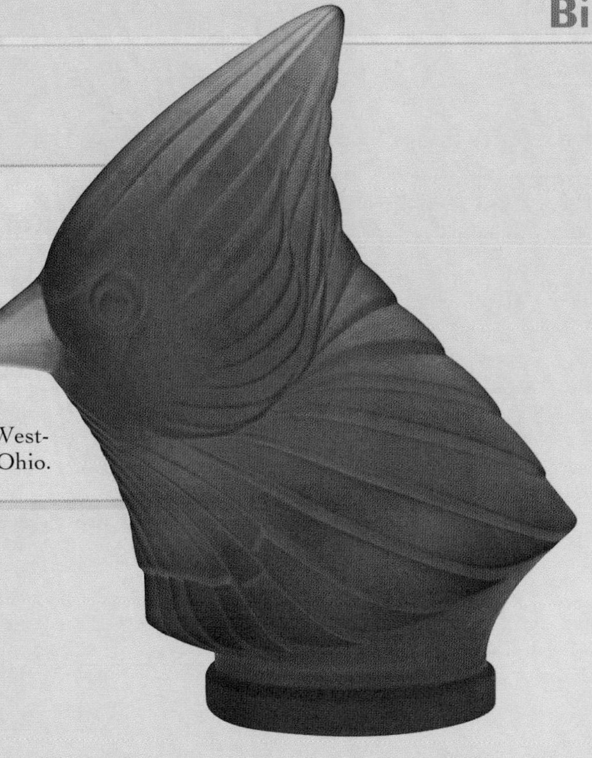

Plate 45
FENTON ART GLASS COMPANY
Cardinal Head. Ruby, 6½" high, after 1986.
$150.00 – 200.00

Other colors: crystal velvet.

Made for Frederick Crawford Museum, Western Reserve Historical Society, Cleveland, Ohio.

Plate 46
FOSTORIA GLASS COMPANY
Cardinal Head. Silver Mist, 6½" high.
$150.00 – 200.00

Other colors: ruby.

The cardinal head was made for the Car Club Collectors as a radiator ornament. It fits the metal cap of the Model A and Model T.

Plate 47
FOSTORIA GLASS COMPANY
Small Bird Candleholders. 1½" high, signed "Fostoria," has small internal knobs to hold candles.
$30.00 – 40.00 pair

Other colors: burgundy, empire green, regal blue and ruby, 1935 – 42; crystal, 1975 – 79; milk glass, 1954 – 58; and ruby, 1981 – 82.

Plate 48
FENTON ART GLASS COMPANY
(Original mold Paden City)
#5197 Happiness Bird. 6½" long, made in multiple colors and decorations.
$30.00 – 45.00, depending on color and decorations

Fenton introduced this item in 1953. Black, 1935 – 55; milk, 1953 – 56.

Paden City originally owned this mold, see Plates 59 and 60.

Plate 49
FENTON ART GLASS COMPANY
#5163 Small Bird. 2¾" tall, 4" long. Custard, circa 1978.
Left: Custard with decoration, $15.00 – 20.00
Right: Custard plain, $10.00 – 15.00

Made in multiple colors with and without decorations.

Plate 50
UNKNOWN MANUFACTURER
Cock-a-Too. Crystal, 10" long.
Seen at $10.00 – 15.00

Hollow back and obviously made as a relish dish. Superb detail.

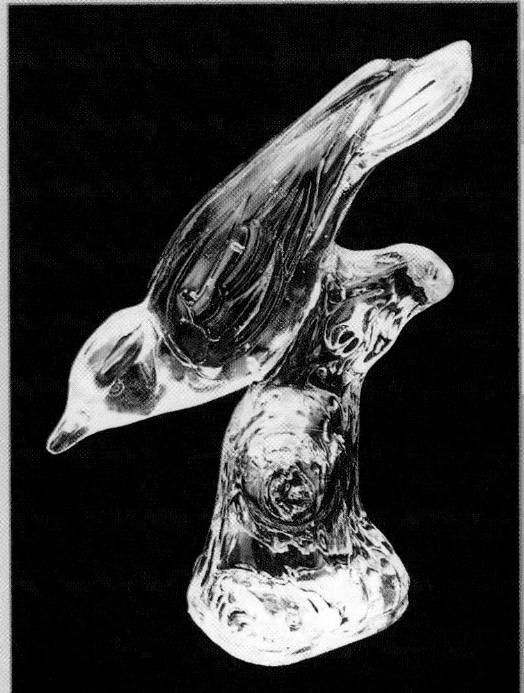

Plate 51
K.R. Haley Glassware Company
Bird (Robin) on Stump. Crystal, 6" high.
$15.00 – 20.00

Other colors: crystal frosted.

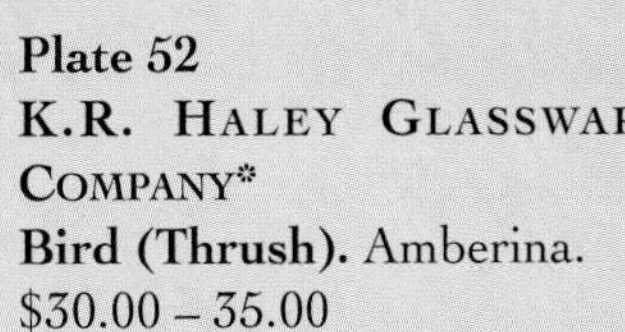

Plate 52
K.R. Haley Glassware Company*
Bird (Thrush). Amberina.
$30.00 – 35.00

*L.E. Smith Glass Co. produced this item from a Haley manufactured mold. Original issue was in crystal and crystal frosted. Circa 1947. Smith has produced this item in several colors and finishes over the years. It was produced in Almond Nouveau in 1980.

Plate 53
K.R. Haley Glassware Company*
Bird (Thrush). Crystal frosted, original issue circa 1947.
$45.00 – 50.00

*Produced by L.E. Smith Glass Co.

Plate 54
HEISEY GLASS COMPANY
Kingfisher Floral Block. Hawthorne, circa late 1920s into early 1930s.
$350.00 – 400.00

Other colors: crystal, moongleam (green), and Flamingo (pink).

Reissues: lavender ice, altered mold. See Plate 56.

Plate 55
HEISEY GLASS COMPANY
Sparrow. Crystal, 2½" high, 4" long (beak to tip of tail), not marked, circa 1942 – 45.
$110.00 – 135.00

Other colors: crystal frosted.

Reissues: multiple colors, but not in crystal by Imperial Glass Co.

Catalogs indicate three different sparrows, #s 1, 2, and 3. This can only be attributed to the angle to which the base was ground. One can find many more than three angles to which the base was ground. This will vary the 2½" height to the tail.

Plate 56
HEISEY GLASS COMPANY (Mold)
Dalzell-Viking production
Kingfisher. Lavender ice.
$55.00 – 60.00

One of the original 12 animals produced by Dalzell-Viking for Heisey Collectors of America in 1993 as part of their "Gem Animal Series." See Plate 84B.

Plate 57
IMPERIAL GLASS COMPANY
Scolding Bird. Crystal frosted, 5" high, circa 1949.
$175.00 – 200.00

Reissues: Imperial produced it in 1964 – 68 and called it "Nosy Jaybird." It was also made in dark jade and black suede. Reissued by Imperial in 1982 and 1983, in glossy finish caramel slag, marked ALIG.

This was part of the Cathay line. Original issue signed "Virginia B. Evans." See Plate 224.

Plate 58
KANAWHA GLASS COMPANY
Bird with Cherry Salt Dip. Amber, 3½" long, circa 1970s – 1980s.
$8.00 – 12.00

Other colors: green, blue, and vintage (amberina).

Plate 59
PADEN CITY GLASS COMPANY
Bird. Crystal, 5" high (at tip of tail)
$40.00 – 50.00

Other colors: light blue.

Reissues: Fenton Art Glass Co., in crystal and multiple colors. Crystal initial was not marked but later issue was marked by Fenton. See Plate 48.

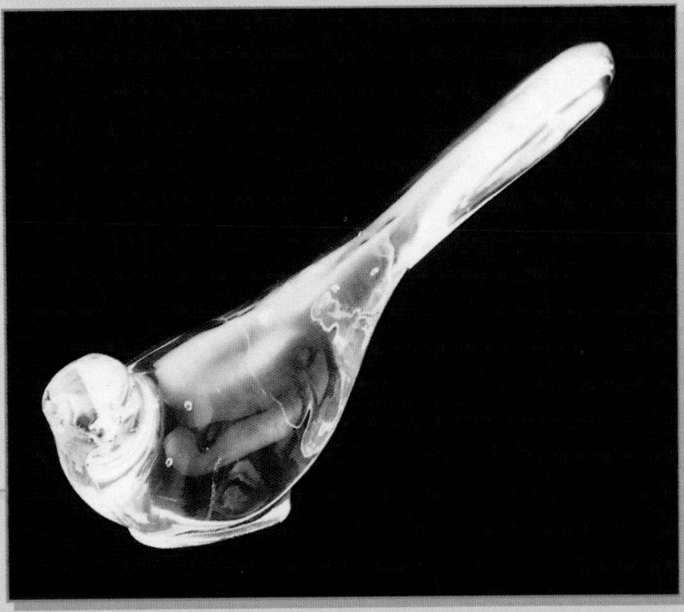

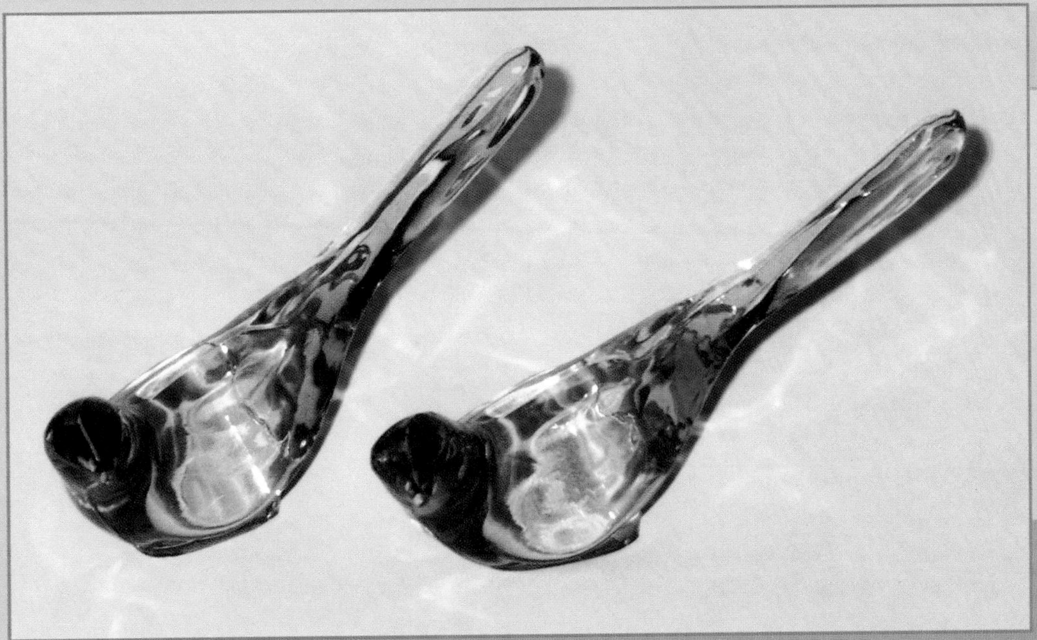

Plate 60
PADEN CITY GLASS COMPANY
Bird. Light blue, 5" high.
$95.00 – 125.00

Other colors: crystal, see Plate 59.

Reissues: Fenton Art Glass Co. in multiple colors. The light blue produced by Fenton was not marked. See Plate 48.

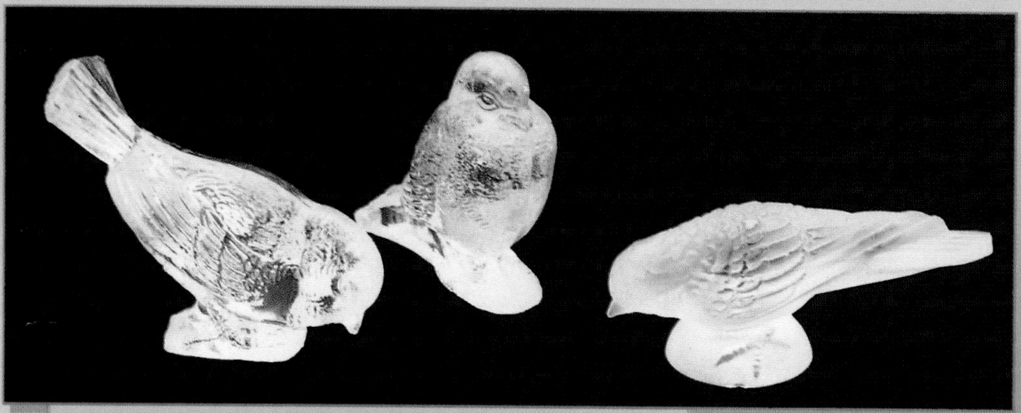

Plate 61
L.E. Smith Glass Company
Sparrow, Head Down. 3½" high, circa 1950s.
$15.00 – 20.00
Sparrow, Head Up. 3½" high, circa 1950s.
$15.00 – 20.00

Other colors: crystal satin, yellow, yellow satin, blue, blue satin, almond nouveau, milk glass, and perhaps others.

Lalique sparrow shown on right for comparison.

Plate 62
L.E. Smith Glass Company
Sparrow, Head Down.
Yellow satin, 3½" high.
$20.00 – 25.00

See Plate 61.

Plate 63
L.E. Smith Glass Company
Mini Bird. Crystal, 2" high, circa 1920s.
$4.00 – 8.00
Mini Bird. Ruby stained, 2" high, circa 1920s.
$5.00 – 9.00

Other colors: crystal frosted and perhaps others.

Plate 64
L.E. Smith Glass Company
#150 Bird, Head-Up. Blue satin, 3", circa 1982.
$30.00 – 35.00
#150 Bird, Head-Down. Blue satin, 3", circa 1982.
$30.00 – 35.00
#840E, Box. Blue satin, 4½", circa 1982.
$45.00 – 50.00

Other colors: almond nouveau, pink satin, crystal satin, and milk glass.

Plate 65
TIFFIN GLASS COMPANY
Lovebirds Lamp. Birds have orange bodies and green heads, 10½" high, circa 1920s.
$450.00 – 550.00

Came with a threaded base and came in other color combinations.

Plate 66
TIFFIN GLASS COMPANY
Lovebirds Lamps. Birds have green bodies and orange heads, 10½" high, circa 1920s.
$450.00 – 550.00

Came with a threaded base and in other color combinations.

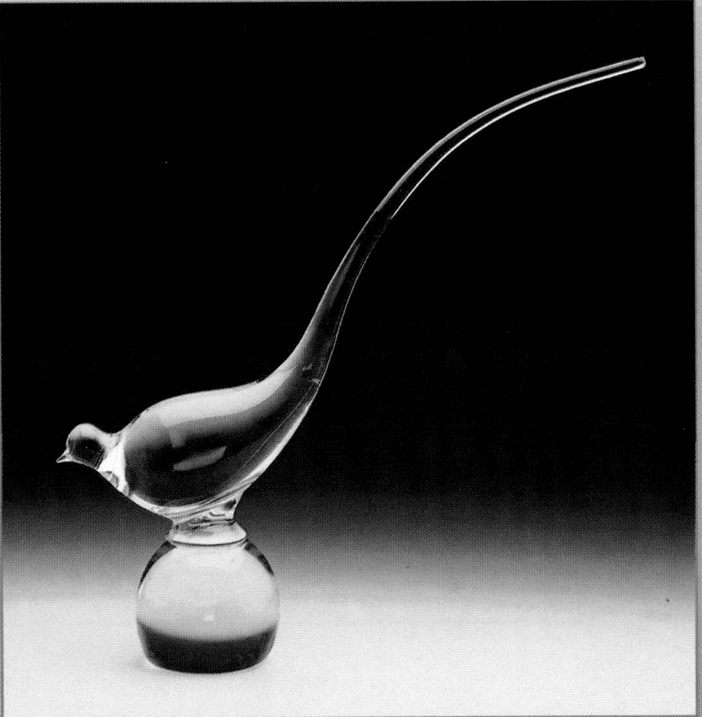

Plate 67
UNKNOWN MANUFACTURER
Bird Long Tail Paperweight. Crystal, 16½" long, 14" high.
Seen at $125.00 – 175.00

This guy has a ground and polished bottom and is of excellent quality. It is very similar to one made by Pairpoint Glass Co.

Plate 68
UNKNOWN MANUFACTURER
Pigeon Relish. Yellow, 13" long, 4½" wide.
Seen at $25.00 – 35.00

This item has excellent detail.

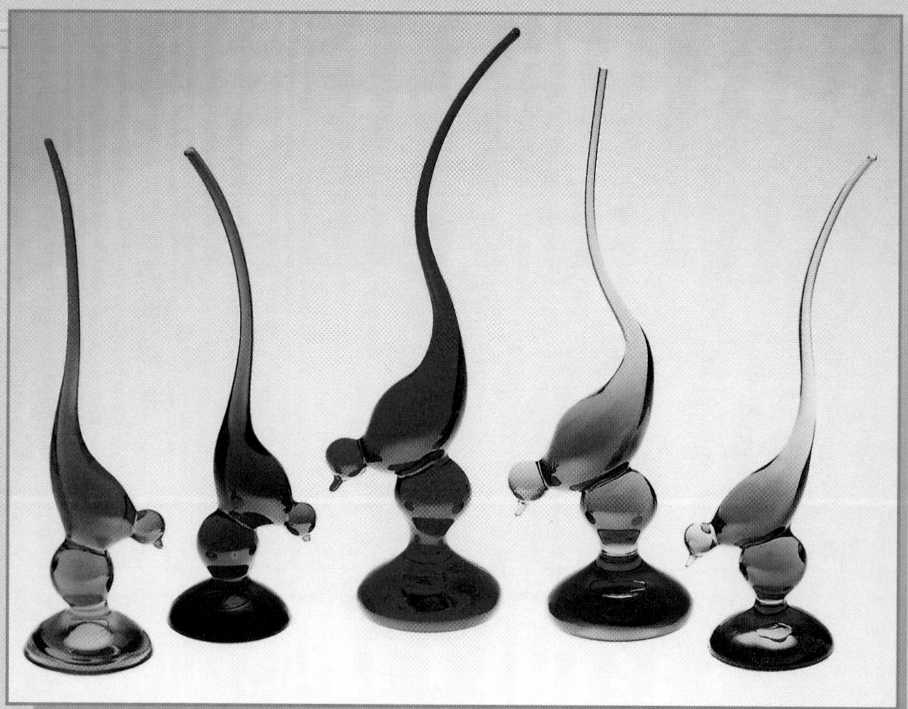

Plate 69
VIKING GLASS COMPANY
#1311 Bird. Orange, 9½" high, circa 1960s.
$30.00 – 45.00
#1311 Bird. Dark medium blue, 9½" high, circa 1960s.
$30.00 – 45.00
#1310 Bird. Ruby, 12" high, circa 1960s.
$55.00 – 65.00
#1310 Bird. Moss Green, 12" high, circa 1960s.
$45.00 – 65.00
#1311 Bird. Orchid, 9½" high, circa 1960s.
$100.00 – 125.00

The Viking catalog shows this bird in crystal and black. In 1991, this bird could be bought in black through the Viking outlet store.

Plate 70
VIKING GLASS COMPANY
Two-Piece Candy Box. Orange, 12" high.
$50.00 – 75.00
#1311 Bird. Amber, 9½" high, circa 1960s.
$35.00 – 45.00

The finial on the candy box is a #1311 bird.

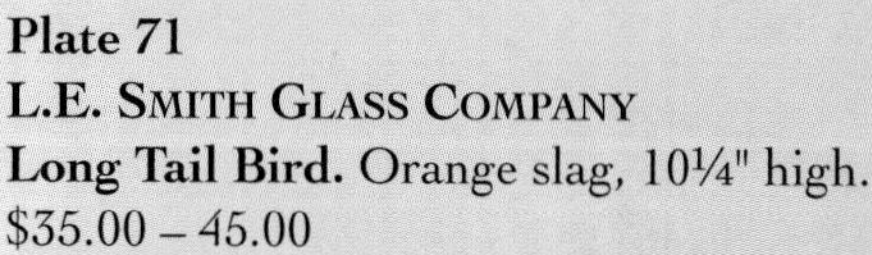

Plate 71
L.E. SMITH GLASS COMPANY
Long Tail Bird. Orange slag, 10¼" high.
$35.00 – 45.00

This bird has an L.E. Smith paper label. Without the label, it could easily be confused with Viking birds.

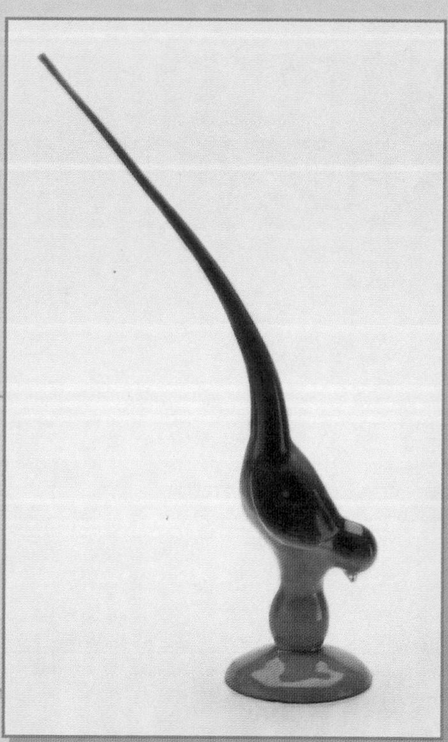

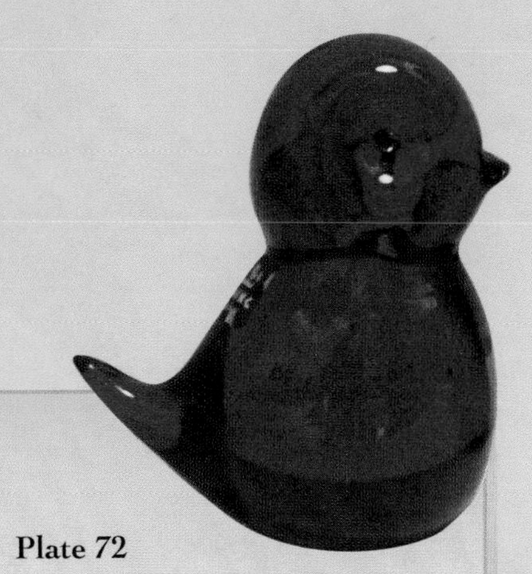

Plate 72
VIKING GLASS COMPANY
#7282 Bird. Ruby, 4" high, circa 1960s – 70s.
$30.00 – 40.00

Made in other Viking colors.

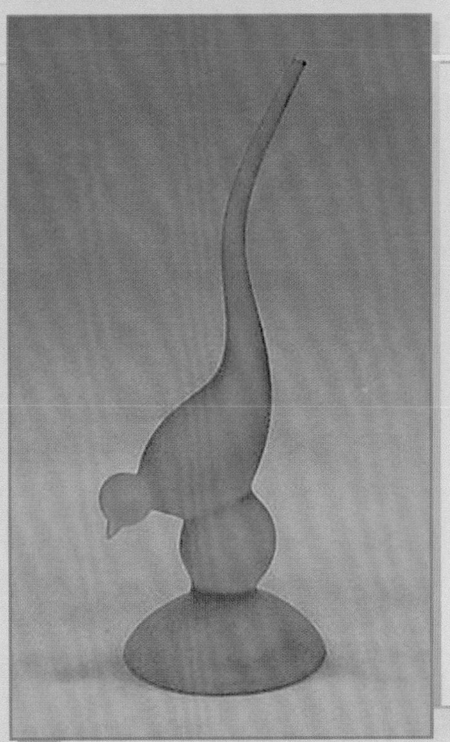

Plate 73
VIKING GLASS COMPANY
#1311 Bird. Blue frosted, 9½" high, circa 1980s – 90s.
$40.00 – 60.00

Plate 74
VIKING GLASS COMPANY
#6807 Bird. Amber, 5" high, circa 1968 – 69.
$25.00 – 30.00

Part of the Epic line. Made in other Viking colors.

Plate 75
VIKING GLASS COMPANY
#7890 Bird. Crystal and satin, 7" tall, 5" wide, circa 1980 – 81.
$15.00 – 25.00

Plate 76
WESTMORELAND GLASS COMPANY
#5 Two-Piece Wren on Perch.
Bird. Green, 3½" long, $15.00 – 20.00
Bird. Blue frosted, 3½" long, $20.00 – 25.00
Perch (base). Milk glass, 3" x 3", $15.00 – 20.00

Other colors: Wren: pink mist, green mist, dark blue mist, apricot mist, almond, and black milk glass. Base: black milk glass and brown wood-like treatment.

Wren has a peg bottom which fits into the branch.

Plate 77
WESTMORELAND GLASS COMPANY
Bird in Flight. Amber marigold, 5" wingspread, 4¼" long.
$45.00 – 55.00

Has a before 1960s label.

Plate 78
WESTMORELAND GLASS COMPANY
#7/1 Robin. Crystal, 3¼" long, 1" ground bottom.
$18.00 – 24.00
#11 Cardinal. Green mist, 5" long.
$22.00 – 28.00

Other colors: Robin: antique blue, milk glass, almond, pink mist, antique blue milk glass, and reissued in cobalt. Cardinal: crystal ruby, purple marble, dark blue mist, apricot mist, ruby carnival, and reissued in ruby, purple carnival, orange slag, and cobalt. Carnival and marble colors demand a higher price.

Plate 79
UNKNOWN MANUFACTURER
Bird. Crystal, 2¼" high, 3" long.
Seen at $8.00 – 12.00

Has excellent quality glass. Suspect it is foreign made.

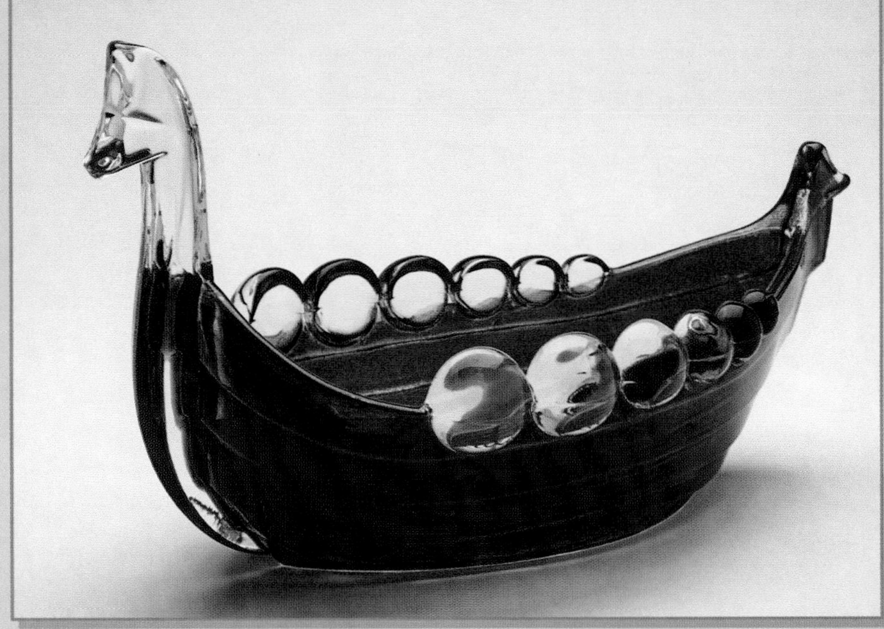

Plate 80
Duncan Glass Company
Viking Boat. Ruby stained, 11½" long, 6½" wide.
$125.00 – 150.00

Other colors: crystal, blue opalescent, and pink opalescent.

Reissues: none.

The boat is very heavy glass with excellent detail.

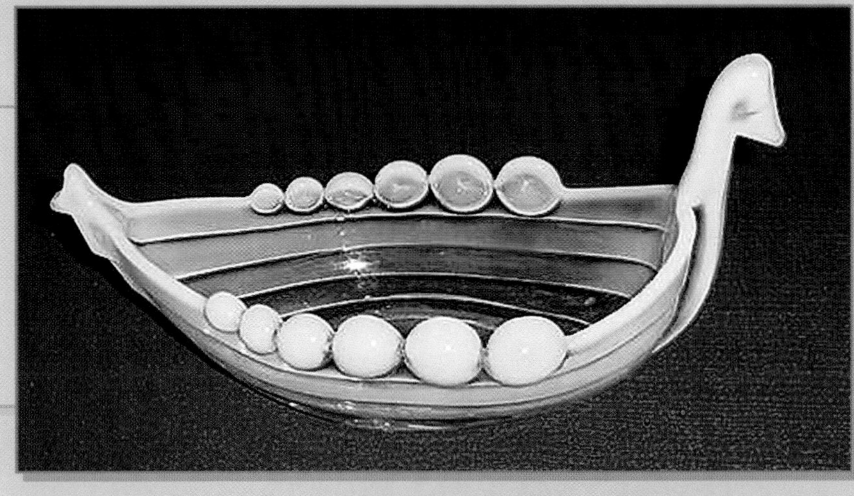

Plate 81
Duncan Glass Company
Viking Boat. Pink opalescent, 11½" long, 6½" wide.
Private collection — Market

This item is very rare. See Plate 80.

Plate 82
Fenton Art Glass Company
Viking Boat. Reissue, plum carnival, 14" long, 6¼" wide, 5" high, circa 1998.
$50.00 – 75.00

Original issue circa 1938, as part of the Viking line. Original issue was made in crystal and crystal satin.

Plate 83
NEW MARTINSVILLE GLASS COMPANY
#499 Clipper Ship Bookends. Crystal, 5¾" high, circa 1938.
$125.00 – 150.00 pair

Reissues: none

Similar bookends were made by U.S. Glass Co., circa 1925, in black or amber satin.

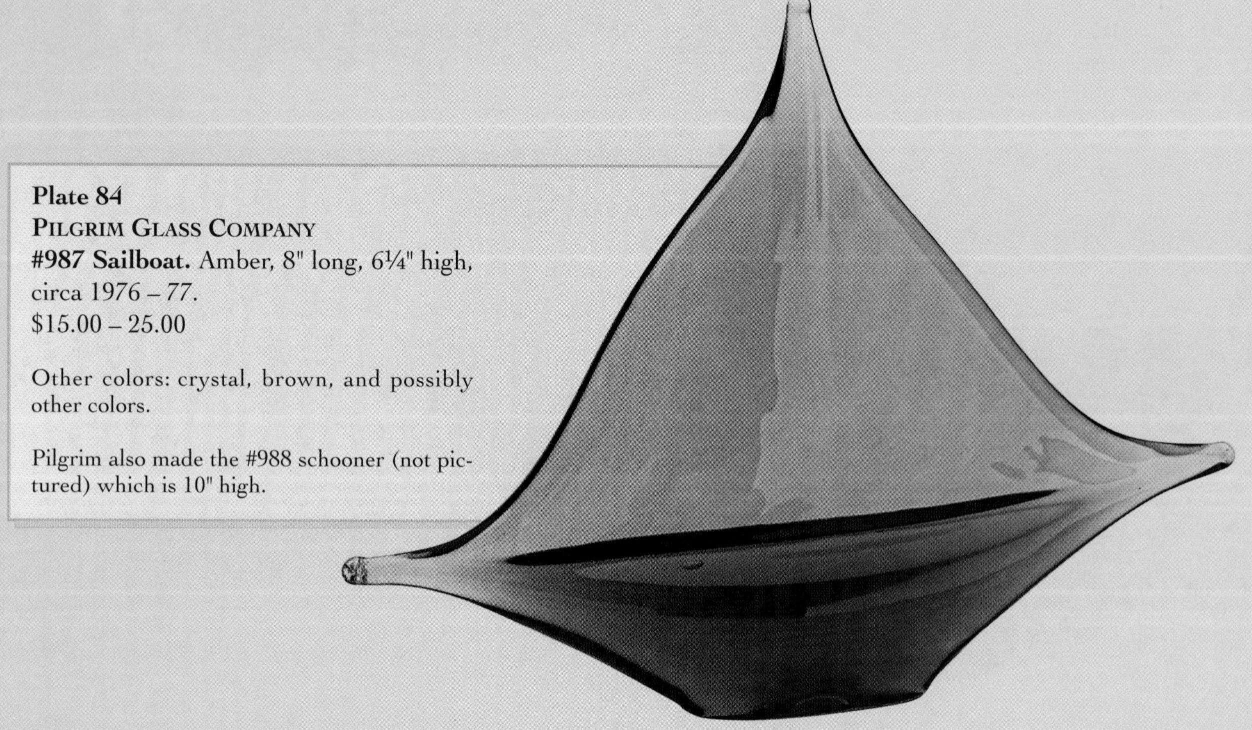

Plate 84
PILGRIM GLASS COMPANY
#987 Sailboat. Amber, 8" long, 6¼" high, circa 1976 – 77.
$15.00 – 25.00

Other colors: crystal, brown, and possibly other colors.

Pilgrim also made the #988 schooner (not pictured) which is 10" high.

Plate 84A
HEISEY GLASS COMPANY
Bull. Crystal, 4" high, 7½" long (tip of tail to front hooves), 1949 – 52, mark appears under right front leg on belly near the base.
$2,400.00 – 2,600.00

Other colors: crystal frosted.

Reissues: Imperial Glass Co., in crystal and multiple colors. Dalzell-Viking in lavender ice as part of the Gem Animal Series. See below.

This figurine is solid glass and has superb detail. This guy demands top price in the market.

HCA "Gem Animal Series"

In 1993, Heisey Collectors of America, Inc., as a fundraising event, had Dalzell-Viking make 450 sets consisting of 12 different animals in the HCA-owned Heisey molds. They were produced in lavender ice. This set of 12 consisted of Bull, Pouter Pigeon, Show Horse, Large Elephant, Medium Elephant, Small Elephant, Rearing Horse Bookend, Mallard (wings up), Mallard (wings down), Mallard (wings ½), Scottie Dog, and King Fisher. These animals were marked HCA 93.

Not part of this original series were the Flying Mare, Tropical Fish, Goose (wings up), Goose (wings down), Goose (wings ½), Mother Rabbit, Heads Up and Heads Down Bunnies, Double Horse Head Paperweight, #1 Madonna, Victorian Girl Bell, Child's Cup, Giraffe, Asiatic Pheasant, Rabbit Paperweight, and perhaps others were made in lavender ice for HCA by Dalzell-Viking.

Some of the items produced in lavender ice, perhaps seconds or overruns, were frosted and will be seen on the market today.

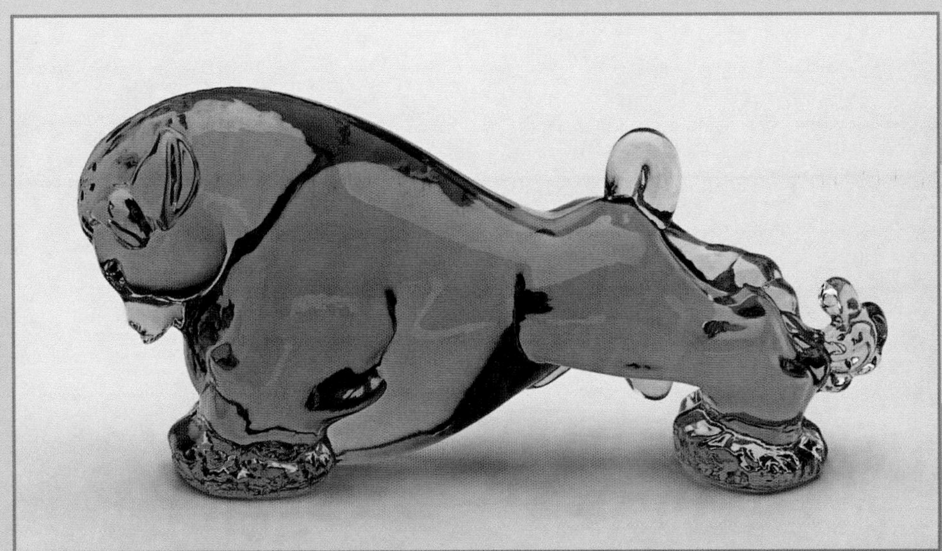

Plate 84B
DALZELL-VIKING GLASS COMPANY (Heisey Glass Co. mold)
Bull. Lavender ice.
$150.00 – 200.00

Camels

Plate 84C
L.E. Smith Glass Company
Camel Lying Down. Crystal, 4½" high, 6" long, raised Shriners emblem on neck, hollow base.
$45.00 – 50.00

Other colors: amber, cobalt, and perhaps others.

This camel has a paper label which reads "Great Lakes Convention, Zenobia Shrine Temple, 1971, Toledo, Ohio."

Plate 84D
L.E. Smith Glass Company
Camel Lying Down. Cobalt, 4½" high, 6" long.
$65.00 – 75.00

Plate 84E
Westmoreland Glass Company
Camel Covered Dish. Pink carnival, 5½" high, 6" long, circa 1924.
$150.00 – 175.00

Commonly referred to as "Humphrey."

Other colors: original colors, green mist, milk glass, yellow mist, antique blue, lilac mist, and cobalt. Original colors are difficult to find.

Reissues: in chocolate glass, milk glass, cobalt, vaseline, mother of pearl, amethyst, light green milk, and possibly others.

Summit Art Glass Co. presently owns the mold.

Plate 84F
Summit Art Glass Company
(original Westmoreland mold)
Camel Covered Dish. Chocolate glass, 5½" high, 6" long, circa 1980s.
$65.00 – 75.00

See Plate 84E.

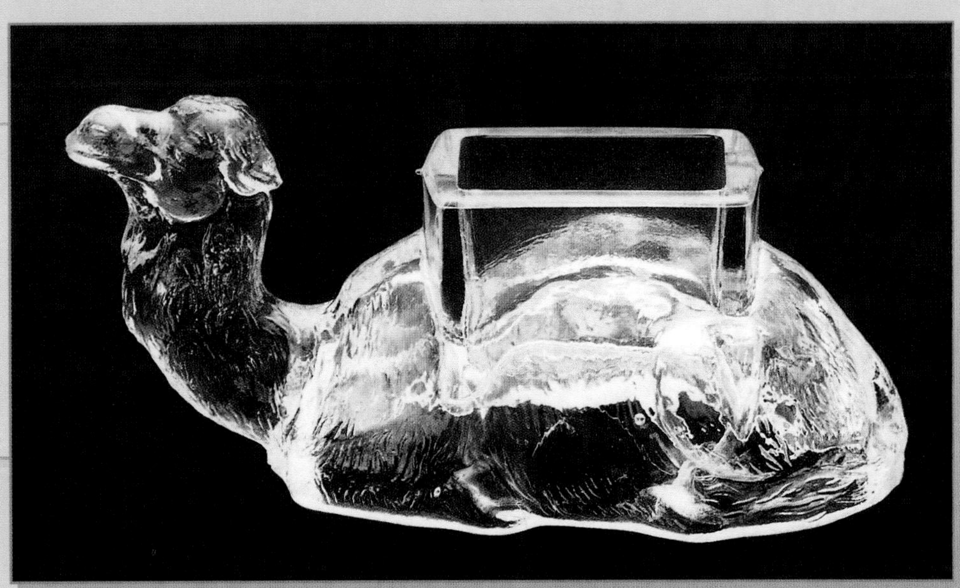

Plate 84G
Unknown Manufacturer
Camel, Lying Down. Crystal, 7" long, circa 1928.
Seen at $55.00 – 65.00

Hollow place on back will hold a package of cigarettes.

Cats

Plate 85
CAMBRIDGE GLASS COMPANY
Cat Bottle. Crystal, 11" high (without lid), 22 oz., circa 1920s.
$45.00 – 55.00

Other colors: peach blo, ritz blue, topaz, and apple green.

This bottle was also made in a smaller size, 8¾" high, 8 oz. Both sizes came with a shot glass lid.

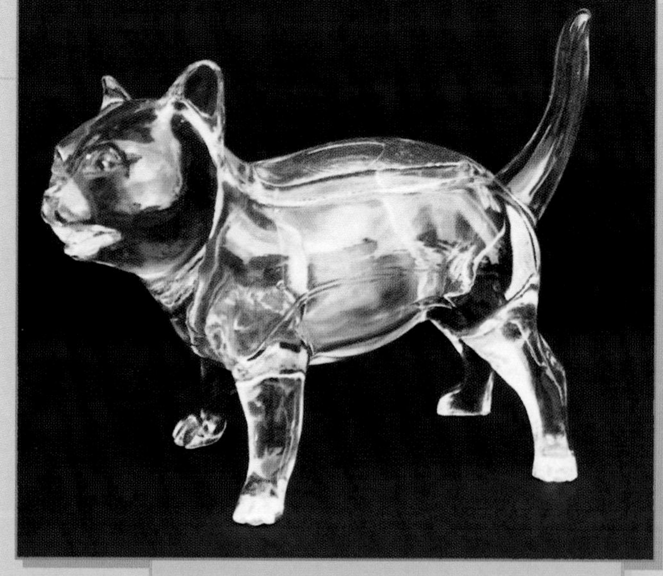

Plate 86
CO-OPERATIVE FLINT GLASS COMPANY
Cat and Cover. Crystal, circa 1927.
$275.00 – 300.00

Other colors: transparent colors and black glass.

Plate 87
FENTON ART GLASS COMPANY
Sitting Cat. Custard, floral decoration, 3¾" high, circa late 1970s.
$35.00 – 40.00

Other colors: made in many Fenton colors with and without decorations.

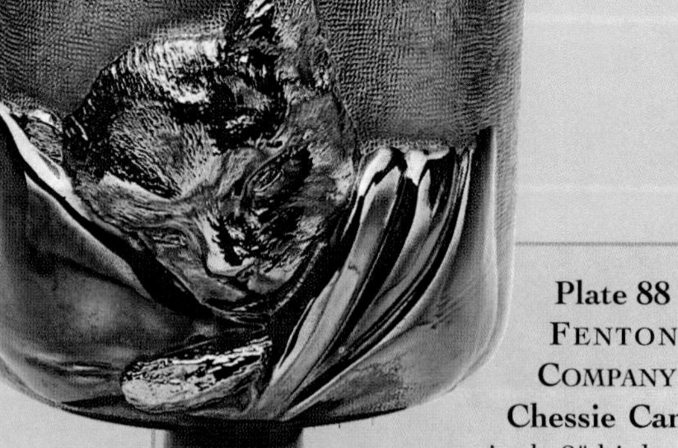

Plate 88
FENTON ART GLASS COMPANY
Chessie Candy Box. Carnival, 8" high, 4½" diameter, circa 1970.
$175.00 – 200.00

Other colors: teal carnival, light purple carnival, shell pink iridized, red carnival, and possibly other colors.

This was made in 1970 for the Chesapeake & Ohio Railroad as a special gift for VIPs. Railroad slogan "Ride the Chesapeake and sleep like a kitten." Fenton's original issue was in rosalene.

Plate 89
FENTON ART GLASS COMPANY
(Reissued from Tiffin Glass Co. mold)
#5177 Alley Cat. First issued in 1970, in amethyst carnival, 11" high.
Left: Velva rose satin, $125.00 – 135.00
Center: Dusty rose carnival, $140.00 – 160.00
Right: Black carnival, $175.00 – 200.00

For original mold details see Plate 99.

Plate 90
FENTON ART GLASS COMPANY
(Reissued from Tiffin Glass Co. mold)
#5177 Alley Cat. 11" high.
Left: Electric blue iridized, $140.00 – 160.00
Center: Ruby marble, $200.00 – 250.00
Right: Purple slag, $135.00 – 140.00

For original mold details see Plate 99.

Plate 91
FENTON ART GLASS COMPANY
(Reissued from Tiffin mold)
Happy Cat. 6½" high, circa late 1990s.
Left to right:
Cobalt satin, $60.00 – 70.00
Topaz iridescent, $65.00 – 75.00
Teal, carnival, $65.00 – 7500
Twilight blue, $60.00 – 70.00

See Plate 102.

Plate 92
FOSTORIA GLASS COMPANY
2821/357 Cat. Olive green, 3¼" high, circa 1971 – 73.
$30.00 – 35.00

Other colors: crystal, lemon and light blue (plain or frosted).

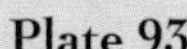

Plate 93
NEW MARTINSVILLE GLASS COMPANY
#1926 Nice Kitty Good Night Set. Green with painted decorations, 10" high, circa 1926, with shot glass lid.
$75.00 – 100.00

Other colors: crystal, black, amber, blue, and rose (plain or frosted).

Cambridge made a very similar decanter, see Plate 85.

Plate 94
NEW MARTINSVILLE GLASS COMPANY
#1926 Nice Kitty Good Night Set. Pink with painted decorations, 10" high, circa 1926.
Without shot glass lid, $45.00 – 55.00

See Plate 93.

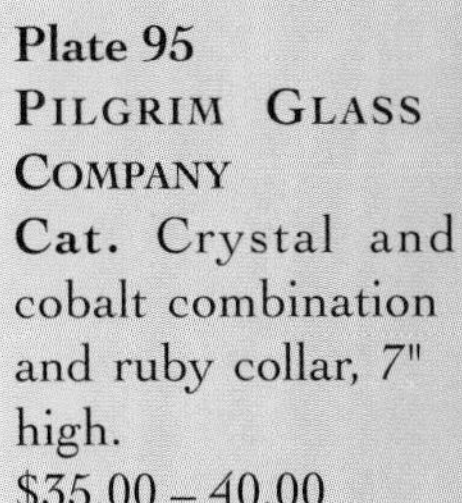

Plate 95
PILGRIM GLASS COMPANY
Cat. Crystal and cobalt combination and ruby collar, 7" high.
$35.00 – 40.00

Plate 96
PILGRIM GLASS COMPANY
Cat. Green, 4¼" high.
$10.00 – 12.00

Plate 97
RAINBOW GLASS COMPANY
Cat. Crystal, 6½" high.
$8.00 – 10.00

Plate 98
L.E. SMITH GLASS COMPANY
Cat. Crystal frosted, 2¾" high, 4" long.
$10.00 – 14.00

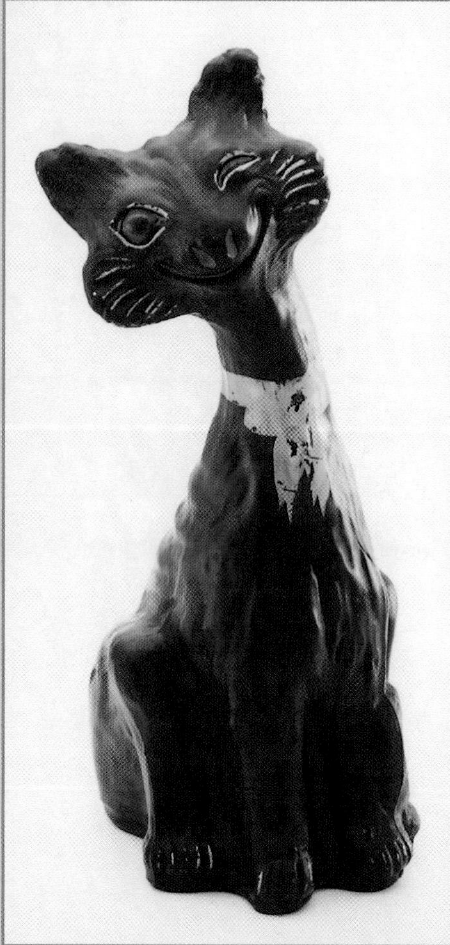

Plate 100
TIFFIN GLASS COMPANY
#9448 Sassy Susie Cat.
Milk glass, 11" high, circa 1929 – 41.
$450.00 to Market

See Plate 99.

Plate 99
TIFFIN GLASS COMPANY
#9448 Sassy Susie Cat.
Black satin, 11" high, circa 1928 – 41.
$175.00 – 200.00

Other colors: milk glass and perhaps other decorations. Also came in shiny and satin finishes.

Reissues: Fenton Art Glass. See Plate 89.

Plate 101
TIFFIN GLASS COMPANY
#9445 Cat. $6\frac{1}{4}$" high, raised bumps, circa 1924, very rare.
$450.00 to Market

Because of the raised bumps it is sometimes referred to as "Bumpy Cat."

Plate 102
TIFFIN GLASS COMPANY
#9446 Grotesque Cat. $6\frac{1}{2}$" high, circa 1920s.
Left: Satin with decorations, $150.00 – 200.00
Right: Shiny finish, $150.00 – 200.00

Other colors: perhaps milk glass.

Reissues: Fenton Art Glass Co. See Plate 91.

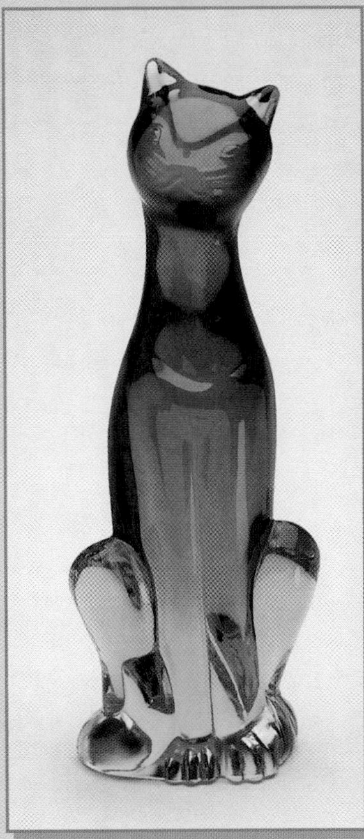

Plate 103
VIKING GLASS COMPANY
#1322 Cat. Orange, 8" high, circa 1960s.
$40.00 – 60.00

Other colors: made in several Viking colors.

Plate 104
VIKING GLASS COMPANY
Paperweight Cat. Ruby, 6" high, circa 1960s.
$25.00 – 30.00

Other colors: made in several Viking colors.

Came in two sizes, 6" and 8½".

Plate 105
VIKING GLASS COMPANY
Cat. Crystal frosted, 6½" high, 4½" long.
$15.00 – 20.00

Plate 106
WESTMORELAND GLASS COMPANY
Cat on Ribbed Base. Milk glass, 4" high, 4" wide.
$35.00 – 45.00

Other colors: blue milk, combination of blue and white milk, and possibly other colors.

Reissues: In the 1990s, produced for P. Rosso, in multiple colors.

Chickens

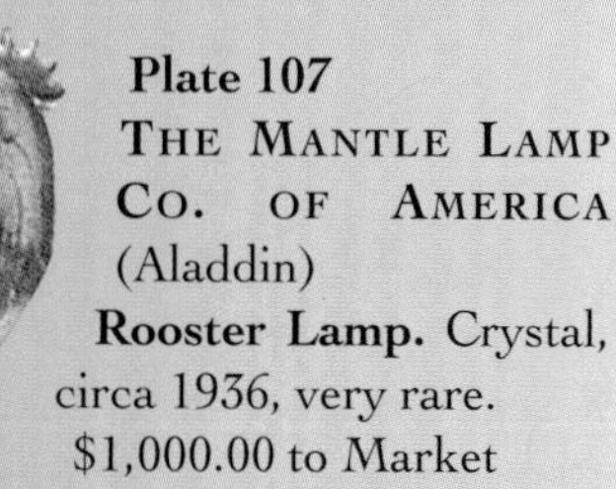

Plate 107
THE MANTLE LAMP CO. OF AMERICA (Aladdin)
Rooster Lamp. Crystal, circa 1936, very rare.
$1,000.00 to Market

Plate 108
ANCHOR HOCKING GLASS COMPANY
Chicken Covered Dish. Crystal, 4" high, 3½" diameter, circa 1950s.
$15.00 – 20.00

Seen in crystal only.

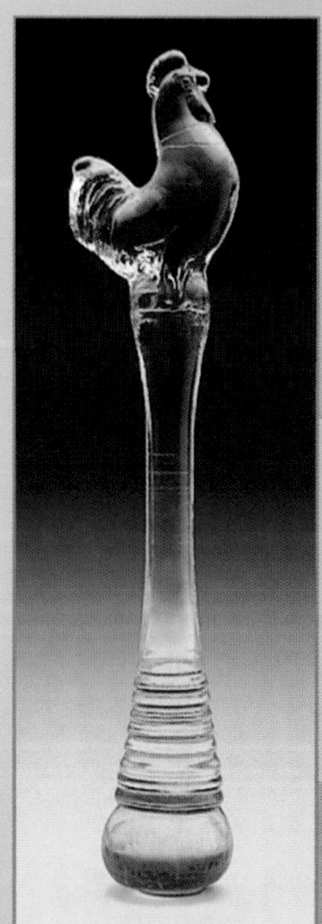

Plate 109
CAMBRIDGE GLASS COMPANY
#2 Rooster Muddler. Crystal, 5¼" high, circa 1930s.
$35.00 – 40.00

Plate 110
FENTON ART GLASS COMPANY
#5188 Chicken Server. Milk glass with amethyst, oval shape, rare.
$300.00 – 325.00

Other colors: milk glass body with green head and milk glass body with black head.

Reissues: Made in 1955 – 56, #5189, in all milk glass.

Plate 111
FENTON ART GLASS COMPANY (Original Paden City mold)
Barnyard Rooster. Sea mist green iridescent, 8¾" high, circa mid-1990s.
$250.00 – 300.00

Other colors: rose mist iridescent.

Reissues: In the 2000s was issued in opal and black with or without decorations and perhaps in other colors.

Plate 112
FENTON ART GLASS COMPANY
(Original Paden City mold)
Barnyard Rooster. Rose mist iridescent, 8¾" high. Circa mid-1990s.
$250.00 – 300.00

See Plate 111.

Plate 113
FENTON ART GLASS COMPANY
#5196 Chick on Basket. 5½" long, 4" high, 4" wide, circa 1953 – 54.
Left: Milk glass bottom, amethyst top, $50.00 – 70.00
Right: Milk glass bottom, green top, $50.00 – 70.00

Plate 114
Fostoria Glass Company
#2629 Chanticleer. Crystal, 10¾" high, circa 1950 – 58.
$200.00 – 250.00

Other colors: black and milk glass.

Reissues: none known.

Plate 115
Fostoria Glass Company
#2629 Chanticleer. Black, 10¾" high, circa 1950 – 58.
$500.00 – 600.00

See Plate 114.

Plate 116
Fostoria Glass Company
#2629 Chanticleer. Milk glass, 10¾" high, circa 1950 – 58.
$600.00 to Market

The milk glass roosters exploded (broke) when taken from the mold; therefore very few survived. In order to save the milk glass production, the mold was altered to make the top tail feathers solid rather than split. See Plates 114 and 115.

Plate 117
Fostoria Glass Company
Two-Piece Covered Hen. Circa 1960s.
Left: Aqua, $100.00 – 125.00
Center: Decorated milk glass, $100.00 – 125.00
Right: Pink, $100.00 – 125.00

The only covered animal dish ever made by Fostoria.

Plate 118
Haley Glass Company (Kemple Glass Co., from Haley mold)
Rooster, Head Down. 9" high, hollow base.
Left: Haley Rooster. Crystal, $45.00 – 55.00
Center: Kemple Rooster. Amber, $45.00 – 55.00
Right: Kemple Rooster. Milk glass decorated, $45.00 – 55.00

John E. Kemple purchased the Haley rooster mold. Kemple glass was produced in the late 1940s and early 1950s, in East Palestine, Ohio, and from the late 1950s through the 1970s in Kenova, West Virginia. Kemple Glass produced this rooster in milk glass, crystal, and colors, with some being decorated.

The Paden City Glass Co. rooster (head down) is almost identical to the Haley/Kemple rooster, but is solid glass. See Plate 130.

Plate 119
A.H. Heisey Glass Company
The Chicken Family.

Rooster. Crystal, 5½" high, 5" long (breast to farthest most point of tail). Seldom marked, but when found, the mark appears on the right side, tip of first feather.
$525.00 – 625.00

Other colors: crystal frosted and amber.

Reissues: Imperial Glass Co., milk glass and amber. Fenton Art Glass Co., Rosalene.

This animal is solid glass and has good detail. It was made only over a two year period and is not seen very often.

Chick, Head Down. Crystal, 1" high, 1⅜" long (tip of tail to top of head), 1948 – 49. There is a possibility that some were marked.
$100.00 – 110.00

Other colors: none.

Reissues: Imperial Glass Co., milk glass. Fenton Art Glass Co., Rosalene.

This animal is solid glass and has very little detail. It is the smallest of the Heisey figurines. It is sometimes confused with the chicks produced by New Martinsville Glass Co. The wings on the Heisey chicks are smooth mounds while the wings on the New Martinsville chicks have an actual line outlining the wings. See Plate 127.

Chick, Head Up. Crystal, 1" high, 1⅜" long (tip of tail to top of head), 1948 – 49. There is a possibility that some were marked.
$100.00 – 110.00

Other colors: none.

Reissues: Imperial Glass Co., milk glass. Fenton Art Glass Co., Rosalene.

This figurine is solid glass and has very little detail. From all appearances the same mold was possibly used for both and the difference is the angle of the grinding on the bottom. Same method as used on the Heisey Sparrow.

Hen. Crystal, 4¼" high, 3¾" long (tip of tail to front of head), 1948 – 49. Seldom marked but when found, it appears on the right side at the tip of the wing.
$425.00 – 525.00

Other colors: none.

Reissues: Imperial Glass Co., in multiple colors. Fenton Art Glass Co., in Rosalene.

This figurine is solid glass and has excellent detail. Like the rest of the Chicken Family, the Hen was made for only two years and is not easily found.

Crystal Animals, Heisey vs. Imperial

A question often asked by collectors is "How do I tell the difference in crystal animals produced by Imperial from the Heisey molds from those produced by Heisey?" The late Clarence Vogel, a pioneer in literature on Heisey, was a firm believer that a black light would show the difference between Heisey and Imperial crystal glass. Mr. Vogel's theory contends that under a black light Heisey crystal will have yellow tones while crystal produced by Imperial would reflect only the color of the light. We, along with many others, have experimented with this and found it to be true on the items tested.

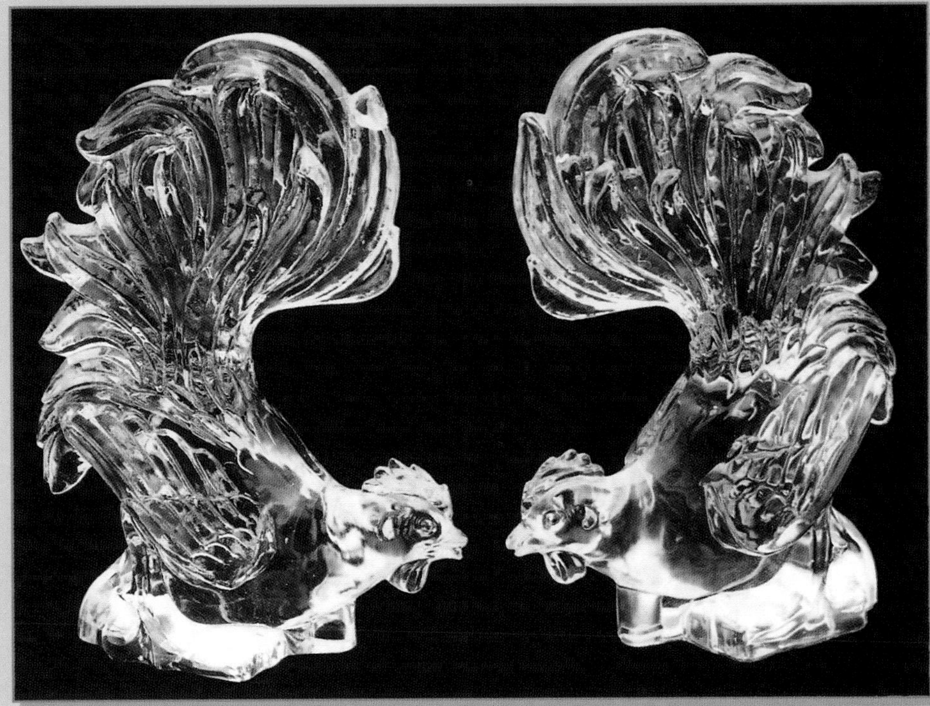

Plate 120
Heisey Glass Company
Fighting Rooster. Crystal, 7½" high, 5½" long (tip of beak to back of tail), 1940 – 46. Seldom marked. When found, it appears on the right side under the wing.
$200.00 – 250.00 each

Other colors: crystal frosted.

Reissues: Imperial Glass Co., in crystal, pink, and pink iridescent.

This figurine is solid glass and has excellent detail except for the tail. The tails are filled with mold marks, perhaps it was difficult to get them out of the molds. Because the beak is extended, they are quite often seen broken or chipped.

Plate 121
Heisey Glass Company
Rooster Vase. 6¼" high, 6" long (front of breast to back of tail), 1939 – 48.
$100.00 – 125.00

Other colors: crystal frosted.

Reissues: none.

This figurine is solid glass except for the back part which forms the vase. A quarter-inch pocket is formed in the base by the outside ridge which it sits on. The detail is excellent, even the feet are quite detailed. They have been seen in crystal frosted. Although the figurine was made by Heisey, we are not sure if they were frosted by Heisey or another company.

Plate 122
HEISEY GLASS COMPANY
Left to right:
Rooster Head Cocktail. Crystal, 5¼" high.
$50.00 – 60.00
Rooster Head Cocktail Shaker. 14" high.
$85.00 – 100.00
Chanticleer Cocktail. 5½" high.
$55.00 – 65.00
Bantam Rooster Cocktail. 4¼" high.
$400.00 – 500.00

The cocktail shaker consists of three pieces, the shaker, a strainer, and the rooster head stopper, which sits down in the strainer. The rooster head is sometimes frosted.

Plate 123
IMPERIAL GLASS COMPANY (from Heisey molds)
The Chicken Family.
Rooster. Milk glass, 5½" high, 1978, made for HCA, IG.
$35.00 – 50.00
Hen. Milk glass, 4½" high, 1978, made for HCA, IG.
$30.00 – 40.00
Chicks. Milk glass, 1" high, 1978, made for HCA, IG.
$15.00 – 20.00 each (Head Up or Head Down)

See Plate 119.

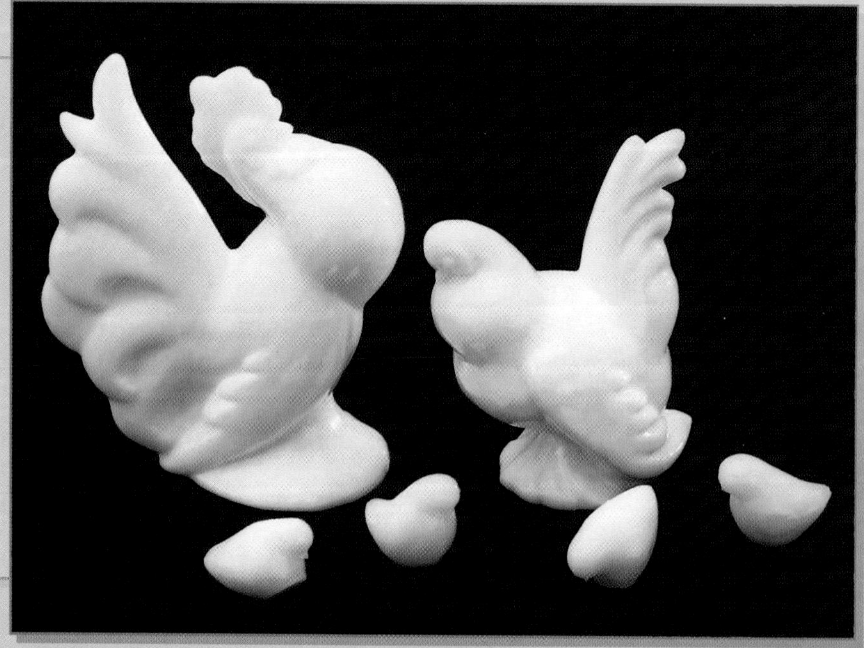

Plate 124
IMPERIAL GLASS COMPANY (Heisey mold)
Hen. Charcoal satin, 4½" high, 1980, feasibility item, marked IG.
$150.00 – 200.00

Plate 125
IMPERIAL GLASS COMPANY (Heisey mold)
Hen. Peach blo, 1960, rare.
$400.00 – 425.00

This figurine is still on the "bust-off" as it came out of the mold.

Heisey Gold Series

In the summer of 1992, HCA, as a fundraiser, contracted with Fenton Art Glass Co. to produce 12 Rosalene animals from Heisey molds. There were to be 450 sets produced and each set numbered. The original 12 Gold Series animals were as follows.

Airdale	Gazelle
Colt, standing	Giraffe
Cygnet	Hen
Duckling, standing	Rabbit paperweight
Filly, head forward	Sow
Fish, bookend	Tiger paperweight

Late in 1992, there were 450 sets each of the Balking and Kicking Colts produced and were considered an add-on to the Gold Series. Although there were other animals produced in Rosalene, they were not considered as part of the Gold Series.

Plate 126
FENTON ART GLASS COMPANY (Heisey mold)
Hen. Rosalene, 4½" high, 1992.
$60.00 – 70.00

See Heisey Gold Series.

Plate 127
New Martinsville Glass Company
The Chicken Family.
#669 Hen. Crystal, 5" high, until 1948.
$55.00 – 65.00
#668 Rooster, with Crooked Tail. Crystal, 7½" high, until 1951.
$65.00 – 75.00
#667 Chick. Crystal, 1" high, until 1948.
$25.00 – 30.00
#667 Chick. Crystal frosted, 1" high, until 1948.
$25.00 – 30.00

Other colors: Chick also came in cobalt and amber.

Reissues: Hen and Rooster reissued by Dalzell-Viking in crystal in 1988. The chicks have also been seen in cobalt and crystal.

Plate 128
New Martinsville Glass Company
#667 Chick. Amber, 1" high.
$55.00 – 65.00

See Plate 119 to compare with the Heisey chicks.

Plate 128A
Morgantown Glass Company
Chanticleer Cocktail. Blue, 3¾" high, circa 1950s.
$35.00 – 40.00 each

Other colors: made in multiple Morgantown colors.

Often confused with Heisey Bantam cocktails. See Plate 122.

Paden City Glass Company
Rooster Cocktail Shaker. Crystal, 12¼" tall.
$140.00 – 160.00

Often confused with Heisey Rooster Head Shaker. See Plate 122.

Although the shaker is often seen with one or more Chanticleer Cocktails, one must remember that they were in fact made by two different companies.

Plate 129
PADEN CITY GLASS COMPANY
Left: **Rooster (Chanticleer).** Pale blue, 9½" high, circa 1940.
$300.00 – 375.00
Right: **Rooster (Elegant).** Pale blue, 11" high, circa 1940.
$350.00 – 400.00

Other colors: both roosters were made in crystal and crystal frosted.

Plate 130
PADEN CITY GLASS COMPANY
Left: **Rooster, Head Down.** Crystal, 8¾" high (Barth Art mold).
$75.00 – 100.00
Right: **Rooster, Barnyard.** 8¾" high.
$125.00 – 150.00

Other colors: Head Down Rooster was made in a dark blue, see Plate 132A. The Barnyard Rooster was made in a darker blue and black. See Plates 131 and 133.

A Rooster similar to Head Down Rooster was made by K.R. Haley and Kemple Glass. See Plate 118.

Plate 131
Paden City Glass Company
Rooster, Barnyard. Dark blue, 8¾" high.
$350.00 – 400.00

Other colors: See Plates 130 and 133.

Plate 132
Paden City Glass Company
Rooster (Chanticleer). Crystal, 9½" high, circa 1940.
$125.00 – 150.00

Plate 132A
Paden City Glass Company
(Barth Art mold)
Rooster, Head Down. Dark blue, 8¾" high.
$300.00 – 350.00

Plate 133
Paden City Glass Company
Rooster, Barnyard. Black, 8¾" high.
$450.00 to Market

Other colors: See Plates 130 and 131.

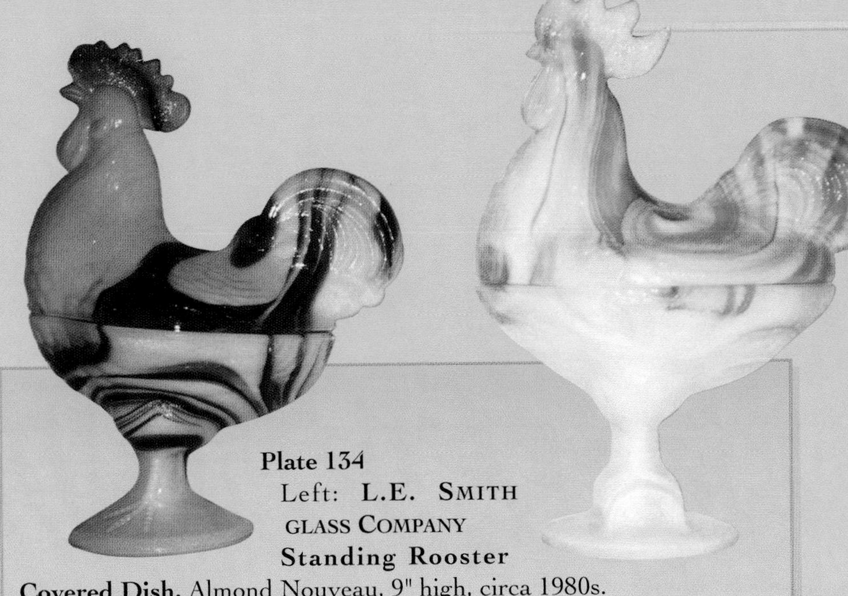

Plate 134
Left: **L.E. Smith Glass Company**
Standing Rooster Covered Dish. Almond Nouveau, 9" high, circa 1980s.
$85.00 – 100.00

Other colors: crystal, blue, black, crystal luster, and perhaps others.

Right: **Kanawha Glass Company**
Standing Rooster Covered Dish. Orange slag, 9½" high, circa 1971.
$75.00 – 95.00

Other colors: azure slag, green slag, mardi gras slag, and perhaps others.

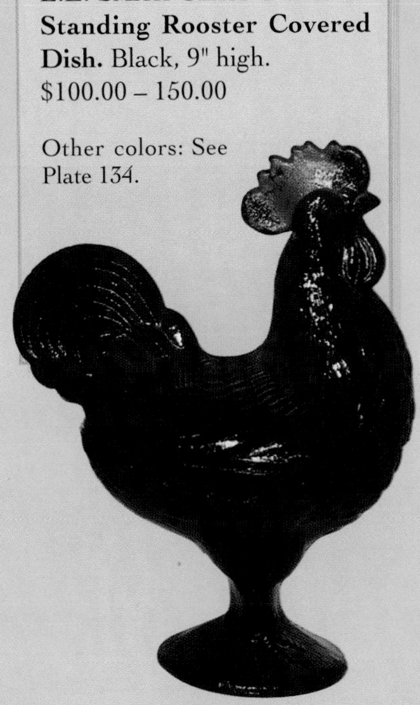

Plate 135
L.E. Smith Glass Company
Standing Rooster Covered Dish. Black, 9" high.
$100.00 – 150.00

Other colors: See Plate 134.

Plate 136
L.E. Smith Glass Company
Fighting Cock. Amberina, 9" high, circa 1960s.
$45.00 – 65.00

Other colors: blue, green, amber, butterscotch slag, and perhaps others.

Plate 137
L.E. Smith Glass Company
Fighting Cock. Butterscotch base slag (brown to red swirls), 9" high, circa 1960s.
$100.00 – 125.00

Other colors: See Plate 136.

Only 200 pairs were made in butterscotch slag.

Plate 138
VIKING GLASS COMPANY
#1321 Epic Rooster. 9½" high, circa 1960s.
Left to Right: Avocado, $40.00 – 50.00
Ruby, $55.00 – 65.00
Orange, $40.00 – 50.00

Other colors: Blunique (dark medium blue), honey (amber), and persimmon (amberina).

Reissues: Rooster made in limited production in 1978, in ruby and crystal.

Plate 139
WESTMORE-LAND GLASS COMPANY
Standing Rooster Covered Dish. Milk glass with painted comb and feet, 8½" high, circa 1950s.
$35.00 – 50.00

Other colors: black milk glass, milk glass with decorations, blue, green, and perhaps others.

Plate 140
UNKNOWN MANUFACTURER
Rooster. Crystal, 9½" high, 10½" long.
Seen at $65.00 – 75.00

This figurine is solid glass and has excellent detail.

Plate 141
UNKNOWN MANUFACTURER
Rooster. 8" high, hollow on rectangular base.
Seen at $55.00 – 65.00

Rooster sold through Sabin's in McKeesport, Pennsylvania, and advertised in *The Crockery & Glass Journal* in 1945.

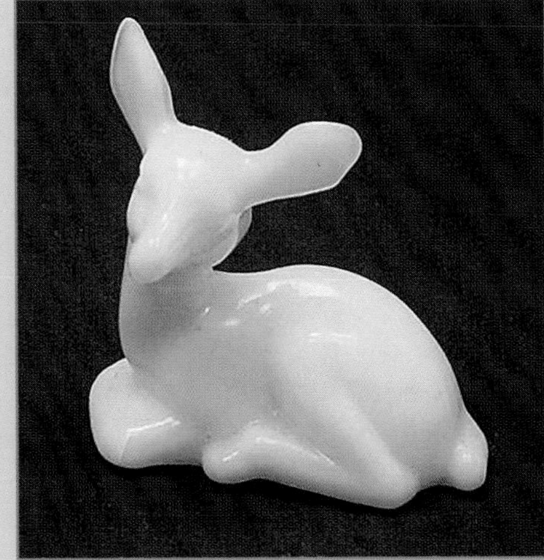

Plate 142
Fenton Art Glass Company
#5160 Fawn. Custard, 3½" high, 3½" long, circa 1983 – 84.
$25.00 – 28.00

Other colors: custard with decorations, crystal, carnival, daisies on cameo satin, and others. Produced up into the 1990s.

Plate 143
K.R. Haley Glassware Company
#251 Deer. 6" high, circa 1940s.
Left: Crystal frosted, $30.00 – 40.00
Right: Crystal, $30.00 – 40.00

Kemple Glass Co. purchased this mold from Haley in 1950. They reissued this item in milk glass, amber, and perhaps others.

Plate 144
Unknown Manufacturer
Deer Bookends. Crystal, 5" high.
Seen at $35.00 – 45.00 pair.

Plate 145
Fostoria Glass Company
#2589 Deer, Standing. Crystal, 4¾" high, circa 1940 – 43.
$35.00 – 45.00
#2589½ Deer, Reclining. Silver mist, 2½" high, circa 1940 – 43.
$35.00 – 45.00
#2589½ Deer, Reclining. Crystal, 2½" high, circa 1940 – 43.
$35.00 – 40.00

Other colors: both Reclining and Standing Deer were made in milk glass, 1954 – 58. See Plate 146.

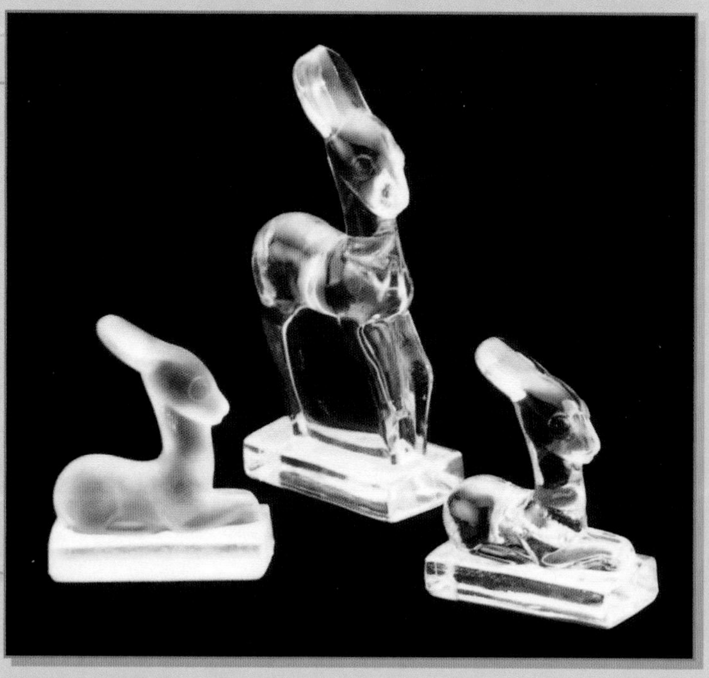

Plate 146
Fostoria Glass Company
#2589 Deer, Standing. Milk glass, 4¾" high, circa 1954 – 58.
$35.00 – 45.00

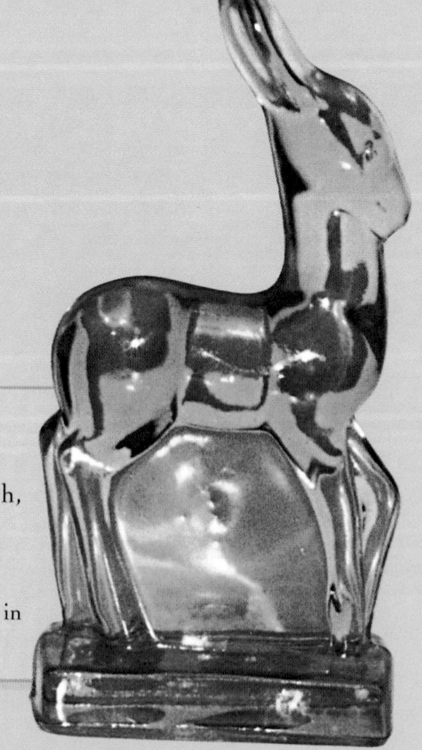

Plate 147
Fostoria Glass Company
#2589 Deer, Standing. Blue, 4¾" high, circa 1977.
$35.00 – 45.00

Made exclusively for Blue Colt Collectibles in 1977. Limited edition of 1,000 made.

Plate 148
HEISEY GLASS COMPANY
Doe Head Bookend. Crystal, 6¼" high, 3¼" wide at the bottom, year of production is unknown, mark appears on the lower left side.
$800.00 – 900.00

Other colors: crystal frosted.

Reissues: None. However, a reproduction of this figurine appeared in the Ohio area in late 1979 – early 1980. It is entirely possible that they could have been reproduced in amber as well as in crystal and crystal frosted.

Plate 149
TIFFIN GLASS COMPANY
Flower Floater with 10" Fawn. Crystal, 14½" long with sockets for three candles, late 1940s.
$125.00 – 150.00

Other colors: citron green, copen blue, smoke, and twilight.

As of 1985 Summit Art Glass owns this mold. Referred to as "Chinese Modern Gazelle and Three-lite Flower Float."

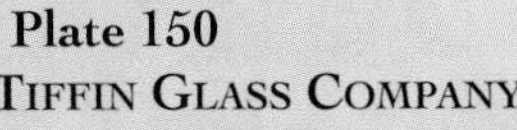

Plate 150
TIFFIN GLASS COMPANY
Flower Floater with 10" Fawn. Citron green, circa late 1940s.
$175.00 – 200.00

See Plate 149.

Dogs

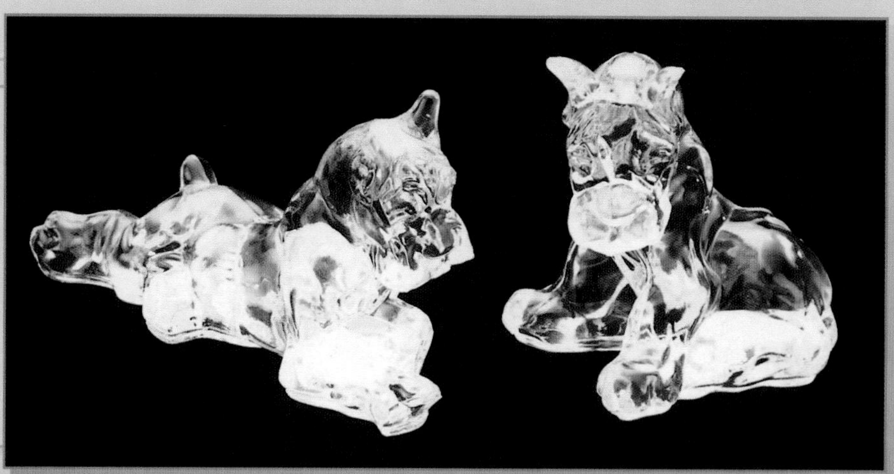

Plate 151
AMERICAN GLASS COMPANY (K.R. Haley design)
Left: **Boxer Dog, Lying.** Crystal, 3⅛" high.
$65.00 – 85.00
Right: **Boxer Dog, Sitting.** Crystal, 4¾" high.
$65.00 – 85.00

Both dogs were produced in frosted with red nose and black eyes.

Plate 152
CAMBRIDGE GLASS COMPANY
Scottie Bookend. Crystal, 6½" high, hollow figurine.
$125.00 – 150.00

Other colors: crystal satin, milk glass, and ebony.

Reissues: 1979 Imperial reissued in black satin for NCC (see Plate 155). Imperial in caramel slag (see Plate 156). Also made in light blue for NCC, by Mosser Glass Co. (see Plate 154).

Plate 153
Left: CAMBRIDGE GLASS COMPANY
Scottie Bookend. Ebony, 6½" high, hollow figurine.
$150.00 – 200.00

See Plate 152.

Right: BOYD CRYSTAL ART GLASS COMPANY
J.B. Scottie Dog. Amethyst, 3" high, 2½" long, circa 1983.
$15.00 – 20.00

Boyd made in several colors.

Plate 154
MOSSER GLASS COMPANY
(Cambridge Glass Co. mold)
Scottie Dog Bookend. Light blue, 6½" high, circa 1999.
$75.00 – 100.00

The National Cambridge Club (NCC), in 1999, had Mosser Glass Co. produce this item as part of a fundraiser for the museum. It is marked NCC 99 M.

Plate 155
IMPERIAL GLASS COMPANY
(Cambridge Glass Co. mold)
Scottie Dog Bookend. Black satin, 6½" high, circa 1979.
$75.00 – 100.00

The National Cambridge Club (NCC), in 1979, had Imperial Glass Co. produce this as a commemorative item. It is marked NCC 1979 LIG.

Plate 156
IMPERIAL GLASS COMPANY (Cambridge Glass Mold)
Scottie Dog Bookend. Caramel slag, 6½" high, circa 1982 – 83.
$100.00 – 150.00 each

See Plate 152.

Plate 157
CAMBRIDGE GLASS COMPANY
Bridge Hound. Circa 1930 – 50. Produced in many colors, including $30.00 – 40.00 range — amber, crystal, dianthus (peach blo), forest green, mandarin gold, and pistachio.
$45.00 – 55.00 range — carmen, crown tuscan, ebony, mocha, moonlight blue, royal blue, and tahoe blue.

Reissues: Guernsey Glass Co. now owns this mold and has reissued this item in heatherbloom, cobalt, green, moonlight blue, red, vaseline, and perhaps others.

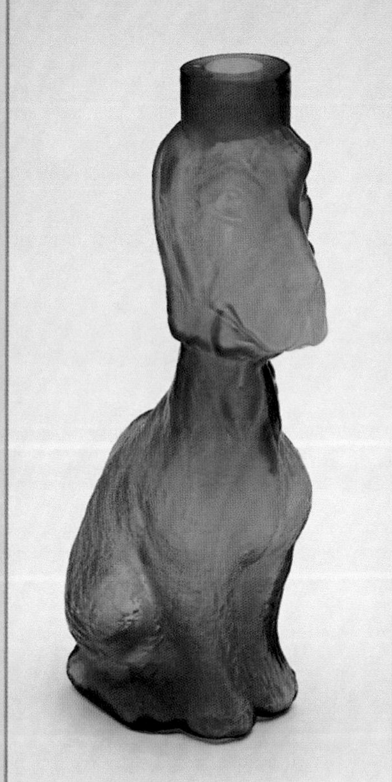

Plate 158
GUERNSEY GLASS COMPANY (Cambridge Glass Company mold)
Dog Bottle, without shot glass cap. Green satin, 8" high.
$45.00 – 55.00

Other colors: blue satin, purple satin, amber satin, and perhaps others.

Information from 1985 shows that this mold is owned by Summit Art Glass Co.

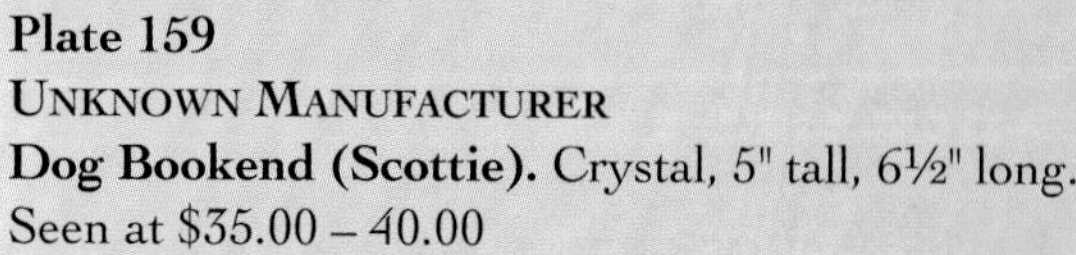

Plate 159
UNKNOWN MANUFACTURER
Dog Bookend (Scottie). Crystal, 5" tall, 6½" long.
Seen at $35.00 – 40.00

The quality of glass in this animal is very poor.

Plate 160
Co-Operative Flint Glass Company
#570 Dog and Cover. Crystal, 5¼" long, circa 1927.
$150.00 – 175.00

Other colors: made in transparent colors and some with hand decorations.

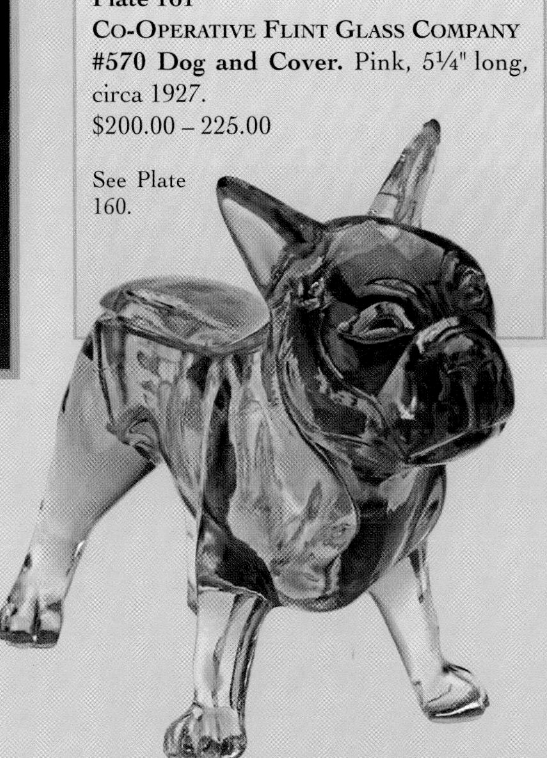

Plate 161
Co-Operative Flint Glass Company
#570 Dog and Cover. Pink, 5¼" long, circa 1927.
$200.00 – 225.00

See Plate 160.

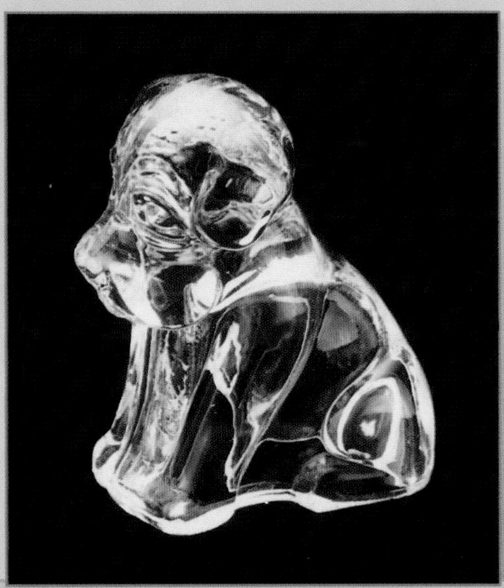

Plate 162
Federal Glass Company
#2565 "Mopey" Dog. Crystal, 3½" high.
$5.00 – 10.00

Federal began in 1900 making handmade glass, changing to automation by the 1920s. Federal became a major supplier of restaurants, motels, etc., and pioneered the decorated tumbler. The company became a division of Federal Paper Board Co. in 1958 and operated until the late 1970s.

Plate 163
Fenton Art Glass Company
RCA Victor Dog. Crystal, 3" high.
$75.00 – 85.00

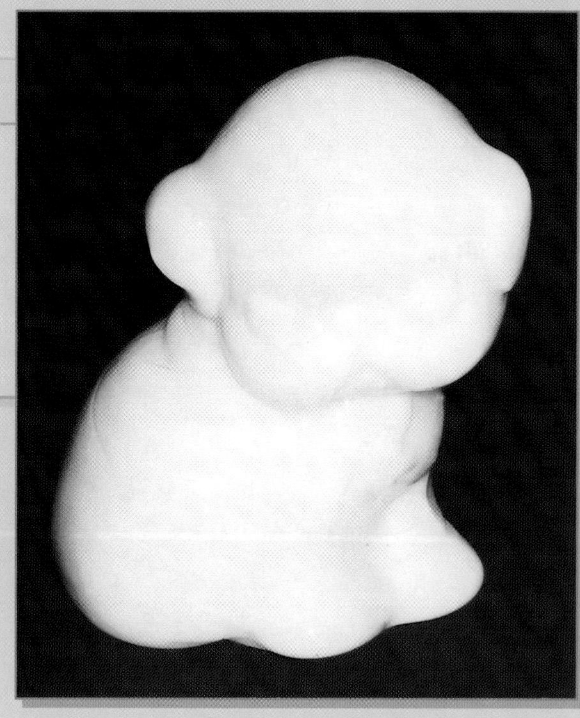

Plate 164
GILLINDER GLASS COMPANY
Sitting Pug Dog. Milk glass, 5¼" high, circa 1990s.
$30.00 – 35.00

This figurine is solid glass.

Plate 165
GILLINDER GLASS COMPANY
Sitting Pug Dog. Black, 5¼" high, circa 1990s.
$30.00 – 35.00

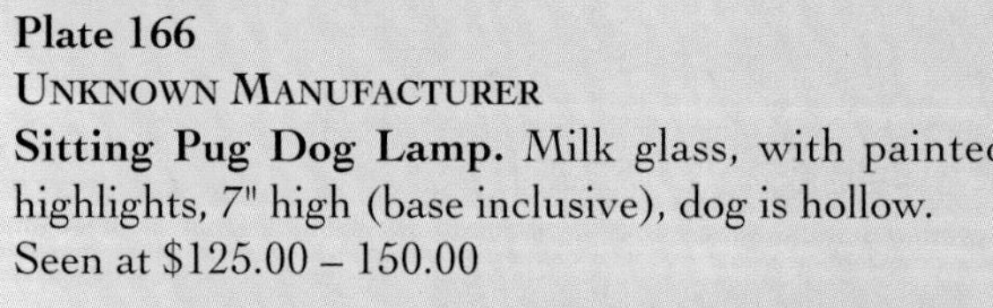

Plate 166
UNKNOWN MANUFACTURER
Sitting Pug Dog Lamp. Milk glass, with painted highlights, 7" high (base inclusive), dog is hollow.
Seen at $125.00 – 150.00

In the *Glass Collector*, issue #4, fall 1982, William Heacock stated "This adorable decorated milk glass puppy dog electric night lamp is a real mystery." He went on to say that it was not U.S. Glass because the base is different, and from the electric fixture it dated it from about 1920. He thought perhaps it was made by Consolidated Lamp and Glass.

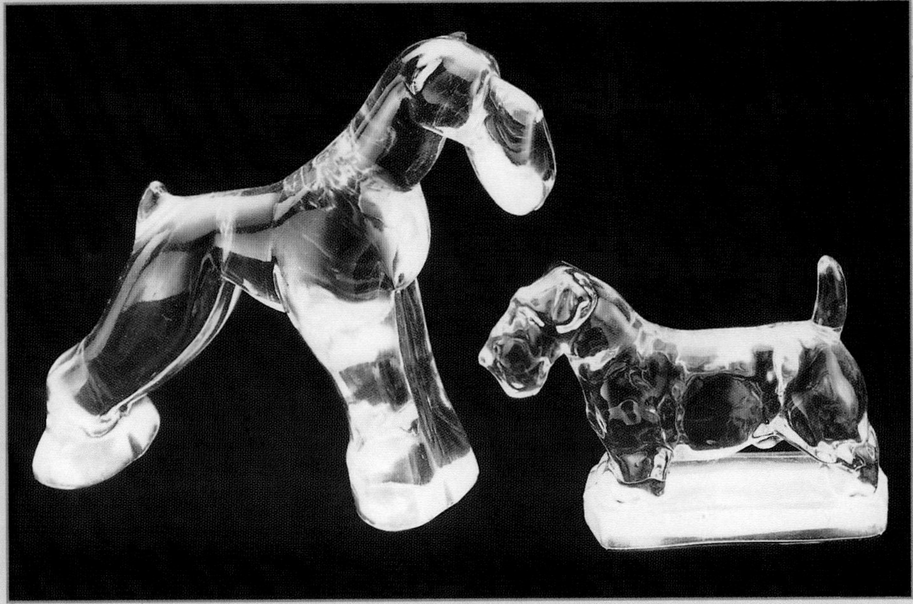

Plate 167
HEISEY GLASS COMPANY
Left: **Airedale.** Crystal, 5¼" high, 6½" long (farthest-most points), 1948 – 49.
$1,400.00 – 1,600.00

Reissues: Imperial Glass Co., in crystal and multiple colors. Fenton Glass Co., in Rosalene as part of the Gold Series. See Plate 126.

Seldom marked, but when mark is found, it appears on the side of the left back leg 1¼" up from the base. Made in crystal only.

Right: **Sealyham Terrier (Scottie).** Crystal, 3½" high, 4¾" long (farthest points), 1941 – 46.
$150.00 – 200.00

Reissues: Imperial Glass Co., in crystal and multiple colors. Dalzell-Viking Glass Co., as part of the Gem Series. See Plate 84B.

Seldom marked, but when mark is found, it appears on the side of the body.

Heisey Collectors of America, Inc., Purchases Original Heisey Molds

In 1985, the Heisey Collectors of America, Inc. purchased all existing Heisey molds in the Imperial Glass factory, except the Old Williamsburg line. The Heisey molds, including the existing animal molds are now, and have been, under the control of H.C.A. They have a board policy not to make items in the same color as originally made by Heisey. In addition each item made has a non-removable mark, generally HCA and the year. H.C.A. has had numerous items made from these molds by several glass companies in order to generate revenue to sustain a world class museum in Newark, Ohio.

Plate 168
IMPERIAL GLASS COMPANY
(Heisey Glass Co. mold)
Left: **Scottie Champ.** Ultra blue clear, 3½" high, circa 1982, marked ALIG.
$75.00 – 100.00

Other colors: Imperial produced this animal in amber and multiple other colors. Dalzell-Viking in lavender ice as part of the HCA Gem Series, see Plate 84B.

This item was made by Imperial Glass Co., for Mirror Images.

Right: **Champ Terrier.** Ultra blue clear, 5¾" high, circa 1982, marked ALIG.
$100.00 – 125.00

Other colors: Imperial produced this animal in multiple colors. Fenton in rosalene as part of the HCA Gold Series. See Plate 126.

This item was made by Imperial Glass Co., for Mirror Images.

Plate 169
IMPERIAL GLASS COMPANY (Heisey Glass Co. mold)
Scottie. Milk glass, 3½" high, circa 1978.
$50.00 – 60.00

This item was produced in milk glass in 1978 by Imperial for HCA and is marked IG.

Plate 170
FENTON ART GLASS COMPANY
(Heisey Glass Co. mold)
Airedale. Rosalene, 5¾" high, circa 1992.
$75.00 – 100.00

This item was produced by Fenton for HCA as part of the Gold Series. See Plate 126.

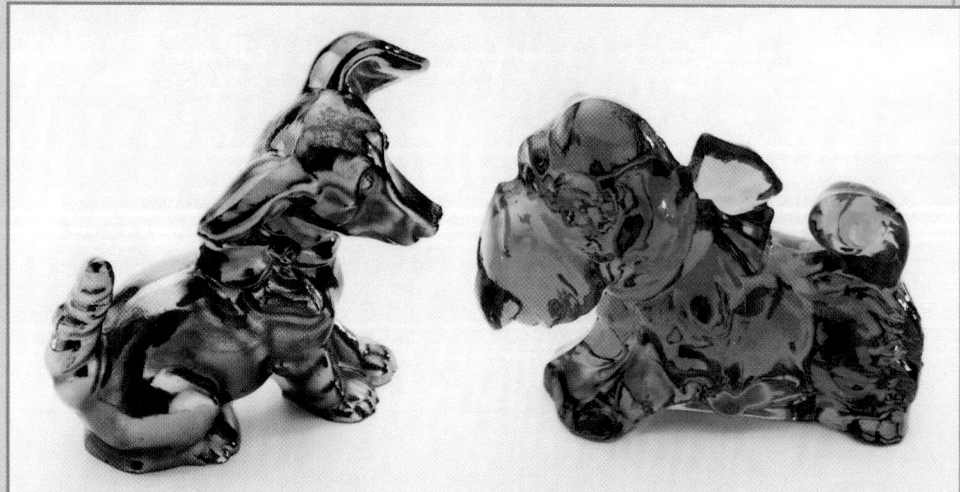

Plate 171
IMPERIAL GLASS COMPANY
Left: **Parlour Pup, Tail Up.** Amethyst carnival, 3½" high, circa 1980.
$50.00 – 55.00

Right: **Parlour Pup, Scottie.** Amber, 2½" high, circa 1983.
$15.00 – 20.00

Other colors: crystal, milk glass, doeskin, caramel slag, and perhaps others.

See Plate 172.

Commemorative issue dated 1983 in raised numbers and the initials NIGCS around the tail.

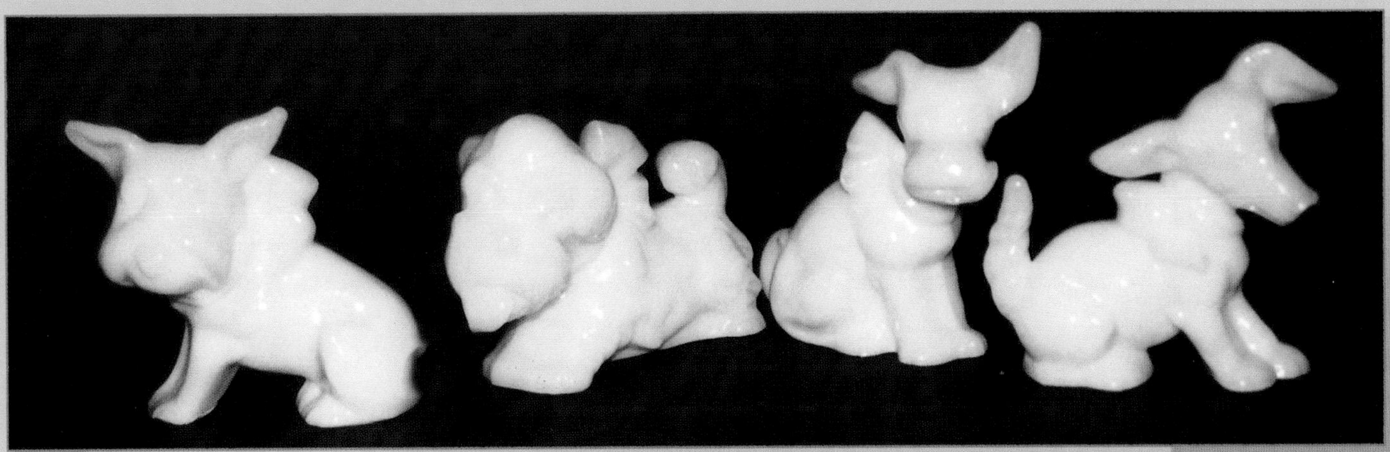

Plate 172
IMPERIAL GLASS COMPANY
Left to right:
Parlour Pup, Bulldog Type. Milk glass, glossy, 3" high, circa 1952. $65.00 – 75.00
Parlour Pup, Scottie Type. Milk glass, glossy, 2½" high, circa 1952. $65.00 – 75.00
Parlour Pup, Terrier, Tongue Out. Milk glass, glossy, 3½" high, circa 1952. $65.00 – 75.00
Parlour Pup, Terrier, Tail Up. Milk glass, glossy, 3½" high, circa 1952. $65.00 – 75.00

Reissues: All four pups were made in ultra blue for Mirror Images in 1983.

Boyd Art Glass Co. has owned all four Parlour Pup molds since 1985, and they bear the Boyd logo.

Plate 173
MOSSER GLASS COMPANY
#193 Collie. Crystal, 3" high, circa 1980s.
$10.00 – 15.00

Other colors: amber, yellow, chocolate slag, and perhaps others.

Plate 174
NEW MARTINSVILLE GLASS COMPANY
#733 Police Dog (German Shepherd). Pink, 6" high, oval base.
$125.00 – 150.00

This was generally used as a lamp base.

Plate 175
NEW MARTINSVILLE GLASS COMPANY
#733 Police Dog (German Shepherd). Crystal, 5" high, circa 1937 – 50.
$50.00 – 75.00

Other colors: none.

Reissues: In 1978 by Viking, with the following appearing on the base: 4/100; the NM incised on side of base; and paper label with Viking emblem. Also reissued in the mid-80s for Mirror Images in ruby, ruby satin, and ruby carnival by Viking (third in a series of five). Limited edition of 500, marked with a "V." See Plate 174.

Plate 176
NEW MARTINSVILLE GLASS COMPANY
#716 Wolfhound. Crystal, 7" high, until 1950.
$75.00 – 95.00

Reissues: Viking in the mid-1980s in ruby plain and carnival for Mirror Images. By Dalzell-Viking in 1988 – 90 in crystal and 1991 in black.

Plate 177
DALZELL-VIKING GLASS COMPANY
(New Martinsville Glass Co. mold)
Wolfhound. Black, 7" high, circa 1991.
$100.00 – 125.00

See Plate 176.

Plate 178
Viking Glass Company
(New Martinsville Glass Co. mold)
Wolfhound. Ruby carnival, 7" high.
$75.00 – 100.00

Made for Mirror Images

See Plate 176.

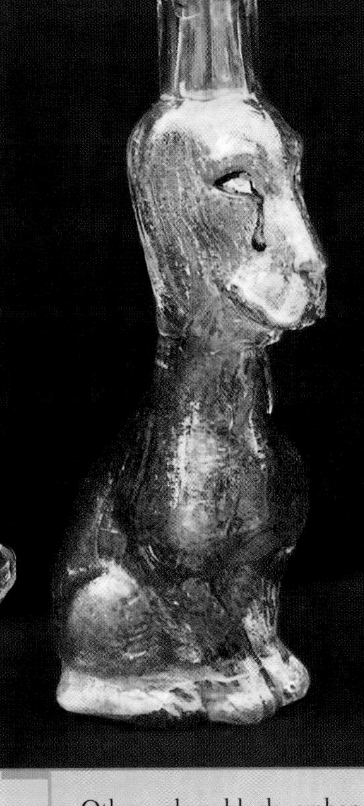

Plate 179
New Martinsville Glass Company
#1926 Volstead Pup Decanter. Crystal, 9½" tall (without hat). Circa 1926.
Without top $45.00 – 55.00

Other colors: black, amber, blue, green, and rose. All decorated.

This pup holds a pint. A tumbler serves as his hat. See Plate 158 for the Cambridge dog decanter.

Plate 180
New Martinsville Glass Company
#1926 Volstead Pup Decanter. Blue, 9½" tall (without hat), circa 1926.
Without top $55.00 – 60.00

See Plate 179.

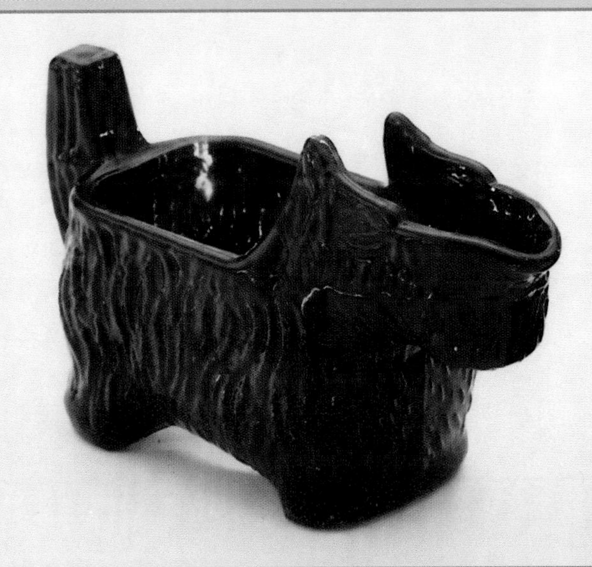

Plate 181
L.E. Smith Glass Company
Scottie Creamer or Pipe Rest. Fired-on black, 5½" long.
$10.00 – 12.00

Other colors: original issue was in crystal. Has been seen in other colors including vaseline.

Plate 182
L.E. SMITH GLASS COMPANY
Scottie Dog. Crystal frosted, 5" high.
$15.00 – 20.00

Made in other colors including black and in a smaller size.

Plate 183
L.E. SMITH GLASS COMPANY
Scottie Dog. Black, 5" high.
$50.00 – 75.00

Plate 184
UNKNOWN MANUFACTURER
Small Dog. Crystal frosted, 3½" high, 4" long.
Seen at $10.00 – 12.00

This dog is often confused with the Imperial Parlour Pups. One seen with a label "Poreg." Suspect they are foreign.

Plate 185
UNKNOWN MANUFACTURER
Small Dog Penholder. Pink penholder base and dog.
Seen at $15.00 – 20.00

The dog mounted on the penholder base is the same as the one shown in Plate 184.

Plate 186
TIFFIN GLASS COMPANY
Dog Pin Holder or Ashtray. Green, 3½" high, 4" diameter, circa 1920s – 30s.
$35.00 – 40.00

Other colors: black satin, gold, and perhaps others.

Plate 187
VIKING GLASS COMPANY
#1323 Dog. Orange, 8" high, circa 1960s.
$45.00 – 65.00

Other colors: leaf green, amber, and perhaps others.

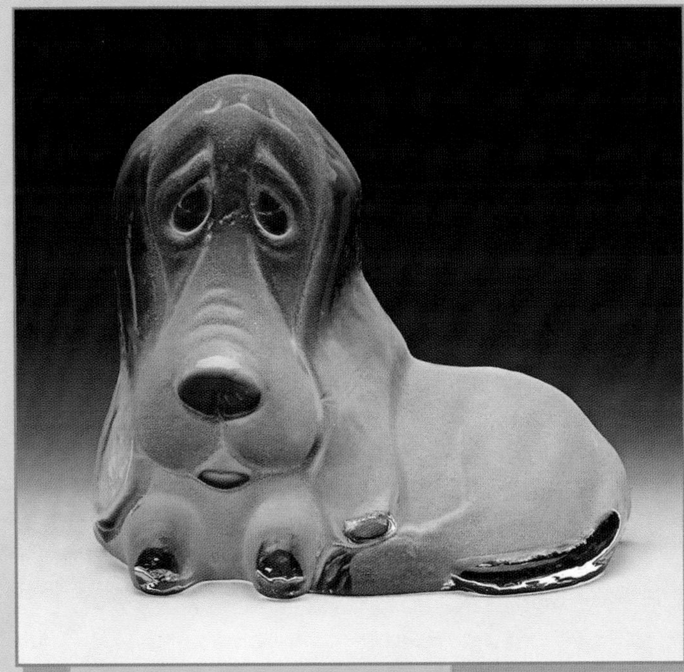

Plate 188
VIKING GLASS COMPANY
#7965 Basset. Crystal satin, 5" high, 6" long, circa 1980 – 81.
$15.00 – 25.00

Plate 189
VIKING GLASS COMPANY
#7754 Dog. Crystal satin, 5½" high, 4¼" long, circa 1980 – 81.
$15.00 – 20.00

Small Bulldog Comparison... The Mystery Deepens!

P.J. Rosso, of Wholesale Glass Dealers, tells us that when going to the old Westmoreland plant to purchase the small bulldog mold, he noticed two small bulldog molds. As one was incomplete, he didn't examine it, and couldn't say which side the collar buckled on. He purchased, and has since reissued, the small bulldog mold as we know it today.

Another source indicates there were also two molds for Tiffin's small bulldog.

It is the author's opinion, based on extensive research, that definite differences are apparent between the Tiffin and Westmoreland small bulldogs, indicating there would have been two or more molds, as opposed to Tiffin having borrowed Westmoreland's mold (as was the case with the large bulldog).

1. The collar of the Westmoreland pup is wider and always buckles on the left side, while Tiffin's buckles on the right and has a narrower collar.
2. From the back, the Westmoreland dog appears to be slouched more to the side than Tiffin's dog.
3. The chin line is slightly longer on the Westmoreland dog.

Tip: A check of original colors, as well as reissue colors of both companies, will help the collector to identify their dog.

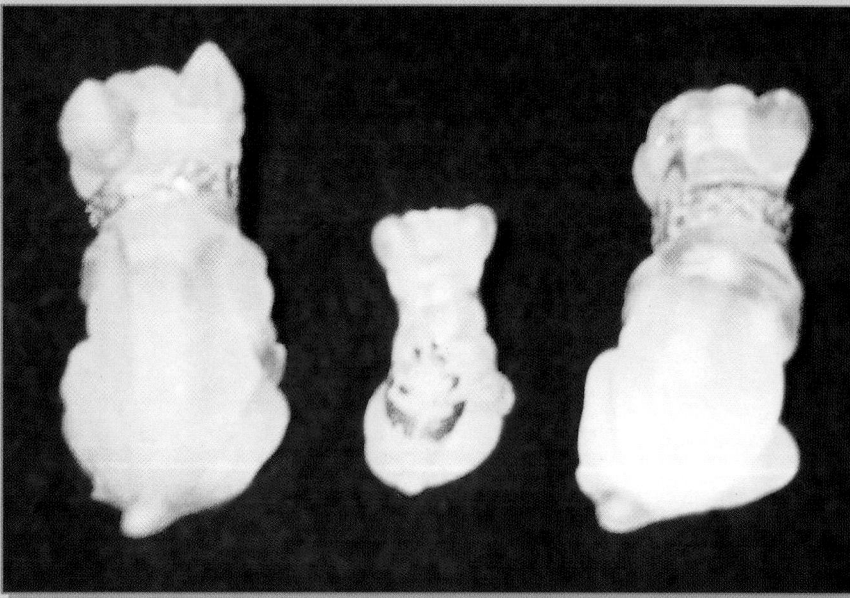

Plate 190
Tiffin's Small Bulldog.
Import Pup, souvenir of Canada.
Westmoreland's Small Bulldog.

Plate 191
Westmoreland's Small Bulldog
(right front paw missing).
Tiffin's Small Bulldog.

Plate 192
WESTMORELAND GLASS COMPANY
#75 Small Bulldog. 2⅝" high, collar buckle on left side.
Black mist, $25.00 – 35.00
Electric blue, $25.00 – 35.00
Brown mist, $25.00 – 35.00
Milk glass, $25.00 – 35.00
Crystal mist, $25.00 – 35.00

Other colors: crystal, black, golden sunset, moss green, ruby, carnival, electric blue carnival, and probably others.

Reissues: Reissued by Rosso Wholesale Glass Dealers after Westmoreland closed in 1984. Colors would include vaseline, cobalt, ruby, black amethyst, milk glass, black with red accents, white with red accents, cobalt with white collar, blue ice, blue ice carnival, blue slag, pink custard, cranberry, and cranberry ice carnival. Reissued in 1992 in green opalescent iridescent. Also reissued by Plum Glass Company in black satin and milk glass.

Plate 193
TIFFIN GLASS COMPANY
Small Bulldog. 2¾" high, collar buckle on right side.
Crystal frosted, $25.00 – 35.00
Black, $25.00 – 35.00

Plate 194
WESTMORELAND GLASS COMPANY
#78 Bulldog Doorstop. Golden sunset mist with green eyes, 8½" high, circa 1916, weighs 5½ lbs.
$350.00 – 450.00

Other colors: black milk glass, white milk glass, black mist, brown mist, moss green (jade reported in 1930s). All of these colors are extremely rare and priced at $350.00 – 450.00. Exceptionally rare is the circa 1925 bulldog with white head and black body. This fellow would be priced at $1,000.00 to Market.

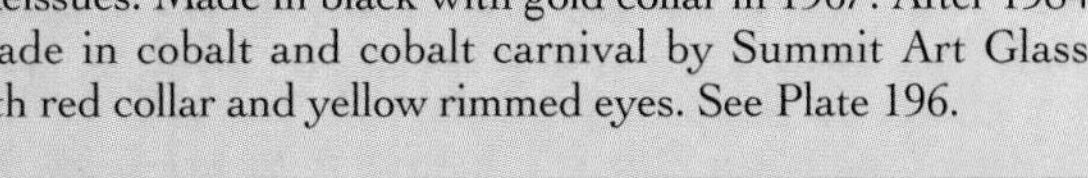

Reissues: Made in black with gold collar in 1967. After 1984, made in cobalt and cobalt carnival by Summit Art Glass, with red collar and yellow rimmed eyes. See Plate 196.

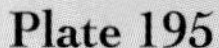

Plate 195
WESTMORELAND GLASS COMPANY
#78 Bulldog Doorstop. Green mist with red glass eyes, 8½" high, solid glass, circa 1916, weighs 5½ lbs.
$350.00 – 450.00

Summit Art Glass Co. purchased the large bulldog mold in 1985 when Westmoreland Glass Company closed.

Plate 196
Left: TIFFIN GLASS COMPANY
#78 Tiffin Bulldog Doorstop. Amber satin with green glass eyes, 8½" high, solid glass, ear missing.
$350.00 – 450.00

Right: SUMMIT ART GLASS COMPANY
#78 Summit Bulldog Doorstop. Cobalt blue with red leather collar and yellow glass eyes, 8½" high, solid glass.
$150.00 – 250.00

Other colors: Summit bulldog also made in cobalt blue carnival.

Plate 197
CAMBRIDGE GLASS COMPANY
#9 Dolphin Candlestick. Emerald, 9½" high, circa mid-1920s.
$100.00 – 125.00

Other colors: crystal, amber, blue bell, ivory, rubina, peach blo, ritz blue, and perhaps others.

Plate 198
CAMBRIDGE GLASS COMPANY
#50 Dolphin Candlestick. Crystal, 7¾" high, circa 1930s.
$75.00 – 100.00

Other colors: crown tuscan, milk glass, amber, carmen, amethyst, forest green, and perhaps others.

Plate 199
CAMBRIDGE GLASS COMPANY
#50 Dolphin Candlestick. Crown tuscan with Charleton decoration, 7¾" high, circa 1930s.
$150.00 – 175.00

See Plate 198.

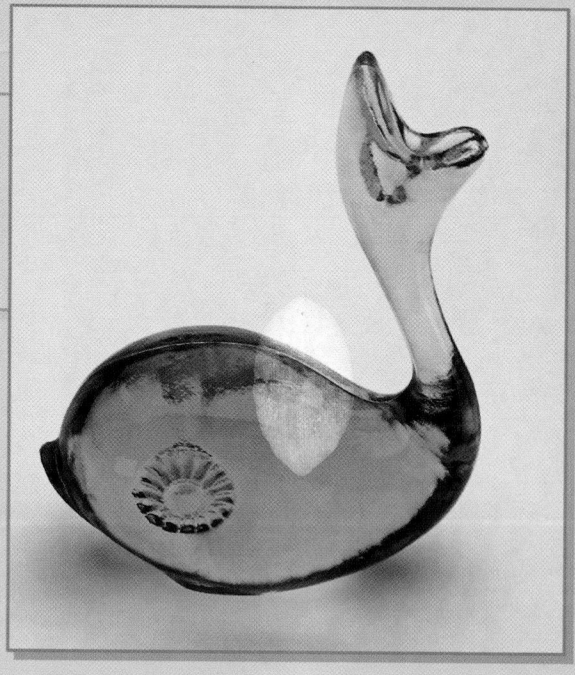

Plate 200
Fostoria Glass Company
2821/410 Dolphin. Blue, 4½" high, 3¾" long, circa 1971 – 73.
$20.00 – 25.00

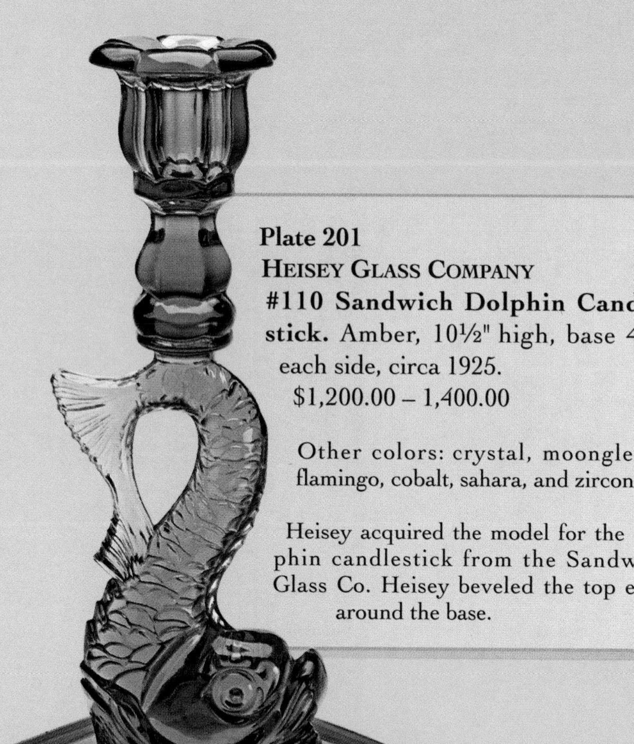

Plate 201
Heisey Glass Company
#110 Sandwich Dolphin Candlestick. Amber, 10½" high, base 4¼" each side, circa 1925.
$1,200.00 – 1,400.00

Other colors: crystal, moongleam, flamingo, cobalt, sahara, and zircon.

Heisey acquired the model for the dolphin candlestick from the Sandwich Glass Co. Heisey beveled the top edge around the base.

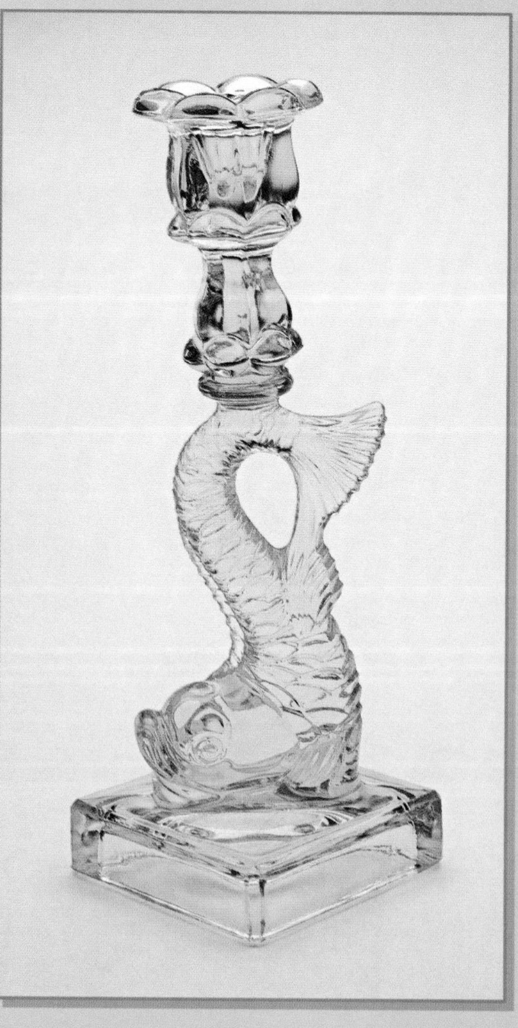

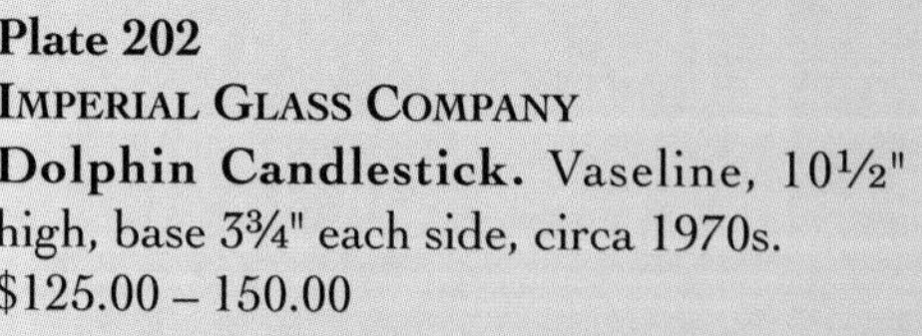

Plate 202
Imperial Glass Company
Dolphin Candlestick. Vaseline, 10½" high, base 3¾" each side, circa 1970s.
$125.00 – 150.00

Other colors: crystal, blue, and teal.

Marked MMA. Was made for Metropolitan Museum of Art, starting in the early 1970s. Copied from Sandwich Glass Co. Base on this candlestick has a smaller base than Heisey and the Dolphin head is solid where the Heisey Dolphin head is hollow. See Plate 201.

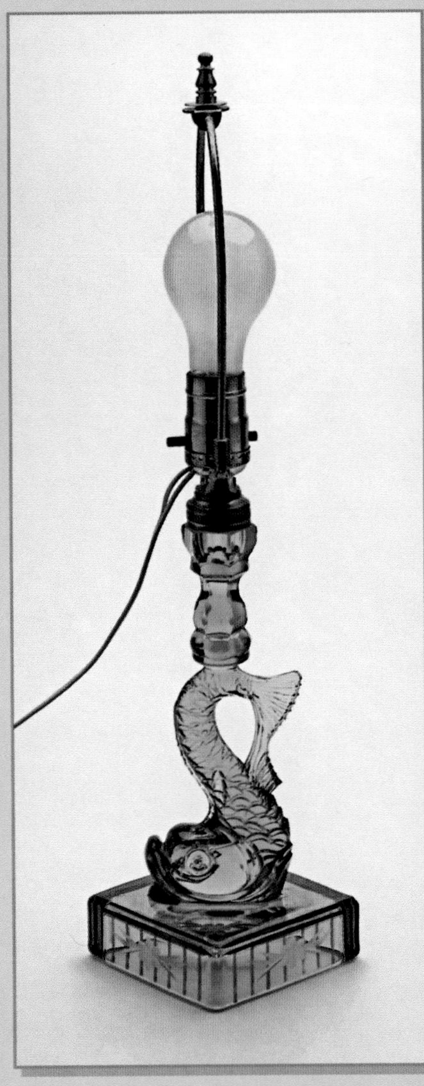

Plate 203
Heisey Glass Company
#110 Sandwich Dolphin Lamp. Moongleam, 9½" high (to the electrical fitting), base 4¼" each side, circa mid-1920s.
$350.00 – 450.00

Other colors: crystal, amber, flamingo, cobalt, sahara, and zircon. These are the colors in which the candlesticks were made.

An inch of the candle socket was cut off and a metal ring applied which holds the electrical fitting. Has a floral cutting on the base. Distribution of these lamps was made through a cut glass company in New York.

Plate 204
Heisey Glass Company
#1401 Empress Dolphin-Footed Candlestick. Moongleam, 6" high, circa 1929.
$150.00 – 200.00

Other colors: crystal, alexandrite, flamingo, and sahara.

Reissues: Imperial Glass Co., 1981 – 82, in sunshine yellow.

When marked, it will be found on the back of one of the dolphin feet.

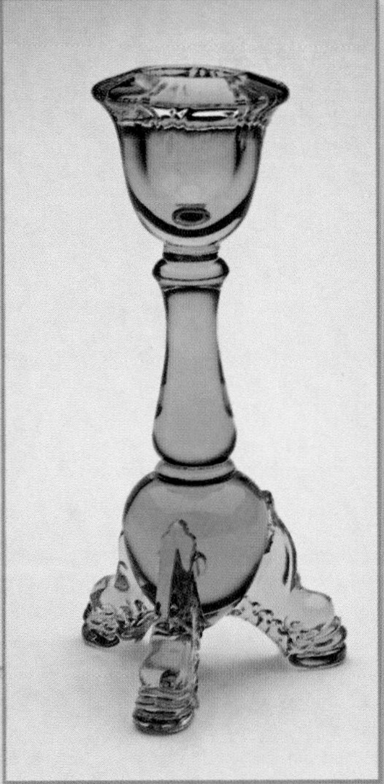

Plate 205
Heisey Glass Company
#1401 Empress Dolphin-Footed Mayonnaise.
Alexandrite, 5½" (top diameter), circa 1932.
$350.00 – 400.00

Other colors: crystal, flamingo, sahara, moongleam, and cobalt.

Reissues: Imperial Glass Co. in crystal.

Plate 206
HEISEY GLASS COMPANY
#109 Petticoat Dolphin Comport. Flamingo, 7¼" high bowl, 7¾" in diameter, circa 1925.
$175.00 – 225.00

Other colors: crystal, moongleam, and sahara.

Heisey designed the candlestick, which serves as the base for this comport, after an earlier candlestick by Northwood or Dugan.

Plate 207
HEISEY GLASS COMPANY
#109 Petticoat Dolphin Comport. Crystal and moongleam, 7¼" high, bowl 7¾" in diameter, circa 1925.
$225.00 – 250.00

See Plate 206.

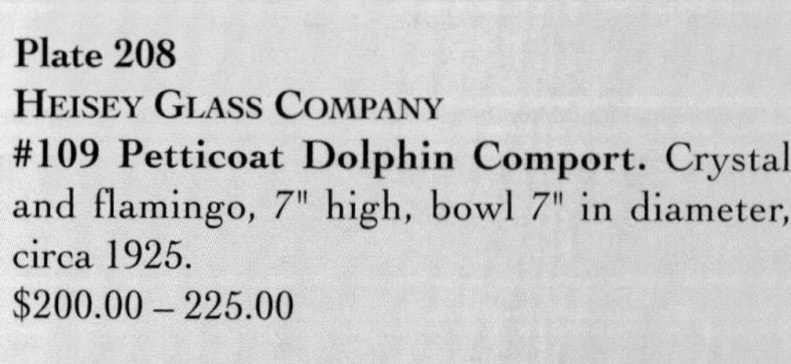

Plate 208
HEISEY GLASS COMPANY
#109 Petticoat Dolphin Comport. Crystal and flamingo, 7" high, bowl 7" in diameter, circa 1925.
$200.00 – 225.00

The bowl on this comport is paneled, as opposed to being plain as are the comports in Plates 206 and 207.

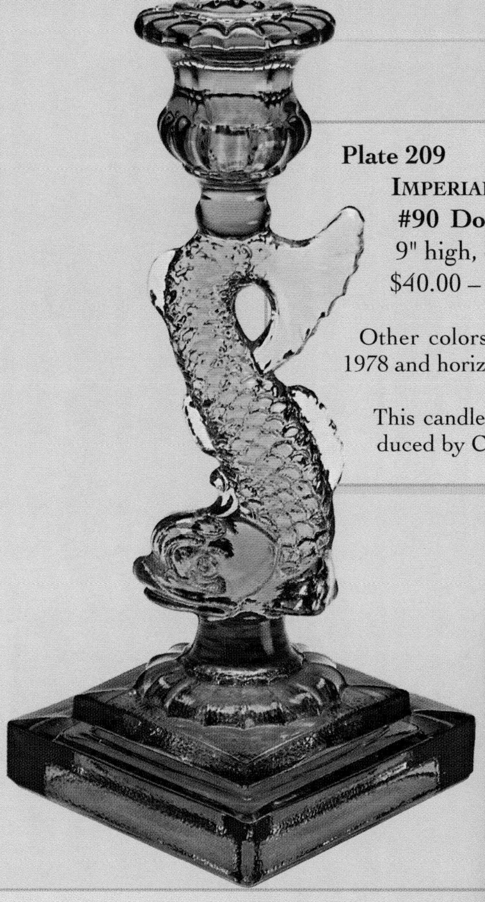

Plate 209
IMPERIAL GLASS COMPANY
#90 Dolphin Candlestick. Amber, 9" high, circa 1970s – 80s.
$40.00 – 50.00

Other colors: nut brown and ultra blue in 1978 and horizon blue carnival in 1970.

This candlestick was copied from one produced by Consolidated.

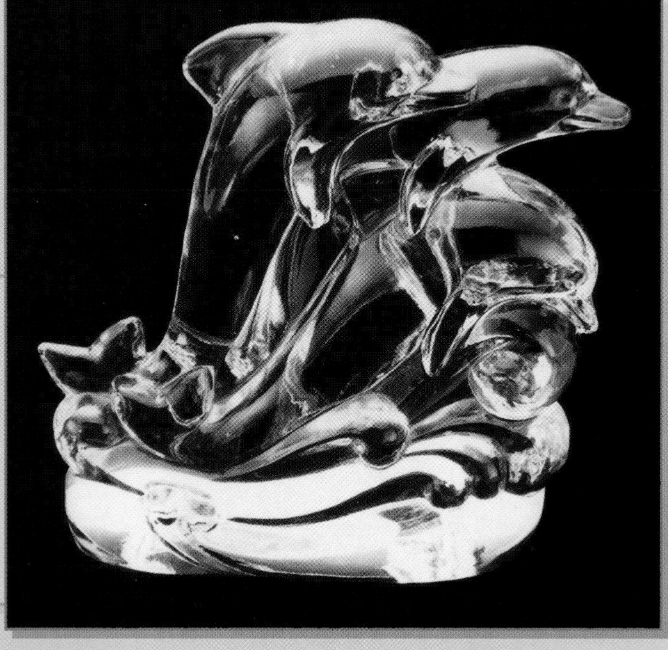

Plate 210
NEW MARTINSVILLE GLASS COMPANY
#766 Porpoise on Wave. Crystal, 6" high, circa 1940s.
Original issue: $350.00 – 400.00

Other colors: clear and frosted combination.

Reissues: 1985 – 86, Viking made a special pour in crystal for Sea World. 1988 – 90, Dalzell-Viking in crystal and frosted. These are marked on the bottom.

Plate 211
PILGRIM GLASS COMPANY
#904 Porpoise. Crystal, 6" high, 9" long, circa 1972.
$25.00 – 35.00

Plate 212
TIFFIN GLASS COMPANY
Dolphin Candlestick. Pink, 7¾" high, circa 1930s.
$35.00 – 45.00

Other colors: crystal, amber, green, blue, and perhaps other Tiffin colors.

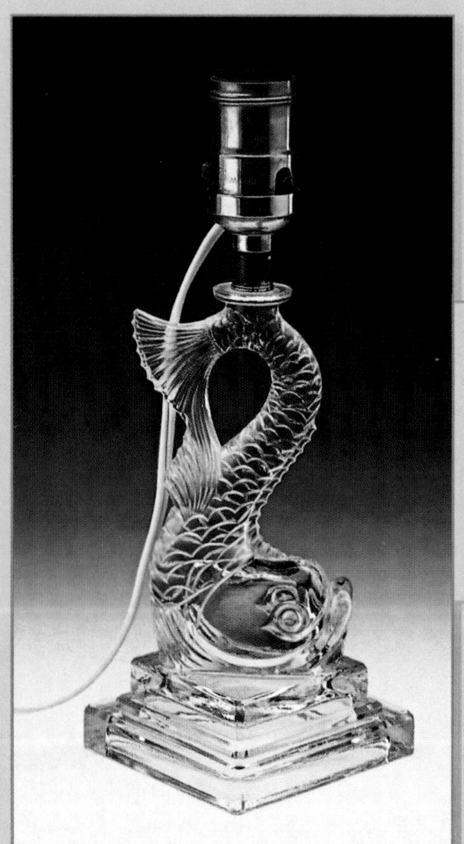

Plate 213
UNKNOWN MANUFACTURER
Dolphin Candlestick. Crystal, 7" high.
Seen at $35.00 – 40.00

This is a confusing collectible. Often labeled as Westmoreland; however, there are strong indications that they are Czechoslovakian.

Plate 214
WESTMORELAND GLASS COMPANY
#1049 Dolphin Comport. 7" high, 6¾" wide, circa 1924.
$45.00 – 55.00

Other colors: crystal, pink, milk glass, and perhaps other Westmoreland colors.

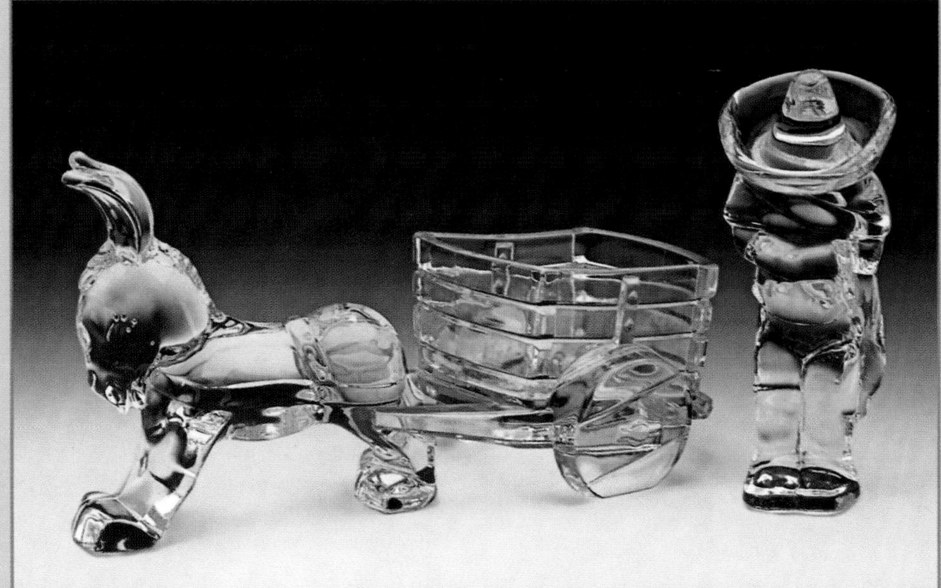

Plate 215
DUNCAN GLASS COMPANY
Donkey, Cart, and Peon.
Donkey, $175.00 – 200.00
Cart, $250.00 – 300.00
Peon, $200.00 – 225.00

All three pieces were made in crystal, crystal satin, and crystal with frosted highlights. It is difficult to find any of the three pieces and even more difficult to find them without any damage.

Donkey: The donkey is 4¾" high, from top of right ear to bottom of front feet. It is 4¾" long from front to back feet. He has a strap representing harness across his back and along both sides. His ears are tilted forward together, with the left being slightly lower than the right. The donkey is solid glass.

Cart: The two wheel car is 3½" wide from wheel to wheel, 5½" long (overall length) and is 3" high. The shafts of the cart, which go on each side of the donkey, are very vulnerable and easily broken. The cart is solid glass except for the inside of the cart box.

Peon: The Peon is 5½" high. His head and face are not visible. It has the appearance of a person with no head, just a hat sitting on a pair of shoulders. This figurine is solid glass.

Reissues: Fenton Art Glass Co. bought the molds for the Donkey and Cart from U.S. Glass Company in 1964 and reissued them as follows: Donkey reissued in white satin, blue satin, crystal satin, custard (with daisies), French opalescent, and burmese. The cart was reissued in white satin, blue satin, crystal satin, and burmese. Fenton made a commemorative donkey and cart for the Duncan Glass Society, Inc., as follows: 1986, blue opalescent donkey; 1987, blue opalescent cart; 1988, topaz opalescent donkey; 1989, topaz opalescent cart; 1991, yellow opalescent donkey and cart.

Plate 216
Left: **KANAWHA GLASS COMPANY**
Donkey. Amber, 4¾" high, 4" long.
$20.00 – 25.00

Came in multiple colors and is often confused with the Duncan Donkey. See Plate 215.

Center: UNKNOWN MANUFACTURER
Donkey. Crystal frosted, 3¾" high, 4" long.
Seen at $8.00 – 10.00

Confusing collectible. Generally seen tagged Duncan or Fenton.

Right: **FENTON ART GLASS COMPANY**
(Duncan Glass Co. original mold)
Donkey. Custard, 4¾" high, 4¾" long.
$35.00 – 40.00

Other colors: See Plate 215.

Plate 217
Fenton Art Glass Company
(Heisey Glass Co. original mold)
Donkey. French opalescent 6½" high, 5" long, circa 1988.
$40.00 – 60.00

Made by Fenton for H.C.A.

Plate 218
Fenton Art Glass Company (Duncan Glass Co. original mold)
Donkey and Cart.
Left: Donkey and Cart were made by Fenton in 1991 as a commemorative item for the Duncan Glass Society. Yellow opalescent. Obviously this is a one of a kind donkey and cart. The cart has been rounded and the ears pulled back. (Compare to the set on the right.)
Rarity prohibits pricing.

Center: **Donkey and Cart**. Blue opalescent. Both were commemorative items for the Duncan Glass Society. Donkey 1986 and the cart 1987.
Set $150.00 – 175.00

Right: **Donkey and Cart.** Yellow opalescent. This set was a commemorative item for the Duncan Glass Society in 1991.
$150.00 – 175.00

See Plate 215.

Plate 219
Heisey Glass Company
Donkey. Crystal, 6½" high, 5" long (from extended upper lip to hind hooves), circa 1944 – 53.
$300.00 – 350.00

When marked, the mark appears on the left hind leg above the hoof.

Other colors: crystal frosted.

Reissues: Imperial Glass Co. in crystal and multiple colors. Fenton Art Glass in French opalescent, green, and perhaps other colors. Mosser Glass Co. in ruby.

Plate 220
Imperial Glass Company
(Heisey Glass Co. original mold)
Wild Jack. Caramel slag, 6½" high, 1969 – 78, IG.
$50.00 – 75.00

Other colors: crystal, black, milk glass, meadow green carnival, and perhaps other colors. Imperial made the donkey in ultra blue for Mirror Images, early to mid-1980s.

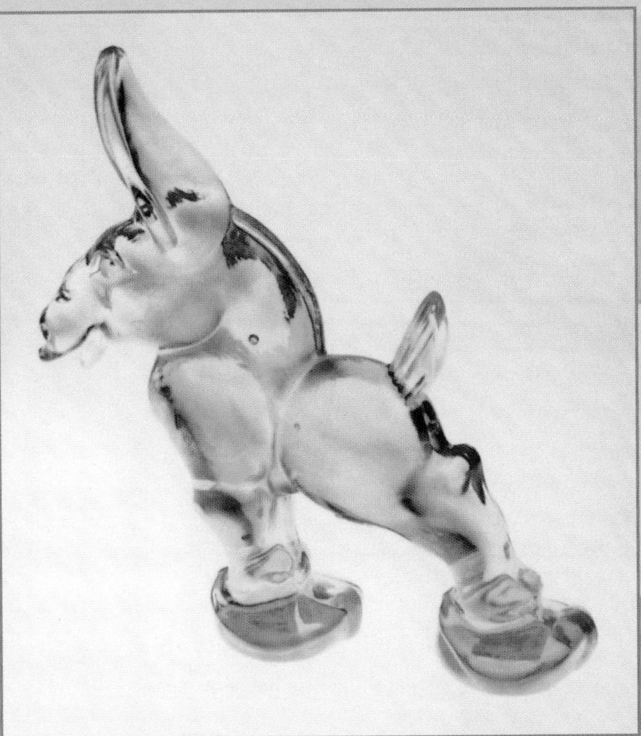

Plate 221
Imperial Glass Company (Heisey Glass Co. original mold)
Wild Jack. Meadow green carnival, circa 1980.
$45.00 – 65.00

The donkey, along with a baby elephant, were made in 1980 in a limited edition of 750 sets, marked LIG and numbered — for Imperial customers and dealers.

Dragons

Plate 223
IMPERIAL GLASS COMPANY
#5011 Wu Ling Ashtray. 5¾" long, 4" wide.
Crystal frosted, $100.00 – 125.00
Jade, $80.00 – 100.00

Other colors: perhaps other Imperial colors.

Produced in the late 1940s and the original issue signed "Virginia B. Evans."

Plate 222
IMPERIAL GLASS COMPANY
#5009 Dragon Candleholder. Crystal frosted, 6¾" high, 6¾" long, circa 1949.
$150.00 – 175.00

Other colors: none seen but is possible they were made in other Imperial colors.

Original issue signed "Virginia B. Evans."

Imperial Glass Company Cathay Line

In 1943, Imperial Glass Co. contracted with nationally known artist and designer Virginia B. Evans to design what was to become known as the Cathay line. All pieces were designed in an ancient Chinese motif, with each piece having a significant meaning. Production started in the late 1940s in crystal frosted and signed "Virginia B. Evans." Production was discontinued in 1957. Imperial later reissued items of the Cathay line in crystal, milk glass, dark jade, black suede, verde green satin, cranberry satin, and although other colors have not surfaced at present, it is entirely possible they exist. Reissues started in 1964, and continued off and on into the 1980s. Cathay items include Concubine Bookends, Cathay Pagoda, Yang and Yin Ashtray, Shang Candy Jar, Lung Ashtray, Dragon Candleholders, Butterfly Ashtray, Junk Flower Bowl, Wu Ling Ashtray, Pillow Cigarette Set, Pillow Candle Bases, Plumb Blossom Ashtray, Bamboo Urn, Peach Blossom Mint/Nut Set, Fu Wedding Vase, Egrette, Ku Ribbon Vase, Ming Jar, Shen Console Set, Fan Sweetmeat Box, Scolding Bird, Wedding Lamps, Empress Bookends, Phoenix Bowl, Candle Servants, Celestial Centerpiece, Lu-Tung Bookends, and Pavilion Tray. Salt and Pepper Shakers were made in feasibility but never put into production.

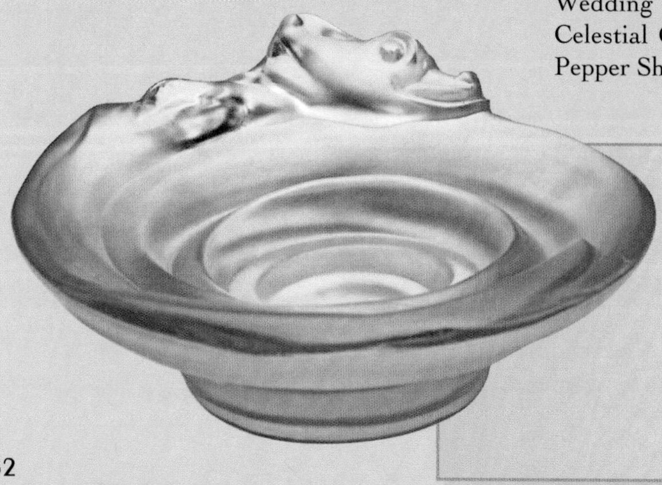

Plate 224
IMPERIAL GLASS COMPANY
#5005 Lung Ashtray. Crystal frosted, 2" high, 6" diameter.
$100.00 – 125.00

Other colors: none seen but it is possible that they were made in other Imperial colors.

Produced in the late 1940s and the original issue signed "Virginia B. Evans."

Plate 225
Paden City Glass Company
Dragon Swan. Crystal, 10" long, 6½" high, circa 1940.
$250.00 – 300.00 each

Other colors: pale blue.

Reissues: none.

Plate 226
Paden City Glass Company
Dragon Swan. Pale blue, 10" long, 6½" high, circa 1940.
$550.00 to Market

Very scarce in pale blue. See Plate 225.

Plate 227
Unknown Manufacturer
Dragon Swan. Crystal, 5½" long, 3½" high.
Seen at $55.00 – 65.00

Excellent quality, believed to be Swedish. Often seen with dealers mark of a U.S. company.

Ducks

Plate 228
Duncan Glass Company
Pall Mall Line.
Duck Smoking Set, three piece. Crystal.
Ashtray. 4" long, 2¼" wide, $20.00 – 25.00
Ashtray. 7" long, 4½" wide, $35.00 – 45.00
Cigarette Box. 6" long, 4" wide, $60.00 – 70.00

Other colors: ruby, ice blue, decorated, ruby stain, black, and opalescent. Unlikely to find a complete set in these colors except for ruby and decorated.

Reissues: Some of the items were reissued by Tiffin and Tiara.

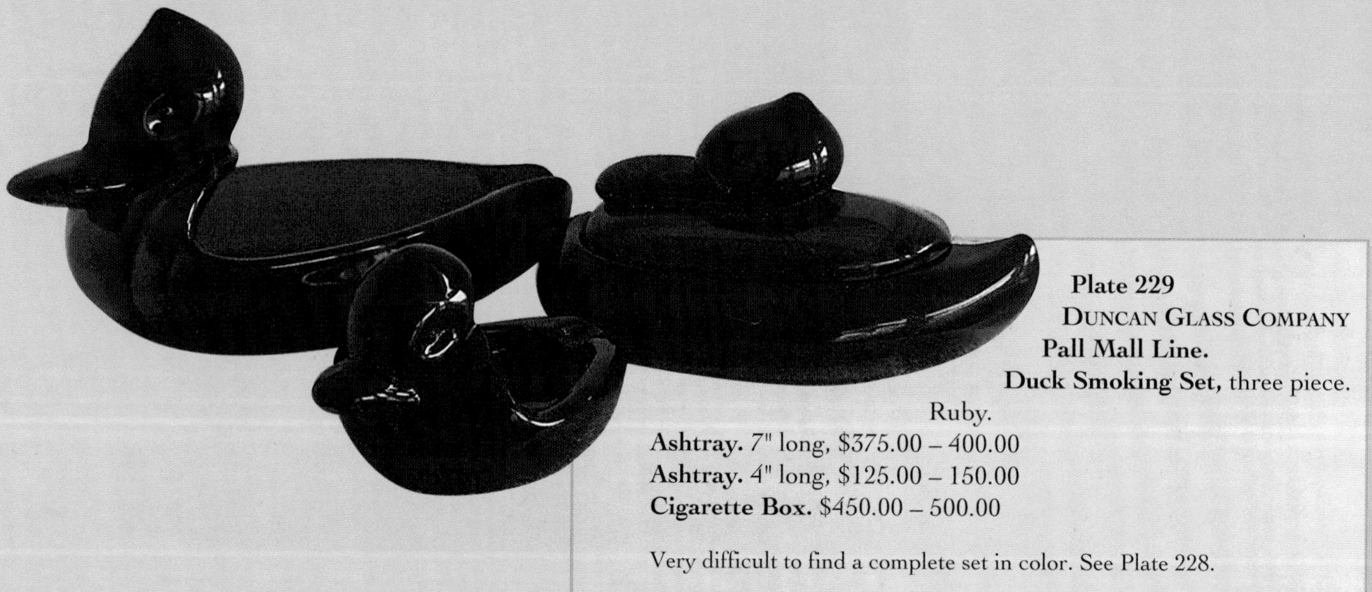

Plate 229
Duncan Glass Company
Pall Mall Line.
Duck Smoking Set, three piece. Ruby.
Ashtray. 7" long, $375.00 – 400.00
Ashtray. 4" long, $125.00 – 150.00
Cigarette Box. $450.00 – 500.00

Very difficult to find a complete set in color. See Plate 228.

Plate 230
Duncan Glass Company
Pall Mall Line.
Duck Ashtray. Ice blue, 4" long, 2½" wide. $225.00 – 250.00

Very scarce and difficult to find.

Plate 231
DUNCAN GLASS COMPANY
Pall Mall Line.
Left: **Duck Ashtray.** Black, 4" long, 2¼" wide.
$125.00 – 150.00
TIFFIN GLASS COMPANY
Right: **Duck Ashtray.** Milk glass, 7" long, 4¼" wide.
$100.00 – 125.00

The Tiffin and Tiara reissues have the ducks' bills pointing down whereas the Duncan ducks' bills are pointing straight out.

Plate 232
DUNCAN GLASS COMPANY
Pall Mall Line.
Left: **Duck Paperweight.** Crystal, 6½" long.
$450.00 – 500.00
Center: **Duck Paperweight.** Crystal, 4" long.
$50.00 – 75.00
Right: **Duck Paperweight.** Crystal, 8" long.
$550.00 – 600.00

Although there are no records documenting the production of the 6½" and 8" ducks, they have the exact lines as the 4" duck and reaction under a black light is identical to that of the 4". The mold did not fill in the tail of the 6½" duck, therefore the tail is not as high in comparison to the other two.

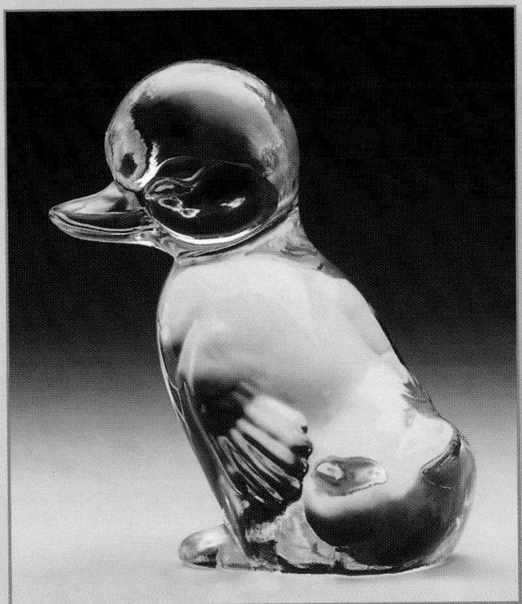

Plate 233
FENTON ART GLASS COMPANY
Duckling. Crystal, 3½" high.
$25.00 – 30.00

Plate 234
FENTON ART GLASS COMPANY
Mallard Duck. Cobalt carnival, 5" long.
$50.00 – 55.00

Other colors: produced in several Fenton colors, many with decorations.

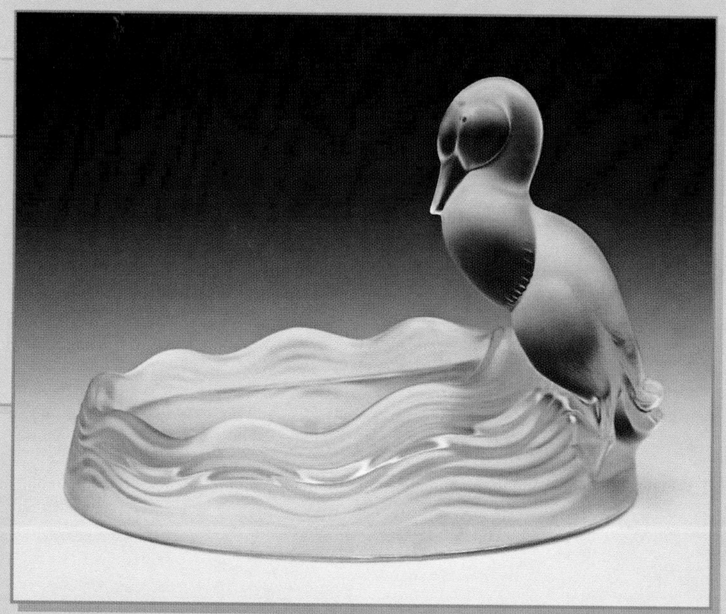

Plate 235
VERLYS OF FRANCE
Duck Ashtray. Crystal satin, 4½" high, 5" long.
$100.00 – 125.00

Signed "Verlys."

AMERICAN HISTORY OF VERLYS

Verlys of France opened a branch office in the USA in 1935. All Veryls items up until that time were imported. The Holophane Co., Newark, Ohio, primarily a lamp fixture company, produced a few Verlys items in the late 1930s. The A.H. Heisey Company obtained permission or leased 19 molds and produced glass from these molds, none of which were signed Verlys or Heisey. Only items produced by Heisey in Limelight color can be positively attributed to Heisey. In the mid-1960s Fenton purchased the molds and started producing glass from these molds in 1968. See Plate 237.

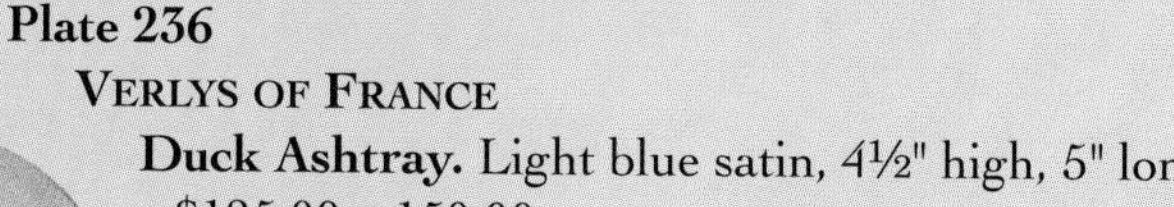

Plate 236
VERLYS OF FRANCE
Duck Ashtray. Light blue satin, 4½" high, 5" long.
$125.00 – 150.00

This color cannot be attributed to Fenton's blue color of production and therefore is attributed to Verlys of France. Item is not signed. Verlys items are sometimes mistakenly marked "Imperial Cathay"' by vendors. See Plates 235 and 237.

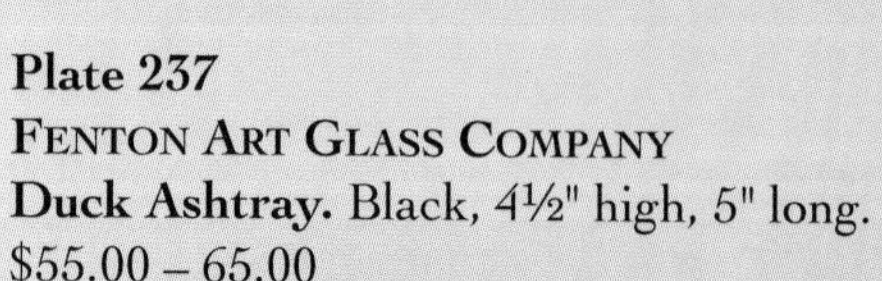

Plate 237
FENTON ART GLASS COMPANY
Duck Ashtray. Black, 4½" high, 5" long.
$55.00 – 65.00

Other colors: circa 1969, colonial amber, colonial blue, colonial green, milk glass, and orange. It was produced in crystal velvet in 1978.

Plate 238
Fostoria Glass Company
2632/404 Mama Duck. Amber frosted, 4" high, circa 1965 – 73.
$35.00 – 45.00
2632/407 Duckling, Head Down. Amber frosted, 1½" high.
$20.00 – 25.00
2632/406 Duckling, Walking. Amber frosted, 2⅜" high.
$20.00 – 25.00
2632/405 Duckling, Head Back. Amber frosted, 2½" high.
$20.00 – 25.00

Other colors: olive green, silver mist, cobalt blue, light blue, and amber, all in plain or frosted. Also reported in ruby and milk glass.

Reissues: crystal in 1991 and emerald green in 1991, for Fostoria outlet stores.

Plate 239
Fostoria Glass Company
2632/407 Duckling, Head Down. Cobalt blue, 1½" high, circa 1965 – 70.
$20.00 – 25.00
2632/404 Mama Duck. Cobalt blue, 4" high.
$35.00 – 45.00
2632/405 Duckling, Head Back. Cobalt blue, 2½" high.
$20.00 – 25.00

Referred to as cobalt blue by Fostoria, but is much darker when frosted.

Plate 240
Fostoria Glass Company
2632/404 Mama Duck. Crystal, 4" high, circa 1950 – 57.
$35.00 – 45.00
2632/405 Duckling, Head Back. Amber, 2½" high, circa 1965 – 73.
$20.00 – 25.00
2632/405 Duckling, Head Back. Cobalt blue, 2½" high, circa 1965 – 70.
$20.00 – 25.00
2632/406 Duckling, Walking. Amber, 2⅜" high, circa 1965 – 73.
$20.00 – 25.00

Plate 241
K.R. Haley Glassware Company
Three Ducks Swimming. Crystal, 9½" long.
$40.00 – 50.00

Other colors: crystal frosted.

Documented as becoming a night light with the addition of a wooden base, with bulb.

Royal Hickman, Designer of Heisey Animals

Royal Hickman, a well-known ceramic designer, was commissioned to design figurines for the Heisey Glass Co. He designed most of the Heisey animals. His extraordinary talent is reflected in these creations.

Plate 242
Heisey Glass Company
Wood Duck Family.
Duckling, Standing. Crystal, 2½" high, 1¾" long (length of base), circa 1947 – 49.
$225.00 – 250.00

Other colors: crystal frosted.

Reissues: Imperial Glass Co. in multiple colors. Dalzell-Viking 1991 in ruby. Fenton Art Glass Co. in rosalene as part of the HCA Gold Series. See Plate 126.

When marked, the mark appears on the left side, above the base behind the feet. Sometimes referred to as "Walking Duckling."

Duckling, Floating. Crystal, 2¼" high, 3¼" long (overall length), circa 1947 – 49.
$225.00 – 250.00

Other colors: crystal frosted.

Reissues: Imperial Glass Co. in multiple colors. Dalzell-Viking, 1991, in ruby.

When marked, mark appears on the left side below the wing. This little guy has about the same profile as the mother.

Mother Wood Duck. Crystal, 4½" high, 6" long (overall length), circa 1947 – 49.
$600.00 – 700.00

Other colors: crystal frosted.

Reissues: Imperial Glass Co. in crystal and multiple colors.

When marked, mark appears on the left side, on the bottom feather.

Plate 243
Heisey Glass Company
Mallards
Wings Half. Crystal, 5" high, 5½" long (wing tip to tip of bill), 1947 – 55.
$225.00 – 250.00

Other colors: crystal frosted.

Reissues: Imperial Glass Co. in crystal and multiple colors. Dalzell-Viking, 1991 in ruby. Dalzell-Viking, 1993, in lavender ice as part of the HCA "Gem Series." See Plate 84.

When marked, mark appears on the left side near the front, above the base.

Wings Up. Crystal, 6¾" high, 4¾" long (tip of bill to tip of tail), 1947 – 55.
$175.00 – 200.00

Other colors: crystal frosted.

Reissues: Imperial Glass Co. in crystal and multiple colors. Dalzell-Viking, 1991, in ruby. Dalzell-Viking, 1993, in lavender ice as part of the HCA "Gem Series." See Plate 84B.

When marked, the mark appears on the left side near the front, above the base.

Wings Down. Crystal, 4½" high, 4½" long (tip of bill to tip of tail), 1947 – 55.
$350.00 – 375.00

Other colors: crystal frosted.

Reissues: Imperial Glass Co., in crystal and multiple colors. Dalzell-Viking, 1991, in ruby. Dalzell-Viking, 1993, in lavender ice as part of the HCA "Gem Series." See Plate 84B.

When marked, mark appears on the left side, near the front, above the base.

Plate 244
Heisey Glass Company
Duck Floral Block.
Left: Flamingo, $225.00 – 250.00
Right: Hawthorne, $275.00 – 300.00

This item is 5" high (including block), 5¼" diameter (block). Circa late 1920s into early 1930s. Not marked.

Other colors: crystal and moongleam.

Reissues: none.

This is a two-piece item. The duck sits in the block which has 10 holes in the top and bottom rims. Heisey also made a candleholder which fits in the block.

Plate 245
IMPERIAL GLASS COMPANY
(original Heisey Glass Co. mold)
Mallards.
Wings Down. Horizon blue, 4½" high, 1980 made for HCA, marked IG.
Wings Up. Horizon blue, 6¾" high, 1980 made for HCA, marked IG.
Wings Half. Horizon blue, 5" high, 1980 made for HCA, marked IG.
Set, $100.00 – 125.00

Other colors: crystal 1964 – 67, horizon blue frosted, caramel slag, amber plain and frosted, wings down in black, wings up in milk glass and other Imperial colors.

Plate 246
IMPERIAL GLASS COMPANY
(original Heisey Glass Co. mold)
Mallards.
Wings Half. Caramel slag, 5" high, 1969 – 78, marked IG.
$35.00 – 50.00
Wings Up. Caramel slag, 6¾" high, 1969 – 78, marked IG.
$35.00 – 50.00

Not shown, mallard, wings down, caramel slag, 4½" high, marked IG, rare.
$175.00 – 225.00

Plate 247
IMPERIAL GLASS COMPANY
(original Heisey Glass Co. mold)
Mallard, Wings Down.
Left: Silver overlay, extremely rare.
$650.00 to Market
Right: Yellow carnival, extremely rare.

These two ducks were obviously a feasibility study, like so many other unique items that came out of the Imperial factory when it closed.

Plate 248
IMPERIAL GLASS COMPANY
(original Heisey Glass Co. mold)
Sittin' Duck. Nut brown, 4½" high, 1983, marked IG.
$100.00 – 110.00
Duckling, Floating. Ultra blue, 2½" high, 1983, made for Mirror Images, marked IG.
$45.00 – 55.00
Duckling, Standing. Sunshine yellow, 2⅜" high, 1983, made for HCA.
$25.00 – 30.00

Other colors: Sittin' Duck, caramel slag, milk glass, pink, sunshine yellow, ultra blue for Mirror Images, and probably other Imperial colors. Standing Duckling, ultra blue for Mirror Images and probably other Imperial colors. Floating Duckling, sunshine yellow for HCA and probably other Imperial colors.

Plate 249
IMPERIAL GLASS COMPANY
(original Heisey Glass Co. mold)
Sittin' Duck. Caramel slag, 4½" high, 1969 – 78, IG.
$35.00 – 45.00

Plate 250
IMPERIAL GLASS COMPANY
(original Heisey Glass Co. mold)
Sittin' Duck. Milk glass, 4½" high, circa 1982.
$400.00 to Market

Very few of these were made.

Plate 251
Imperial Glass Company
#43920 Duck on Nest. Caramel slag, 4½" wide, circa 1970s.
$35.00 – 45.00

Other colors: jade slag and purple slag, glossy or satin finish. In 1980 was issued in blue satin, pink satin, and custard satin.

Plate 252
L.E. Smith Glass Company
Duck Ashtray. Black, 6½" long.
$8.00 – 12.00

Other colors: original issue was in crystal.

Ashtray is part of a three-piece set, two ashtrays and two-piece mother.

Plate 253
Vallerysthal/Portieux Glass Company
Covered Duck Butter Dish. Amber, 5" long, 4¾" high, circa 1903.
$65.00 – 75.00

Vallerysthal located in Lorraine, France, produced glass from 1470 until the factory was bombed in WWII. Molds have been copied by numerous American glass companies.

Plate 254
Viking Glass Company
#1316 Duck. 5½" high, circa 1960s.
Amber, $20.00 – 30.00
Moss green, $20.00 – 35.00
Orange, $20.00 – 35.00
#1317 Duck. Moss green, 9" high, circa 1960s.
$50.00 – 55.00

Small duck also used as a finial on two-piece round candy box. See Plate 255.

Plate 255
VIKING GLASS COMPANY
Round Candy Box. Amber, 9" high, circa 1960s.
$45.00 – 55.00

Other colors: also made in Viking colors.

The #1316 5½" Duck was used as the finial for this item. A bird was also used as the finial for this item, see Plate 70.

Plate 256
VIKING GLASS COMPANY
#1317 Duck, Head Up. Orange, 13½" high, circa 1960s.
$75.00 – 85.00

Other colors: made in Viking colors.

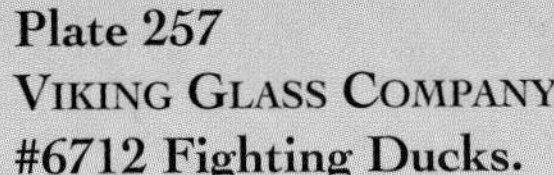

Plate 257
VIKING GLASS COMPANY
#6712 Fighting Ducks.
Left: Head Down. Crystal, 2½" high, circa 1967.
$45.00 – 50.00
Right: Standing. Crystal, 4½" high, circa 1967.
$45.00 – 55.00

Other colors: made in Viking colors, tinted crystal and ruby for only one year.

Plate 258
WESTMORELAND GLASS COMPANY
Duck Individual Nut/Salt. Pink frosted, decorated, 5" long, circa 1920s.
$25.00 – 35.00

Other colors: crystal, amber, green, and blue.

Eagles

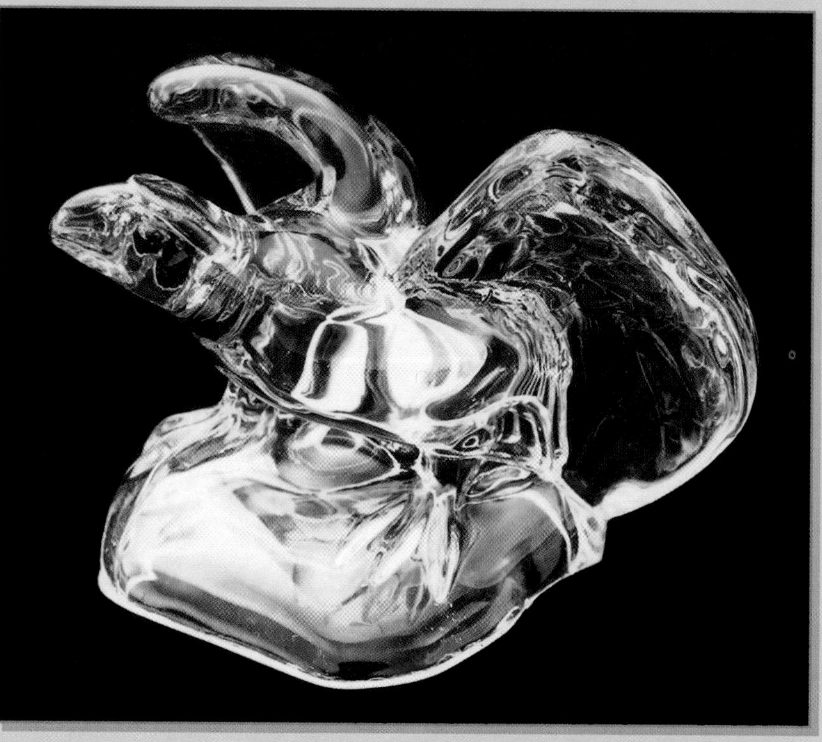

Plate 259
CAMBRIDGE GLASS COMPANY
Eagle Bookend. Crystal, 5½" high (wingtip to bottom of base), 4" long, and 4" wide (base).
$75.00 – 100.00

Other colors: crystal satin. Pictured in first edition in crystal and crown tuscan, experimental.

Reissues: Cambridge in crystal (1964 – 68) and Mosser Glass Company, 1986, in cobalt for NCC. See Plate 260.

Plate 260
MOSSER GLASS COMPANY
(original Cambridge Glass Co. mold)
Eagle Bookend. Cobalt, 5½" high.
1986 selling price, $30.00

This bookend was made by Mosser Glass Company for the National Cambridge Collectors as a commemorative item.

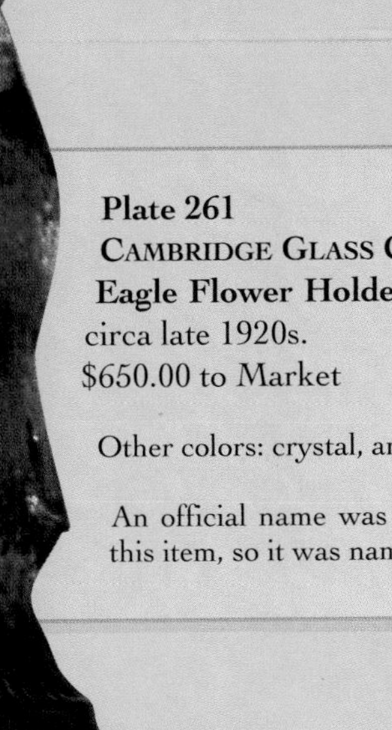

Plate 261
Cambridge Glass Company
Eagle Flower Holder. Dianthus (peach blo), 5⅜" tall, circa late 1920s.
$650.00 to Market

Other colors: crystal, amber, and emerald.

An official name was not found in Cambridge records for this item, so it was named Eagle by collectors.

Plate 262
Cambridge Glass Company
#1675 Eagle Three-Part Relish. Crystal, 8".
$50.00 – 60.00

Other colors: none known.

Cambridge also made in this line the #1676 6" ashtray with eagle handle and the #1144 eagle figure on a ball, 5½" tall. Because of its similarity to Heisey's crystolite pattern, the relish is often seen with a dealer sticker marked "Heisey."

Plate 263
Duncan Glass Company
Federal Mirror Bookend. Crystal, 6½" high, 5" wide.
$1,400.00 – 1,600.00 pair

Other colors: none.

Reissues: none.

These bookends are rare. They were designed after the wall-hanging Federal mirror. When found, these bookends generally have a monogram in the center of the mirror portion. Fortunately the pair pictured do not have a monogram.

Plate 264
Fostoria Glass Company
#2585 Eagle Bookend. Crystal, 7" high, circa 1940 – 43.
$100.00 – 125.00

Other colors: silver mist, 1939 – 43.

Plate 265
Imperial Glass Company
Federal Column Bookend. Crystal, 5" high base.
Base and eagle, $200.00 – 250.00

This is the old style bookend with the medallion on the center column. This base is accompanied by a Candlewick eagle adapter with peg bottom. See Plates 266 and 268.

Plate 266
Imperial Glass Company
Federal Column Bookend. Crystal, 4½" high base.
Base and eagle, $200.00 – 250.00

This is the later style bookend which is more often seen. The medallion was removed from the front of the column and stars were added to the top of the columns. The eagle adapters were also made with a candle well behind the eagle for use as a candleholder or for flowers. See Plates 265 and 268.

Plate 267
Imperial Glass Company
Original magazine ad

This ad was from an early 1950s magazine introducing the "Black Suede" line.

See Plate 268.

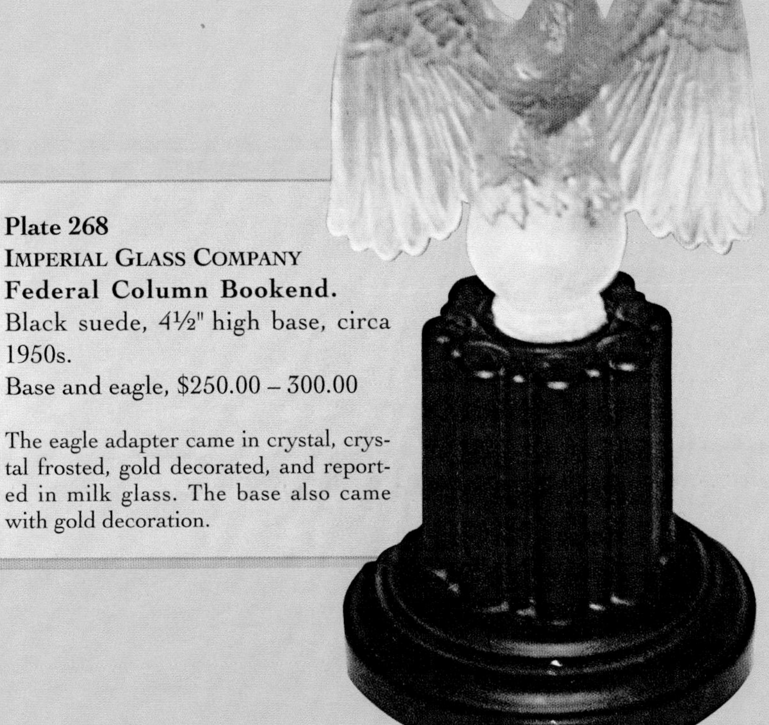

Plate 268
Imperial Glass Company
Federal Column Bookend.
Black suede, 4½" high base, circa 1950s.
Base and eagle, $250.00 – 300.00

The eagle adapter came in crystal, crystal frosted, gold decorated, and reported in milk glass. The base also came with gold decoration.

Plate 269
Imperial Glass Company
31776/3 Candlewick Eagle Mirror. Black milk glass, 6½" high, circa 1942 – 50.
$125.00 – 150.00

Other colors: crystal, crystal with bright gold trim, frosted crystal, and antique blue.

Plate 270
Imperial Glass Company
Top: **Candlewick Eagle Ashtray.** Milk glass, 6½" high, circa 1950s.
$75.00 – 85.00

Bottom: **Candlewick Eagle Mirror.**
See Plate 269.

Plate 271
Imperial Glass Company
Left: **Candlewick Eagle Cigarette Holder.** Crystal, 4" high.
$25.00 – 35.00
Right: **Candlewick Eagle Ashtray.** Crystal frosted, 6½" high.
$50.00 – 60.00

Other colors: crystal, crystal frosted, milk glass, black milk glass, antique blue, carnival, and perhaps others.

Plate 272
NEW MARTINSVILLE GLASS COMPANY
#509 Eagle. Crystal, 8" high, circa 1938.
$65.00 – 75.00

Reissues: Dalzell-Viking in crystal and crystal frosted, 1988, 1990, and 1991.

Plate 273
PADEN CITY GLASS COMPANY
American Eagle Head Bookends. Crystal, 7½" high.
$500.00 – 550.00 pair

Other colors: crystal frosted (Plate 274).

These are solid glass with a flat back and weigh 4 lbs. each.

Plate 274A
WESTMORELAND GLASS COMPANY
Eagle. Crystal mist, 7½" high.
$200.00 – 275.00

This eagle was made for only a few months and is therefore extremely scarce.

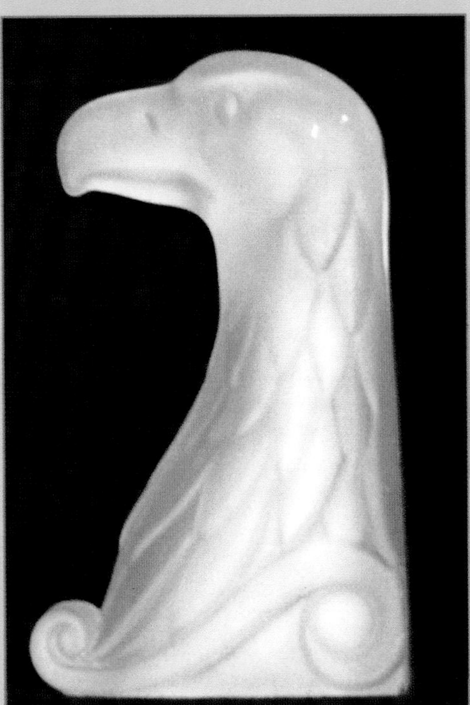

Plate 274
PADEN CITY GLASS COMPANY
American Eagle Head Bookend. Crystal frosted, 7½" high.
$250.00 – 275.00

See Plate 273

EGRETS

Plate 275
IMPERIAL GLASS COMPANY
Egret. Crystal satin, 9½" high, circa 1949.
$450.00 – 550.00

Signed "Virginia B. Evans." See Plate 224.

Other colors: cranberry satin (1964 – 66), verde green satin (1964 – 66), and crystal (1964 – 68).

Plate 276
IMPERIAL GLASS COMPANY
Egret. Cranberry satin, 9½" high, circa 1964 – 66.
$200.00 – 225.00

Plate 277
FOSTORIA GLASS COMPANY
Stork. Blue, 2" high, 2¾" long, circa 1963.
$20.00 – 25.00

Other colors: crystal, green, and other Fostoria colors. Made in clear and frosted. Blue made 1971 – 73.

Plate 278
VIKING GLASS COMPANY
#1315 Egret. 9½" to 12", ranges in height depending on length of neck, circa 1960s.
Orange, $40.00 – 50.00
Dark medium blue, $40.00 – 50.00
Ruby, $70.00 – 80.00
Amber, $30.00 – 40.00

Other colors: made in Viking colors.

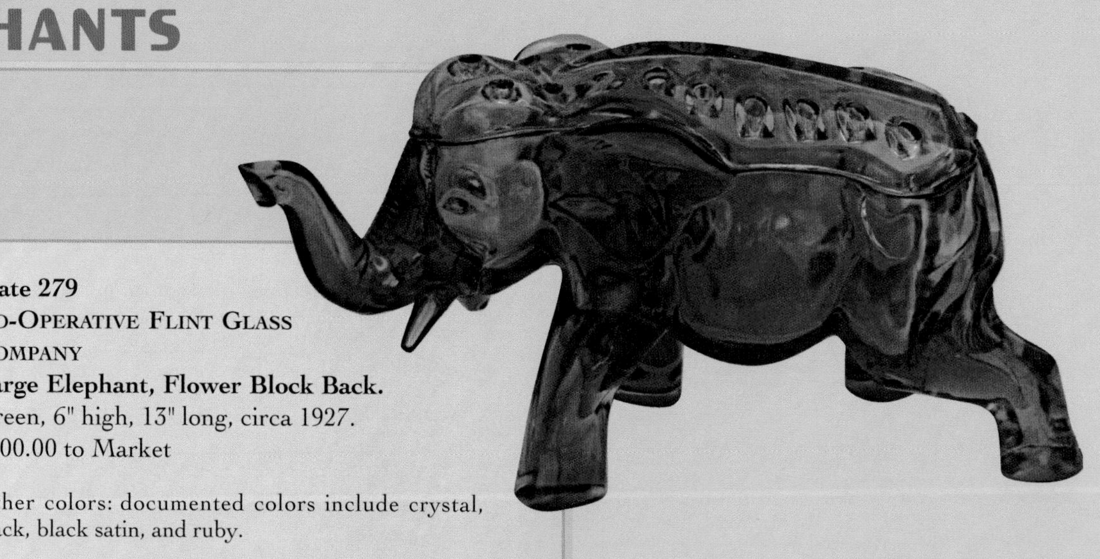

Plate 279
Co-Operative Flint Glass Company
Large Elephant, Flower Block Back. Green, 6" high, 13" long, circa 1927.
$600.00 to Market

Other colors: documented colors include crystal, black, black satin, and ruby.

Plate 280
Co-Operative Flint Glass Company
Large Elephant, Flat Back. Black, 6" high, 13" long, circa 1927.
$600.00 to Market

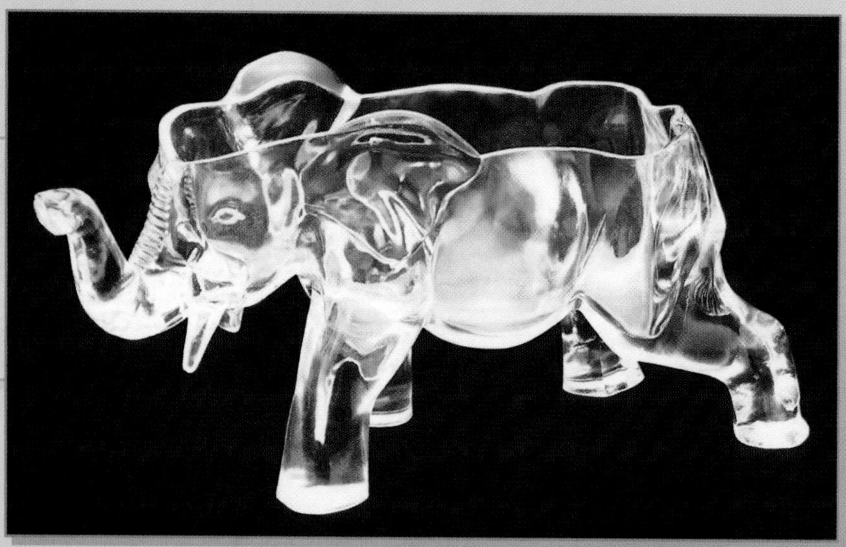

Plate 281
Co-Operative Flint Glass Company
Large Elephant (No Lid). Crystal, 6" high, 13" long, circa 1927.
Complete $300.00 – 350.00

Plate 282
Co-Operative Flint Glass Company
Large Elephant Oil Lamp. Black, 6" high, 13" long, circa 1927.
Rarity prohibits pricing

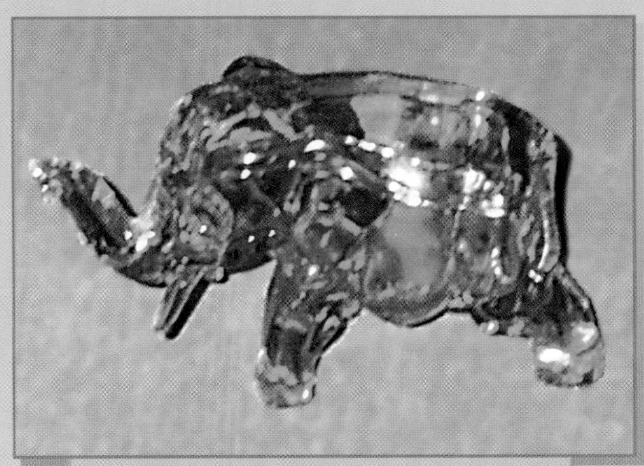

Plate 283
Co-Operative Flint Glass Company
Small Elephant, Flat Back. Ritz blue, 4½" high, 7" long, circa 1930.
$300.00 – 350.00

Other colors: crystal, amber, rose, and black.

Elephants came with variations of the backs, flat back, ashtray, and flower frog. Indiana Glass made a copy of this elephant with a variation in the back in the 1980s. See Plates 286 and 287.

Plate 284
Co-Operative Flint Glass Company
Small Elephant, Flower Frog Back. Amber, 4½" high, 7" long, circa 1930.
$350.00 – 400.00

Plate 285
Co-Operative
Flint Glass Company
Small Elephant, Ashtray Back. Amber, 4½" high, 7" long, circa 1930.
$350.00 – 400.00

Plate 286
Left: Indiana Glass Company
Small Elephant and Cover. Pink, 4" high, circa 1980s.
$50.00 – 75.00
Center: Co-Operative Flint Glass Company
Small Elephant, Flat Back. Black with jeweled decorations, 4½" high, 7" long, circa 1930.
$300.00 – 350.00
Right: Indiana Glass Company
Small Elephant and Cover. Crystal, 4" high, circa 1980s.
$40.00 – 50.00

Plate 287
Indiana Glass Company
Small Elephant and Cover. Pink, 4" high, circa 1980s.
$50.00 – 75.00

In 1981, this elephant was produced in crystal and filled with red, white, and blue jelly beans for the republicans. Other clear colors were made. In 1983, Tiara Glass (Division of Indiana Glass) made the elephant in frosted colors of pink, blue, and mint green. In the 1990s an almost identical elephant appeared on the scene in ruby, pink, and cobalt. It was believed to be imported.

Plate 288
Fenton Art Glass Company
Elephant. Pink, 3" high, circa 1970s.
$95.00 – 110.00

Other colors: made in a variety of Fenton colors.

This is an offhand production and will therefore vary in size.

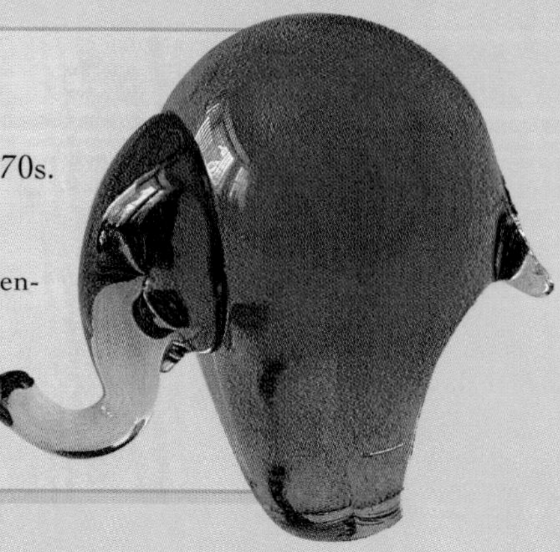

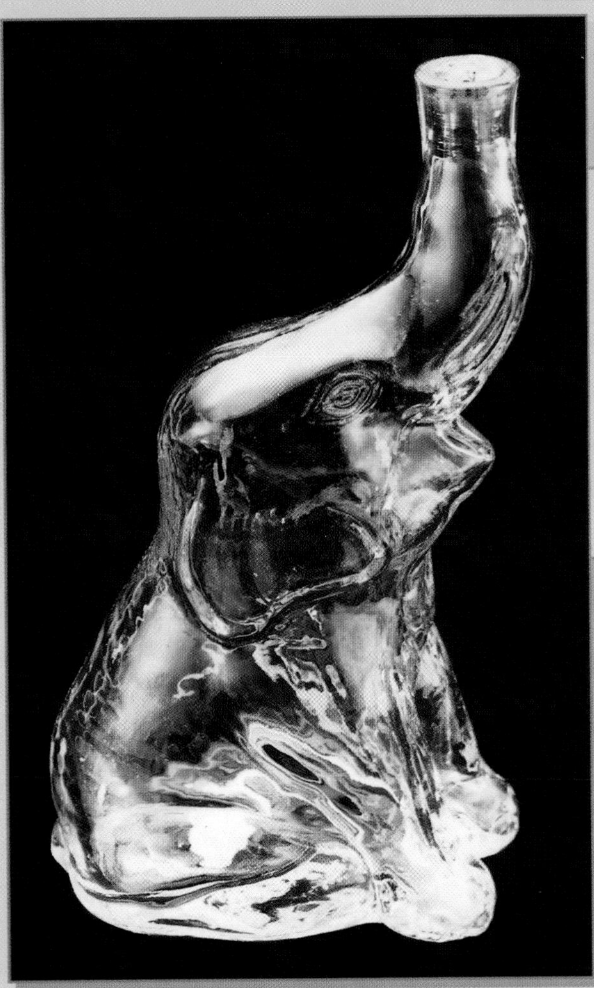

Plate 289
FENTON ART GLASS COMPANY
Elephant Whiskey Bottle. Crystal, 8" high, circa 1935.
$325.00 – 350.00

Other colors: periwinkle. Only one is known.

Printed on the bottle "Federal Law Prohibits the Sale or Reuse of this Bottle." This bottle is considered rare.

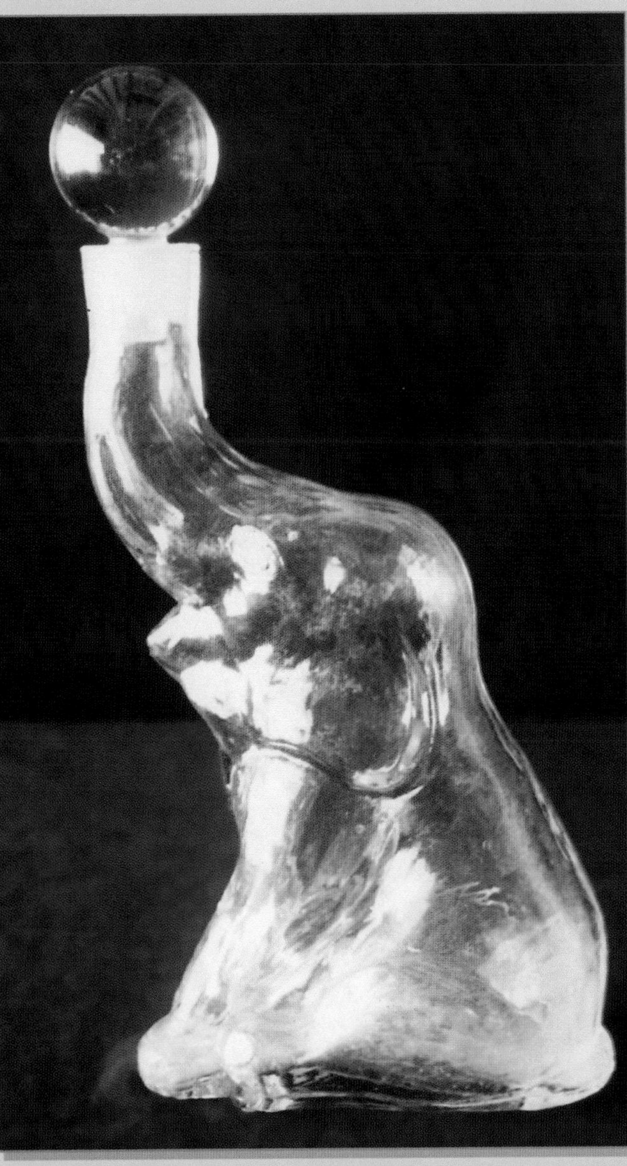

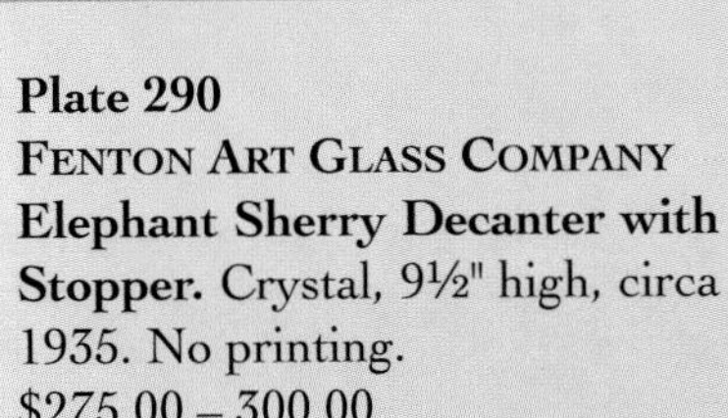

Plate 290
FENTON ART GLASS COMPANY
Elephant Sherry Decanter with Stopper. Crystal, 9½" high, circa 1935. No printing.
$275.00 – 300.00

Plate 291
Fenton Art Glass Company
#1618 Elephant Flower Bowl.
Black satin, 6½" high x 9" long, circa 1929, very rare.
$600.00 to Market

Other colors, opaque: teal blue, black, and jade green; transparent: crystal, green, amethyst, and rose.

Plate 292
Fenton Art Glass Company
#1618 Elephant Flower Bowl.
Teal blue, 6½" high x 9" long, circa 1929.
$450.00 – 500.00

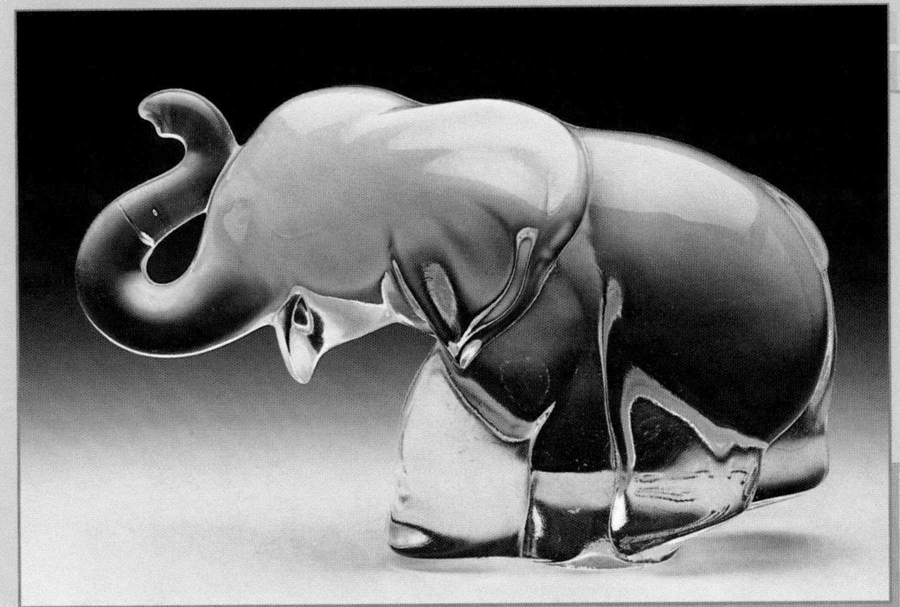

Plate 293
FENTON ART GLASS COMPANY (original Heisey Glass Company mold)
Large Elephant (Papa). Crystal opalescent, 5" high, 6½" long, circa 1988 for HCA.
$75.00 – 100.00

See Plate 301.

Plate 294
FENTON ART GLASS COMPANY (original Heisey Glass Company mold)
Small Elephant (Baby). 4½" high, 5" long.
Left: Crystal opalescent.
$50.00 – 75.00
Right: Sea mist green.
$50.00 – 75.00

See Plate 301.

Plate 295
FOSTORIA GLASS COMPANY
#2580 Elephant Bookend. Crystal, 6½" high, circa 1940 – 43.
$100.00 – 125.00

Other colors: original, silver mist.

Reissues: 1980 in ebony and 1990 in crystal for Fostoria outlet stores.

Plate 296
GREENSBURG GLASS WORKS
Elephant Ashtray. Black, 6½" diameter, circa 1920s.
$35.00 – 45.00

Other colors: crystal, amber, pink, and green.

Greensburg Glass Works became part of L.E. Smith Glass Company before the 1930s.

Plate 297
GREENSBURG GLASS WORKS
Elephant Ashtray. Green, 6½" diameter, circa 1920s.
$35.00 – 45.00

See Plate 296.

Plate 298
L.J. Houze Glass Company
Elephant Rocker Blotter. Black, 2¼" high, 3¼" long, circa 1931.
$40.00 – 50.00

Also made with horse, dog, and sailboat in yellow, black, green, and blue.

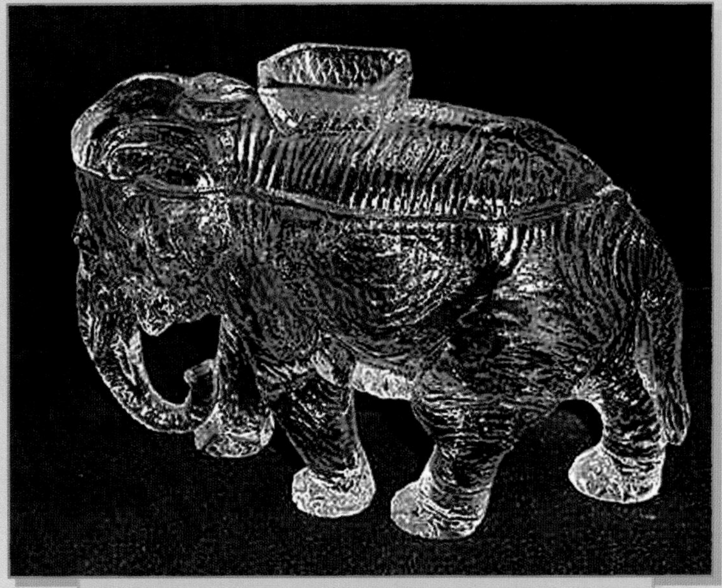

Plate 299
Hocking Glass Company
Pachyderm. Crystal, 6½" long, 4½" high, 2¼" wide, two piece, circa 1920s.
Private collection — Market

Other colors: green, rose, crystal satin, and vitrock.

Hocking Glass Company's name was changed to Anchor Hocking Glass Company in 1969.

Plate 300
Hocking Glass Company
Pachyderm. Green, 6½" long, 4½" high, 2¼" wide, two piece, circa 1920s.
Private collection — Market

Other colors: crystal, rose, crystal satin, and vitrock.

See Plate 299.

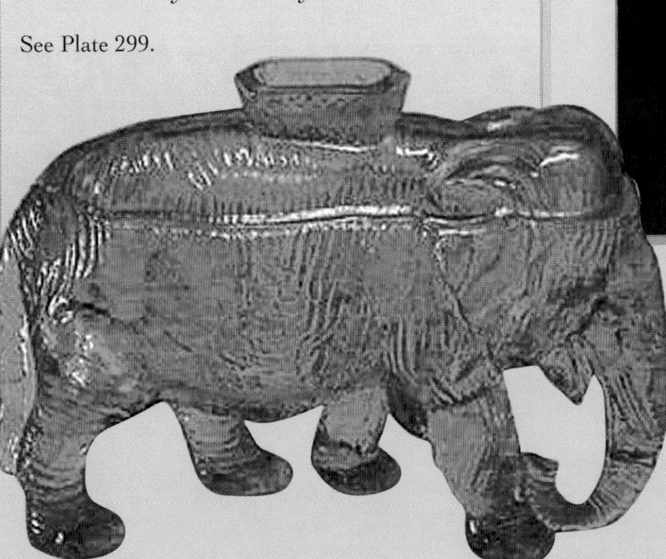

Plate 300A
Hocking Glass Company
Pachyderm. Rose, 6½" long, 4½" high, 2¼" wide, two piece, circa 1920s.
Private collection — Market

Other colors: crystal, green, crystal satin, and vitrock.

See Plate 299.

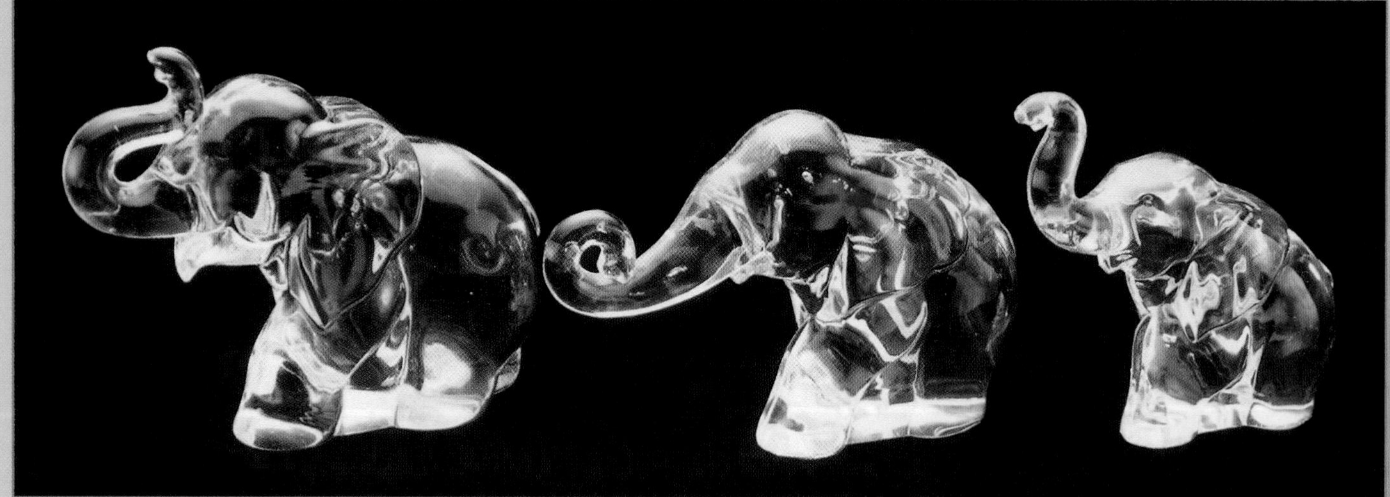

Plate 301
Heisey Glass Company
Elephant Family
Left: **Large Elephant (Papa).** Crystal, 5" high, 6½" long, circa 1944 – 53.
$450.00 – 475.00

Other colors: crystal frosted and amber.

Reissues: Imperial in crystal, amber, milk glass, caramel slag, and other Imperial colors. Fenton in crystal opalescent. Dalzell-Viking in lavender ice as part of the Gem Series. See Plate 84B.

When marked, mark appears on the left side, between the legs, near the base.

Center: **Medium Elephant (Mama).** Crystal, 4" high, 6½" long (overall length), circa 1944 – 55.
$350.00 – 395.00

Other colors: crystal frosted and amber.

Reissues: Imperial in crystal and multiple Imperial colors. Fenton in crystal opalescent. Dalzell-Viking in lavender ice as part of the Gem Series. See Plate 84B.

When marked, mark appears on the left side, between the legs, near the base. The trunk is down whereas the trunks on the large and small elephants are up in the air.

Right: **Small Elephant (Baby).** Crystal, 4½" high, 5" long, circa 1944 – 53.
$275.00 – 325.00

Other colors: crystal frosted and amber.

Reissues: Imperial in crystal and multiple Imperial colors. Fenton in crystal opalescent. Mosser in cobalt. Dalzell-Viking in lavender ice as part of the Gem Series. See Plate 84B.

When marked, mark appears on the left side, between the legs, near the base.

Plate 302
Heisey Glass Company
Medium Elephant (Mama). Amber, 4" high, 6½" long (overall length).
$2,400.00 – 2,600.00

Plate 303
Imperial Glass Company (original Heisey Glass Company mold)
Small Elephant. Pink satin, 4½" high, circa 1980, marked LIG.
$55.00 – 65.00

Other colors: In 1980s crystal, meadow green, pink plain or iridized, milk glass, horizon blue, nut brown, caramel slag, and salmon/pink. In charcoal as a feasibility item. Charcoal horizon blue, milk glass, and nut brown came in plain and/or frosted.

Reissues: Fenton in crystal opalescent with hand-painted flowers and in sea mist green, plain or frosted. Mosser in cobalt and Dalzell-Viking in lavender ice as part of the Gem Series. See Plate 84B.

Plate 304
Imperial Glass Company (original Heisey Glass Company mold)
Medium Eminent Elephant. Caramel slag, 4" high, circa 1980s, IG.
$65.00 – 85.00

Plate 305
Imperial Glass Company (original Heisey Glass Company mold)
Medium Eminent Elephant. Milk glass, 4" high, circa 1980s.
$375.00 – 425.00

Very scarce in milk glass.

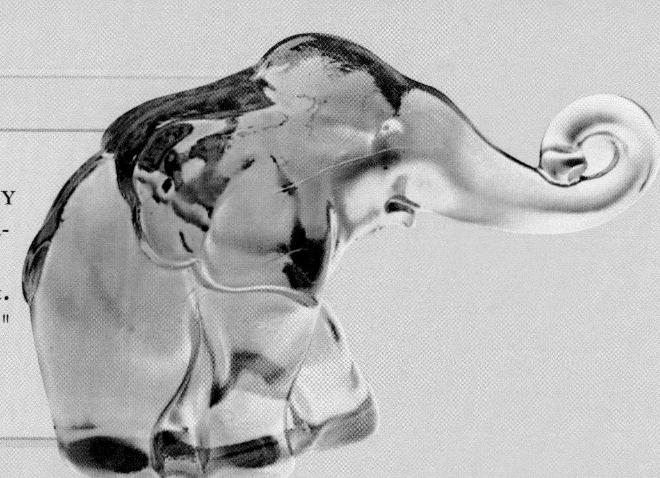

Plate 306
IMPERIAL GLASS COMPANY (original Heisey Glass Company mold)
Medium Eminent Elephant. Meadow green carnival, 4" high, circa 1980s.
$65.00 – 75.00

Plate 307
IMPERIAL GLASS COMPANY (original Heisey Glass Company mold)
Child's Fairy Tale Mug. Aurora jewels, 5" high.
$35.00 – 45.00

Other colors: Imperial in fern green, ruby slag, green slag, caramel slag, sea mist iridized, helios, and many other Imperial colors. Fenton in rosalene,. Dalzell-Viking in lavender ice.

Heisey made this mug in crystal only.

Plate 308
UNKNOWN MANUFACTURER
Elephant. Crystal, 6½" high.
Seen at $150.00 – 175.00

This elephant is of superior quality and is very similar to those produced by Steuben.

Plate 309
New Martinsville Glass Company
#201 Elephant Incense Burner. Green with decorations, 6" high, circa 1940.
$350.00 – 400.00
#198 Elephant Cigarette Holder. Pink with decorations, 5" high, circa 1940.
$300.00 – 350.00

Other colors: black amethyst and blue.

Plate 310
New Martinsville Glass Company
#198 Elephant Cigarette Holder.
Green, 6" high, circa 1940.
$300.00 – 350.00

Plate 311
New Martinsville Glass Company
#237 Elephant Bookend. Crystal, 5½" high, circa 1990s.
$70.00 – 90.00

Other colors: none.

Plate 312
PILGRIM GLASS COMPANY
Elephants.
Left: crystal, 4¼" high, circa 1980, #917. $15.00 – 20.00
Center: crystal, 6" high, circa 1960s. $40.00 – 45.00
Right: lilac, 5" high, circa 1950 – 60s, #917. $35.00 – 45.00

These are offhand animals and will vary in size.

Plate 313
L.E. SMITH GLASS COMPANY
Elephant. Crystal, 1¾" high, 2¼" long. Circa 1950s.
$8.00 – 10.00

Sometimes seen with decorations, ruby stain, gold highlights, etc.

Plate 314
STEUBEN GLASSWORKS
#7231 Elephant Flower Frog.
Crystal satin, 8" high, circa 1932.
Private collection — Market

Figurine has a peg bottom which fits into the flower holder base.

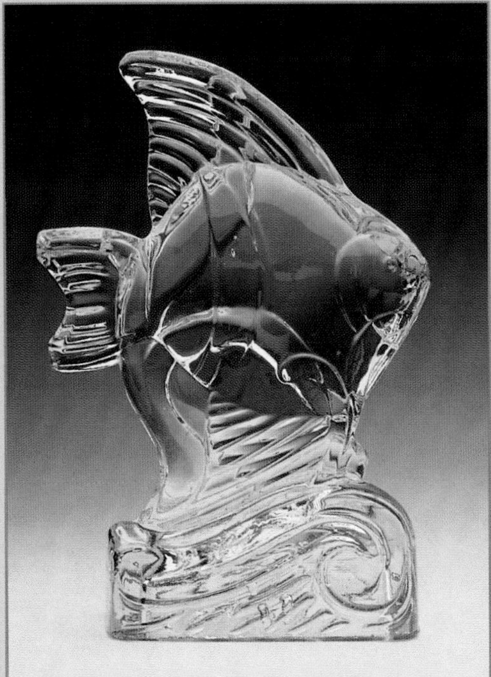

Plate 316
ANCHOR HOCKING GLASS COMPANY
Fish Covered Dish. Crystal, $3\frac{1}{2}$" high, circa 1940s.
$10.00 – 12.00

Also made this covered dish as a shell, chicken, and turtle.

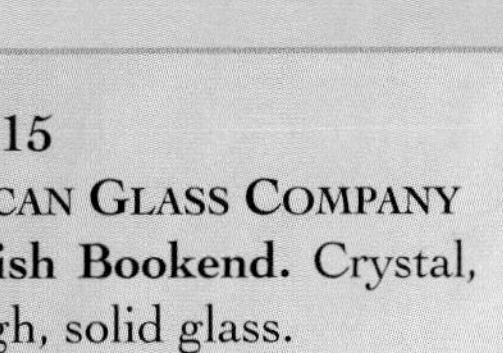

Plate 315
AMERICAN GLASS COMPANY
Angelfish Bookend. Crystal, $8\frac{1}{4}$" high, solid glass.
$50.00 – 75.00 each.

K.R. Haley design. See Haley Glass Company in Glass Factories.

Plate 318
UNKNOWN MANUFACTURER
Fish Vase. Crystal and green, 13" high, 19" long.
Seen at $50.00 – 75.00

This fish vase generally bears a price tag that says "Blenko," however, the tail, props, and mouth are all different from the Blenko fish in Plate 317.

Plate 317
BLENKO GLASS COMPANY
Fish Vase. Crystal and green, 13" high, 15" long, circa 1960s.
$100.00 – 125.00

Plate 320
Co-Operative Flint Glass Company
Whale and Cover. Green, circa 1927.
Private collection — Market

See Plate 319.

Plate 319
Co-Operative Flint Glass Company
Whale and Cover. Crystal, circa 1927.
Rarity prohibits pricing.

Other colors: crystal and transparent colors.

This mold was scrapped during World War II.

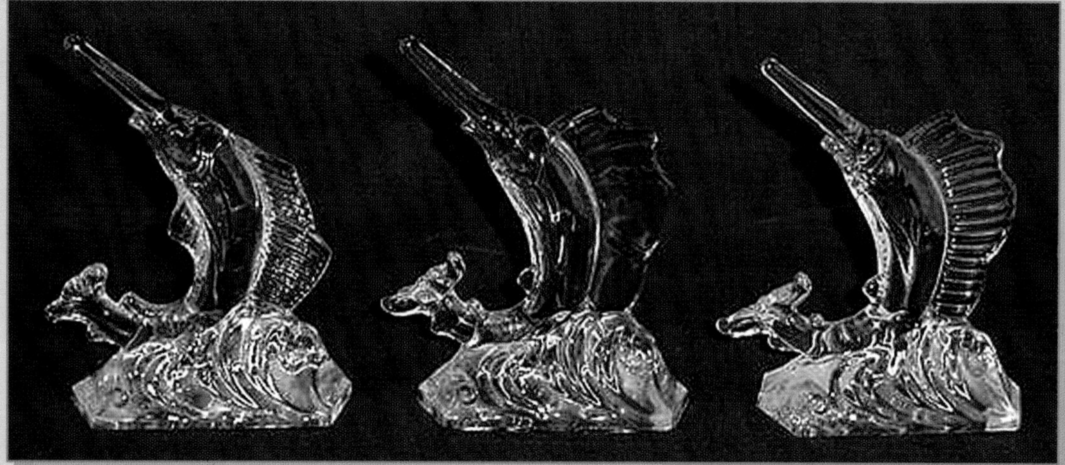

Plate 321
Duncan Glass Company
Pall Mall Line Sail Fish. Crystal, 5" high, circa 1940s.
Left and right: $200.00 – 275.00 each
Center: $375.00 – 400.00

Center fish is very difficult to find.

Other colors: crystal frosted and blue opalescent.

Plate 322
Duncan Glass Company
Pall Mall Line Sail Fish. Blue opalescent, 5" high, circa 1940s.
$500.00 – 600.00 each

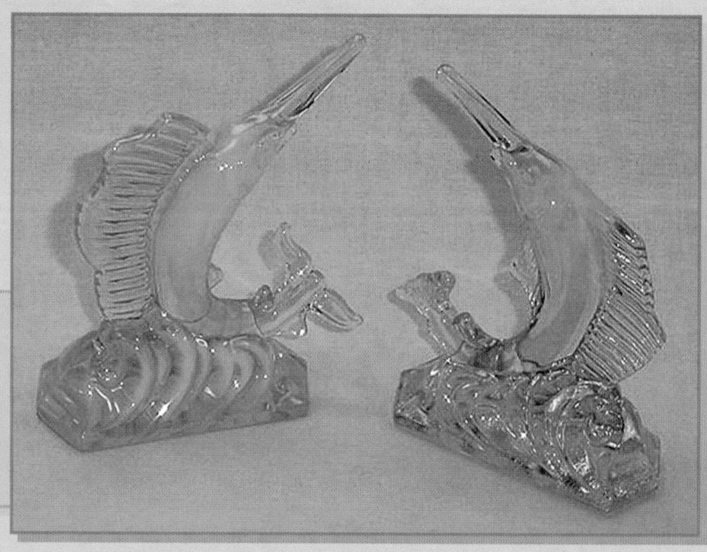

Plate 323
DUNCAN GLASS COMPANY
Sanibel Tropical Fish Ashtray. 3½" long.
Blue opalescent, $65.00 – 75.00
Yellow opalescent, $75.00 – 100.00
Pink opalescent, $65.00 – 75.00

Other colors: crystal.

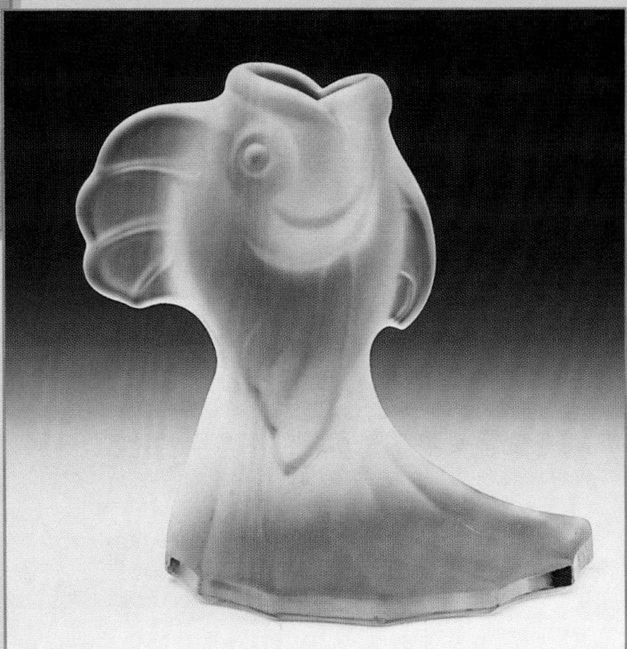

Plate 324
DUNCAN GLASS COMPANY
Tropical Fish Candleholder. Crystal frosted, 5" high.
$550.00 – 600.00

Other colors: crystal, blue opalescent, and pink opalescent.

Plate 325
FENTON ART GLASS COMPANY
#5156 Fish Vase. Milk glass with black tail and eyes, 7" high, circa 1953, rare.
$400.00 – 450.00

Other colors: black with white tail and eyes, and milk glass with black tail.

Reissues: In 2000 and 2001.

Plate 326
FENTON ART GLASS COMPANY
#5156 Fish Vase. Milk glass, black and white, 7" high, circa 2000 – 01.
$125.00 – 150.00

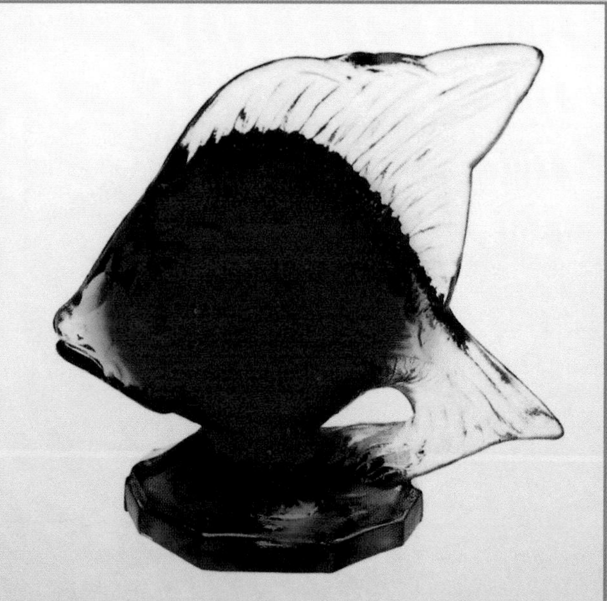

Plate 328
FENTON ART GLASS COMPANY
#5193 Fish Paperweight. Carnival, 4½" high, circa 1970s.
$45.00 – 65.00

Special pour of fish paperweight, 500 each of ruby plain, pink carnival, and green carnival. Has been reissued in other Fenton colors.

Plate 327
FENTON ART GLASS COMPANY
#306 Novelty Fish. Ruby with amberina type tail and fins, 2½" high.
$65.00 – 75.00

Reissues: Rechristened "Sun Fish" in 1992 and issued in pearlized colors of rose, jade, blue, twilight blue, pink, and red carnival.

Also known as "Li'l Fish." This fish was made for S.S. Kresge Company, in royal blue, ruby, jade, crystal etched, and green.

Plate 329
FOSTORIA GLASS COMPANY
Goldfish. Crystal, circa 1950 – 57.
#2633B Vertical. 4" high, $150.00 – 200.00
#2633A Horizontal. 4" long, $100.00 – 150.00

Plate 330
CONFUSING COLLECTIBLE
Goldfish, Foreign Made. Crystal, 3" long.
Seen at $10.00 – 15.00

Has original "Oneida" sticker. These are often seen at shows and shops labeled "Fostoria," obviously confused with the horizontal goldfish. See Plate 329.

Plate 331
CONFUSING COLLECTIBLE
Goldfish, Foreign Made. Crystal, 3½" long.
Seen at $8.00 – 10.00

Made in Japan. These are often seen at shows and shops labeled "Fostoria," obviously confused with the horizontal goldfish. See Plate 329.

Plate 332
FOSTORIA GLASS COMPANY
#2497 Flying Fish Vase. Circa 1965.
Lavender, 6½" high, $65.00 – 75.00
Teal green, 7½" high, $40.00 – 50.00
Ruby, 6½" high, $55.00 – 65.00

Height of vases will vary.

Plate 333
FOSTORIA GLASS COMPANY
#2497½ Seafood Cocktail Creamer. Empire green, 3¼" high, circa 1934 – 40.
$45.00 – 55.00

Other colors: crystal, burgundy, royal blue, silver mist, and ruby.

Plate 334
FOSTORIA GLASS COMPANY
#2534 Fish Ashtray. Empire green, 5" long, circa 1935 – 39.
$30.00 – 40.00

Other colors: crystal, regal blue, and burgundy.

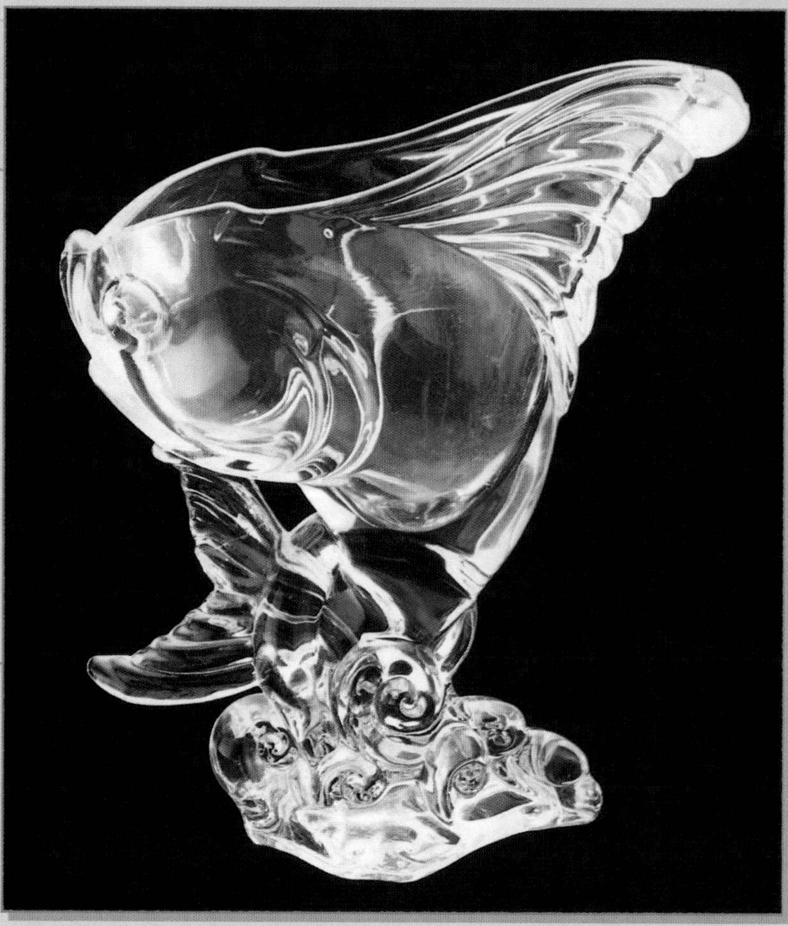

Plate 335
Heisey Glass Company
Fish bowl. Crystal, 9½" high, 8½" long (from front to back at the top), circa 1941 – 46. Marked in the middle of the bottom. $600.00 – 675.00

Reissues: none.

The base is solid glass up to the fish which is hollow and holds one pint of liquid. The glass is generally wavy and has numerous mold marks. Decorating companies decorated them by applying bright colors such as red, gold, white, and black to various features or applied ruby stain.

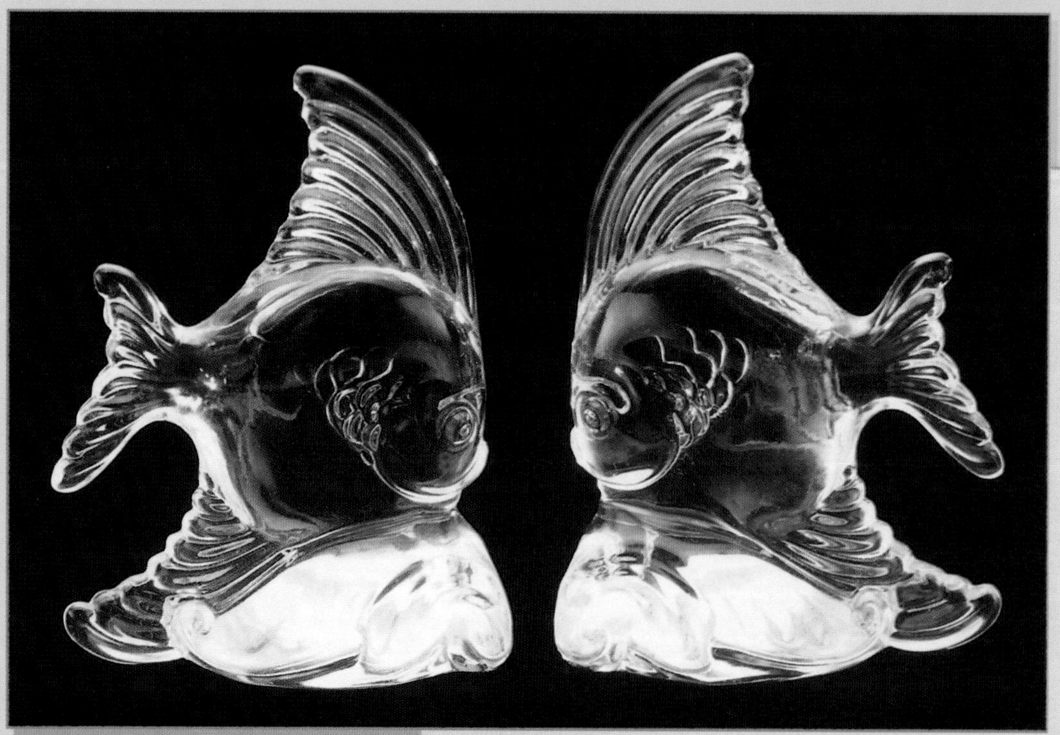

Plate 336
Heisey Glass Company
Fish Bookends. Crystal, 6½" high, 5" long (from front of base to end of lower fin), circa 1942 – 52. $350.00 – 375.00 pair

Other colors: crystal frosted and highlighted.

Reissues: Imperial Glass Company in multiple colors. Fenton in rosalene as part of the HCA Gold Series. See Plate 126. Some of the rosalene seconds were frosted and are sometimes referred to as plumstone. See Plate 342.

When marked, mark appears on the left side above the base in the middle. Decorating companies also decorated the bookends with bright colors.

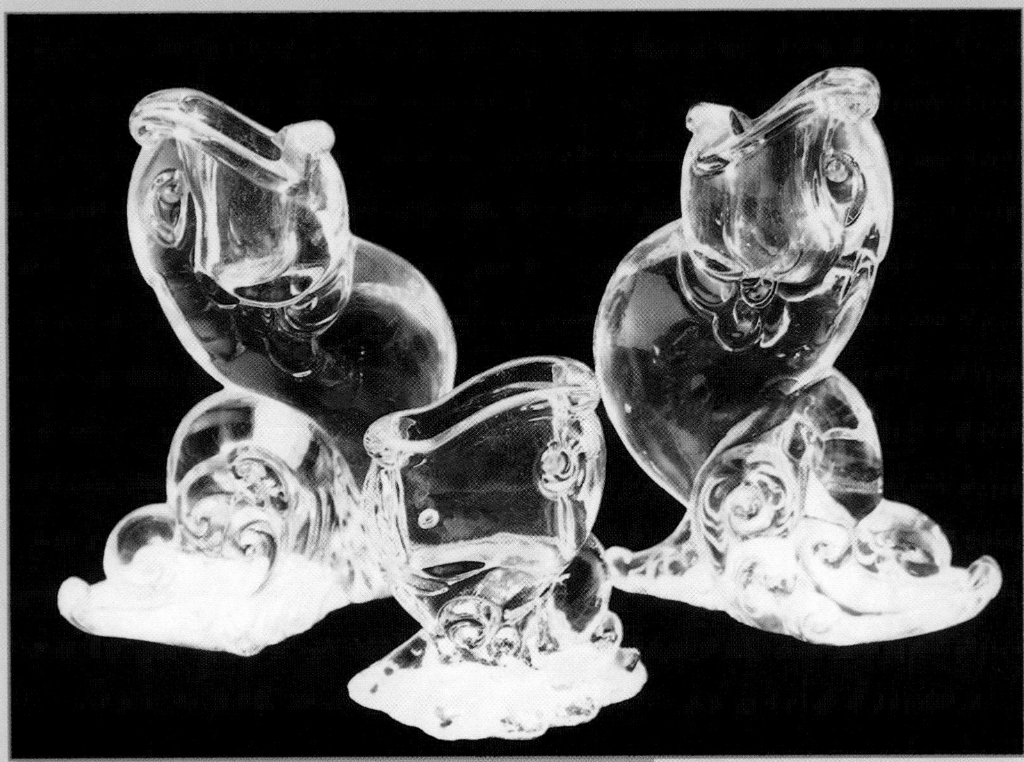

Plate 337
HEISEY GLASS COMPANY
Fish Candlestick. Crystal, 5" high, 4" long (at the base), circa 1941 – 48, not marked.
$350.00 – 400.00 pair

Other colors: none.

Reissues: Imperial Glass Company in sunshine yellow and sunshine yellow frosted. Dalzell-Viking in light blue and cobalt.

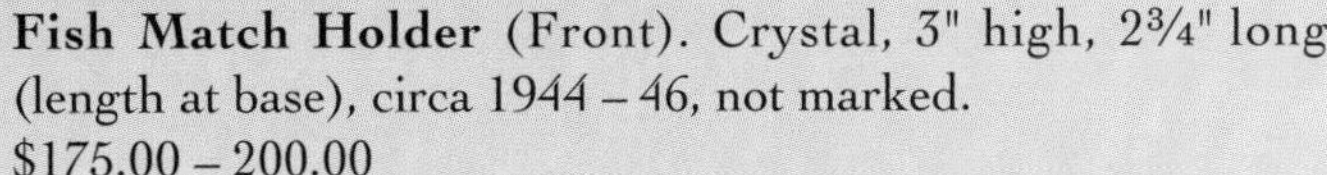

Fish Match Holder (Front). Crystal, 3" high, 2¾" long (length at base), circa 1944 – 46, not marked.
$175.00 – 200.00

Other colors: none.

Reissues: Imperial Glass Company in sunshine yellow and sunshine yellow frosted.

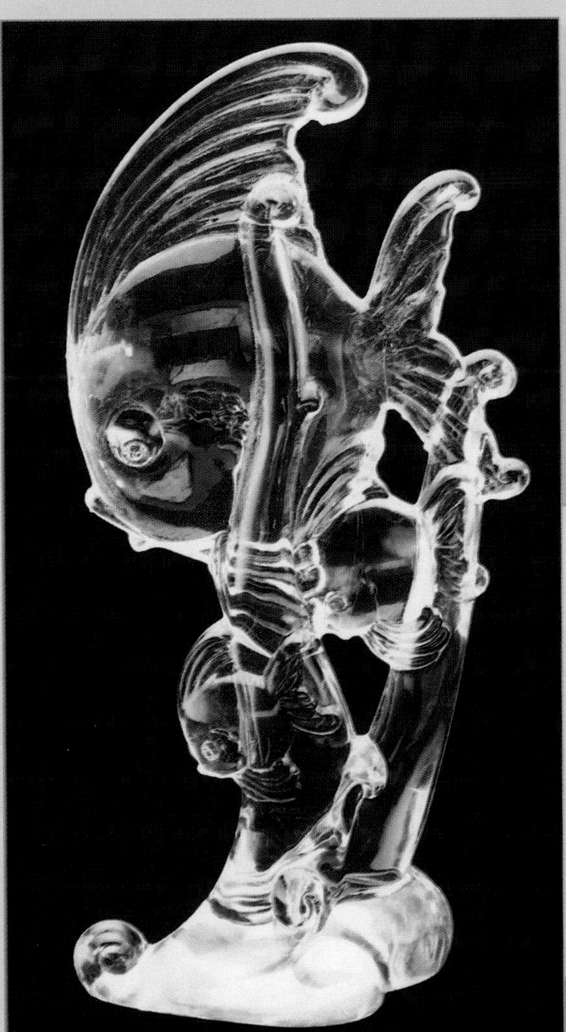

Plate 338
HEISEY GLASS COMPANY
Tropical Fish. Crystal, 12" high, 6½" long, circa 1948 – 49.
$2,000.00 – 2,200.00

Other colors: crystal frosted.

Reissues: Imperial Glass Company in crystal and amber. Dalzell-Viking in yellow and lavender ice.

When marked, mark appears on the right side, near the bottom of the back stalk of seaweed. If you look close, you can actually see three fish mounted on the two stalks of seaweed.

Plate 339
HEISEY GLASS COMPANY
Fish Bookend. Crystal, 6½" high, 5" long, circa 1942 – 53.

This item is repeated here in order to do a side-by-side comparison with the Viking Angelfish, Plate 340. For details on this item see Plate 336.

Plate 340
VIKING GLASS COMPANY
#1303 Angelfish. Crystal, 6½" high.
$65.00 – 75.00

This item is shown here in order to do a side-by-side comparison with the Heisey Fish Bookend, Plate 339. For all details on this item, see Plate 359.

Plate 341
IMPERIAL GLASS COMPANY (original Heisey Glass Company mold)
Angelfish Bookend. Ruby, 6½" high, circa 1984.
$325.00 – 375.00

See Plate 336.

Plate 342
FENTON ART GLASS COMPANY (original Heisey Glass Company mold)
Fish Bookend. Plumstone, 6½" high, circa 1992.
$100.00 – 125.00

After the Gold Series was produced in rosalene for HCA in 1992, some of the seconds or overruns were frosted and they became known as "plumstone." See Plate 126 for information on the Gold Series.

Plate 344
HARMON GLASS COMPANY
Crackle Glass Fish Vase.
Green, 13" long, 8½" high, circa 1940.
$85.00 – 95.00

Other colors: topaz and possibly other colors.

Plate 343
IMPERIAL GLASS COMPANY (original Heisey Glass Company mold)
Left: **Fish Candlestick.** Sunshine yellow, 5" high, circa 1982, for HCA, IG.
$35.00 – 45.00
Right: **Fish Match Holder.** Sunshine yellow, 3" high, circa 1982, for HCA, IG.
$20.00 – 25.00

Both items were produced in sunshine yellow frosted.

Plate 345
IMPERIAL GLASS COMPANY
#12 Offhand Fish Ornament. Opalescent crystal, 12" long, 6" high, circa 1964.
$175.00 – 200.00

Other colors: opalescent green, opalescent pink, and iridescent rubigold.

Plate 346
KANAWHA GLASS COMPANY
#903 Venetian Fish. Crystal with blue fins and eyes, 7" long, 5¼" high.
$40.00 – 50.00

Other colors: crystal with red fins and eyes.

Fish

Plate 347
PILGRIM GLASS COMPANY
Angelfish. Emerald green with orange mouth, 9" high.
$55.00 – 65.00

Creation of Alessandro and Robert Moretti.

Plate 348
PILGRIM GLASS COMPANY
"Murano" Fish. Smoke, 9" long, 7" high, circa 1950 – 60.
$75.00 – 95.00

The color is end of day brown (smoke) with milk glass chips.

Plate 349
SILVERBROOK ART GLASS
Fish Head Up. Crystal, 8½" high.
$125.00 – 150.00

Plate 350
SILVERBROOK ART GLASS
Fish Head Down. Crystal, 8" high, 11" long.
$125.00 – 150.00

Plate 351
L.E. Smith Glass Company
King Fish Aquarium. Green, 7¼" high, 15" long, circa mid-1920s.
$400.00 – 450.00

Other colors: crystal.

The aquarium also came with a high base, 10" high, 15" long, in green or crystal.

Plate 352
L.E. Smith Glass Company
Queen Fish Aquarium. Crystal, 7¼" high, 15" long, circa mid-1920s.
$300.00 – 350.00

Other colors: green.

Queen Fish Aquarium has a ribbed body.

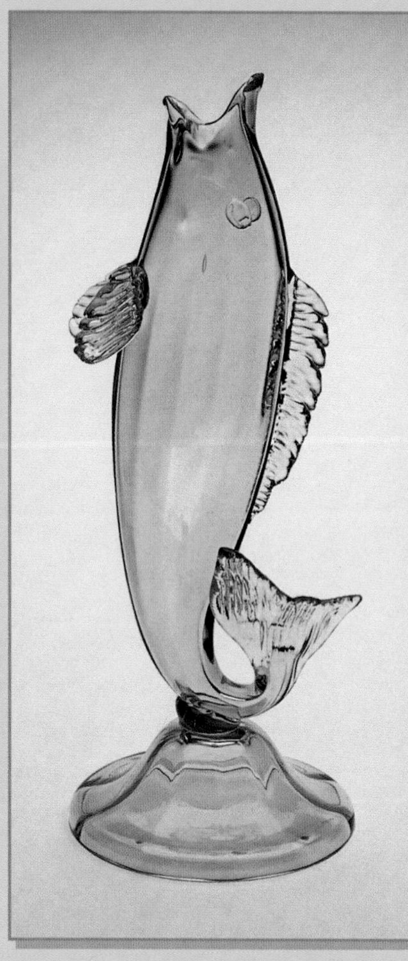

Plate 353
Steuben Glass Works
#6421 Fish Vase. Blue, 11½" high, blown, circa 1920s.
$400.00 – 450.00

Other colors: crystal and transparent colors.

Came in swirl optic or plain.

Plate 354
Steuben Glass Works
#6421 Fish Vase. Lavender, 12¾" high, blown, swirl optic, circa 1920s.
$400.00 – 450.00

Other colors: crystal and transparent colors.

Came in swirl optic or plain.

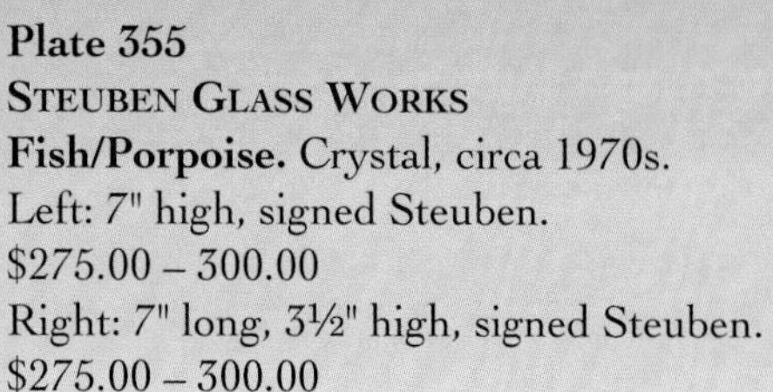

Plate 355
Steuben Glass Works
Fish/Porpoise. Crystal, circa 1970s.
Left: 7" high, signed Steuben.
$275.00 – 300.00
Right: 7" long, 3½" high, signed Steuben.
$275.00 – 300.00

Plate 356
Steuben Glass Works
#7064 Double Fish Flower Holder. Crystal base, satin figures, 7½" high, circa 1930s.
Private collection — Market

Plate 357
TIFFIN GLASS COMPANY
#6043 Fish. Crystal, 9" high, 10" long, circa 1946 – 47.
$350.00 – 400.00

Other colors: copen blue.

Plate 358
TIFFIN GLASS COMPANY
Fish, Controlled Bubbles.
$700.00 – 750.00 pair

Plate 359
VIKING GLASS COMPANY
#1301 Angelfish. Milk glass, 6½" high.
$250.00 to Market

Other colors: crystal, amber, ebony, and light blue.

Reissues: Dalzell-Viking in crystal in 1991.

Plate 360
VIKING GLASS COMPANY
#1301 Angelfish.
Light blue, 6½" high.
$175.00 – 200.00

See Plate 359.

Plate 361
VIKING GLASS COMPANY
#1320 Fish on Base. Dark medium blue, 10" high, circa 1960s.
$45.00 – 65.00

Other colors: made in Viking colors.

Plate 362
VIKING GLASS COMPANY
#7274 Whale. Dark medium blue, 5" long, circa 1960s.
$30.00 – 40.00

Other colors: made in Viking colors.

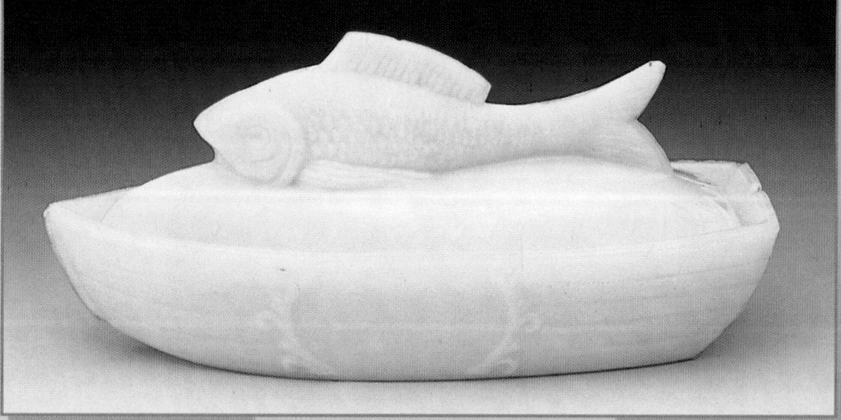

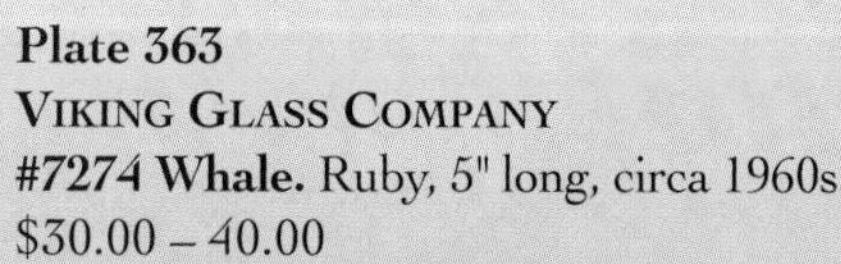

Plate 363
VIKING GLASS COMPANY
#7274 Whale. Ruby, 5" long, circa 1960s.
$30.00 – 40.00

Other colors: Made in Viking colors.

Plate 364
UNKNOWN MANUFACTURER
Fish on a Skiff. Milk glass, 7½" long, circa early 1900s.
Seen at $50.00 – 60.00

Plate 365
Pilgrim Glass Company
#176 Blossom Holder. Cranberry and crystal, 10" long, circa 1984.
$45.00 – 55.00

Other colors: crystal and probably other Pilgrim colors.

Plate 366
Pilgrim Glass Company
#140 Table Flowers. 7" long, circa 1976 – 77.
Green, $25.00 – 30.00
Blue, $25.00 – 30.00
Amber, $35.00 – 40.00
Amberina, $40.00 – 45.00

Used for table decor.

Plate 367
VIKING GLASS COMPANY
Long Stem Rose. Amberina, 6" long, 4½" wide, circa 1970s, very scarce.
$225.00 – 250.00

Other colors: ritz blue, amethyst, ruby, orange, green, amber, and perhaps other Viking colors.

Plate 368
VIKING GLASS COMPANY
Long Stem Rose. Green, 6" long, 4½" wide, circa 1970s.
$225.00 – 250.00

See Plate 367 for other colors.

Plate 369
VIKING GLASS COMPANY
Long Stem Rose. Amber, 6" long, 4½" wide, circa 1970s.
$225.00 – 250.00

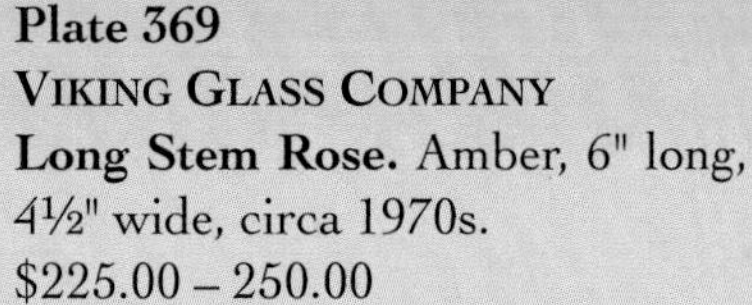

See Plate 367 for other colors.

Plate 370
VIKING GLASS COMPANY
Long Stem Rose. Orange, 6" long, 4½" wide, circa 1970s.
$225.00 – 250.00

See Plate 367 for other colors.

Plate 371
Viking Glass Company
Fruit Paperweights:
#7295 Apple Paperweight. Blue and green, 4" high, circa 1971.
$30.00 – 40.00
#7296 Pear Paperweight. Orange, 6" high, circa 1971.
$30.00 – 40.00

Other colors: both made in other Viking colors.

The height of these items will vary.

Plate 372
Unknown Manufacturer
Mushroom Paperweights:
Confusing Collectibles
Amber, 6". Seen at $25.00 – 35.00
Crystal frosted, 2½", $8.00 – 10.00
Crystal and cobalt, 3", $10.00 – 15.00

The two smaller mushrooms have foreign labels and the amber mushroom, although not marked, is probably also an import.

Plate 372A
Morgantown Glass Company
Mushroom Covered Boxes.
Left: #1412, ruby and milk glass, 7" high.
$70.00 – 90.00
Right: #1413, ruby and milk glass, 11" high.
$100.00 – 125.00

Other colors: crystal, white and ebony, nutmeg, and moss.

Came in three sizes, 6" not pictured.

Plate 373
Pilgrim Glass Company
#170 Mushroom Paperweight. Amber and crystal, 3", circa 1976 – 77.
$20.00 – 25.00

Other colors: crystal stems with colored caps, amber, red, blue, green, and perhaps others.

Also made #172 mushroom, which is 4½". All are handmade.

Plate 374
Viking Glass Company
Mushroom Paperweights. Crystal, circa 1971, 3½", 5½", and 2¾".
Left: #6941, medium, $25.00 – 35.00
Center: #6942, large, $30.00 – 35.00
Right: #6940, small, frosted, $20.00 – 25.00

Other colors: amber, medium green, blue, orange, yellow green, crystal, crystal frosted, and possibly other Viking colors.

Mushrooms have polished bottoms and gills under the caps. Sizes will vary. Size refers to height.

Plate 375
Viking Glass Company
Mushroom Paperweight. Amber, circa 1971.
Left: #6941, medium, $30.00 – 35.00
Right: #6940, small, $20.00 – 25.00

See Plate 374 for details.

Plate 376
Viking Glass Company
Mushroom Paperweights. Blue, circa 1971.
Left: #6941, medium, $30.00 – 35.00
Right: #6940, small, $25.00 – 30.00

See Plate 374 for details.

Plate 377
VIKING GLASS COMPANY
Mushroom Paperweights. Yellow green, circa 1971.
Left: #6942, large, $40.00 – 45.00
Center:, #6940, small, $25.00 – 30.00
Right: #6941, medium, $30.00 – 35.00

See Plate 374 for details.

Plate 378
VIKING GLASS COMPANY
Mushroom Paperweights. Orange, circa 1971.
Left: #6941, medium, $30.00 – 35.00
Right: #6940, small, $25.00 – 30.00

See Plate 374 for details.

Plate 379
VIKING GLASS COMPANY
Mushroom Paperweights. Medium green, circa 1971.
Left: #6942, large, $40.00 – 45.00
Right: #6941, medium, $30.00 – 35.00

See Plate 374 for details.

Plate 380
Fenton Art Glass Company
#5226 Fox. Red carnival iridized, 4" high, circa mid-1990s.
$55.00 – 75.00

Other colors: 1989 in crystal, crystal velvet, and others. Also made in multiple colors in the mid-1990s.

Plate 381
Heisey Glass Company
Sleeping Fox Ashtray. $6\frac{1}{4}$" long, 4" high, circa 1940s.
$400.00 – 450.00

Other colors: none.

Reissues: Dalzell-Viking, 1993, lavender ice, as commemorative item for opening of museum expansion. Mosser, 1999, cobalt with silver highlights, as commemorative item, 25th anniversary of Heisey Museum.

Plate 382
Cambridge Glass Company
Frog. Crystal satin, 1¼" high, circa 1930s.
$35.00 – 45.00

Other colors: crystal, light emerald, light emerald satin, and probably other Cambridge colors.

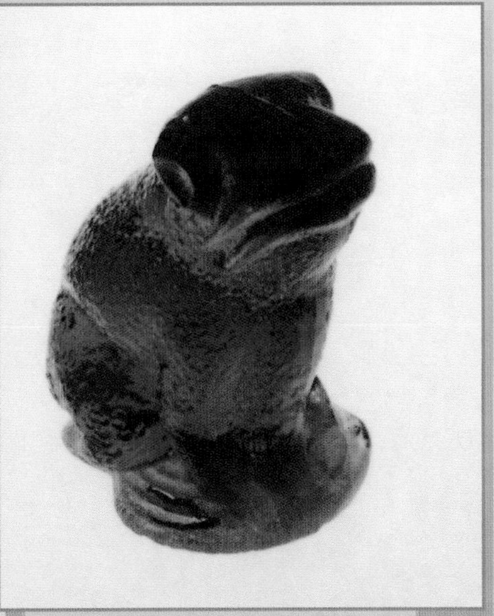

Plate 383
Cambridge Glass Company
Frog. Emerald satin, 1¼" high, circa 1930s.
$45.00 – 55.00

See Plate 382.

Plate 384
Co-Operative Flint Glass Company
Frog and Cover. 4" high, 5½" long, circa 1927.
Crystal frosted, $200.00 – 225.00
Pink, $250.00 – 275.00

Other colors: crystal and transparent colors.

Reissues: Erskine Glass Company, 1969, in amber and green.

Can be found in milk glass, produced by Vallerysthal in the 1920s.

Plate 385
Fenton Art Glass Company
#5166 Frog. Lime green satin, 4" long, 2¼" high, circa 1979 – 80.
$35.00 – 40.00

Other colors: crystal velvet, blue satin, custard, custard decorated, and perhaps others.

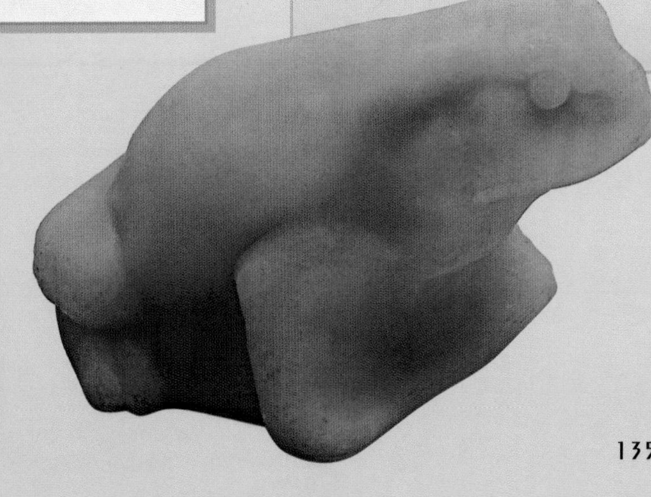

Plate 386
Fostoria Glass Company
#2821/420 Frog. Lemon, 1⅞" high, 3½" long, circa 1971 – 73.
$30.00 – 35.00

Other colors: crystal and olive green, plain or frosted, and probably other Fostoria colors.

Plate 387
Fostoria Glass Company
#2821/420 Frog. Olive green, 1⅞" high, 3½" long, circa 1971 – 73.
$30.00 – 35.00

See Plate 386.

Plate 388
Heisey Glass Company
Frog Handled Cheese Tray. Flamingo, 7¼" wide (top of handle to bottom), circa 1929 – 33.
$100.00 – 125.00

Other colors: crystal, moongleam, and marigold.

Not marked.

Plate 389
Tiffin Glass Company
#72 Frog Candlestick. Black satin, 5½" high, circa 1924 – 34.
$100.00 – 125.00 each

Sometimes used as a child's napkin ring.

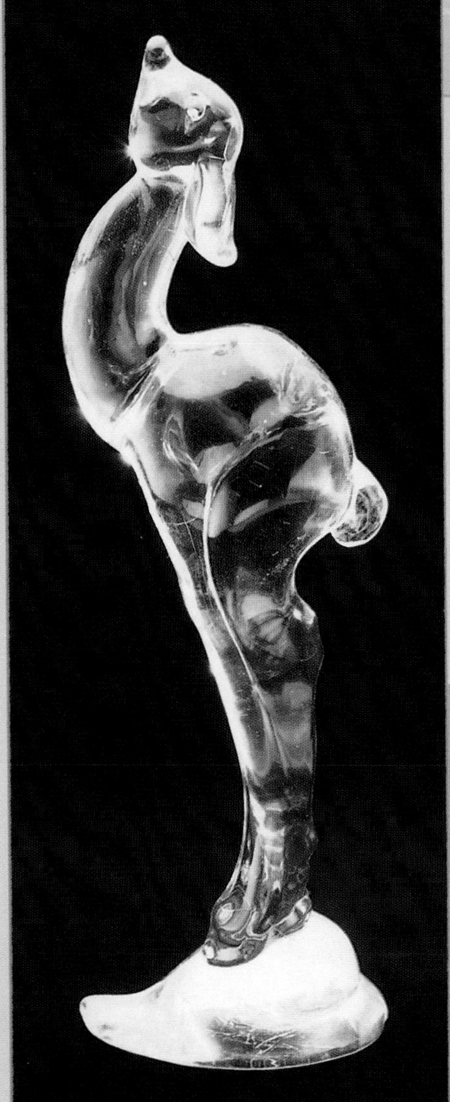

Plate 390
Heisey Glass Company
Gazelle. Crystal, 10¾" high, 3¼" long (length of base), circa 1947 – 49. Mark appears on the side of the left hoof.
$1,400.00 – 1,800.00

Other colors: crystal frosted.

Reissues: Imperial Glass Company in crystal, ultra blue (for Mirror Images), ultra blue satin, and black. Fenton Art Glass Company in rosalene as part of the HCA Gold Series. See Plate 126.

This elegant figurine is solid glass and has excellent detail. It is sometimes confused by collectors with the Tiffin Fawn (Plate 149). Imperial Glass Company produced this animal in cobalt (ultra blue) without removing the Heisey mark (Diamond H). This has caused a tremendous amount of confusion and many think this was a Heisey production simply because of the mark. The crystal refers to the late Imperial reissue before the factory closed.

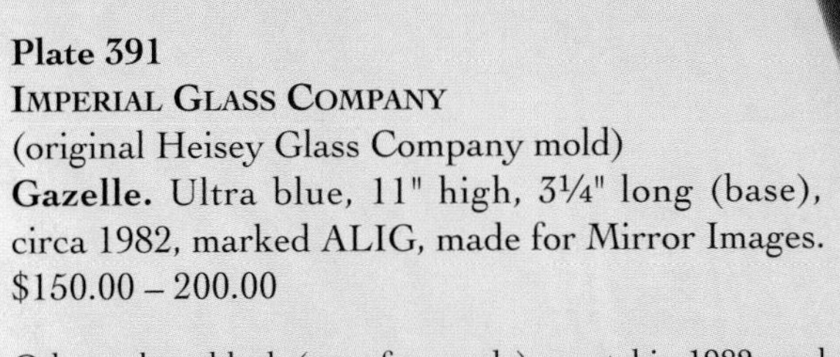

Plate 391
Imperial Glass Company
(original Heisey Glass Company mold)
Gazelle. Ultra blue, 11" high, 3¼" long (base), circa 1982, marked ALIG, made for Mirror Images.
$150.00 – 200.00

Other colors: black (very few made), crystal in 1982 marked ALIG, and ultra blue frosted.

When Imperial first made this item in ultra blue, they did not take the Diamond H out of the mold and the first ones are marked with the Heisey mark. However, Heisey only made the Gazelle in crystal and crystal satin and not in cobalt.

Plate 392
Owens-Illinois Glass Company
Gazelle Bookend. Frosted crystal.
Private collection — Market

Owens Bottle Machine Company, Toledo, Ohio, founded in 1903, merged with Illinois Glass Company in 1929, and became Owens-Illinois. Under the ownership of Libbey Glass Company since 1936.

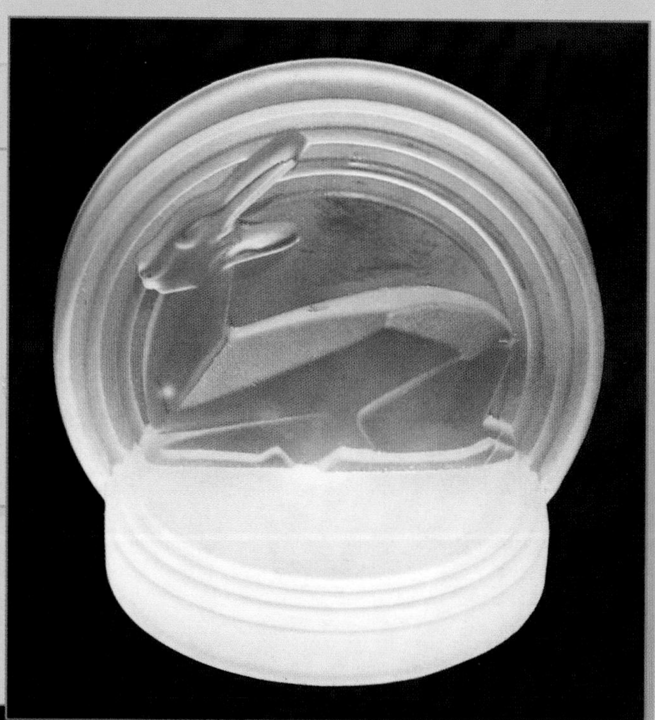

Plate 393
Steuben Glass Works
Gazelle Bookend. Crystal and crystal frosted, 6½" high, 8" long, circa 1930s.
$400.00 – 500.00 each

Plate 394
New Martinsville Glass Company
Gazelle, Leaping. Crystal, 8¼" high.
$55.00 – 65.00

Other colors: crystal with frosted base and all crystal frosted.

Reissues: Viking Glass Company, 1998, before factory closed, in ruby for Mirror Images.

Plate 395
DUNCAN GLASS COMPANY
Fat Goose. Crystal, 6½" high (to tip of bill), 6" long (breast to tip of tail).
$250.00 – 300.00

Other colors: none.

Reissues: none.

This figurine is solid glass and is very heavy. It had many uses including a bookend and a doorstop.

Plate 396
PADEN CITY GLASS COMPANY
Goose. Pale blue, 5" high, circa 1940.
$100.00 – 125.00

Other colors: crystal and crystal frosted.

Plate 397
L.E. SMITH GLASS COMPANY
Goose. Crystal frosted, 4½" high, 4½" long, circa 1920s.
$20.00 – 30.00

Other colors: crystal.

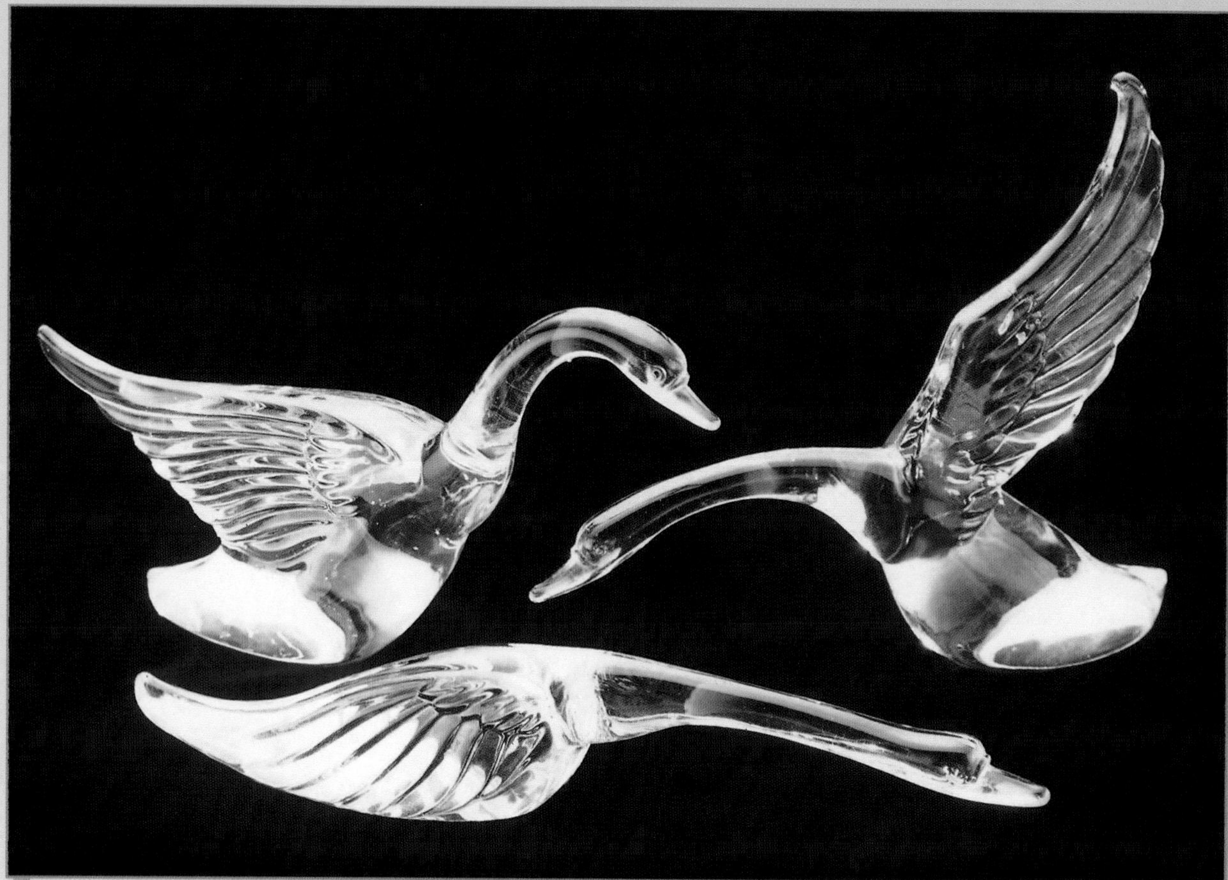

Plate 398
HEISEY GLASS COMPANY
Geese.
Left: **Wings Half.** Crystal, 4½" high, 8½" long (tip of tail to tip of bill), circa 1942 – 53.
$100.00 – 125.00

Other colors: crystal frosted.

Reissues: Imperial Glass Company in crystal and ultra blue. Dalzell-Viking in lavender ice. Mosser Glass Company in red.

When marked, the mark appears midway on the left side near the base. It is sometimes seen with floral decorations. This goose is seen more often than the other two, perhaps it was not as easily broken.

Center: **Wings Down.** Crystal, 2" high, 10¼" long (tip of tail to tip of bill), circa 1942 – 53. When marked, the mark appears on the left side, third feather near the base.
$450.00 – 500.00

Other colors: crystal frosted.

Reissues: Imperial Glass Company, none. Dalzell-Viking Glass Company, lavender ice. Mosser Glass Company, red.

The neck is very easily broken which probably accounts for its scarcity.

Right: **Wings Up.** Crystal, 6½" high, 7½" long (tip of tail to tip of bill), circa 1942 – 53. When marked, the mark appears midway on the left side near the base.
$100.00 – 125.00

Other colors: crystal frosted.

Reissues: Imperial Glass Company, crystal. Dalzell-Viking Glass Company, lavender ice. Mosser Glass Company, red.

Because the wings are extended upwards, it is easily knocked over and generally the wing tip will break. Although the wings up is seen more often than the wings down, it is seen less often than the wings half.

As lovely as a Christmas star —Heisey CRYSTAL

A For dispensing good cheer *what* could be more appropriate than the Heisey creations displayed here?

B Graceful epergnes, gleaming candelabra, intriguing penguin cordial sets—all betoken gracious living.

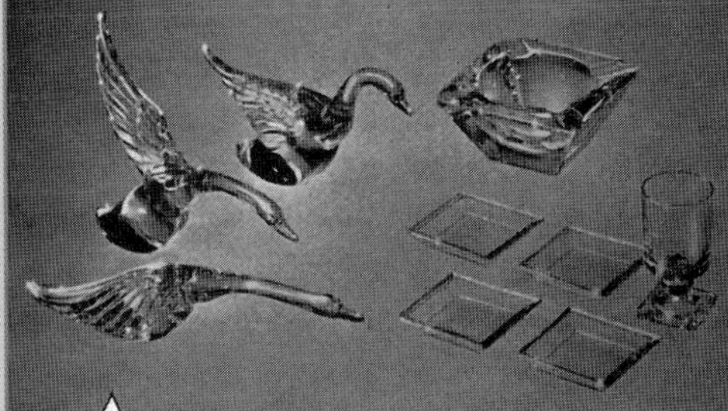

C Here, the famous crystal swans admire a few of Heisey's smart smokers' accessories.

The sparkle of Christmas itself is captured—and preserved—in Heisey Crystal. Whether for gifts or for your very own, choose Heisey Crystal, knowing it will become a proud possession. Handmade by America's finest craftsmen. See it at better stores everywhere. A. H. HEISEY & CO., NEWARK, OHIO.

Buy War Bonds, too! HEISEY'S HAND-WROUGHT CRYSTAL

Original Heisey magazine ad.

Caption under the bottom picture refers to the Heisey geese as "Swans."

Plate 399
HEISEY GLASS COMPANY
Large Goose Decanter and Stems.
Decanter. Crystal, frosted stopper and tail, 13¾" high, circa 1940s.
$400.00 – 450.00
Sherry. Crystal, frosted stem.
$200.00 – 225.00
Sherry. Crystal, crystal stem.
$200.00 – 225.00

Stems also made in amber.

Plate 400
HEISEY GLASS COMPANY
Small Goose Decanter and Stems.
Decanter. Crystal, no frosting, 12" high, circa 1940s.
$400.00 – 425.00
Cordial. Crystal, 1 oz.
$200.00 – 225.00 each.

Stems also made in amber.

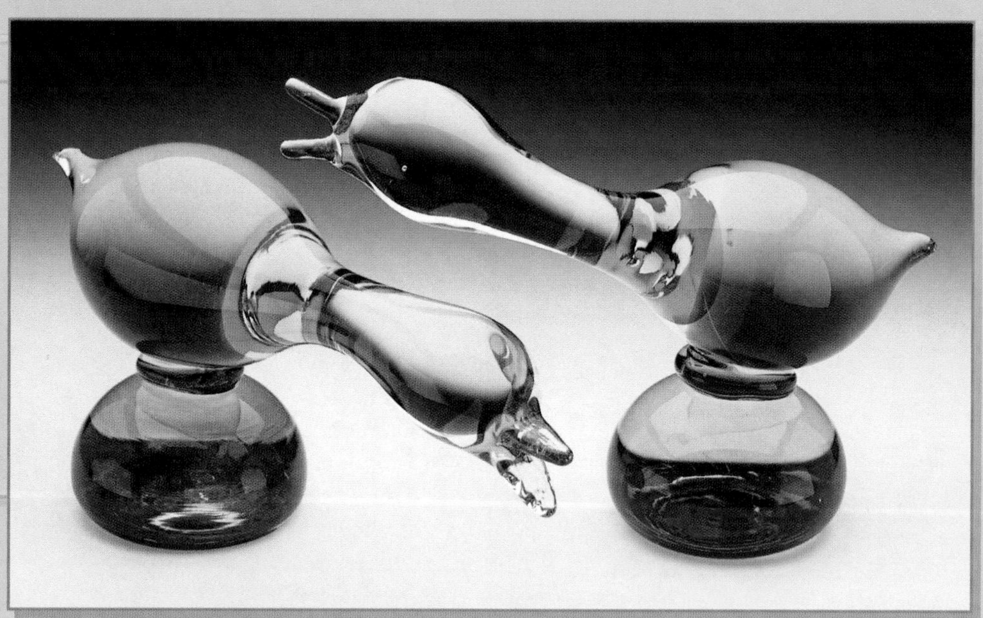

Plate 401
TIFFIN GLASS COMPANY
Geese. Crystal.
Left: **Head Down.** 11½" long, 5" high, circa 1940s.
$350.00 – 400.00
Right: **Head Up.** 10" long, 7" high, circa 1940s.
$350.00 – 400.00

These are off-hand made animals and are rare.

Plate 402
TIFFIN GLASS COMPANY
Goose. Copen blue, circa 1930s.
$500.00 to Market

This animal is very rare.

Plate 403
STEUBEN GLASS WORKS
#8338 Gander. Crystal, 5¼" high, circa 1980 – 81, signed.
$225.00 – 275.00

Came with #8348, Preening Goose (not shown). Pair referred to as Goose and Gander. Designed by Lloyd Atkins. Given as wedding gifts, as they represent "Faithful Pair."

Plate 404
HEISEY GLASS COMPANY
Giraffe. Crystal, 10¾" high, 3" long (length of base), circa 1942 – 52.
$275.00 – 300.00

When marked, the mark appears on the right side of the front leg, near the base.

Other colors: crystal frosted and amber.

Reissues: Imperial Glass Company, 1980 – 82, in crystal, crystal frosted, amber, black, and sunshine yellow. Fenton Art Glass Company in rosalene as part of the Heisey Gold Series. See Plate 126. Was also made in rosalene with satin finish. Dalzell-Viking in lavender ice.

They are listed in the catalog as being produced in amber by Heisey, but they have not been seen. The neck was hand shaped after they were removed from the mold, therefore, the head may be facing different directions and the height may vary.

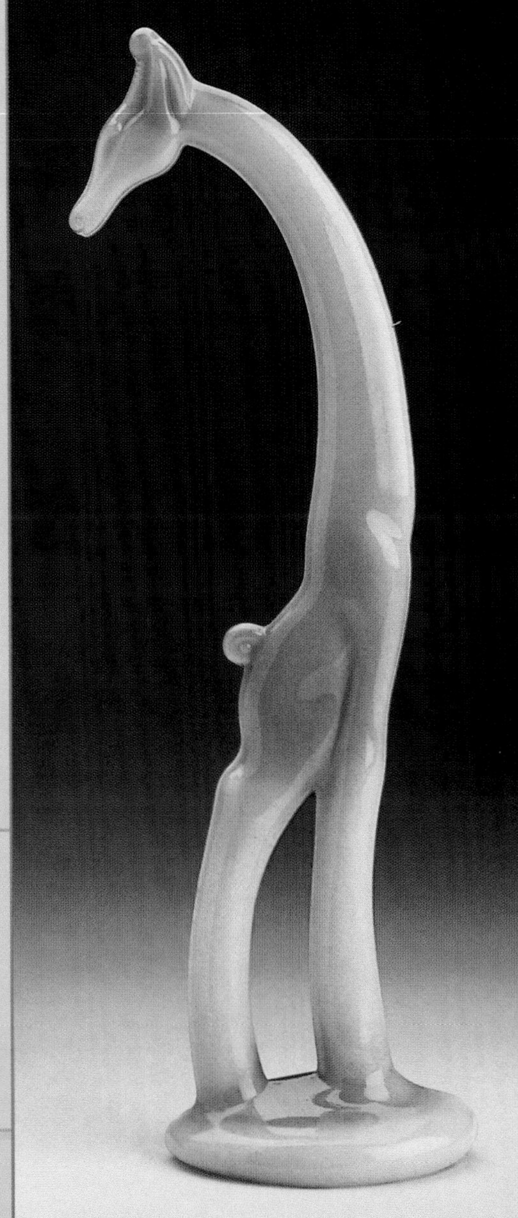

Plate 405
FENTON ART GLASS COMPANY (original Heisey Glass Company mold)
Giraffe. Rosalene, 10¾" high, 3" long.
$100.00 – 125.00

This was part of the HCA Gold Series. See Plate 126. For all reissues see Plate 404.

Grouse

Plate 406
Duncan Glass Company
Ruffled Grouse. Crystal with frosted highlights, 6½" high, 7½" long (from tip of tail to breast), circa 1930s. $1,400.00 – 1,600.00

Other colors: crystal, crystal frosted, and crystal with frosted highlights on tail and collar, as shown.

Reissues: none.

This figurine is extremely rare. Because of its design with tail extended, obviously many were broken. This coupled with the fact that only a small number were made accounts for its rarity.

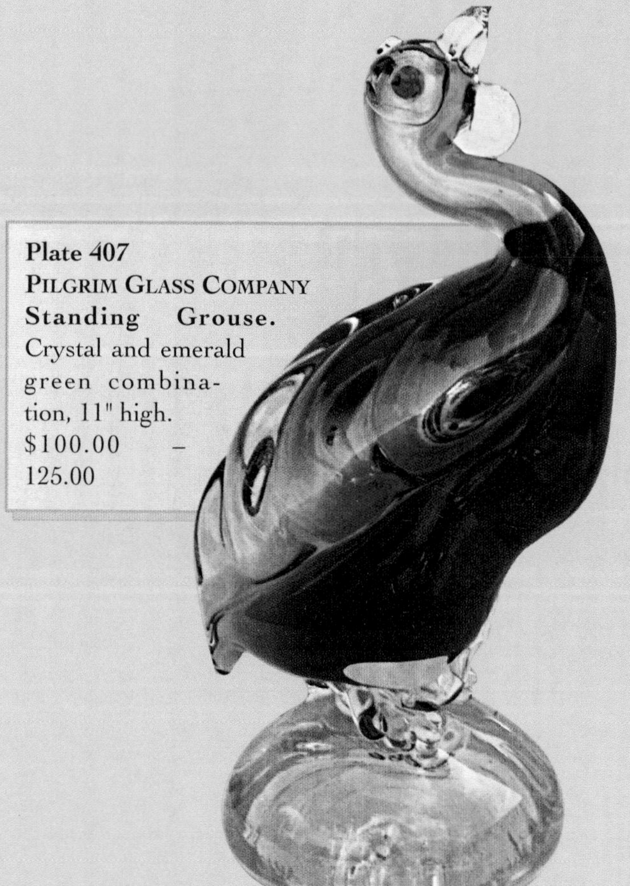

Plate 407
Pilgrim Glass Company
Standing Grouse. Crystal and emerald green combination, 11" high. $100.00 – 125.00

Plate 408
Unknown Manufacturer
Grouse. Crystal, 5½" high, 5" wide. Seen at $200.00 – 225.00

This figurine is solid, excellent quality glass with a ground and polished bottom. It has excellent detail.

Plate 409
Circa early 1900s, crystal with black pistol grips and silver overlay, length 5", advertising on barrel "WALDEK BALMAR RYE BALTO."
$100.00 – 125.00

Plate 410
Circa early 1960s – 1970s, established by the Westmoreland sticker on the pistol grip, solid black, length 5".
$75.00 – 100.00

Plate 411
Contemporary, cobalt, length 5", comes in vaseline and possibly other colors, produced by Summit Art Glass.
$15.00 – 25.00

Plate 411 has a squared off and flat barrel. Plates 409 and 410 have indented barrels.

Heron

Plate 412
Cambridge Glass Company
Heron Flower Holders. Crystal.
Left: 12" high, circa 1920s, $140.00 – 160.00
Right: 9" high, circa 1930s, $75.00 – 95.00

Other colors: The 9" produced in milk glass. 12" none.

Reissue: 12" none. 9" in milk glass, in 1950s.

The sides of the base are fluted on the 9" whereas the base is smooth on the 12". The small Heron is sometimes confused with the Heron produced by Duncan. See Plate 413.

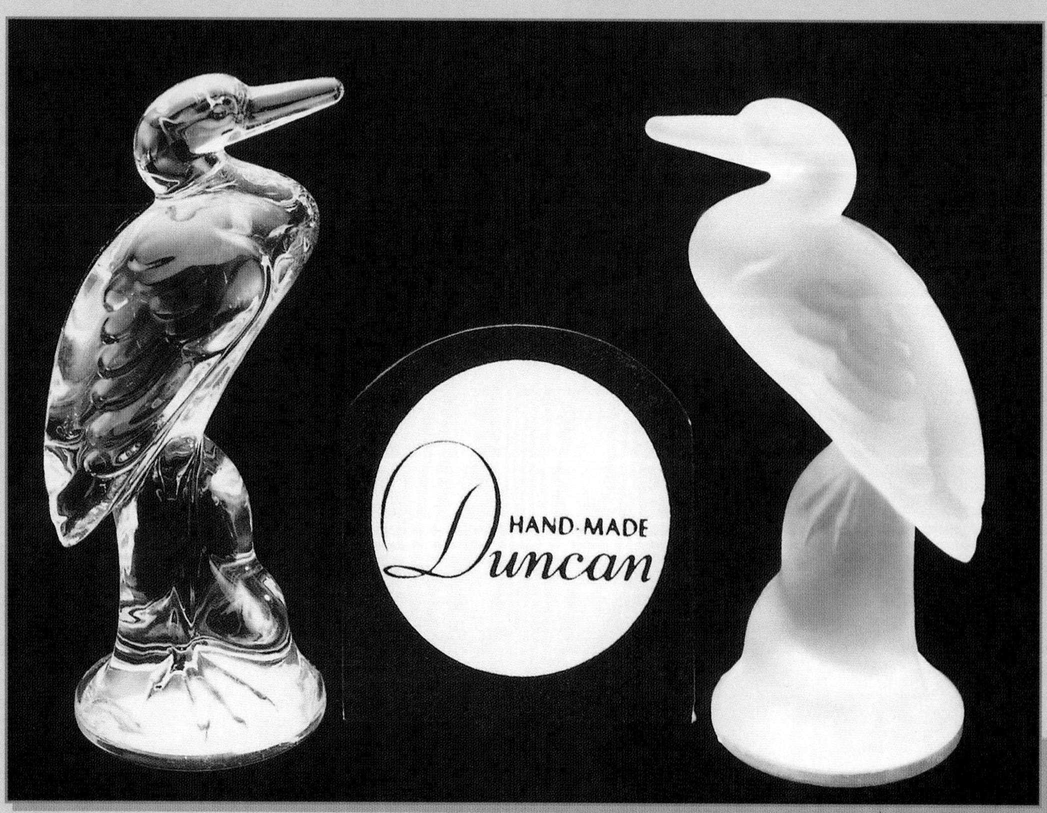

Plate 413
Duncan Glass Company
Heron. Crystal and crystal satin, 7" high, base 2½" diameter, circa 1930s.
$100.00 – 125.00 each

Other colors: none known.

Reissues: none known.

This figurine's right leg and foot are extended to the ground whereas the left leg is drawn up against the body and only the foot is visible. Sometimes this Heron is confused with the small Cambridge Heron. See Plate 412 for the difference.

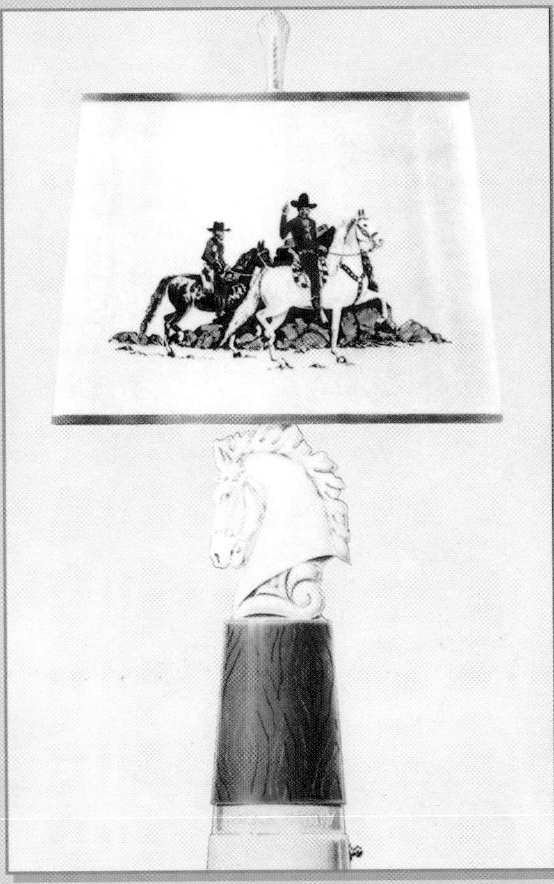

Plate 414
Mantle Lamp Company of America (Aladdin)
G335C Hoppy Horse Head Lamp. Alacite, circa 1951.
$425.00 – 475.00

Value is for lamp with original shade.

Plate 415
American Glass Company
Jumping Horse Bookend. Crystal, 8" high.
$50.00 – 60.00

Other colors: crystal frosted.

The base of this figurine is hollow.

Plate 416
Federal Glass Company
#2563 Horse Head. Pastel frosted, 5½".
$15.00 – 20.00

Other colors: crystal and crystal frosted, both of which are frequently seen with various decorations.

This figurine is hollow, has a cardboard bottom, and is sometimes filled with candy.

Comparison of Rearing Horse Bookends

There were four companies that made Rearing Horse bookends that have similarities and sometimes are confusing. We can eliminate Heisey from the confusion very easily. The Heisey Rearing Horse has a flowing mane and the head and nose are high in the air. For photo and complete details on the Heisey horse, see Plate 431.

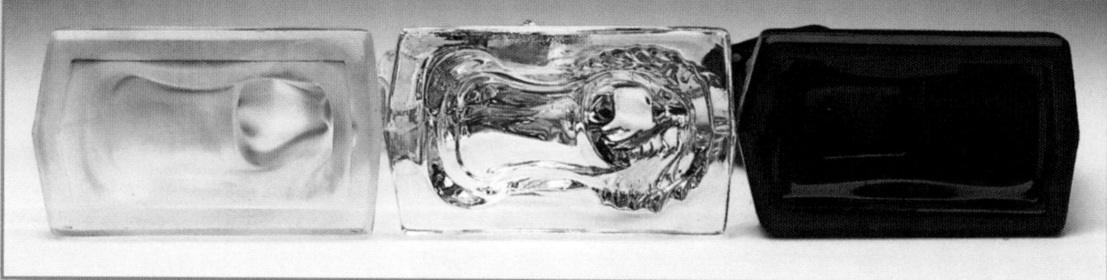

Plate 417
Rearing Horse Bookends
Left: **Fostoria,** crystal frosted.
$60.00 – 70.00 each
Center: **New Martinsville,** crystal.
$75.00 – 85.00 each
Right: **L.E. Smith,** black.
$45.00 – 50.00 each

Left: The horse made by Fostoria is 7¾" tall with a 5½" long base. It has a close-cropped mane and like the other three has the front legs folded under. Unique to the Fostoria horse is the rectangular opening on the bottom of the base. It measures 4½" long, 2¼" wide, and ⅛" deep. This creates a ledge before the start of the hollow in the animal. The hollow runs further up into the figurine than that of New Martinsville. A small but notable features is that the right ear is smaller than the left ear. See Plate 418.

Center: The horse made by New Martinsville is 7½" high and the base is 5½" long. It has a close-cropped mane and a flowing tail like the other three. The clarity of glass in the New Martinsville horse is somewhat better than that of Fostoria. The bottom of the base is ground smooth to the hollow which does not go as far up into the animal as does Fostoria. Addie Miller once told us this animal has that "Roman nose," which gives the appearance of pointing down further than the nose of the Fostoria horse. See Plate 469.

Right: The horse made by L.E. Smith is 8" tall, 5¾" base. It is easy to tell from the other three horses, by simply looking at the mane. It is the only one of the four that is beaded. See Plate 476.

Plate 418
FOSTORIA GLASS COMPANY
Rearing Horse Bookend. Crystal, 7¾" high, circa 1939 – 58.
$60.00 – 70.00 each

Other colors: silver mist 1939 – 43, ebony (few sold in outlet stores) 1980, reissued in 1991 in crystal only for Fostoria outlet

Plate 419
FOSTORIA GLASS COMPANY
Rearing Horse Lamp. Figurine: crystal, 7¾" high.
$100.00 – 125.00

Fostoria made the figurine, but the lamp was made by a lamp company who actually put them together and sold them.

Plate 420
FOSTORIA GLASS COMPANY
#2589 Colt Reclining. Crystal, 2¼" high, 2¾" long, circa 1940s.
$20.00 – 25.00

Other colors: silver mist and milk glass.

Reissues: reissued in milk glass in the 1950s.

#2589 Colt Standing. Crystal, 3⅞" high, circa 1940s.
$35.00 – 45.00

Other colors: silver mist and cobalt.

Reissues: Limited edition of 1,000 made in 1977 for Blue Colt Collectibles.

Plate 421
K.R. Haley Glassware Company
Trail's End Indian and Pony. Crystal, 7½" high, circa 1946.
Rarity prohibits pricing.

Designed by Walter Przybylek, a prominent designer for multiple glass companies. This figurine is extremely rare.

Plate 422
K.R. Haley Glassware Company
Jumping Horse. Crystal, 9½" long, 7½" high, circa 1947.
$55.00 – 65.00

The base is hollow. Kemple Glass Company purchased this mold in the 1950s. See Plate 423.

Plate 423
Kemple Glass Company (original K.R. Haley Glassware Co. mold)
Jumping Horse. Milk glass, 9½" high, 7½" long, circa 1950 – 60.
$75.00 – 95.00

Other colors: amber and amethyst.

For information and photo on the Guernsey Glass Company Spark Plug Horse, see Plate 697.

Plate 424
K.R. Haley Glassware Company
Horse and Rider Bookend. Crystal, 6" high, 6" long.
$45.00 – 55.00 each

Other colors: crystal frosted.

Commonly known as Lady Godiva bookends.

Plate 425
K.R. Haley Glassware Company
Horse and Cart. Crystal.
Left: Small Horse and Cart, $10.00 – 15.00
Right: Large Horse and Cart, 4½" high, $20.00 – 25.00

Other colors: Large Horse and Cart also made in milk glass.

Reissues: Reissues of these items in almost every color and there are far too many to document.

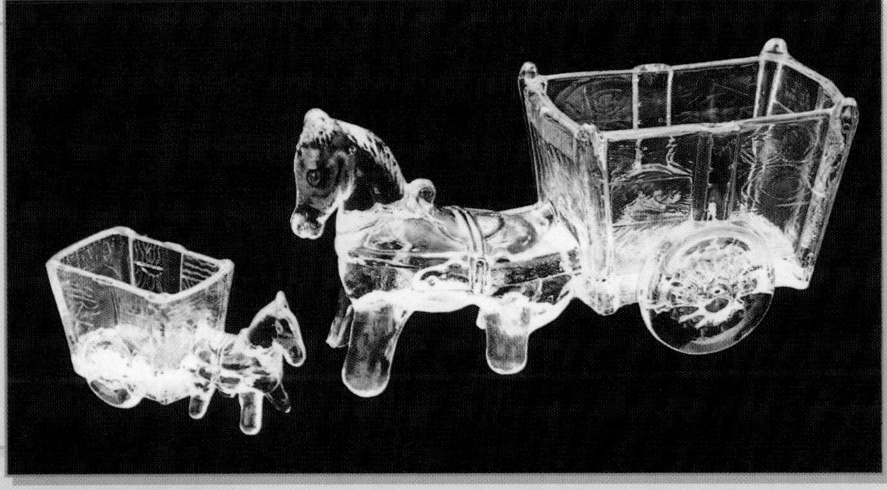

Plate 426
K.R. Haley Glassware Company
Pacemaker Ashtray. Crystal, 3½" high.
$10.00 – 15.00

Other colors: fired mellotint colors in red, light amber, and apple green; fired Chinese red, green, pink, and blue with black Pacemaker colt in center.

Produced by Knox Glass Company, later by American Glass in the early 1940s, this little ashtray was selected by Randolph Hearst to be given out to tourists as a souvenir of their visit to Hearst Castle. In May 1974 these were sold at Roosevelt Raceway in New York. The mold is in the possession of Reikes Crystal, but has not been reissued.

Plate 427
Heisey Glass Company
Clydesdale. Crystal, 7½" high, 7" long (front to back at base), circa 1942 – 48.
$475.00 – 525.00

Other colors: crystal frosted and amber.

Reissues: Imperial Glass Company in crystal satin, 1978 and in the 1980s in amber, amber satin, salmon, antique blue, verde green, verde green satin, and ultra blue satin. Imperial in ultra blue for Mirror Images in 1984. Dalzell-Viking in lavender ice. Mosser in cobalt blue and perhaps in other colors for Lonaberger.

Seldom marked, but when found, the mark appears on the extreme lower right back leg.

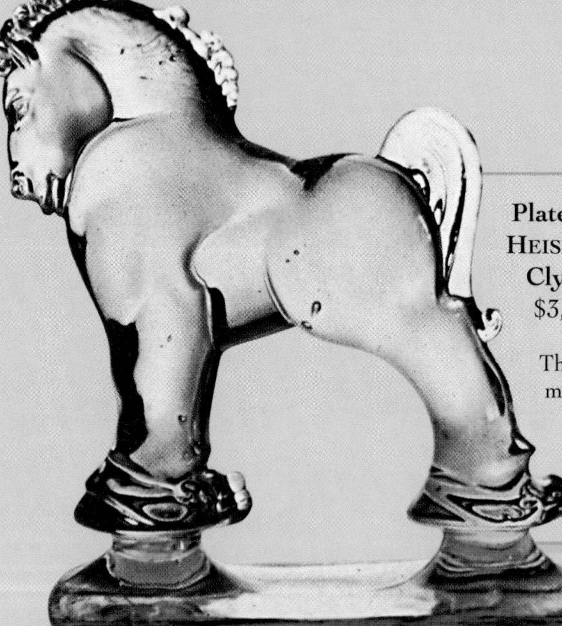

Plate 428
Heisey Glass Company
Clydesdale. Amber on bust-off, circa 1942 – 48.
$3,000.00 – 3,500.00

This amber Clydesdale is still on the bust-off as it came out of the mold. Because of its poor quality, it should have been destroyed (remelted) but obviously some worker took it home with them. This guy is a beautiful light amber and stands proudly in the Heisey Museum in Newark, Ohio. It was purchased in an auction by a Heisey study club and donated to the museum.

Plate 429
Heisey Glass Company
Clydesdale. Crystal with decorations, 7½" high, 7" long, circa 1942 – 48.
$450.00 – 475.00

This Clydesdale has been decorated by a decorating company. Gold, black, red, and white paint has been applied to various places on the animal.

See Plate 427, for details of colors and reissues of the Clydesdale.

Plate 430
Heisey Glass Company
Left: **Filly, Head Backwards.** Crystal, 8⅛" high, 5¼" long (from front to back at base), circa 1948 – 49.
$1,300.00 – 1,400.00

Other colors: none.

Reissues: Imperial Glass Company, in crystal, amber, verde green plain and satin, and black.

When marked, the mark appears on the lower abdomen. Imperial had a habit of turning the head and it does not always appear straight back on their reissues.

Right: **Filly, Head Forward.** Crystal, 8½" high, 5¼" long, circa 1948 – 49.
$1,200.00 – 1,400.00

Other colors: None

Reissues: Imperial Glass Company, in crystal, crystal satin, salmon, black, and in amber for Mirror Images. Fenton Art Glass Company in rosalene as part of the HCA Gold Series. See Plate 126.

Plate 431
Heisey Glass Company
Rearing Horse Bookend. Crystal, 7½" high, 6½" long, circa 1940s.
$2,000.00 – 2,500.00

Other colors: none.

Reissues: Imperial Glass Company in black and black satin. Dalzell-Viking in red and in lavender ice as part of the HCA Gem Series. See Plate 84B.

This animal was not marked. It is solid glass except under the rear feet and tail, which is hollow. The head is raised and looks straight ahead, this alone makes it easily identified when compared to figurines made by other companies. See Plate 417 for comparison.

Plate 432
Heisey Glass Company
Show Horse. Crystal, 7⅜" high, 7½" long (farthest point), circa 1948 – 49.
$1,250.00 – 1,450.00

Other colors: crystal frosted.

Reissues: Imperial Glass Company in crystal and amber. Dalzell-Viking in cobalt (1995) and lavender ice as part of the HCA Gem Series, see Plate 84B. Mosser Glass Company in ruby (2000).

Plate 433
Heisey Glass Company
Flying Mare. Amber, 9" high, 12" long, circa 1951 – 52.
$4,800.00 – 5,200.00

Other colors: crystal and crystal frosted.

Reissues: Imperial Glass Company in amber, crystal, amber satin, and sunshine yellow. Dalzell-Viking in lavender ice, cobalt, and dark green.

When marked, the mark appears on base, left side, under flank. It is seen more often in amber than in crystal.

Plate 434
Heisey Glass Company
Plug Horse. Crystal, 4" high, 4" long, circa 1941 – 46.
$100.00 – 125.00

Other colors: crystal frosted, amber, and cobalt.

Reissues: Imperial Glass Company in crystal, caramel slag, pink with a carnival finish, and in multiple colors for HCA souvenirs (see Plate 458). In multiple colors by Fenton and Viking as HCA souvenirs (see Plate 458).

When marked, the mark appears between the front legs. This animal is often referred to as Oscar or Sparkie.

Plate 435
Heisey Glass Company
Plug Horse. Crystal with decorations, 4" high, 4" long, circa 1941 – 46.
$90.00 – 110.00

The colorful decorations were applied by a decorating company. In most instances the decorations lower the value of the figurine as opposed to the non-decorated items.

Plate 436
Heisey Glass Company
Horse Head Bookend. Crystal and crystal frosted, 6⅞" high, 6¼" long (nose to mane), circa 1937 – 55.
Crystal, $150.00 – 175.00 each
Crystal frosted, $100.00 – 125.00 each

Other colors: amber.

Reissues: Imperial Glass Company in pink.

This figurine is very heavy and has excellent detail. It was the first of what is known as Heisey animals. When marked, the mark appears on the side of the neck, immediately above the base.

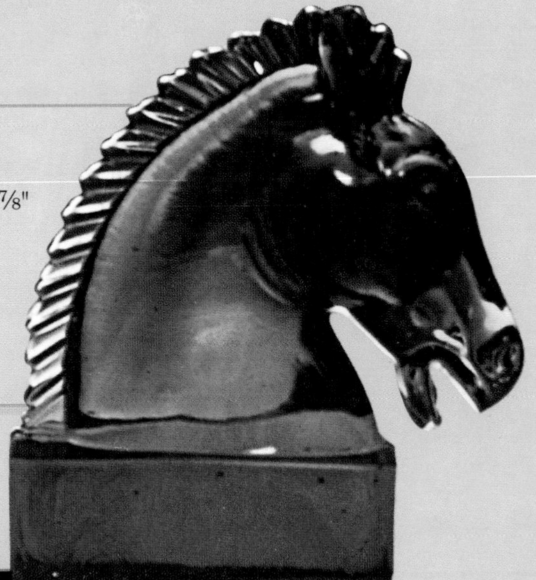

Plate 437
Heisey Glass Company
Horse Head Bookend. Amber, 6⅞" high, 6¼" long, circa 1937 – 55.
$5,000.00 to Market

This figurine is extremely rare. For other details on this figurine see Plate 436.

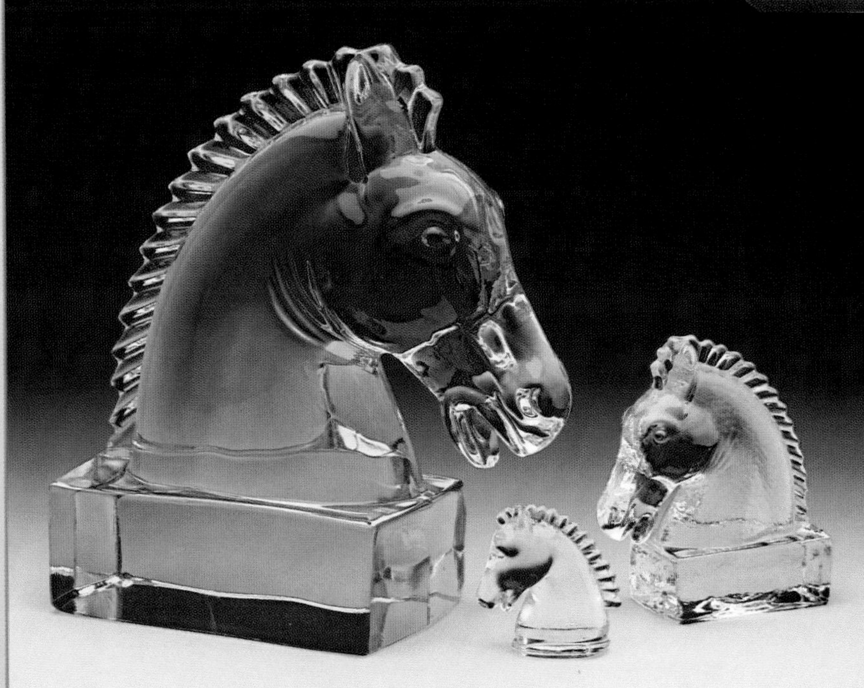

Plate 438
Heisey Glass Company
Horse Head Comparison:
Left: **Horse Head Bookend.** 6⅞" high. See Plate 436.
Center: **Horse Head Finial.** 2" high. This was used as a finial for cigarette boxes, ashtray center, etc. Came in crystal, crystal frosted, and cobalt.
Crystal, $45.00 – 65.00
Right: **Toy Horse Head Bookend.** 3½" high. This item was not made by Heisey. See Plate 465.

Plate 439
HEISEY GLASS COMPANY
Balking, Standing, and Kicking Colts.

Colt, Balking. Crystal, 3½" high, 3½" long, 1941 – 45.
$250.00 – 275.00

Other colors: amber and cobalt.

Reissues: Imperial Glass Company in crystal, caramel slag, amber, ultra blue, and horizon blue and sunshine yellow, both with satin finish. Fenton in rosalene as an add-on to the Gold Series. Viking in ruby and ruby satin. Mosser in willow blue and black for Lonaberger.

When marked, the mark appears between the legs of the left side.

Colt, Standing. Crystal, 5" high, 3" long (front of head to tip of tail), 1940 – 52.
$90.00 – 110.00

Other colors: amber and cobalt.

Reissues: Imperial Glass Company in crystal, caramel slag, black, amber, horizon blue clear/frosted, milk glass, nut brown, sunshine yellow clear/frosted, and ultra blue. Viking in ruby clear/frosted. Fenton in rosalene for HCA Gold Series. Mosser in willow blue, cobalt, and black.

Mark appears on the right side between the legs near the base.

Colt, Kicking. Crystal, 4" high, 3½" long (tip of ear to back of base), 1941 – 45.
$250.00 – 275.00

Other colors: amber and cobalt.

Reissues: Imperial Glass Company in crystal, caramel slag, amber, black, horizon blue clear/frosted, sunshine yellow clear/frosted, amber, and ultra blue. Viking in ruby clear/frosted. Fenton in rosalene as an add-on to the Gold Series. Mosser in willow blue, cobalt, and black.

Mark appears behind the legs.

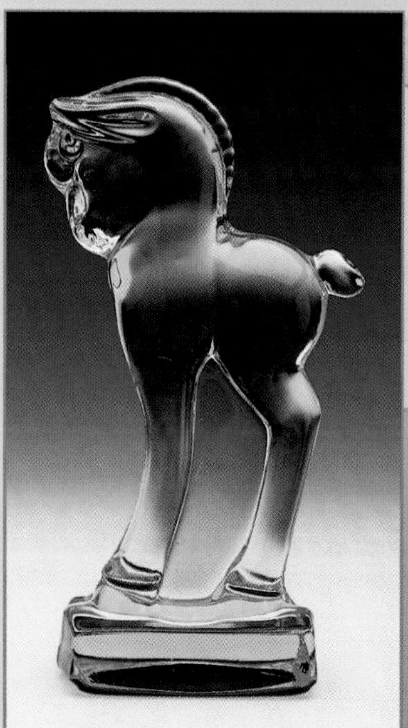

Plate 440
HEISEY GLASS COMPANY
Colt Standing. Amber, 5" high, 3" long, circa 1940 – 52.
$600.00 – 700.00

This colt is rare and expensive. It is seen more often in amber than cobalt.

Plate 441
HEISEY GLASS COMPANY
Colt Standing. Cobalt, 5" high, 3" long, circa 1940 – 52.
$1,000.00 – 1,200.00

Very rare and expensive. Seldom seen.

Plate 442
Heisey Glass Company
Horse Head Cigarette Box. Crystal, 4¼" long, 4" high, circa 1940s.
$75.00 – 85.00

Other colors: finial made in crystal frosted.

The horse head finial is mounted on the #1489 Puritan cigarette box.

Plate 443
Heisey Glass Company
Horse Head Cigarette Box. 6¼" long, 4" high, circa 1940s.
$100.00 – 125.00

Other colors: finial also made in crystal frosted and cobalt. Cobalt is very rare and very expensive.

Plate 444
Heisey Glass Company
Sitting Pony Cigarette Box. 6¼" long, 4½" high, circa 1940s.
Rarity prohibits pricing.

This item is extremely rare.

Plate 445
Unknown Manufacturer
Horse Head Bookend. Crystal, 5" high, 7" long.
Seen at $35.00 – 40.00 each

We do not advocate this horse head bookend as being Heisey. The mold for this item was found in the Imperial factory when Heisey Collectors of America purchased the Heisey molds. The mold carried the same number found in Heisey records for a horse head bookend. It has been reported that they were made also by Corning Glass in Pittsburgh. The glass is very poor quality, except for a pair once displayed in the Heisey Museum, which appeared to be much better quality than others seen. We saw one pair which had a label from Ovington's, Fifth Avenue, New York. Where was Ovington's getting them? Certainly not from Heisey based on the quality of glass as compared to other Heisey animals.

Plate 446
Left: Mosser Glass Company
Right: Heisey Glass Company
Mosser. 5½" high, stands on an oval base, open between front and hind legs and has a wavy mane (see Plate 468).
Heisey. 5" high, stands on a rectangular base, has solid glass between front and hind legs and has a cropped mane (see Plate 439).

These two figurines often confuse collectors and are sometimes mismarked by dealers even though Mosser is marked with a "M."

Plate 447
Heisey Glass Company
Horse Head Covered Candy. Crystal, 7½" diameter, circa 1940s.
$1,600.00 – 1,800.00

Other colors: none.

This item falls in the #1540 Lariat pattern. They are rare and sometimes seen with a cutting.

Plate 448
Heisey Glass Company
Horse Head Ashtray. Crystal, 4½" square, circa 1940s – 50s.
$70.00 – 80.00

Other colors: Horse Head also came in crystal frosted.

The horse head was mounted in a #1489 Puritan pattern ashtray.

Plate 449
Heisey Glass Company
Cocktail Shaker/Large Horse Head Stopper. Crystal, stopper 4½" high.
$150.00 – 175.00

The Horse Head stopper fits into a glass strainer which fits into the shaker.

Standing Pony Cocktail. Crystal, 5½" high, circa 1940s.
$500.00 – 600.00

Other colors: none.

This is a rare item.

Plate 450
Heisey Glass Company
Cocktail Shaker/Small Horse Head Stopper. Crystal, stopper 4" high.
$100.00 – 125.00

Reissues: Made in the early 1980s, *not from a Heisey mold.* The bottom is larger and does not fit the glass strainer.

Horse Head Cocktail. Crystal, 4¼" high, circa 1940s.
$350.00 – 450.00

Plate 451
DALZELL-VIKING GLASS COMPANY (altered Heisey Glass Company mold)
Double Horse Head Paperweight. Ruby, 3" high, circa 1996.
$40.00 – 50.00

Reissues: Dalzell-Viking in lavender ice, 1993, limited to 225, seconds frosted base. Also made in 1994, in green mist by Dalzell-Viking.

This mold was found when HCA purchased the Heisey molds from Imperial. It was actually #1589 Double Horse Head Ashtray (never used) and was altered to be a paperweight.

Plate 452
DALZELL-VIKING GLASS COMPANY (original Heisey Glass Company mold)
Kicking Colt. 4" high, circa 1990.
$60.00 – 65.00
Balking Colt. 3½" high, circa 1990.
$60.00 – 65.00
Standing Colt. 5" high, circa 1990.
$60.00 – 65.00

Also made in ruby satin. See Plate 439 for details and reissues of the three Colts.

Plate 453
DALZELL-VIKING GLASS COMPANY (original Heisey Glass Company mold)
Rearing Horse Bookend. Lavender ice, 7½" high, circa 1993.
$100.00 – 125.00

Made as part of the HCA Gem Series. See Plate 84B. For all details and reissues of this item see Plate 431.

Plate 454
DALZELL-VIKING GLASS COMPANY (original Heisey Glass Company mold)
Show Horse. Cobalt, 7⅜" high, circa 1995.
$175.00 – 200.00

See Plate 432 for detail of this item as well as reissues.

Plate 455
DALZELL-VIKING GLASS COMPANY (original Heisey Glass Company mold)
Flying Mare. Lavender ice, 9" high, 12" long, circa 1993.
$450.00 – 500.00

For all details on this animal, see Plate 433.

Plate 456
DALZELL-VIKING GLASS COMPANY (original Heisey Glass Company mold)
Flying Mare. Cobalt, 9" high, 12" long, circa 1990s.
$600.00 – 800.00

For all details on this animal, see Plate 433.

Plate 457
FENTON ART GLASS COMPANY (original Heisey Glass Company mold)
Filly, Head Forward. Rosalene, 8½" high, circa 1992.
$125.00 – 150.00

Made for HCA as part of the Gold Series, see Plate 126. For all details including reissues, see Plate 430.

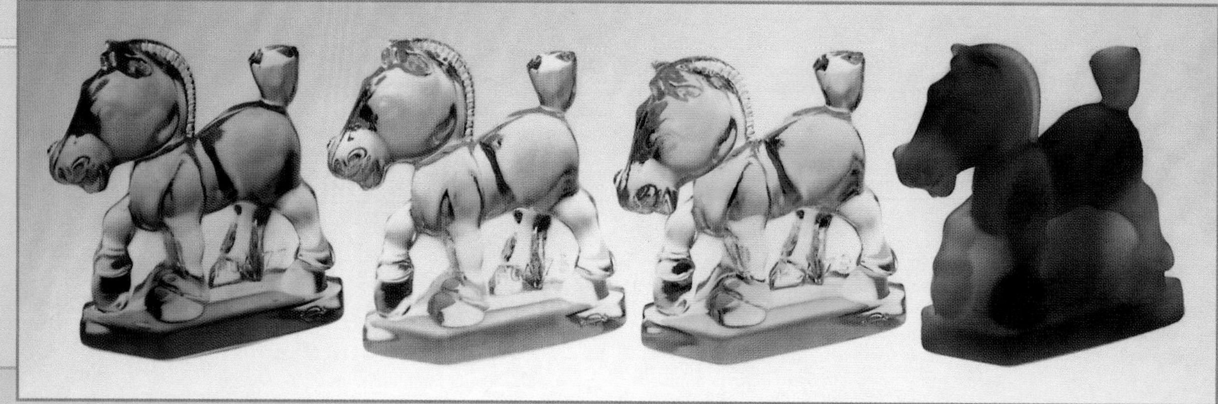

Plate 458
Imperial, Viking, and Fenton (original Heisey Glass Company mold)
Oscar Souvenirs
Left to right: fern green, Imperial, 1977; rose pink, Imperial, 1978; sunshine yellow, Imperial, 1979; heather frosted, Imperial, misdated 1979.
Except for mistakes, average price for Oscars $35.00 – 45.00 each

What is an Oscar?

An Oscar is the Heisey plug horse, Sparkie Spark Plug, or called the Pony Stallion when made by Imperial. Since the Heisey salesmen had named it "Oscar" when it was first made, and because it was listed that way in one catalog, HCA decided to call it "Oscar" when it became the Heisey Collectors of America souvenir mascot.

The figurine was very popular with HCA members, as well as collectors, and one of the biggest fundraisers. All Oscars initially sold for $25.00 at date of issue. After a number of years of Oscars, members wanted a different item and 1995 was the last year for this item. The following chart is a complete listing of the Oscars from 1977 through 1995.

Year	Color	Made By	# Made
1977	fern green	Imperial	2,115
1978	rose pink	Imperial	2,838
1979	sunshine yellow	Imperial	2,663
1979*	heather, misdated	Imperial	1,099
1980	heather	Imperial	2,930
1980	heather, frosted	Imperial	441
1981	light blue	Imperial	2,642
1982	emerald green	Imperial	2,274
1983	tangelo orange	Viking	2,262
1983***	tangelo frosted	Viking	310
1983*	ruby, misdated	Viking	251
1984	ruby	Viking	2,164
1984	ruby, frosted	Viking	208
1985**	antique blue	Imperial	446
1985	black opaque	Imperial	1,500
1986	clematis alexandrite	Viking	1,548
1987	crystal opalescent	Fenton	1,500
1988	opal white	Fenton	1,461
1989	teal blue/green	Fenton	1,200
1990	rosalene	Fenton	1,267
1990	peach	Fenton	559
1991	sapphire blue opalescent	Fenton	1,154
1991	sapphire blue opalescent frosted	Fenton	405
1992	burmese, shiny	Fenton	1,077
1992	burmese, frosted	Fenton	Unk
1993	Biscayne blue plain and frosted	Viking	Unk
1994	green mist, plain and frosted	Viking	Unk
1995	goodness gracious brown, plain and frosted	Viking	Unk

* When the company made the first turn of these, they had forgotten to change the date. Rather than let the lot be sold as factory seconds, HCA bought the Oscars and sold them by special drawing.
** Imperial was having trouble making the antique blue color. HCA took the 446 and sold them by special drawing. The regular Oscar was made in opaque black.
*** Overruns were frosted and sold by drawing.

Plate 459
IMPERIAL GLASS COMPANY (original Heisey Glass Company mold)
"3 Sons." Ultra blue, circa 1976.
Kicking. 1,500 made.
$35.00 – 50.00
Standing. 1,000 made.
$50.00 – 75.00
Balking. 1,500 made.
$35.00 – 50.00

This was a special order for Dan Fortney. Many people refer to Imperial's ultra blue as "cobalt" but there is little resemblance to Heisey's cobalt when compared. For details on the original Heisey molds for these colts, see Plate 439.

Plate 460
IMPERIAL GLASS COMPANY (original Heisey Glass Company molds)
Caramel Slag.
Left: **Kicking Colt,** 4" high.
$150.00 – 175.00
Center: **Standing Colt,** 5" high.
$45.00 – 55.00
Right: **Pony Stallion,** 4" high.
$45.00 – 55.00

The above figurines are marked "IG." For details on the Pony Stallion, see Plate 434.

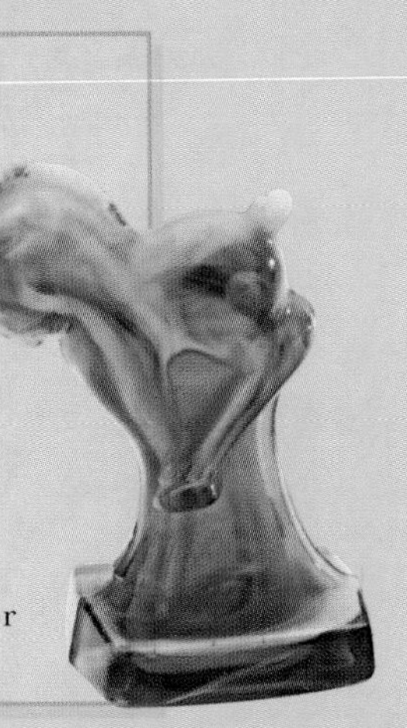

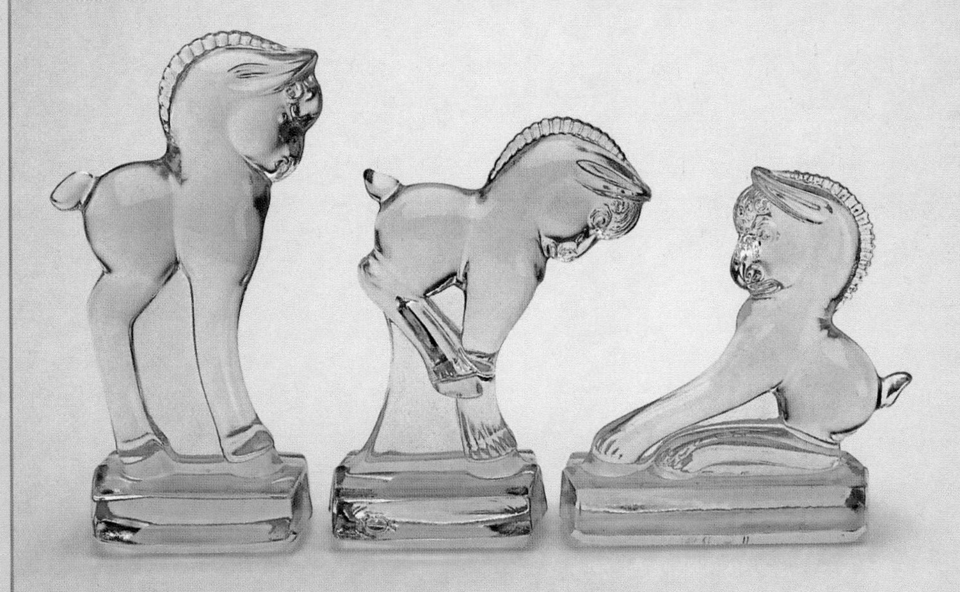

Plate 461
IMPERIAL GLASS COMPANY (original Heisey Glass Company mold)
Standing, Kicking, and Balking Colts.
Horizon blue, circa 1979.
Set of three, $90.00 – 120.00

Imperial made these colts as a special order for HCA.

For details on the original molds for these colts, see Plate 439.

Plate 462
IMPERIAL GLASS COMPANY (original Heisey Glass Company mold)
Imperial Logo. Found in cobalt and crystal.
Clydesdale. Ultra blue, 5¼" high, circa 1984, marked ALIG.
$150.00 – 200.00

Imperial made this horse for Mirror Images.

The Clydesdale made in antique blue had a blistery and bubbly effect covering the entire animal — none were sold to customers. For details on the Clydesdale original, reissues, etc., see Plate 427.

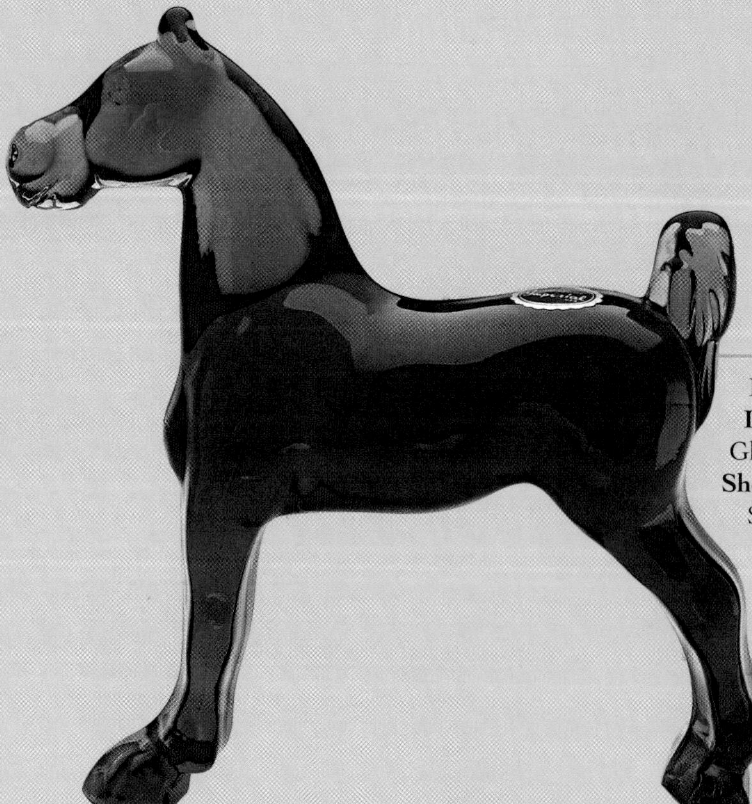

Plate 463
IMPERIAL GLASS COMPANY (original Heisey Glass Company mold)
Show Horse. Amber, 7⅜" high, 7½" long.
$400.00 – 450.00

Imperial made the Show Horse in several colors (see Plate 432) but the amber Show Horse seems to bring the highest price.

Plate 464
Imperial Glass Company
Filly, Head Forward. Crystal frosted, 8½" high, circa 1982.
$90.00 – 110.00
Filly, Head Forward. Amber, 8½" high, circa 1982.
$200.00 – 225.00

These two horses are marked ALIG.

For details on this animal including original issue, colors, and reissues, see Plate 430.

Plate 465
Viking Glass Company (Heisey Collectors of America mold)
Toy Horse Head Bookend. 3½" high, 3" long (from tip of nose to back of base).
1984 crystal plain and frosted.
1985 cobalt plain and frosted.
1986 ruby plain and frosted.
1987 light blue plain and frosted.
$20.00 – 35.00 each

This item is not from a Heisey mold. In 1984, Heisey Collectors of America, Inc., had this mold made with the intentions of selling them as a fundraiser. After the mold was made, Viking Glass Company made the horse heads. The figurine is scaled down from the Heisey Horse Head Bookend. To see a comparison of size, see Plate 438. Those produced in 1984 have a ⅞" diameter x ⅛" deep indentation on the very bottom which bears the mark "1984." Thereafter they were marked HCA and the year.

Plate 466
Indiana Glass Company
Horse Head Bookend. Crystal, 6" high, circa 1940s.
$40.00 – 50.00 pair

Other colors: milk glass.

The horse head has a hollow back.

Plate 467
Indiana Glass Company
Horse Head Bookend. Milk glass, 6" high, circa 1940s.
$65.00 – 75.00 pair

See Plate 466.

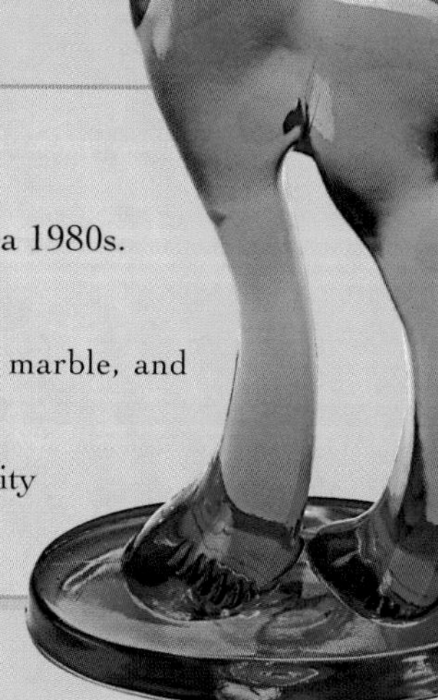

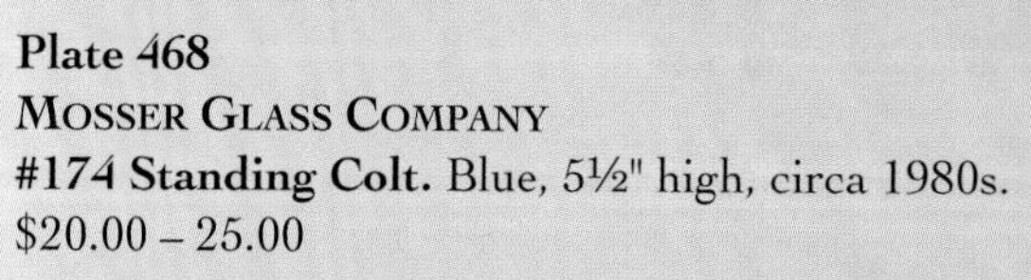

Plate 468
Mosser Glass Company
#174 Standing Colt. Blue, 5½" high, circa 1980s.
$20.00 – 25.00

Other colors: amber, custard yellow, blue marble, and vaseline.

This colt looks like a scaled down Paden City Colt. For comparison with the Heisey standing colt see Plate 446.

Plate 469
New Martinsville Glass Company
Rearing Horse Bookend. 7½" high, 5½" long.
Left: Crystal satin, circa 1940s.
$70.00 – 80.00 each
Right: Crystal decorated, circa 1940s.
$65.00 – 75.00 each

Other colors: crystal, pink, and peach satin.

The decorations on this horse were done by a decorating company. For a comparison of Rearing Horse Bookends, see Plate 417.

Plate 470
New Martinsville Glass Company
Rearing Horse Bookend. Pink, 7½" high, 5½" long, circa 1940s.
Private collection — Market

This horse is very rare in pink.

Plate 471
New Martinsville Glass Company
Horse, Head Up. Crystal, 8" high, 7" long (tail to front legs).
$100.00 – 125.00

Has a hollow base up to the horse's belly. Detail is excellent. This is a fairly scarce animal.

Plate 473
PADEN CITY GLASS COMPANY
Tall Pony. Pale blue, 12" high, circa 1940.
$200.00 – 225.00

Other colors: crystal, crystal and frosted combination, and black.

Reissues: Viking Glass Company in aqua blue and amber. Dalzell-Viking in crystal in 1990, marked Dalzell on the bottom.

Mosser Glass Company now owns the mold and has reissued in cobalt, vaseline, and jadite. Is marked with an "M" in a circle.

Originally this was a Barth Art mold.

Plate 472
PADEN CITY GLASS COMPANY
Rearing Horse. Crystal, 10" high.
$325.00 – 350.00

This is a Barth Art mold. "The Museum of Industrial Arts in Prague credits this design to Mario Petrucci, an Italian sculptor, produced by a North Bohemian glass factory in the 20s. . . " (Mary Van Pelt). However, we have only seen this horse with the Barth Art label.

Plate 475
PADEN CITY GLASS COMPANY
Left: **Tall Pony.** Crystal, 12" high, circa 1940.
$125.00 – 150.00

MOSSER GLASS COMPANY
Right: **#174 Standing Colt.** Vaseline, 5½" high, circa 1980s.
$20.00 – 25.00

This photo shows the difference between the horses without saying a word. For details on the Mosser Pony see Plate 468.

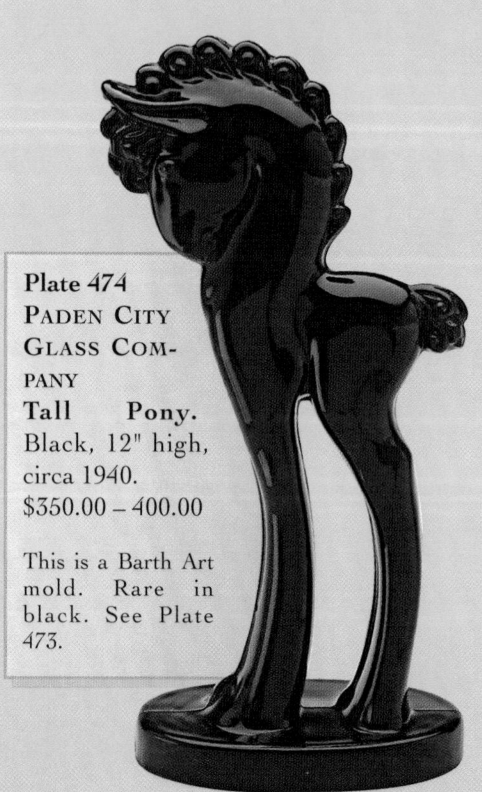

Plate 474
PADEN CITY GLASS COMPANY
Tall Pony. Black, 12" high, circa 1940.
$350.00 – 400.00

This is a Barth Art mold. Rare in black. See Plate 473.

Plate 476
L.E. Smith Glass Company
Rearing Horse Bookend. Emerald green, 8" high.
$45.00 – 50.00 each

Other colors: 1940s original issue crystal or crystal frosted. Later colors were amberina, green, blue, amber, black, almond nouveau, and probably other Smith colors.

For comparison of Rearing Horse Bookends see Plate 417.

Plate 477
L.E. Smith Glass Company
Rearing Horse Bookend. Black, 8" high.
$45.00 – 50.00 each

See Plate 476 for other colors.

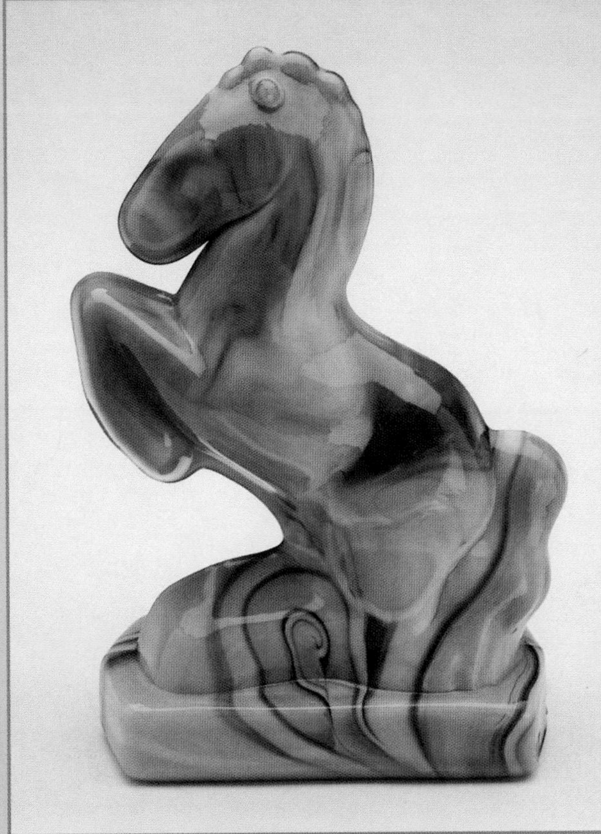

Plate 478
L.E. Smith Glass Company
Rearing Horse Bookend. Almond nouveau, 8" high.
$55.00 – 60.00 each

See Plate 476 for other colors.

Plate 479
L.E. Smith Glass Company
Horse, Lying Down. Amber, 9" long, 4¾" high, circa 1968.
$150.00 – 175.00

Other colors: blue, green, and amberina.

This horse was made for only a short period of time and is scarce.

Plate 480
L.E. Smith Glass Company
Horse, Lying Down. Amberina, 9" long, 4¾" high, circa 1968.
$225.00 – 250.00

Other colors: blue, green, and amber.

This horse was made for only a short period of time and is scarce.

Plate 481
L.E. Smith Glass Company
Horse, Lying Down. Green, 9" long, 4¾" high, circa 1968.
$150.00 – 175.00

Other colors: blue, amber, and amberina.

This horse was made for only a short period of time and is scarce.

Plate 482
L.E. Smith Glass Company
Miniature Horse. Crystal, circa 1920s.
Left: **Horse, Standing.** 2" long, 2¼" high, circa 1920s.
$10.00 – 15.00
Right: **Horse, Rearing.** 1½" long, 2⅜" high, circa 1920s.
$10.00 – 15.00

Miniatures usually marked with copyright mark and a small "S" beside it.

Plate 483
Viking Glass Company
Horse Head. Crystal satin, 5½" wide, circa 1980s.
$20.00 – 25.00

Other colors: possibly made in Viking colors.

Plate 484
Viking Glass Company (original ownership of mold unknown)
Four Horse Head Ashtray. Crystal with frosting, 7" point to point, marked Viking.
$65.00 – 75.00

Other colors: crystal and amber.

The following was related by Louise Ream. "The foreman of the etching dept. at Heisey remembered etching the ashtray. Believe G. Dalton Miller, mold maker at Heisey, created the mold. Heisey reportedly produced the ashtray one time. Lucille Kennedy, while working at Viking, reported that a man named John Gottfried brought the mold to Viking for a special order. Mr. Gottfried reportedly worked at Heisey at one time. The mold remained at Viking until they closed in 1985. Ashtrays also known to have been produced at Tiffin in crystal and amber." Imperial Glass Company never made this item.

Plate 485
Viking Glass Company (original Paden City Glass Company)
#1302 Horse. Aqua blue, 11½" high, circa 1957.
$100.00 – 125.00
#1302 Horse. Amber, 11½" high, circa 1957.
$100.00 – 125.00

Reissues: Dalzell-Viking in 1989, in crystal. Marked Dalzell on bottom.

See Plate 473 for details on the original Paden City Pony.

Plate 486
Viking Glass Company
#7275 Horse. Green, circa 1974 – 76.
$20.00 – 25.00

Other colors: blue, orange, moss green, crystal satin, and possibly other colors.

Plate 487
Cambridge Glass Company
Lion Bookend. Crystal, 6" high, 5" long, circa 1920s.
$200.00 – 225.00

Other colors: none.

Reissues: 1978 in amber as a NCC commemorative item. See Plate 488.

Plate 488
Lenox-Imperial Glass Company
Lion Bookend. Amber, 6" high, 5" long, circa 1978.
$65.00 – 75.00

This item was produced for N.C.C., and was marked N.C.C. 1978 L.I.G.

Plate 489
Fenton Art Glass Company
#5241 Lion. Red carnival, 2¾" high, 5" long.
$40.00 – 50.00

Other colors: blue royale, black, and shell pink.

Plate 490
Heisey Glass Company
Lion Covered Trinket Box. Crystal, 4½" high, 6½" long.
$500.00 – 550.00

Other colors: none.

Reissues: Reissued by Imperial Glass Company in amber.

This item is part of the #1519 Waverly pattern. This item was produced late in the life of the Heisey factory and was probably still in production at the time of closing.

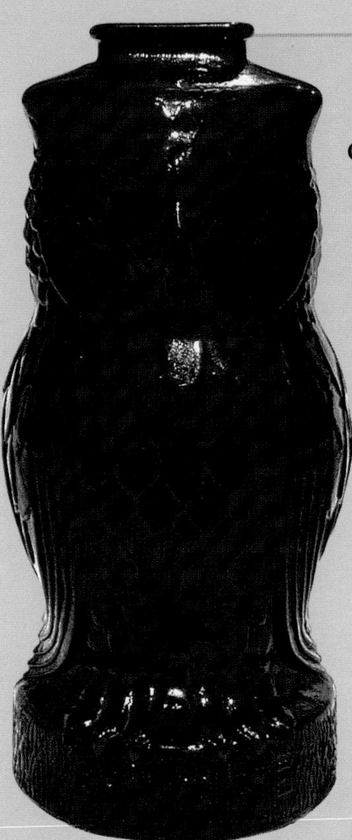

Plate 490A
ANCHOR HOCKING GLASS COMPANY
Owl Bank. Ruby, 7" high.
$250.00 – 300.00

Is marked with an anchor and "H." Also says "Royal Ruby Anchorglass." On the front at the bottom it says "Be Wise."

Plate 491
BLENKO GLASS COMPANY
#6813 Owl Bookend. Crystal, 7" high, 5½" wide, circa 1984.
$20.00 – 25.00

Other colors: amber.

Plate 492
BLENKO GLASS COMPANY
#6813 Owl Bookend. Amber, 7" high, 5½" wide, circa 1984.
$25.00 – 30.00

This bookend is very heavy and weighs nearly five pounds.

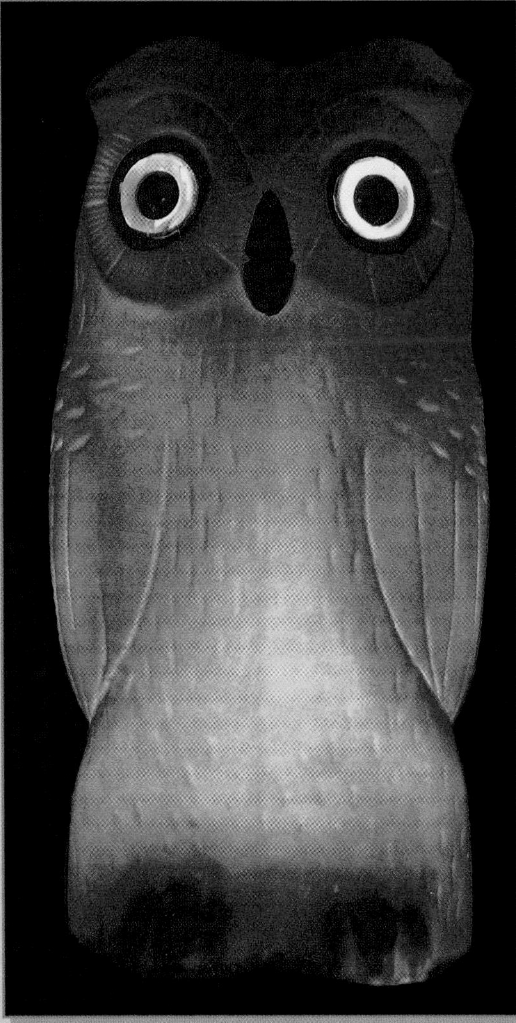

Plate 493
CAMBRIDGE GLASS COMPANY
Owl Lamp. 13½" high, ivory with brown enameling.
$1,250.00 to Market

The owl sits on an ebony base. The lamp is lighted, therefore does not appear brown. This guy is very rare.

Plate 494
Fenton Art Glass Company (original U.S. Glass Company mold)
#5178 Owl. Green iridized, 6½" high, circa 1971 – 80.
$75.00 – 85.00

Other colors: original issue, 1971, in dark amethyst carnival, in 1980 in electric blue carnival and springtime green carnival. Also made in other Fenton colors.

Plate 495
Fostoria Glass Company
#2615 Owl Bookend. Crystal, 7½" high, circa 1943.
$150.00 – 200.00 each

Other colors: A few were made in ebony in 1980 and sold through the outlet stores.

Original issue in crystal made for one year only.

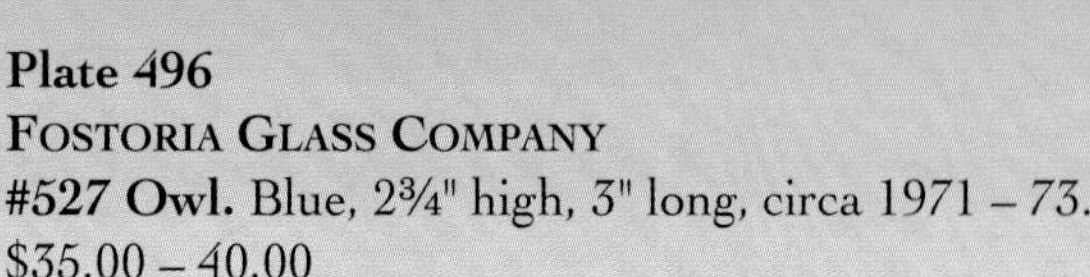

Plate 496
Fostoria Glass Company
#527 Owl. Blue, 2¾" high, 3" long, circa 1971 – 73.
$35.00 – 40.00

Other colors: crystal, silvermist, lemon, and olive green, sometimes frosted.

Plate 497
Fostoria Glass Company
Miniature Owl. Crystal, 2½" high, circa 1980s – 90s.
$10.00 – 12.00

These were sold through the outlet stores.

Plate 498
CONFUSING COLLECTIBLE
Left: **Owl.** Crystal, 3¼" high, 3" wide.
Seen at $10.00 – 15.00

This figurine has a sticker "Made in Sweden." Is sometimes confused with the Imperial owl.

IMPERIAL GLASS COMPANY
Right: **#51940S Owl.** Crystal frosted, 4" high, 3" wide, circa 1979 – 80.
$20.00 – 25.00

Other colors: crystal and crystal frosted.

Part of Little Pals animal gift ware. See Plate 498A.

Plate 498A.
Original Imperial ad for Little Pals gift ware.

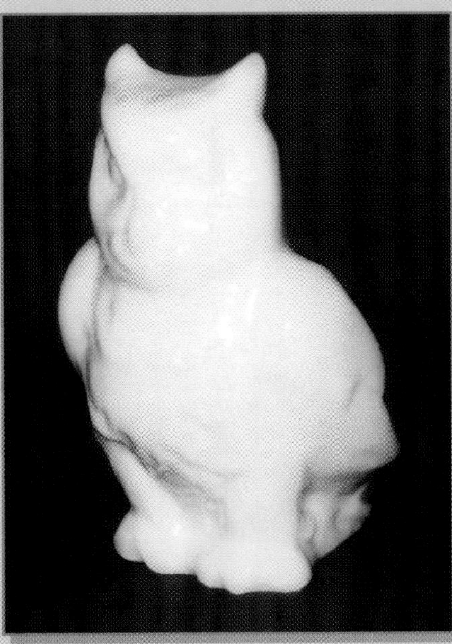

Plate 499
IMPERIAL GLASS COMPANY
#18 Hoot Less Owl. Milk glass, 4" high, circa 1950s – 60s.
$35.00 – 45.00

Other colors: initial issue in crystal, mid-60s slag colors, caramel slag, jade slag, purple slag, and ruby slag.

Plate 500
IMPERIAL GLASS COMPANY
#18 Hoot Less Owl. Caramel slag, 4" high, mid-1960s – 70s.
$50.00 – 55.00

For other colors, see Plate 499.

Plate 501
UNKNOWN MANUFACTURER
Owl Decanter. Crystal, 7½" high.
Seen at $35.00 – 45.00

The owl has good detail and the top appears to be made for a shot glass cap.

Plate 502
IMPERIAL GLASS COMPANY
Two-Piece Owl Jar. Caramel slag, 6½" high, original issue.
$85.00 – 95.00
Two-Piece Owl Jar. Horizon blue carnival, with glass eyes, 6½" high, late issue.
$55.00 – 65.00

Other colors: purple and jade slag, glossy or satin finish, mid-1970s. Milk glass and doeskin (frosted milk glass). Later colors include pink and meadow green iridized. Summit Art Glass Company now owns this mold.

Plate 503
IMPERIAL GLASS COMPANY
#335 and #336 Owl Creamer and Sugar. Caramel slag, 3½" high, circa 1970s.
$85.00 – 95.00 pair.

Other colors: 1955 – 60 milk glass, 1970s in end-of-day ruby slag, jade slag, purple slag. Came in glossy or satin finish.

These items were made as a "go with" the two-piece owl jar (Plate 502). These molds are now owned by Summit Art Glass Company.

Plate 504
LIBBEY GLASS COMPANY
Wise Old Owl Bank. Crystal, contemporary.
$10.00 – 12.00

Other colors: crystal frosted, smoke, amber, and brown.

Marked "Wise Old Owl" on the bottom.

Plate 505
MOSSER GLASS COMPANY
#124 Owl. 4½" high, circa 1980s.
$10.00 – 15.00

Other colors: amber, green, crystal, cobalt carnival, and yellow.

Plate 506
MOSSER GLASS COMPANY
#137 Owl. Green, 4" high, circa 1980s.
$10.00 – 15.00

Other colors: blue, amethyst, crystal, amber, cobalt, chocolate, and purple carnival.

Plate 507
MOSSER GLASS COMPANY
#127 Owl Fairy Lamp. Amber, 6¼" high, circa 1980s.
$45.00 – 50.00

Other colors: cobalt and possibly others.

Plate 508
NEW MARTINSVILLE GLASS COMPANY
Wise Old Owl Pitcher. 4½" high, circa 1927.
Crystal, $20.00 – 25.00
Pink, $25.00 – 30.00

Other colors: amber, blue, green, amethyst, and jade green.

Usually has "Pat. Applied For" on its base.

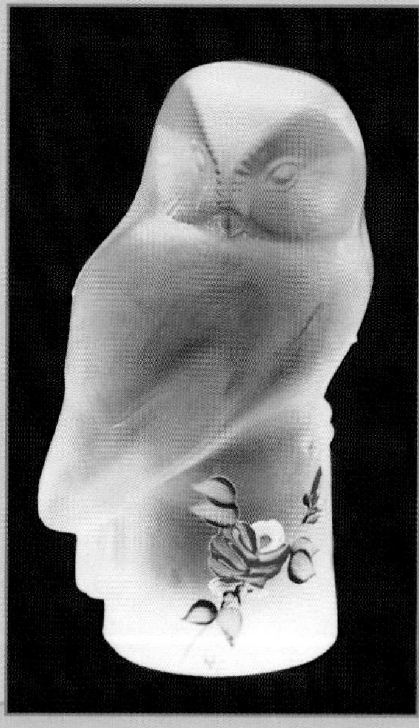

Plate 509
L.E. SMITH GLASS COMPANY
Owl on Stump, with Rose.
Crystal frosted, 3½" high.
$14.00 – 17.00

Other colors: crystal was the original issue, circa 1960s.

Plate 510
L.E. SMITH GLASS COMPANY
Owl Tumbler. Crystal, 4¾" high, circa 1985.
$10.00 – 12.00

Plate 511
SUMMIT ART GLASS COMPANY
#530 Owl. Crystal frosted, 4" high, circa 1972.
$15.00 – 20.00

Other colors: chocolate, vaseline, malachite (emerald green slag), amethyst slag, cobalt, and probably others.

Plate 512
Tiffin Glass Company
#E-1 Owl Lamp. Brown, 9" high, circa 1924 – 29. $550.00 – 650.00

Other colors: cobalt blue and one known in albino or milk glass.

This lamp has a screw-on black base.

Plate 513
Tiffin Glass Company
#E-1 Owl Lamp. Cobalt blue, 9" high, circa 1924 – 29, rare.
$1,000.00 to Market

Plate 514
Viking Glass Company
Owl Bookend. Crystal and crystal frosted, 5½" high, 4½" wide, circa 1980s.
$15.00 – 20.00 each.

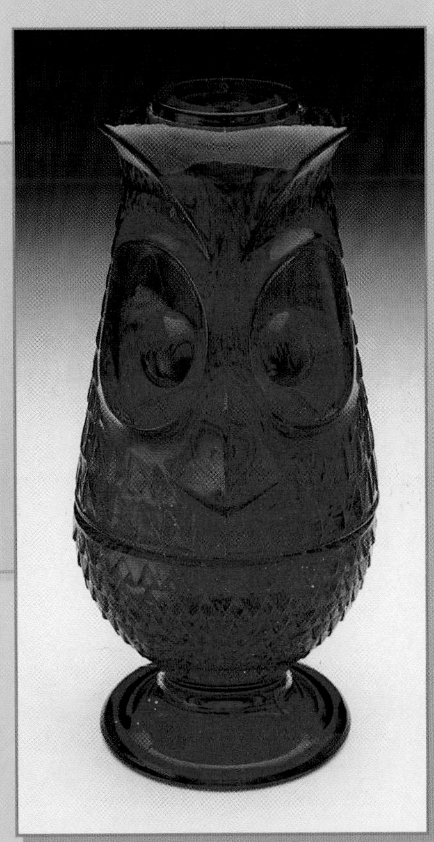

Plate 515
Viking Glass Company
#6900 Owl Glimmer Candleholder. Ruby, 7" high, circa 1980s.
$35.00 – 40.00

Other colors: blue, amber, green, orange, and perhaps other Viking colors.

This is a two-piece figurine.

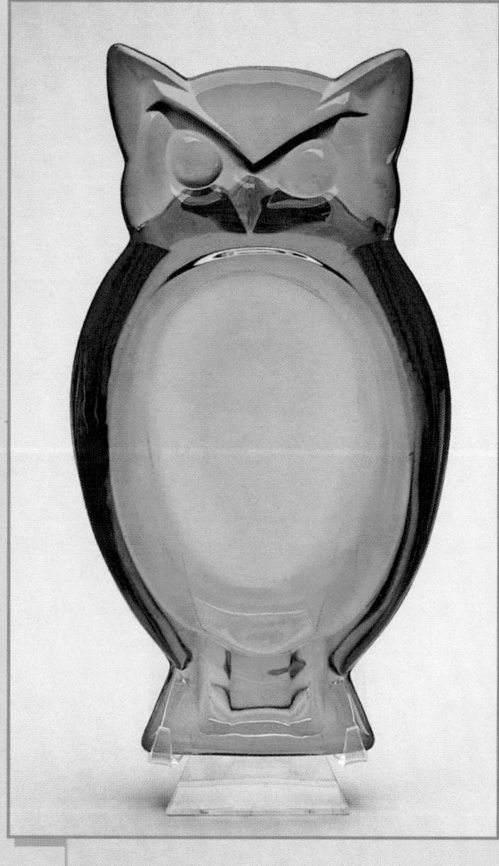

Plate 516
VIKING GLASS COMPANY
#6944 Owl Ashtray. Orange, 8" long, circa 1980s.
$10.00 – 15.00

Other colors: ruby and probably other Viking colors.

Plate 517
VIKING GLASS COMPANY
Left: **#7277 Owl.** Blue, 5" high, circa 1970s.
$15.00 – 20.00

Other colors: ruby, brown, crystal, blue, and other Viking colors.

Right: Confusing collectible. **Owl.** Crystal, 3" high.
Seen at $8.00 – 10.00

This owl has a foreign sticker. Generally seen labeled

Plate 518
VIKING GLASS COMPANY
Owl Bottle. Ruby, 7" high, circa 1960s.
$20.00 – 25.00

Other colors: amber, red, and possibly other colors.

Has a Viking label, but was probably made by subsidiary Rainbow.

Plate 519
WESTMORELAND GLASS COMPANY
#62 Owl Toothpick. Milk glass, 3" high.
$20.00 – 25.00

Other colors: dark blue mist, green slag, purple slag, crystal, moss green, pink, and others.

This mold is presently owned by Phil Rosso, Port Vue, Pennsylvania.

Plate 520
WESTMORELAND GLASS COMPANY
#10 Owl on Two Books. With rhinestone eyes, 3½" high. Left: almond. Right: ruby.
$25.00 – 35.00

Other colors: 1960s – 1970s green mist, dark blue mist, light blue mist, antique blue, mint green, pink opaque, and many other Westmoreland colors.

Reissues: has been reissued in many colors, but do not have rhinestone eyes.

Plate 521
WESTMORELAND GLASS COMPANY
Owl Bookend. Green mist, 6" high, 4" wide, circa 1926.
$125.00 – 150.00 each

Other colors: crystal and possibly other Westmoreland colors.

Very few have obviously survived over the years. They are very scarce and hard to find.

Plate 522
WESTMORELAND GLASS COMPANY
#1 Owl with Glass Eyes. Crystal mist, 5½" high, circa 1970s.
$40.00 – 45.00

Other colors: mid-1970s amber mist, dark blue, antique gold, topaz, purple marble, caramel mother of pearl, antique blue mist, yellow mist, and almond mist. 1980s crystal mother of pearl, almond mother of pearl, milk glass with gold feathers, milk glass, ruby, and ruby carnival.

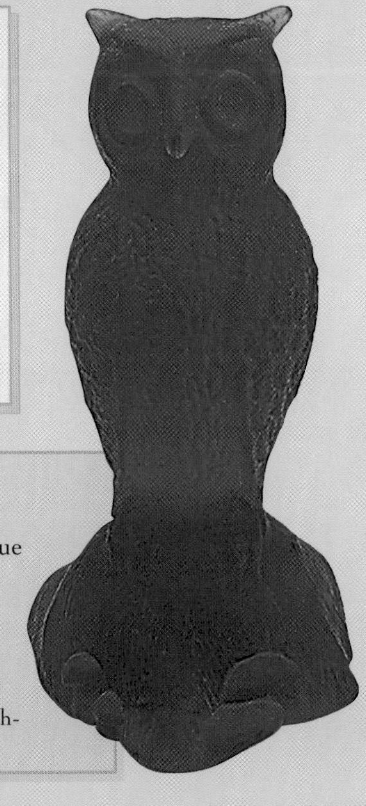

Plate 523
WESTMORELAND GLASS COMPANY
#1 Owl with Glass Eyes. Antique blue mist, 5½" high, circa mid-1970s.
$40.00 – 45.00

Other colors: See Plate 522.

Owl stands on a grassy base with mushrooms.

Panthers

Plate 524
Indiana Glass Company
Walking Panther. Blue, 3" high, 7" long, circa 1930s, very rare.
$400.00 – 450.00

Other colors: amber.

Plate 525
Indiana Glass Company
Walking Panther. Amber, 3" high, 7" long, circa 1930s, rare.
$300.00 – 350.00

Other colors: blue.

The base under the animal in this picture has been applied.

Plate 526
Duncan Glass Company
Bird of Paradise. Crystal, 8½" high, 13" long, circa 1030s.
$650.00 – 750.00

Reissues: none.

The bird of paradise is sometimes referred to as a Peacock. The figurine is solid glass and has excellent detail. It is rarely seen.

Plate 527
Fenton Art Glass Company
#711 Peacock Bookends. Crystal satin, 5¾" high.
$300.00 – 350.00 pair

Other colors: black and French opalescent. Both are extremely rare.

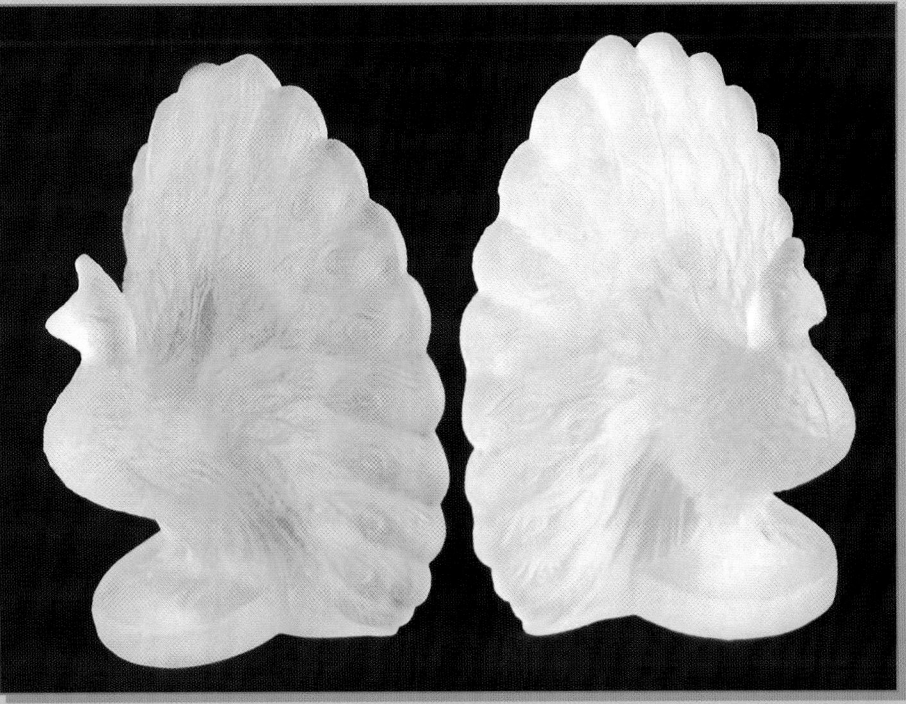

Pelicans

Plate 528
Fostoria Glass Company
#2531 Pelican. Crystal, 3⅞" high, circa 1935 – 1944.
$75.00 – 85.00.

Other colors: Topaz, 1935 – 1936; silvermist, 1936 – 1943; gold tint, 1937 – 1939. Topaz was changed to gold tint in 1937.

Plate 529
Fostoria Glass Company
Commemorative Pelican. Depression green, circa 1990.
$65.00 – 75.00

This pelican has a card around its neck stating "Tenth Anniversary 1980 – 1990 Fostoria Glass Society."

Plate 530
Fostoria Glass Company
Commemorative Pelican. Cobalt Blue, circa 1989.
$100.00 – 125.00.

The pelican was introduced at the 1987 convention by the Fostoria Glass Society of America as "Mascot." It was produced as follows: 1987, amber; 1988, opal/opal iridescent; 1989, cobalt; 1990, Depression green; 1991, pink; 1992, raspberry ice.

Plate 531
Paden City Glass Company
Pelican. Crystal, 10" high, circa early 1940s, rare.
$650.00 – 750.00

Other colors: none.

Reissues: none.

This pelican is from a Barth Art mold. Generally referred to as the "Barth Art Pelican."

Plate 532
New Martinsville Glass Company
#761 Pelican. Crystal, 8" high, early 1940s – 1945.
$100.00 – 125.00

Other colors: pink.

Reissues: 1990 in crystal by Dalzell-Viking.

Plate 533
New Martinsville Glass Company
#761 Pelican with Elongated Neck.
Pink, 11" high.
Private collection – Market

Extremely rare, probably one of a kind.

Penguins

Plate 534
Fostoria Glass Company
#2531 Penguin. Crystal, 4⅝" high, circa 1935 – 1943.
$75.00 – 85.00

Other colors: silver mist and topaz.

Plate 535
Fostoria Glass Company
#2531 Penguin. Topaz, 4⅝" high, circa 1935 – 1936.
$100.00 – 125.00

Other colors: See Plate 534.

Plate 536
Heisey Glass Company
Small Penguin Decanter. Crystal 8½" high.
$350.00 – 400.00

Also came in a larger size, #4039, quart size. The penguin head stoppers are seen more often than the complete decanter.

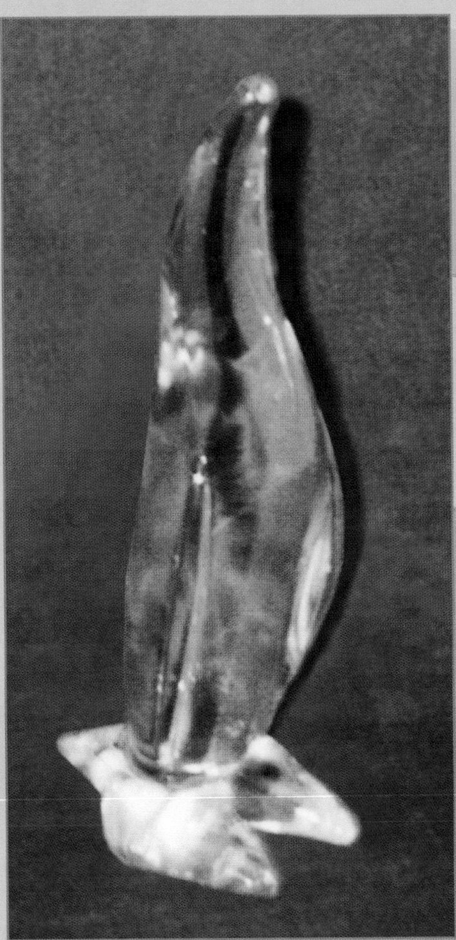

Plate 537
Viking Glass Company
#1319 Penguin. Crystal, 7" high, circa 1960s.
$25.00 – 35.00

Other colors: made in other Viking colors.

Plate 538
Westmoreland Glass Company
Penguin on Ice Floe. Brandywine blue mist, 3¾" high, circa 1970s.
$35.00 – 45.00

Other colors: crystal mist with a plain crystal ice floe.

Rumor has it that this fellow was made for a Kool cigarette advertisement.

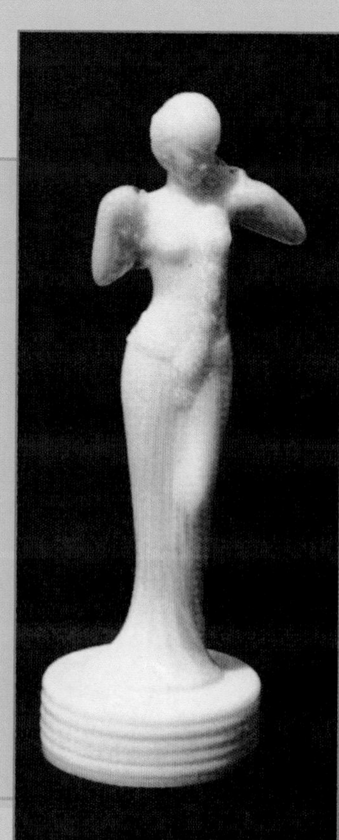

Plate 539A
MANTLE LAMP COMPANY (ALADDIN)
G-16 Figurine. Alacite, five-ring base, circa 1940.
$650.00 to Market

Other colors: opalique which is a bright clear glass, almost luminescent, finished with a smooth satin etch. Quite different from Aladdin's crystal with a satin finish, which appears almost opaque.

Plate 539
AKRO AGATE COMPANY
Colonial Lady Puff Box. 6½" high, circa 1939 – 42.
Turquoise opaque, $100.00 – 110.00
Milk, $90.00 – 100.00

Other colors, opaques: white, pink, lime green, and blue. Five different blue shades; transparent colors: crystal, amber, ice blue, and others. Pumpkin opaque is a rare color.

This item sold mainly in dime stores. Woolworths was Akro's largest customer.

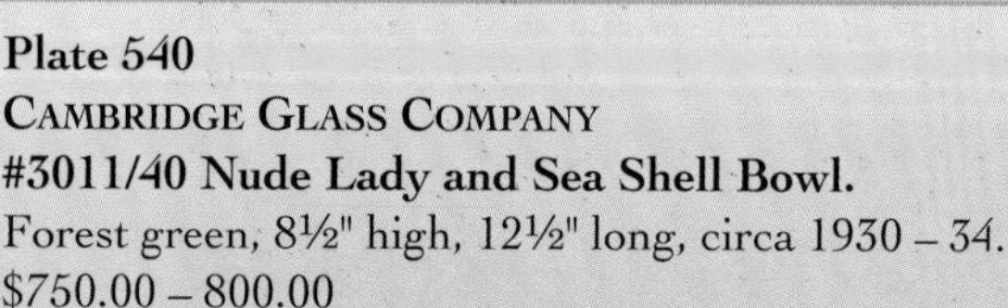

Plate 540
CAMBRIDGE GLASS COMPANY
#3011/40 Nude Lady and Sea Shell Bowl.
Forest green, 8½" high, 12½" long, circa 1930 – 34.
$750.00 – 800.00

Other colors: crown tuscan, carmen, windsor blue, amethyst, crystal, and crystal frosted.

Plate 541
CAMBRIDGE GLASS COMPANY
Dresden Lady Figurine or Lamp. Circa 1930s – 50s.
Frosted, $125.00 – 145.00
Crystal, $100.00 – 120.00

Reissues: Imperial Glass Company 1981 in dark blue, marked LIG. Made in other colors later, marked ALIG.

Summit Art Glass Company produced "Melanie," a 5¼" high copy of Dresden Lady in multiple colors.

Cambridge Glass Company made a number of figural flower holders from the mid-1920s until the factory closed in 1958. These flower holders are commonly referred to as "frogs." Many of the molds were scrapped by Cambridge as part of the war effort in the 1940s; however, some of the molds survived and went to Imperial Glass Company, where some of the frogs were reissued. Imperial changed the base and instead of being smooth they put vertical ribs on the base. After Imperial closed, the flower frog molds were sold, but the bases still had the vertical ribs. The following photos reflect the various flower holders made. Leading the parade are the Elegant Ladies that are so popular among collectors today.

Plate 542
CAMBRIDGE GLASS COMPANY
Rose Lady. 8½", low base, amber satin, sitting in a floral/candleholder centerpiece (see Rose Lady, Plate 555 for colors, sizes, and prices).

Plate 543
CAMBRIDGE GLASS COMPANY
Mandolin Lady. 9½" crystal satin, sitting in a floral/candleholder centerpiece (see Mandolin Lady, Plate 559 for colors, sizes, and prices).

The Draped Lady figural flower holder is seen more often than any of the other Cambridge figural flower holders, except for perhaps the Seagull. She came in three sizes, 8½", 12¾", and 13¼". The latter has a vertical fluted base, in other words, it is not perfectly round. The 8½" figurine was reissued by Imperial Glass Company during 1962 in crystal with a lalique finish. The Imperial reissues have vertical ribs around the base. They have also been reissued by other companies since Imperial closed, in light blue, cobalt, and ruby. They also have vertical ribs around the base.

Plate 544
CAMBRIDGE GLASS COMPANY
Draped Lady. 8½" high, dianthus (peach blo).
$150.00 – 175.00

Plate 545
CAMBRIDGE GLASS COMPANY
Draped Lady. 8½" high, satin finish.
Left to right: light emerald, $150.00 – 175.00; amber, $200.00 – 225.00; dianthus (peach blo), $125.00 – 150.00; gold krystol, $200.00 – 250.00

Plate 546
Cambridge Glass Company
Draped Lady. 8½" high.
Left to right: crystal, $50.00 – 75.00; amber, $175.00 – 200.00; ivory, $1,000.00 to Market; light emerald, $85.00 – 125.00; and crystal, $50.00 – 75.00

Plate 547
Cambridge Glass Company
Draped Lady. 8½" high.
Left to right: gold krystol, $200.00 – 250.00; dianthus (peach blo), $125.00 – 150.00; crown tuscan, rarity prohibits pricing; moonlight blue, $325.00 – 375.00; amber, $175.00 – 200.00

Plate 548
Cambridge Glass Company
Draped Lady. 12¾", satin.
Left to right: light emerald, $225.00 – 250.00; crystal, $175.00 – 200.00; and amber, $275.00 – 325.00

Plate 549
Cambridge Glass Company
Draped Lady. 13¼" high base (fluted).
Left to right: amber, $350.00 – 400.00; bluebell, $1,500.00 to Market; ivory, $1,300.00 to Market; light emerald, $225.00 – 250.00; and crystal, $175.00 – 200.00

Bashful Charlotte was produced by Cambridge in two sizes, 6½" and 11½". This elegant flower holder is a lady who is partially covered with a towel or cloth and appears to be struggling to cover herself. She is bent forward with her right hand holding the cloth over her breast and her left arm and hand extended downward towards her right knee. Both sizes have been reissued. Imperial Glass Company has been given credit for altering the mold and adding vertical ribs to the bases, hollowing out the bases, and removing the holes in the 6½" figurine. Imperial referred to this figurine as "Venus Rising" when producing for Mirror Images. The 6½" Bashful Charlotte has been reissued in multiple colors and the 11½" in cobalt and possibly vaseline. Imperial reissued the 6½" in seven different colors, ruby sunset, caramel slag, midnight magic, pink pixie, green goddess, forever amber, and bluebell (plain, frosted, or carnival in all colors). These have IG-181 in the base.

Plate 550
Cambridge Glass Company
Bashful Charlotte. Moonlight blue, 11½" high.
$950.00 to Market

Plate 551
Cambridge Glass Company
Bashful Charlotte. 6½" high.
Left to right: moonlight blue, $500.00 – 600.00; amber, $400.00 – 500.00; crystal (side view), $75.00 – 100.00; light emerald, $250.00 – 300.00; crystal (front view), $75.00 – 100.00; and dianthus (peach blo), $250.00 – 300.00

Plate 552
Cambridge Glass Company
Bashful Charlotte. 11½".
Left to right: moonlight blue, $950.00 to Market; dianthus (peach blo), $400.00 – 500.00; crystal, $150.00 – 175.00; and moonlight blue satin, $950.00 to Market

Plate 553
Cambridge Glass Company
Bashful Charlotte. 11½".
Left to right: amber satin, $500.00 – 550.00; light emerald, $350.00 – 375.00; amber (light), $500.00 – 550.00

Cambridge produced the Rose Lady in two sizes, the low base being 8½" high and the high base 9¾" high. Both sizes were produced in multiple colors. The figurine is a lady holding a bouquet of flowers, presumably roses. Her right hand is chest high above the flowers and her left arm and hand are waist high cradling the flowers. Her head is down as if she is admiring her flowers. The Rose Lady has not been reissued.

Plate 554
CAMBRIDGE GLASS COMPANY
Rose Lady. 8½" high, light emerald.
$225.00 – 250.00

Plate 555
CAMBRIDGE GLASS COMPANY
Rose Lady. 8½" high.
Left to right: amber, $225.00 – 250.00; light emerald satin, $250.00 – 275.00; dianthus (peach blo), $225.00 – 250.00; light emerald, $225.00 – 250.00; dianthus (peach blo) satin, $250.00 – 275.00; and crystal satin, $200.00 – 225.00

Plate 556
Cambridge Glass Company
Rose Lady. 9¾" high, high base.
Left to right: amber satin, $325.00 – 350.00; dianthus (peach blo), $250.00 – 275.00; ivory, $1,150.00 to Market; amber, $275.00 – 300.00; crystal, $175.00 – 200.00; light emerald, $250.00 – 275.00

Plate 557
Cambridge Glass Company
Draped Lady and Rose Lady. Very scarce and rare opaques.
Left to right: Draped Lady, 8½", ivory, $1,000.00 to Market; Draped Lady, crown tuscan, rarity prohibits pricing; Draped Lady, 13¼", ivory, $1,300.00 to Market; Rose Lady, 9¾", ivory, $1,150.00 to Market

Cambridge produced the Mandolin Lady in one size only, 9½" high. This figurine was produced in crystal, light emerald, and dianthus (peach blo). Each was also available in satin. This flower holder is a lady playing a mandolin. Her right hand is holding the neck of the instrument while she is playing it with her left hand. The Mandolin Lady has not been reissued.

Plate 558
CAMBRIDGE GLASS COMPANY
Mandolin Lady. 9½" high,
dianthus (peach blo)
$375.00 – 425.00

Plate 559
CAMBRIDGE GLASS COMPANY
Mandolin Lady. 9½" high.
Left to right: crystal (side view bent), $200.00 – 250.00; dianthus (peach blo) satin, $375.00 – 425.00; crystal (head forward), $200.00 – 250.00; dianthus (peach blo), $375.00 – 425.00; crystal (head turned), $200.00 – 250.00; light emerald, $350.00 – 400.00

People

Cambridge produced the Two-Kid flower holder in only one size, 9¼" high. Some were produced with an oval base but they were the same height. This figurine was produced in multiple colors. The Two-Kid flower holder is a youngster cradling a small animal (presumably a baby goat based on terminology) in its arms. The Two-Kid was not reissued.

Plate 560
CAMBRIDGE GLASS COMPANY
Two-Kid. 9¼" high, light emerald satin.
$325.00 – 350.00

Plate 561
CAMBRIDGE GLASS COMPANY
Two-Kid. 9¼" high.
Left to right: amber satin, $350.00 – 400.00; dianthus (peach blo), $250.00 – 275.00; crystal, $175.00 – 200.00; amber, $300.00 – 325.00; light emerald, $325.00 – 350.00; dianthus (peach blo), $250.00 – 275.00

Plate 562
Cambridge Glass Company
Two-Kid. 9¼" high, moonlight blue.
$1,800.00 to Market

This figurine is very rare.

Plate 563
Cambridge Glass Company
Two-Kid. 9¼" high, ivory.
$2,000.00 to Market

This figurine is very rare.

Plate 564
Cambridge Glass Company
Two-Kid. Cut off, light emerald.
$250.00 – 275.00

This two-kid was cut off to be mounted on a lamp, but for some reason didn't make it.

Cambridge made some of the flower frogs with oval bases. Most commonly seen is the Draped Lady.

Plate 565
CAMBRIDGE GLASS COMPANY
Flower Frogs with Oval Bases.
Draped Lady, left to right: dianthus (peach blo), 8½", $275.00 – 300.00; light emerald, 8½", $275.00 – 300.00; crystal, 8½", $175.00 – 200.00; crystal satin, 8½", $200.00 – 225.00
Two-Kid: dianthus (peach blo), 9", $350.00 – 375.00; light emerald, 9", $300.00 – 325.00
Draped Lady, dianthus (peach blo), 8½", $275.00 – 300.00

Cambridge produced two types of Geisha flower holders, one-bun 12" high and two-bun 11¾" high. They were produced in multiple colors, including opaques of jade, ivory, and perhaps others. All one has to do is look at their hair style to determine if they are a one-bun or a two-bun. The bottom of the figurine is threaded and screws into the base. This figurine was not reissued.

Plate 566
CAMBRIDGE GLASS COMPANY
Geishas: One-bun, 12" high, amber, $750.00 – 850.00
Two-bun, 11¾" high, crystal, $450.00 – 550.00
One-bun, 12" high, crystal, $450.00 – 550.00

Cambridge made several of the figural flower frogs into figurines and figurals for lamps. The Geishas and Buddhas had screw bottoms which screwed into a base. The Two-Kid and Bashful Charlotte were smooth on the bottom and have been seen affixed to night light lamps. One would assume that the figurine was glued to the base. The Draped Lady lamp was a molded one-piece figurine and base. The base is hollow and has a hole in it for the cord. A brass tube was attached to the base behind the figurine and extended upwards and held the light socket and shade. Cambridge made these in crystal only. They have been reissued in green.

Plate 567
Cambridge Glass Company
Draped Lady Lamp. Crystal.
$150.00 – 175.00

Plate 568
Cambridge Glass Company
Figurines or Figurals for Lamps.
Bashful Charlotte, crystal satin.
$150.00 – 200.00
Draped Lady, light emerald satin.
$200.00 – 250.00
Draped Lady, crystal satin.
$150.00 – 200.00

Plate 569
CAMBRIDGE GLASS COMPANY
Rose Lady Flower Frog/Bowl. Ivory, circa 1930s.
Rarity prohibits pricing

The Rose Lady Flower Frog base has been factory altered to fit the center of the bowl she sits in. Very rare. Perhaps one of a kind.

Plate 570
CAMBRIDGE GLASS COMPANY
#1191 Cherub Candlestick. Crystal, 6" high, circa 1930 – 34.
$150.00 – 175.00

Other colors: crystal frosted, light emerald, and probably other colors.

Also came with a 12" vase insert.

Plate 571
CAMBRIDGE GLASS COMPANY
#29 Shell Mint. Amber, 4" high, circa 1930s.
$350.00 – 400.00

The shell is mounted on a #3011 Statuesque stem.

Plate 572
CAMBRIDGE GLASS COMPANY
#3011 Statuesque Goblet. Topaz, crackle glass table goblet, circa 1950s.
$450.00 – 550.00

Cambridge Collectors of America owns the molds for the #3011 Statuesque 7" comport, cocktail, table goblet, 4" mint and paste molds ¾ blown tops.

Plate 573
Cambridge Glass Company
#3011/25 Ivy Ball. Crown Tuscan, 9½" high, circa 1930s.
$150.00 – 200.00

Other colors: crystal, carmen, smoke, royal blue, and amethyst, all with crystal stems. Probably made in other colors.

Ivy bowl is mounted on a statuesque line stem, commonly known as "Nude Stem."

Plate 574
Cambridge Glass Company
#3011 Candlestick. Crown tuscan with decorations, circa 1930s.
$275.00 – 300.00 each

Other colors: made in other Cambridge colors.

Candlestick is part of the #3011 Statuesque line and is 8½" high.

Plate 576
Mosser Glass Company (original Cambridge Glass Company mold)
Ladyleg Bookend. Custard, 8" high, circa late 1970s.
$75.00 – 95.00 pair

See Plate 575 for reissues and details on original issue.

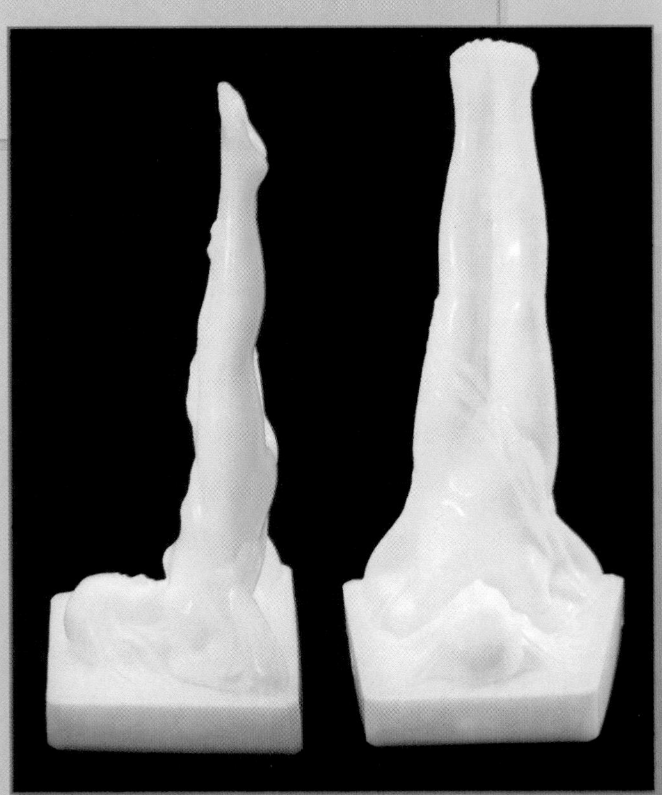

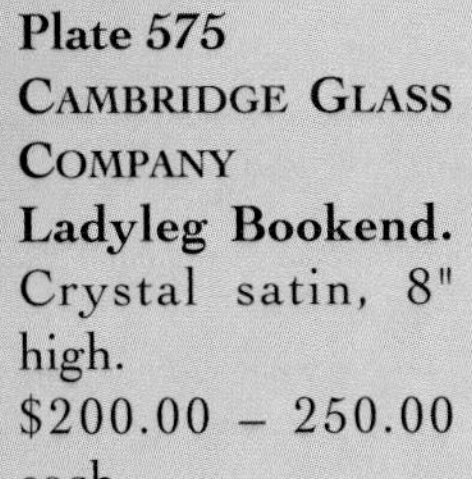

Plate 575
Cambridge Glass Company
Ladyleg Bookend. Crystal satin, 8" high.
$200.00 – 250.00 each

Other colors: crystal.

Reissues: Mosser Glass Company in 1977, in medium blue for National Cambridge Collectors, as a commemorative item. Also reissued in green carnival and custard.

Plate 577
Fenton Art Glass Company
#1645 September Morn Nymphs. 6¼" high, with flower frog base, circa 1928. Left to right: ruby, $200.00 – 250.00; moonstone, $200.00 – 225.00; jade, $200.00 – 225.00; pink, $100.00 – 125.00; milk glass, $175.00 – 200.00

Other colors: Chinese yellow, Pekin blue, aquamarine, black, amberina, crystal, dark green, light green, lilac, Mandarin red, rose, royal blue, and a custard color.

Plate 578
Fenton Art Glass Company
#1645 September Morn Nymph. Pekin blue, 6¼" high, circa 1928. $1,500.00 to Market

The figurine is sitting in a #9193 mini arranger base (flower/candle). This September Morn in Pekin blue is very rare.

Plate 579
Fenton Art Glass Company
September Morn Souvenir Items.
Left: Peachaline with black arranger, circa 1990 – 91, $75.00 – 100.00
Right: Roseline with opal arranger, circa 1990 – 91, $75.00 – 100.00

The bases are #9193 mini arranger bases for flowers/candles.

Plate 580
Fostoria Glass Company
#2634 Mermaid. Crystal, 10⅛" high, circa 1950 – 58. $140.00 – 160.00

This figurine was used in #2634 13" floating garden bowl.

Plate 581
Fostoria Glass Company
Chinese Lotus, Chinese Buddha, and Chinese Lute.
Left: #2626 Chinese Lotus Figurine, ebony with gold, 12¼" high, circa 1953 – 57, $300.00 – 350.00
Center: #2298 Chinese "Buddha" Bookend, ebony with gold, 7½" high, circa 1953 – 57, $500.00 – 600.00 pair
Right: Chinese Lute Figurine, ebony with gold, 12½" high, circa 1953 – 57, $300.00 – 350.00

Other colors: lute and lotus came in crystal and silver mist.

Plate 582
American Glass Company
(K.R. Haley mold)
#8 Colonial Lady with Bonnet. Crystal, 5" high, circa 1948.
$15.00 – 25.00

Other colors: milk glass decorated.

This came as a set of three "belles." The other two were Victorian lady and the Southern Belle.

Plate 583
Heisey Glass Company
Doulton Girl. Crystal, 4½" high, circa 1940s.
$800.00 – 900.00

Reissues: Imperial Glass Company in crystal and colors. Mosser Glass Company for HCA as convention souvenirs, 1998 vaseline and 1999 teal green.

Generally referred to as "Dinky Do."

Plate 584
Heisey Glass Company
Victorian Bell. Crystal, 4¼" high, 2¾" diameter (bottom), circa 1944 – 48.
$100.00 – 125.00

Other colors: crystal frosted.

Reissues: Imperial in multiple colors. Dalzell-Viking in clematis/purple, clear and frosted, and perhaps other colors.

Plate 586
Heisey Glass Company
#111 Cherub Candleholder. Flamingo, 11½" high, circa 1926 – 29.
$450.00 – 550.00 each.

Other colors: crystal and moongleam. All came clear or frosted. Not marked.

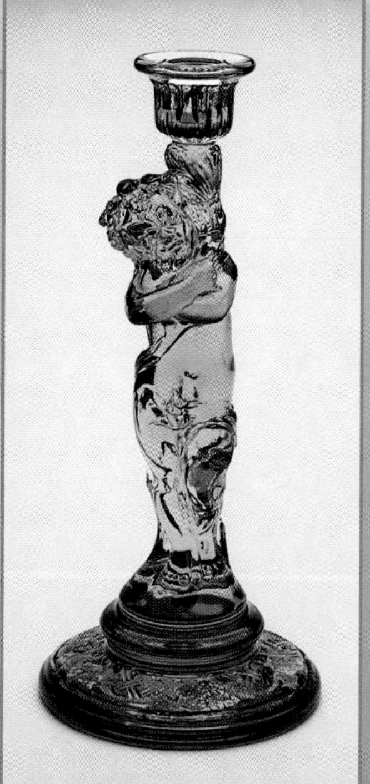

Plate 585
Heisey Glass Company
Cherub Lamp. Moongleam, circa 1926 – 29.
$550.00 – 600.00

This lamp was factory made by clipping the candle socket from the #111 cherub candleholder. See Plate 586 for other colors.

Plate 587
Heisey Glass Company
Girl Head Stopper and Dancer's Leg Stem.
Left: Cocktail Shaker with Girl Head Stopper. Crystal, stopper is 4¾" high, circa 1940s.
$400.00 – 425.00

Very scarce as was made for only a short period of time. Supposedly Clarence Heisey disapproved of them so they were not put into production.

Right: Dancer's Leg Goblet. Crystal, 7¼" high, very rare.
$1,500.00 to Market

Plate 588
Imperial Glass Company
#80 Vinelf Candleholder. Forget-me-not blue, 7½" high, circa 1955 – 58.
$45.00 – 55.00 each

Also came in milk glass. Was made to go with the Vinelf comport. This comport was inspired by the 1880s Atterbury glass comport.

Plate 589
Imperial Glass Company (altered Cambridge Glass Company mold)
"Venus Rising"
6½" high, circa 1981 – 82.
Left to right: Midnight Magic, $45.00 – 55.00
Green Goddess, $35.00 – 45.00
Sunmaid, $35.00 – 45.00
Carmelita, $65.00 – 75.00

Other colors: circa 1981 – 82 colors, glossy and satin. Ruby Sunset, Pink Pixie, Forever Amber, Blue Belle, Irish Lass, Azure Princess, Empress Jade, and Crystal Gal.

These were made by Imperial for Mirror Images and are marked IG-81.

Plate 590
Imperial Glass Company (altered Cambridge Glass Company mold)
Draped Lady. Ruby sunset, 8½" high, circa 1985, marked IG.
$85.00 – 90.00

Other colors: Made for Mirror Images by Imperial with ribbed base and holes, in cobalt, vaseline (plain, frosted, or iridized), by Viking, in mid-1980s in alexandrite and ruby glossy. By Viking in 1992 – 93, in vaseline and cobalt. By Mosser in 1996, in caprice blue.

Plate 591
Imperial Glass Company
#5029 Empress Book-Stops. Jade green, 7" high.
$175.00 – 200.00 pair

Other colors: Original issue in crystal frosted and signed "Virginia B. Evans." The jade bookstops were a later issue.

These are part of the Cathay line. See Plate 224 for more information on Cathay.

Plate 592
Imperial Glass Company
Salt/Pepper Shaker, Cathay Line. Crystal, 3¼" high.
$400.00 – 450.00 each

Made as feasibility only and never placed in full production. Rumor has it that they applied frosted highlights to some.

Plate 594
Kanawha Glass Company (original U.S. Glass Company mold)
#933 Lady with Dog Figurine. Blue slag, 8½" high, circa 1980 – 81.
$75.00 – 100.00

Other colors: green slag, red slag, transparent amber, transparent blue, and probably others.

This mold was purchased by Kanawha from U.S. Glass Co., Glassport, PA.

Plate 593
Imperial Glass Company
#809 Colonial Belle. White carnival (bell), 7½" high, circa 1974 – 75.
$45.00 – 55.00

Other colors: original issue 1950s in milk glass. Also made in frosted colors, pink, blue, ivory, and crystal. Carnival pink, horizon blue, and white. Transparent colors, ultra blue, verde green, and nut brown. Possibly other colors.

Also seen with a base and is referred to as "Colonial Belle Box."

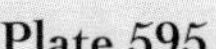

Plate 595
Kanawha Glass Company (original U.S. Glass Company mold)
#933 Lady with Dog Figurine. 8½" high.
Left to right: green slag, $75.00 – 100.00; red slag, $100.00 – 125.00; amber, $50.00 – 75.00

See Plate 594 for all details on this figurine.

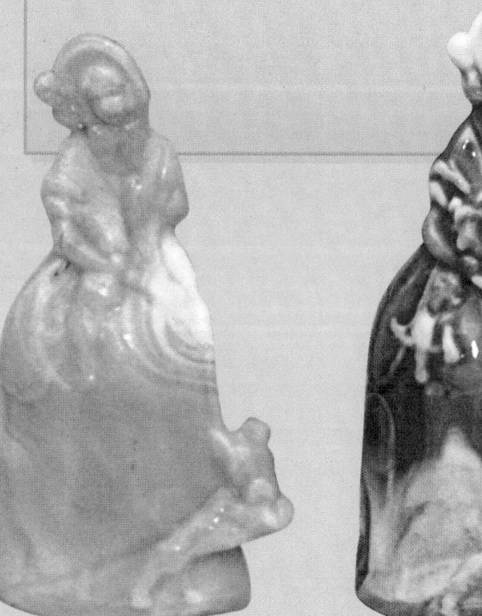

Plate 596
New Martinsville Glass Company
Dancing Lady Flower Frog. Pink satin, 6¼" high, circa 1940s.
$750.00 to Market

Other colors: crystal satin.

This figurine is very rare. Rumor has it that Isadora Duncan served as a model for this figurine.

Plate 597
New Martinsville Glass Company
Lady Face Bookend. Crystal, 5¼" high (rare).
$250.00 – 300.00 pair

These have also been seen marked "Czechoslovakia" on back of base at bottom; however, the base is slightly different on these. See Plate 598 for the base difference. The base on the back is shaved off at about a 45 degree angle.

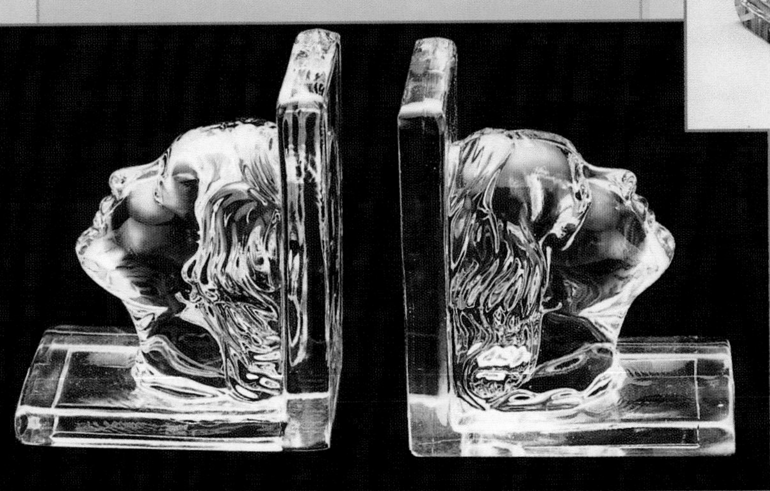

Plate 598
Foreign Manufacturer
Little Old Lady Bookends. Crystal, 5½" high, and 4½" wide.
Seen at $300.00 – 350.00 pair

These are marked "Czechoslovakia" on the bottom at the back. These are excellent glass and are of the New Martinsville style and are generally labeled "New Martinsville" when offered for sale. We could find nothing to attribute them to New Martinsville.

Plate 599
L.E. Smith Glass Company
Goose Girl: original issue.
Left to right: Crystal, 6" high, circa 1950s, $25.00 – 30.00
Crystal, 8" high, circa 1950s, $25.00 – 30.00
Crystal satin, 6" high, circa 1950s, $25.00 – 30.00

Other colors: later colors, 1970s, both sizes, in amber, green, blue, and flame.

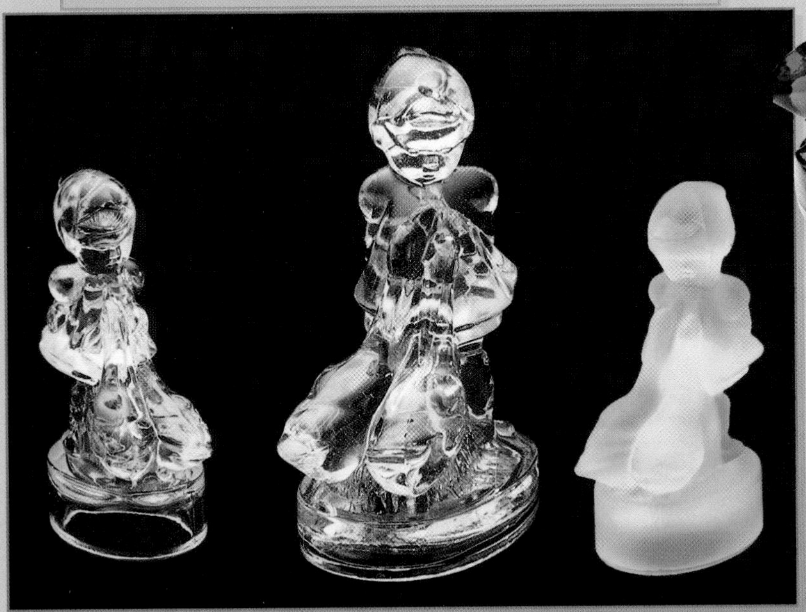

Plate 600
L.E. Smith Glass Company
Goose Girl. Circa 1970s.
Blue, 8" high, $45.00 – 65.00
Amber, 8" high, $45.00 – 65.00

See Plate 599 for all colors.

Plate 601
Steuben Glass Works
#6495 Kneeling Girl Flower Block. All crystal, 8" high, circa 1932.
Private collection — Market

Other colors: crystal base with frosted figurine.

Plate 602
Steuben Glass Works
#6483 Diving Lady. Satin finish, 13½" high, circa 1930s.
Private collection — Market

Other colors: blue satin with crystal flower block.

Figurine is on a peg which fits into the hand-blown crystal base.

Plate 603
Steuben Glass Works
#6495 Kneeling Girl Flower Block. Satin figurine with crystal base, 7½" high, circa 1932.
Private collection — Market

For other colors see Plate 601.

Plate 604
STEUBEN GLASS WORKS
#7039 Lady in Circle. Satin figurine, in a crystal base, 9½" high, circa 1930s, rare.
Private collection — Market

Plate 605
TIFFIN GLASS COMPANY
#E-3 Girl Lamp. Decorated pink, 10½" high, circa 1923.
$450.00 – 500.00

Other colors: hand-decorated pink, green, and yellow.

Known as "The Colonial Dame," sits on a black glass base.

Plate 606
TIFFIN GLASS COMPANY
#9313 Dancing Girl Puff Box. Pink satin, 6" high, circa 1924.
$150.00 – 175.00

Other colors: possibly came in other satin colors.

Plate 607
Cambridge Glass Company
Melon Boy. 9¾" high.
Center: light emerald satin, $850.00 to Market
Left and right: dianthus (peach blo), $850.00 to Market

Other colors: plain and satin.

There was a variance in the dianthus, a range from light to dark, even though the figurine on the right appears to be amber, it is dianthus (peach blo). Sometimes referred to as "Boy Child." The figurine is that of a young boy holding what appears to be half of a melon. It was not reissued.

Plate 608
Duncan Glass Company
Peon. Crystal, 5½" high, circa 1940.
$200.00 – 225.00

Other colors: crystal frosted.

Reissues: none.

This is part of the three-piece peon, donkey, and cart set. See Plate 215.

Plate 609
Duncan Glass Company
Toby Glass and Pitcher.
Glass: Crystal, $25.00 – 35.00. The glass was also produced in pink opalescent and cobalt.
Pitcher: Crystal, 7½" high, $175.00 – 225.00. Was also produced in pink opalescent and cobalt.

This is known as "Old Charlie," and was a copy of an English Toby. Duncan only made one turn of the pitchers, less than 200. Some of the pitchers were decorated by a decorating company and are now considered rare.

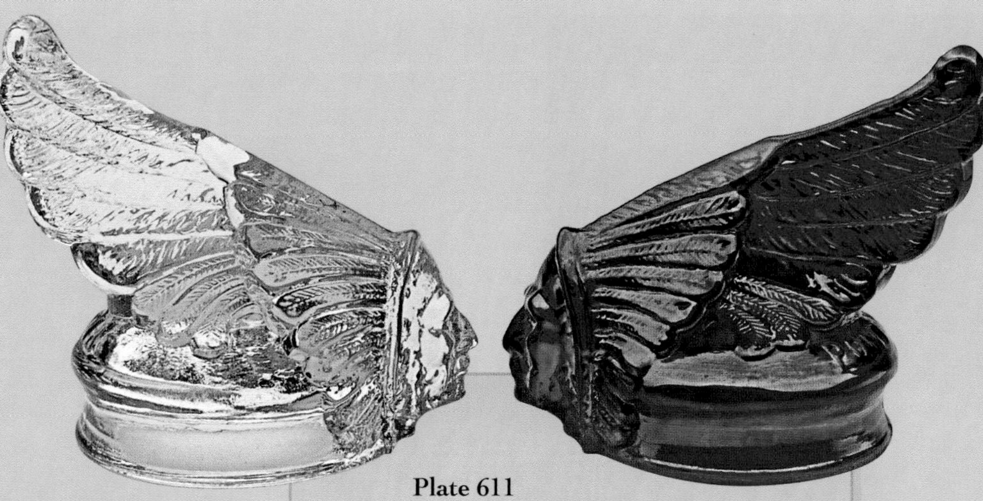

Plate 610
FENTON ART GLASS COMPANY
#5106 Santa Two-Piece Fairy Lamp. Milk glass, 5½" high, circa 1971 – 79.
$30.00 – 35.00

Other colors: ruby, 1971 – 79; lime sherbet, 1974 – 75; colonial green, 1971 – 74; and custard satin, 1974 – 75.

Plate 611
GUERNSEY GLASS COMPANY
Pontiac Chief Paperweight. 5¼" high, 4" wide, circa 1981. Pink iridized and red carnival.
$22.00 – 28.00 each

Other colors: cobalt carnival, white carnival, green, mint green, and light blue.

Designed after an old car radiator cap. Marked with a "B" inside a triangle.

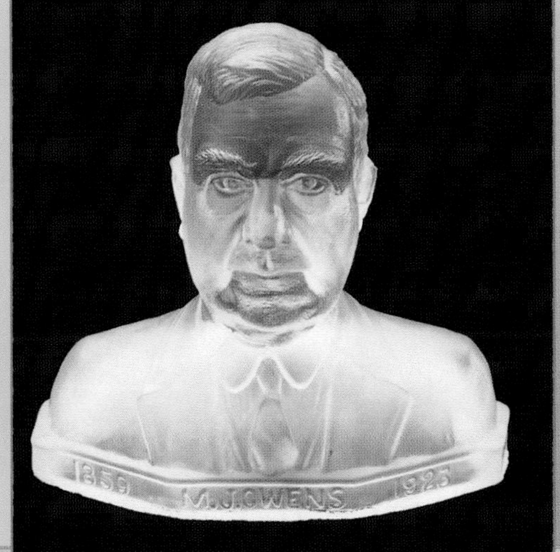

Plate 612
HEISEY GLASS COMPANY
Mike Owens Bust. Crystal frosted, 4½" high, 5⅛" long, circa 1923.
$40.00 – 50.00

Other colors: moongleam and flamingo.

Mike Owens invented machinery which automated the production of glass in the early 1900s. His first machine was made specifically for bottles but later was expanded into other phases of glassmaking. Mike Owens was a partner at the time of his death in 1923 with Edward Drummond Libbey, in the Libbey-Owens Glass Company. Edward Libbey commissioned Heisey Glass Company to produce the bust of Mike Owens in 1923.

Plate 613
IMPERIAL GLASS COMPANY
Lu-Tung Book Holders. Crystal frosted, 7¼" high, circa 1949.
$250.00 – 300.00 each

Part of Imperial's Cathay line. Signed "Virginia B. Evans." For details on Cathay, see Plate 224.

Plate 614
McKee Glass Company
Jolly Golfer Glass. Canary, 4" high, circa 1926.
$125.00 – 135.00

Other colors: white opal, green, rose pink, canary, blue, amber, and crystal, either clear or frosted.

Jolly Golfer Set, designed by cartoonist Tony Sarg, consisted of decanter and glasses with removable hats. Jeanette Glass Co. acquired the mold and reissued for private request orders in the 1960s. Reportedly was issued as "one turn" which means four hours of production.

Plate 615
Westmoreland Glass Company
#1872 Santa Lid on Sleigh. Emerald green opalescent, 5½" long, circa 1960s – 70s.
$25.00 – 30.00

Other colors: brandywine, blue opalescent, milk glass decorated, purple carnival, and antique blue. The green opalescent (pictured) was produced in the 1970s for Levay Glass Co.

Sleigh was originally sold without the lid. Summit Art Glass Company now owns this mold.

Plate 616
Morgantown Glass Company
Top Hat Cocktail. Harlequin pastel blue, 5" high, 4½" oz., circa 1950s.
$55.00 – 60.00

Other colors: all crystal, cobalt, ruby, stiegel green, and Harlequin pastels.

Made for Knickerbocker Hotel.

Plate 617
Morgantown Glass Company
Jockey Stem. Amber, 5½" high, 6 oz., circa 1950s.
$50.00 – 55.00

Other colors: all crystal or topaz/amber stem with crystal bowl and foot.

Made for Gulfstream Race Track.

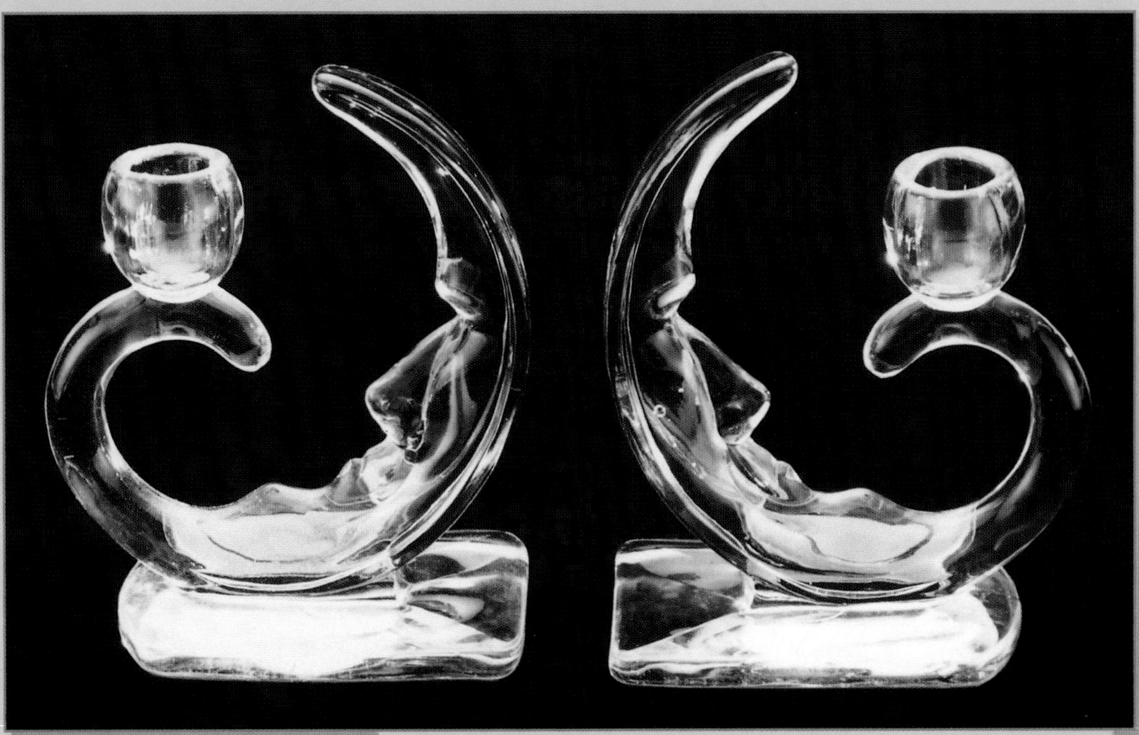

Plate 618
Undetermined Glass Company
Man in the Moon Candlesticks. Crystal, 6½" high, circa 1940s.
$300.00 – 350.00 pair

There is speculation that perhaps New Martinsville Glass company designed and produced these candlesticks. However, there have been several pair show up with Barth Art labels, which indicates that this was a Barth Art mold and could have very well been made at Paden City Glass Company. Nonetheless, the candlesticks are unusual, scarce, and very desirable.

Plate 619
New Martinsville Glass Company
#497 Hunter/Woodsman. Crystal, 7⅜" high, on square base.
$80.00 – 100.00

Other colors: crystal only.

Reissues: In crystal probably by Dalzell-Viking.

Plate 621
VIKING GLASS COMPANY
#7878 Sea Captain. 7" high, circa 1970s – 80s.
Amber, $22.00 – 24.00
Crystal/highlights, $25.00 – 30.00

Other colors: perhaps made in other Viking colors.

Plate 620
VIKING GLASS COMPANY
Happy and Sad Clown Figurines. Crystal with crystal frosted accents, 7" high, circa 1970s – 80s.
$18.00 – 22.00 each

Other colors: perhaps made in other Viking colors.

Plate 622
VIKING GLASS COMPANY
Cowboy with Ten Gallon Hat. Crystal/textured, 9½" high, circa 1970s – 80s.
$25.00 – 30.00

Other colors: perhaps made in other Viking colors.

Plate 623
VIKING GLASS COMPANY
Gay Nineties Man. Crystal/textured, 7¾" high, circa 1970s – 80s.
$24.00 – 28.00

Other colors: perhaps made in other Viking colors.

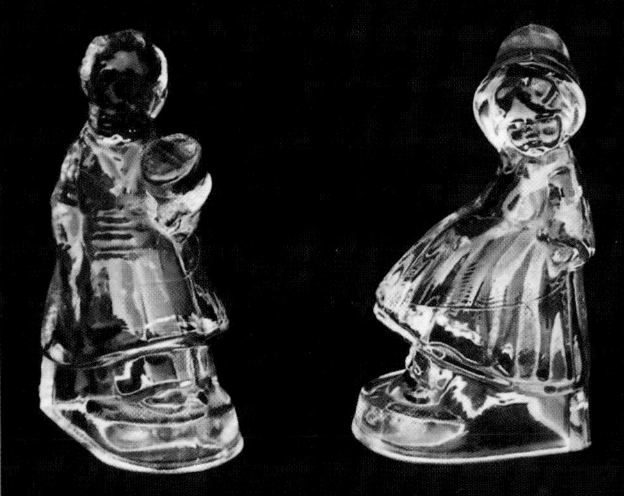

Plate 623A
American Glass Company (K.R. Haley mold)
Victorian Boy and Girl Bookends. Crystal, 5½" high.
$65.00 – 75.00 pair

Reissues: Wheaton Glass Company in multiple colors.

Plate 624
Fenton Art Glass Company
#5100 Praying Boy and Girl. White satin and jade green, 3¾" high.
White satin, 1972, $75.00 – 95.00 pair
Jade green, 1980, $40.00 – 50.00 pair

Other colors: black, peking blue, custard satin, lime satin, blue satin, purple carnival, and perhaps other Fenton colors.

Plate 625
Imperial Glass Company
#5033/34 Candle Servants. Crystal frosted, 9" high, circa 1949.
$250.00 – 275.00 each

Part of Imperial's Cathay line. Original issue signed "Virginia B. Evans" in script. See Plate 224 for details on the Cathay line.

Plate 626
Undetermined Glass Company
Spanish Dancers.
Crystal, frosted, 10¼" high, circa 1920s or 1930s.
$175.00 – 195.00

Reportedly thought to have been made by Fostoria Glass Company. Mold was designed by Walter Przybylek, who was known for his work with Consolidated Glass Company.

Pheasants

Plate 627
HEISEY GLASS COMPANY
Left: **Asiatic Pheasant.** Crystal, 10½" high, 7½" long (wing tip to tip of beak), circa 1945 – 55.
$400.00 – 450.00

Other colors: crystal frosted.

Reissues: Imperial Glass Company, crystal, crystal frosted, and amber. Dalzell-Viking in lavender ice.

This figurine is generally marked and it appears midway on the right side of the base.

Right: **Ringneck Pheasant.** Crystal, 5" high, 12" long (tip of tail to beak), circa 1942 – 53.
$145.00 – 165.00

Other colors: crystal frosted.

Reissues: Imperial Glass Company in crystal, 1964 – 67; in black carnival, 1985; and amber, 1983.

Seldom marked but when marked it appears on left side of base, midway under wing. Often found with non-Heisey decorations, bright red, gold, white, black, and sometimes found with floral decorations.

Plate 628
IMPERIAL GLASS COMPANY (original Heisey Glass Company mold)
Ringneck Pheasant. Amber, 5" high, 12" long, circa 1983.
$250.00 – 275.00

See Plate 627.

Plate 629
AMERICAN GLASS COMPANY
(K.R. Haley mold)
Ringneck Pheasant. Crystal, 11½" long, circa 1947.
$40.00 – 50.00

Other colors: crystal frosted.

Reissues: Kemple Glass Company, in amber and slag.

Plate 630
PADEN CITY GLASS COMPANY
Pheasant (Chinese). Crystal, 13½" long, circa 1940.
$100.00 – 125.00

Other colors: made in two different shades of blue, light and dark.

Plate 631
PADEN CITY GLASS COMPANY
Pheasant (Chinese). Light blue, 13½" long, circa 1940.
$175.00 – 200.00

See Plate 630

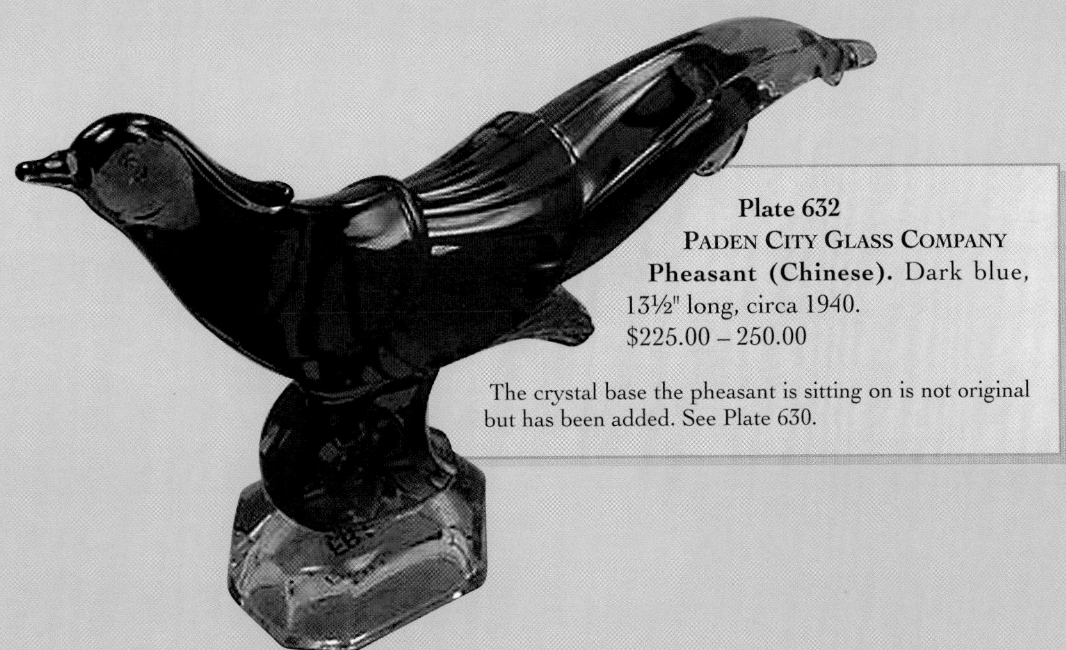

Plate 632
PADEN CITY GLASS COMPANY
Pheasant (Chinese). Dark blue, 13½" long, circa 1940.
$225.00 – 250.00

The crystal base the pheasant is sitting on is not original but has been added. See Plate 630.

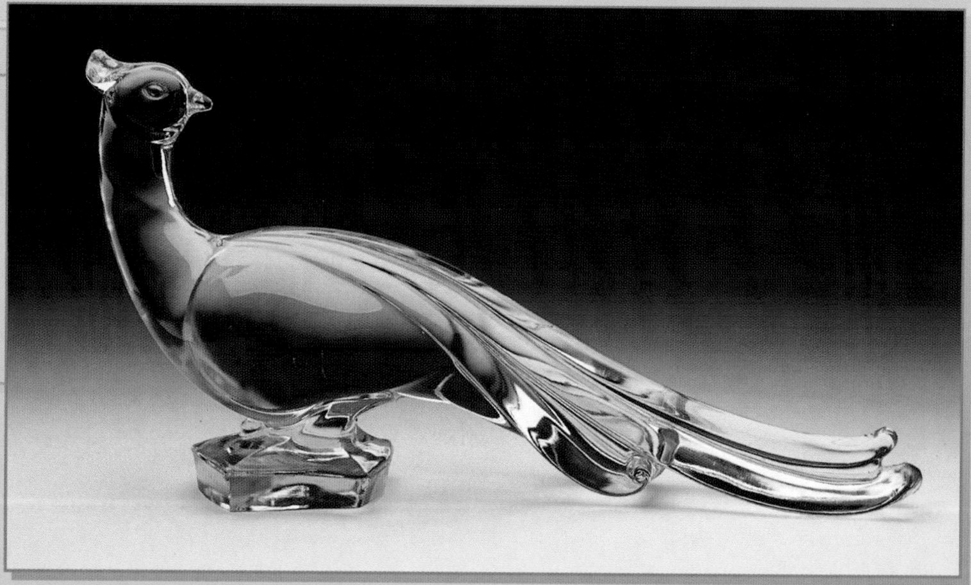

Plate 633
PADEN CITY GLASS COMPANY
Pheasant, Head Turned.
Crystal, 12" long, circa 1940.
$100.00 – 125.00

Other colors: made in a pale blue.

Reissues: none.

Plate 634
PADEN CITY GLASS COMPANY
Pheasant, Head Turned. Pale blue, 12" long, circa 1940.
$200.00 – 225.00 each

See Plate 633.

Plate 635
TIFFIN GLASS COMPANY
Pheasant Paperweights.
Left: #6042 Female, head down. Crystal, on 3" ball, 8¾" high at tail, 13" long, circa 1935.
$175.00 – 200.00
Right: #6042 Male, head up. Crystal on 3" ball, 7¼" high at head, 11" long, circa 1935.
$175.00 – 200.00

Other colors: crystal with controlled bubbles, Copen blue, wisteria, and twilight.

The measurements on the pheasants vary, as they are free-hand pieces. The early pheasants were larger in diameter in the body; the later pieces were slimmer in the body.

Plate 637
Tiffin Glass Company
Pheasant Paperweight. Crystal, controlled bubbles, 7½" high, 16" long, on ball.
Private collection — Market

Very difficult to make and very few made.

Plate 636
Tiffin Glass Company
#6042 Head Down Pheasant Paperweight.
Copen blue, 16" long, 7½" high, circa 1935.
$275.00 – 300.00

For other colors, see Plate 635.

Plate 639
Undetermined Manufacturer
Pheasant Ashtray. Crystal pheasant and crystal ashtray with bubbles.
Seen at $100.00 – 125.00

The pheasant is 7" long and the ashtray is 6" in diameter and contains bubbles. Tiffin was ruled out and then thought perhaps to be Silverbrook but unable to confirm.

Plate 638
Tiffin Glass Company
Pheasant Paperweights. Crystal, controlled bubbles, 12" long.
Left: Female, $250.00 – 275.00
Right: Male, $250.00 – 275.00

These are shorter than the earlier pheasants, which were 16". The later pheasants measure approximately 12". Since these are handmade, they will all vary in size.

Phoenix Birds

Plate 640
Imperial Glass Company
Phoenix Bowl. Crystal and satin, 5" high, 7" long, original issue.
$300.00 – 350.00

Signed "Virginia B. Evans." For details on Imperial's Cathay line, see Plate 224.

Other colors: 1954 – 55, black suede; 1960 – 61, dynasty jade; 1964 – 66, cranberry satin and verde green satin; 1981, dark jade; and 1980s, black suede; marked "ALIG."

Reissues: in crystal, for sale in Fostoria's outlet stores, in 1990. Item not marked except with the Fostoria red, white, and blue label.

Plate 641
Imperial Glass Company
Phoenix bowl. Black suede, 5" high, 7" long, unmarked, circa 1954 – 55.
$175.00 – 200.00

For other reissues and colors see Plate 640. For details on Cathay line see Plate 224.

Plate 642
Imperial Glass Company
Phoenix Bowl. Cranberry satin, 5" high, 7" long, circa 1964 – 66.
$170.00 – 190.00

For other reissues and colors, see Plate 640. For details on Imperial's Cathay line see Plate 224.

Plate 643
Imperial Glass Company
Phoenix Bowl. Verde green satin, 5" high, 7" long, circa 1964 – 66.
$170.00 – 190.00

For other reissues and colors, see Plate 640. For details on Imperial's Cathay line see Plate 224.

Plate 644
Lancaster Colony Glass Company
Phoenix Bowl. Crystal, 5" high, 7¾" long, circa 1990.
$50.00 – 60.00

Item purchased in the Fostoria outlet store, in early 1990s. Has a red, white, and blue Fostoria label. The neck is pulled forward on these, making it longer in overall length than those made by Imperial.

Pigeons

Plate 645
Cambridge Glass Company
Pouter Pigeon Bookend. Crystal, 5½" high, 5" wide, circa 1940s.
$75.00 – 100.00 each

Other colors: milk glass and crown tuscan.

Reissues: none.

The bird itself is solid glass but the base is hollow.

Plate 646
Indiana Glass Company
Pouter Pigeon Bookend.
Crystal, 5½" high.
$30.00 – 35.00 each

Other colors: crystal frosted.

Also seen with "Czechoslovakia" in raised letters on the base.

Plate 647
Indiana Glass Company
Pouter Pigeon Bookend.
Crystal frosted, 5½" high.
$25.00 – 30.00 each

Other colors: crystal.

See Plate 646.

Plate 648
Heisey Glass Company
Pouter Pigeon. Crystal, 6½" high, 7½" long, circa 1947 – 49.
$1,000.00 – 1,200.00

Other colors: crystal frosted.

Reissues: Imperial Glass Company in crystal. Dalzell-Viking in lavender ice (part of HCA Gem Series, see plate 84B), lavender ice frosted, and emerald green.

Marked on left side ¾" above base, between wing and leg.

Plate 649
Dalzell-Viking Glass Company (original Heisey Glass Company mold)
Pouter Pigeon. Lavender ice, 6½" high, 7½" long.
$90.00 – 100.00

This was part of HCA Gem Series, see Plate 84B. For details on original issue see Plate 648.

Plate 650
Original Heisey Glass Company Photo.
This is an original photo that was from the files left in the factory when Heisey closed. It was used to produce magazine and other advertisements of Heisey glassware.

Plate 651
Paden City Glass Company (Barth Art mold)
Pouter Pigeon Bookend. Crystal, 6¼" high, circa 1940.
$100.00 – 110.00 each

Other colors: none.

Reissues: none known.

Figurine stands on a base which is solid glass, ground and polished.

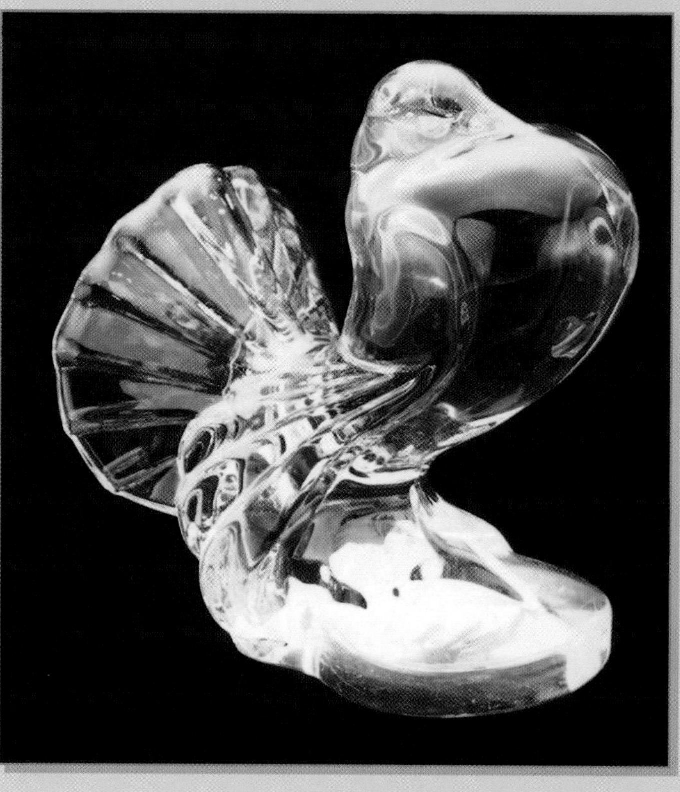

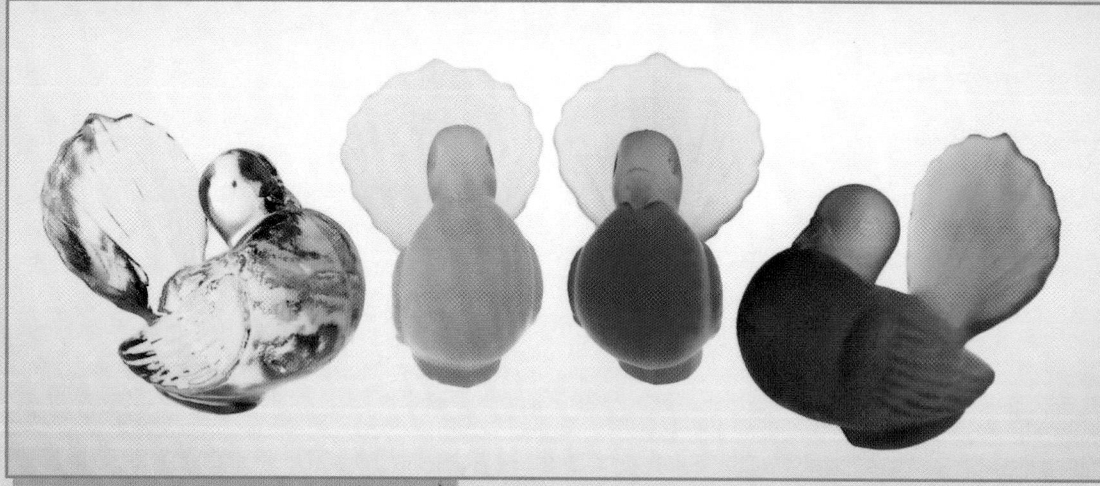

Plate 652
Westmoreland Glass Company
#9 Pouter Pigeon. 2½" high, circa 1970s.
Left to right: Crystal, $20.00 – 25.00
Pink mist, $25.00 – 35.00
Blue mist, $25.00 – 35.00
Apricot mist, $25.00 – 35.00

Other colors: Other 1971 colors include amber, amethyst mist, blue, green mist, lilac, lilac mist, dark blue mist, and perhaps others. Black in 1984 (experimental).

Plate 653
Westmoreland Glass Company
#9 Pouter Pigeon. 2½" high, circa 1971, amethyst mist.
$25.00 – 35.00

For other colors and details see Plate 652.

Plate 654
FENTON ART GLASS COMPANY
#5220 Pig. 2½" high, 3" long, circa 1985.
$25.00 – 30.00

Other colors: 1985 – 86 crystal velvet, crystal iridized, blue slag, and Heaven 'N Nature sign decoration. 1989 pink and other colors.

Plate 655
PILGRIM GLASS COMPANY
#943 Pig. Crystal, 2" high, 3¼" long, circa 1980s.
$10.00 – 12.00

Other colors: amber, cobalt, and probably others.

This is an off-hand style.

Plate 656
WESTMORELAND GLASS COMPANY
Porky Pig. Milk glass, 3" long, 1½" wide, circa late 1970s.
$15.00 – 20.00

Other colors: crystal mist, dark blue mist, mint green, yellow opaque, cobalt carnival, blue opaque, and ruby. Reissued in cobalt, milk glass, milk glass with mother-of-pearl, and some hand-painted pieces.

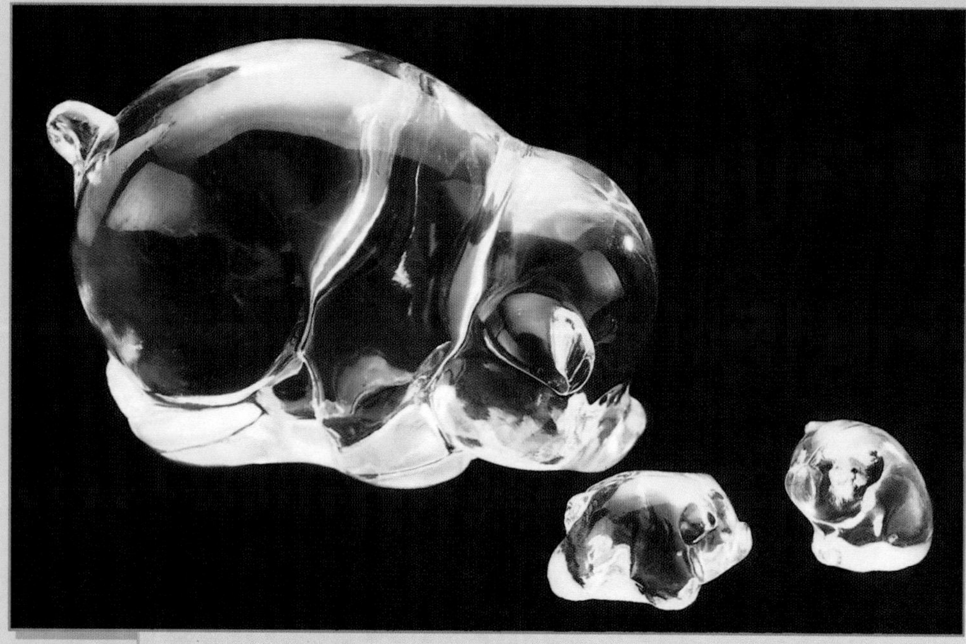

Plate 657
HEISEY GLASS COMPANY
Sow, Piglet Walking, and Piglet Sitting

Sow. Crystal, 3" high, 4½" long (tip of tail to nose), circa 1948 – 49, $1,200.00 – 1,400.00

Other colors: none.

Reissues: Imperial Glass Company in crystal, crystal frosted, black, amber, amber frosted, pink, ruby, milk glass, milk glass carnival, ruby frosted, verde green, ultra blue satin finish, ultra blue carnival, salmon, and salmon frosted. Made by another company for Imperial and Mirror Images in ultra blue. Fenton in rosalene as part of the HCA Gold Series (see Plate 126). Dalzell-Viking in lavender ice and lavender ice frosted.

Seldom marked, but when marked it appears on the right side, near the base between the legs.

This figurine is solid glass and has good detail. She is sometimes confused with New Martinsville #2 Mama Pig. See Plate 662 for the differences.

Piglet, Walking. Crystal, ⅞" high, 1½" long (tip to tip), circa 1948 – 49, $100.00 – 125.00

Other colors: none.

Reissues: Imperial Glass Company in crystal, amber, ruby, ultra blue carnival, and ultra blue frosted. Made for Imperial and Mirror Images by another company in crystal, emerald green, horizon blue, and ultra blue. Fenton Art Glass Company in rosalene. Dalzell-Viking in lavender ice.

Seldom marked, but when marked it appears on the left side near the base between the legs.

In the 1980s there were piglets, very similar to the Heisey piglets appearing on the market, from the Ohio area, in multiple colors. These were not made from the original Heisey molds. The Walking Piglet is sometimes referred to as the Standing Piglet.

Piglet, Sitting. Crystal, 1⅛" high, 1⅛" long (nose to tail), circa 1948 – 49, $100.00 – 125.00

Other colors: none.

Reissues: Imperial Glass Company in crystal, pink, ruby, and amber. Fenton Art Glass Company in rosalene. Dalzell-Viking in lavender ice.

Seldom marked but when found, it appears on the right side between the legs.

See note in Piglet, Walking, above, for information on similar piglets on the market.

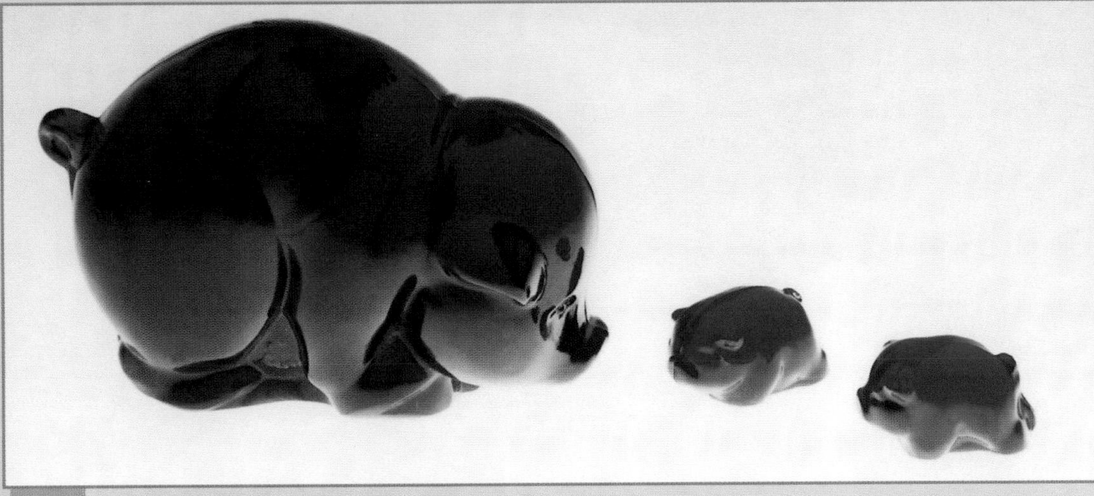

Plate 658
IMPERIAL GLASS COMPANY (original Heisey Glass Company mold)
Mother Pig and Walking Piglet
Mama Pig. Ultra blue, 3" high, 4½" long, circa 1983.
$155.00 – 175.00

This item was made for Mirror Images through Imperial Glass Co. (actually made by another company for Imperial).

Walking (Standing) Piglet. Ultra blue, ⅞" high, 1½" long, circa 1983.
$20.00 – 25.00 each

This item was made for Mirror Images through Imperial Glass Company (actually made by another company for Imperial).

For all details on the Mama Pig and Piglets, colors, reissues, etc., see Plate 657.

Plate 659
IMPERIAL GLASS COMPANY (original Heisey Glass Company mold)
Piglets, Sitting, and Walking (Standing). Amber, sitting, 1⅛" high, walking, ⅞" high, circa 1984.
$50.00 – 75.00 pair

For details on original, reissues, and colors, see Plate 657.

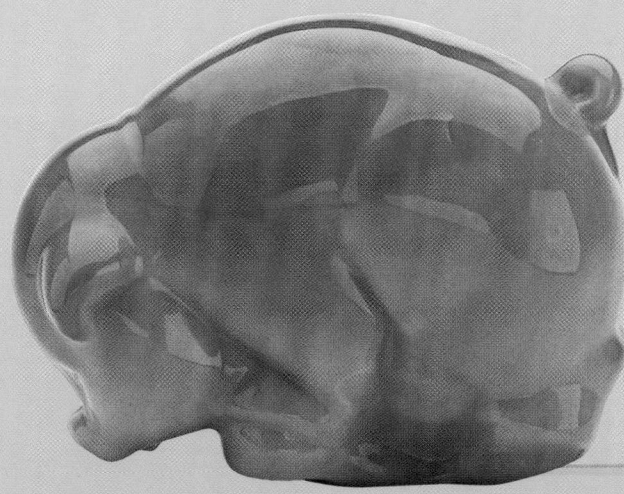

Plate 660
FENTON ART GLASS COMPANY (original Heisey Glass Company mold)
Mama Pig. Rosalene, 3" high, 4½" long, circa 1992.
$75.00 – 100.00

This figurine was produced for HCA as part of the Gold Series. See Plate 126.

Plate 661
NEW MARTINSVILLE GLASS COMPANY
Mama Pig, Design #1. Crystal, 3¼" high, 6" long, circa 1940.
$1,200.00 – 1,400.00

Other colors: none.

Reissues: none.

After production started this original design was considered to be in "bad taste," and production was stopped after approximately 200 were made. Mama Pig and Piglets were redesigned. See Plate 662.

Plate 662
NEW MARTINSVILLE GLASS COMPANY
#762 Mama Pig, Design #2. #763 Piglets. Crystal.
Mama Pig. 4" high, 6½" long, circa 1941 – 53.
$300.00 – 325.00

Other colors: crystal frosted.

Reissues: Dalzell-Viking, 1990 in crystal, 1991 in black.

Piglet. 2" long, 1⅛" high, circa 1941 – 53.
$175.00 – 200.00 each

Reissues and other colors: none.

These piglets are very difficult to find.

Plate 663
NEW MARTINSVILLE GLASS COMPANY
#2 Mama Pig, Design #2. Crystal frosted, 4" high, 6½" long, circa 1941 – 53.
$250.00 – 275.00

At some time during the life of this mold, it was altered. Note the difference in this pig's tail as compared with the tail on the pig in Plate 662.

Plate 664
Blenko Glass Company
Rabbit. 6½" high, circa 1970s.
Crystal, $12.00 – 14.00
Amber, $14.00 – 18.00

Blenko animals were designed by Joel Myers.

Plate 665
Cambridge Glass Company
Rabbit Covered Box. Crystal, 7" long, new style.
$275.00 – 300.00

Other colors: dianthus (peach blo), amber, and probably others.

There are two styles and two sizes of these covered boxes. The old style has much more detail than the newer style. When Cambridge re-worked the molds they took out some of the fine detail.

Plate 666
Cambridge Glass Company
Rabbit Covered Box. Amber, 5" long, new style.
$325.00 – 350.00

Other colors: crystal, dianthus (peach blo), and probably others.

Compare to old style. See Plate 667.

Plate 667
CAMBRIDGE GLASS COMPANY
Rabbit Covered Box. 5" long, old style, dianthus (peach blo).
$350.00 – 400.00

Compare to new style reflected in Plate 666.

Plate 668
FENTON ART GLASS COMPANY
#5162 Bunny. 3" high, 3" long, circa 1978.
Custard, $20.00 – 25.00
Crystal, $20.00 – 25.00

Other colors: crystal velvet, blue satin, lime sherbet, lavender satin, and others.

Plate 669
FENTON ART GLASS COMPANY
#5162 Bunny. Purple slag, 3" high, 3" long, circa 1981.
$30.00 – 35.00

Made for Levay Distributing Company.

Plate 670
FENTON ART GLASS COMPANY
Bunny. Sea mist green, 1½" high, 2" long.
$8.00 – 10.00

Plate 671
FENTON ART GLASS COMPANY
#5174 Large Hollow Rabbit. Electric blue carnival, 5¾" high, circa 1980.
$65.00 – 75.00

Other colors: first issued in 1971 in amethyst carnival. Made for Levay Distributing Co., 1978, springtime green carnival and in 1980 in electric blue carnival.

This mold is a former U.S. Glass mold now owned by Fenton. See Plate 672.

Plate 672
TIFFIN GLASS COMPANY
Rabbit Lamp E-8. Brown on black base, 8" high, circa 1926 – 35.
$1,400.00 – 1,600.00

This lamp is rare. Tiffin Glass was factory "R" of the U.S. Glass Company.

Plate 673
FOSTORIA GLASS COMPANY
Left to right: **#2821/628 Mama Rabbit.** Light blue, 2" high, 4" long, circa 1971 – 73, $35.00 – 40.00
#2821/627 Baby Rabbit. Light blue, 1½" high, 3" long, circa 1971 – 73, $30.00 – 35.00

Other colors: olive green, lemon, crystal, and probably others.

Plate 674
FOSTORIA GLASS COMPANY
Left to right: **#2821/627 Baby Rabbit.** Olive green, 1½" high, 3" long, circa 1971 – 73, $30.00 – 35.00
#2821/628 Mama Rabbit. Crystal, 2" high, 4" long, circa 1971 – 73, $35.00 – 40.00
#2821/628 Mama Rabbit. Lemon, 2" high, 4" long, circa 1971 – 73, $35.00 – 40.00

Plate 675
SUMMIT ART GLASS COMPANY (original Atterbury/Imperial mold)
#155 Large Rabbit Covered Dish. Cobalt, 10" long, 4" high.
$30.00 – 40.00

Other colors: cobalt carnival, princess purple, vaseline plain or iridized, and milk glass.

This mold was originally an Atterbury and Company mold, produced in opaque white and blue glass. Imperial Glass Company obtained the mold in the 1950s and produced it in milk glass as part of the Belknap Collection. Summit acquired the mold after Imperial closed.

Plate 676
Heisey Glass Company
Rabbit Paperweight. Crystal, 2¾" high, 3¾" long, circa 1941 – 46.
$200.00 – 225.00

Other colors: crystal frosted.

Reissues: Imperial Glass Company in milk glass and horizon blue. Dalzell-Viking 1996, ice blue, HCA convention souvenir, 1997, lavender ice, HCA convention souvenir. Was dubbed "Bonnie Bunny" by HCA. Fenton Art Glass Company in rosalene as part of the HCA Gold Series.

Plate 677
Imperial Glass Company (original Heisey Glass Company mold)
Rabbit Paperweight. Milk glass, 2¾" high, 3¾" long, circa 1977.
$35.00 – 45.00

For all details on the paperweight, see Plate 676.

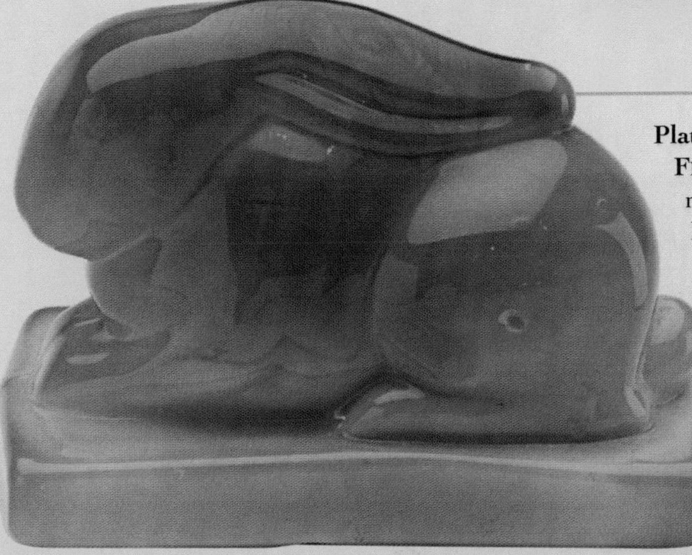

Plate 678
Fenton Art Glass Company (original Heisey Glass Company mold)
Rabbit Paperweight. Rosalene, 2¾" high, 3¾" long, circa 1992.
$70.00 – 75.00

Made for HCA as part of the HCA Gold Series. For details see Plate 126.

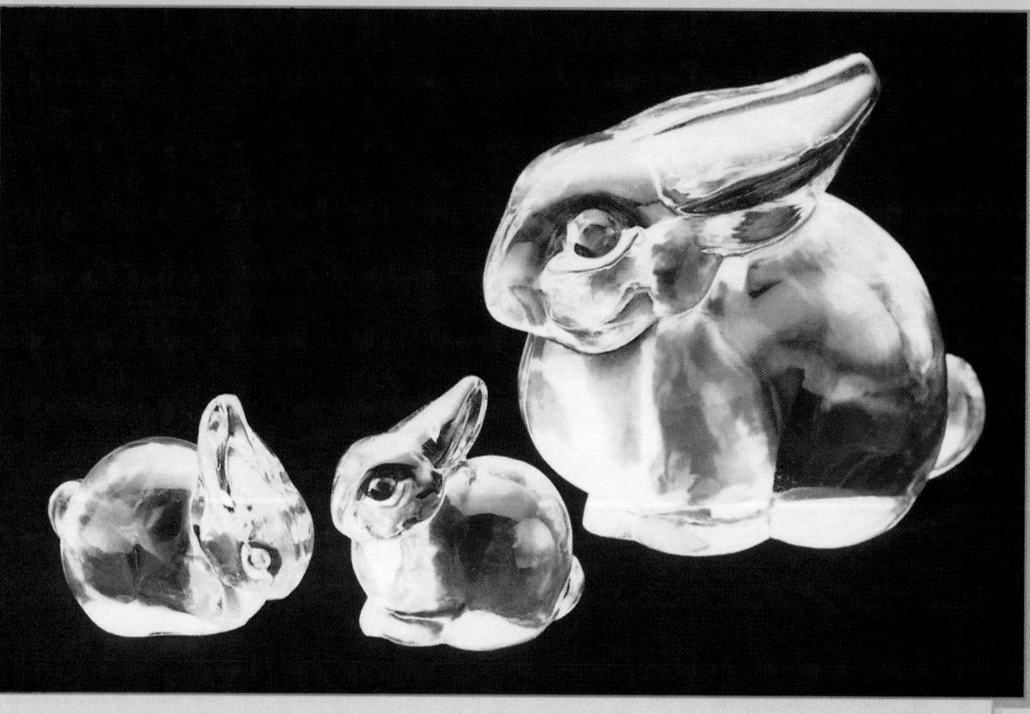

Plate 679
Heisey Glass Company
Rabbit Family. Crystal.
Bunny, Head Down. 2½" high, 3" long (tip of tail to front of head), circa 1948 – 52.
$275.00 – 300.00

Other colors: crystal frosted.

Reissues: Imperial Glass Company, ultra blue, sunshine yellow, caramel slag, and in milk glass for HCA. Dalzell-Viking in red and lavender ice. Fenton in pink.

Seldom marked, but when found the mark is located on the left side near the front on the base.

Bunny, Head Up. 2½" high, 2½" long (tip of nose to tail), circa 1948 – 49.
$300.00 – 325.00

Other colors: crystal frosted.

Reissues: Imperial Glass Company in ultra blue and milk glass for HCA. Dalzell-Viking in red and lavender ice. Fenton in pink.

The head up Bunny was made for a shorter period of time than the head down Bunny and demands a slightly higher price.

Mother Rabbit. 4½" high, 5½" long (tip of nose to tail), circa 1948 – 52.
$1,500.00 – 1,700.00

Other colors: crystal frosted.

Reissues: Imperial Glass Company in milk glass for HCA, sunshine yellow, caramel slag, red, verde green, and ultra blue. Dalzell-Viking in red and lavender ice. Fenton in pink.

Seldom marked, but when found mark appears on the left side near the front on the base.

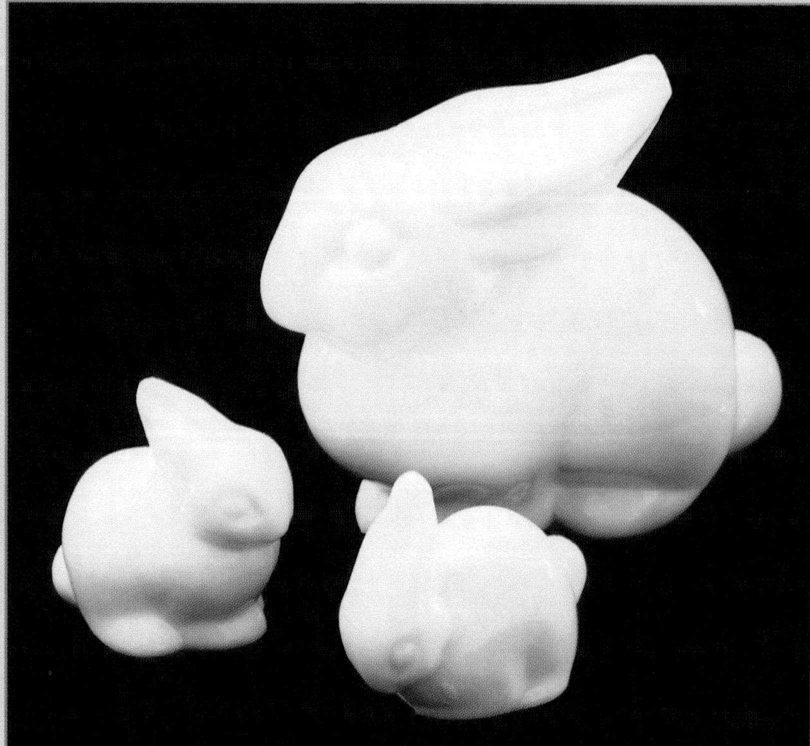

Plate 680
Imperial Glass Company (original Heisey Glass Company mold)
Rabbit Family. Milk glass.
Mother Rabbit. 4½" high, 5½" long, circa 1978, made for HCA, IG.
$40.00 – 50.00
Bunny, Head Up. 2½" high, 2½" long, circa 1977, made for HCA, IG.
$25.00 – 30.00
Bunny, Head Down. 2½" high, 3" long, circa 1977, made for HCA, IG.
$25.00 – 30.00

For details on the Rabbit Family, reissues, colors, etc., see Plate 679.

Plate 681
New Martinsville Glass Company
#764 Large Mama Rabbit. Crystal, 2½" high, circa until 1945.
$350.00 – 375.00
Bunny, Head Up, Ears Back. Amber, 1" high.
$100.00 – 125.00
Bunny, Ears Up. Amber, 1" high.
$100.00 – 125.00

Other colors: Bunnies were made in crystal, cobalt, and red.

Reissues: Reissued in 1986 by Viking for Mirror Images in ruby plain, satin, or carnival, fifth in a series of five, limited edition of 500, marked with a "V." Dalzell-Viking reissued the mama rabbit in 1988 – 90 in crystal and frosted and in black in 1990.

Plate 682
New Martinsville Glass Company
#764 Large Mama Rabbit. Crystal, 2½" high, circa until 1945.
$350.00 – 375.00
Bunny, Head Up, Ears Back. Crystal, 1" high.
$70.00 – 90.00
Bunny, Ears Up. 1" high.
$70.00 – 90.00

For details on reissues and other colors, see Plate 681.

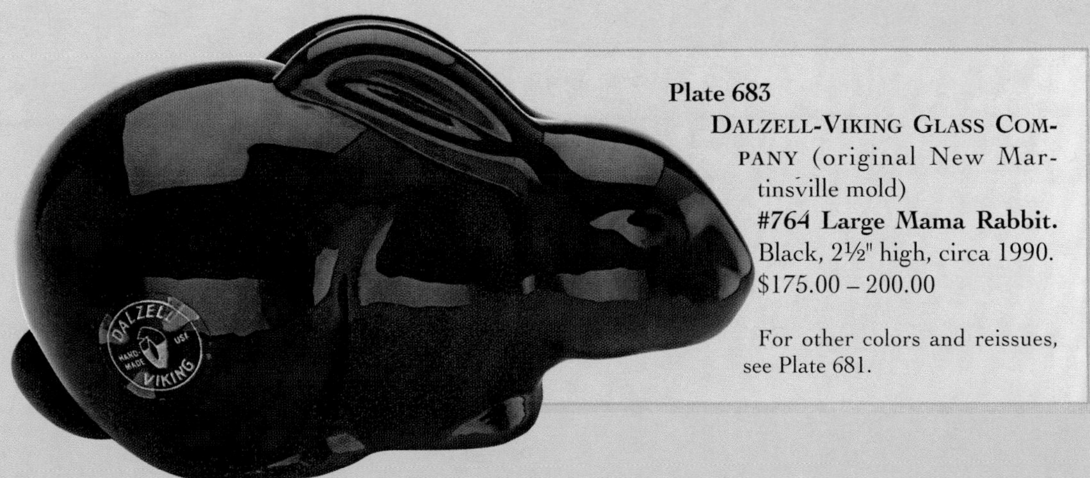

Plate 683
Dalzell-Viking Glass Company (original New Martinsville mold)
#764 Large Mama Rabbit. Black, 2½" high, circa 1990.
$175.00 – 200.00

For other colors and reissues, see Plate 681.

Plate 684
Paden City Glass Company
Bunny "Cotton Tail" Dispensers.
Left to right: Ears Up. Frosted blue, $250.00 – 300.00
Ears Down. Frosted blue, $200.00 – 225.00
Ears Up. Frosted blue, $250.00 – 300.00

Other colors: crystal, pink, or blue transparent, frosted pink, or crystal and milk glass.

Plate 685
Paden City Glass Company
Bunny "Cotton Tail" Dispensers. Ears back, 5" high.
Left to right: Pink frosted, $200.00 – 225.00
Pink transparent, $200.00 – 225.00
Crystal transparent, $175.00 – 200.00
Blue frosted, $200.00 – 225.00

Plate 686
Viking Glass Company
#6808 Rabbit (aka Thumper).
Crystal, 6½" high, circa 1968.
$30.00 – 35.00

Other colors: amber, green, and other Viking colors.

Plate 687
Viking Glass Company
#6808 Rabbit (aka Thumper).
Green, 6½" high, circa 1960s.
$35.00 – 40.00

Other colors: Made in Viking colors.

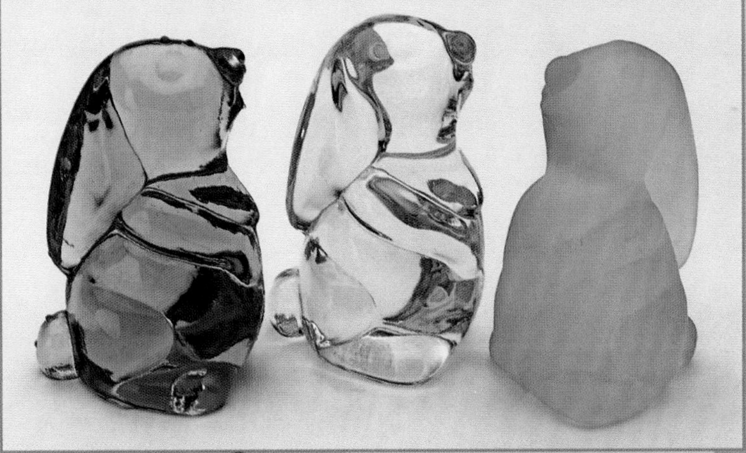

Plate 688
Viking Glass Company
Epic Line "Special Pour."
Double "b" marked bunnies, $35.00 – 40.00 each

In 1978, the #6808 Rabbit was made for a private company in 500 each of the following colors: vaseline, blue milk glass, cobalt, custard, crystal, sapphire blue, green, pink, lime green slag, lemon custard slag, blue milk slag, and ruby. The special pour bunnies are marked with a double "b" on the bottom as well as an incised rosette, distinguishing them from the Viking issue with plain polished bottom.

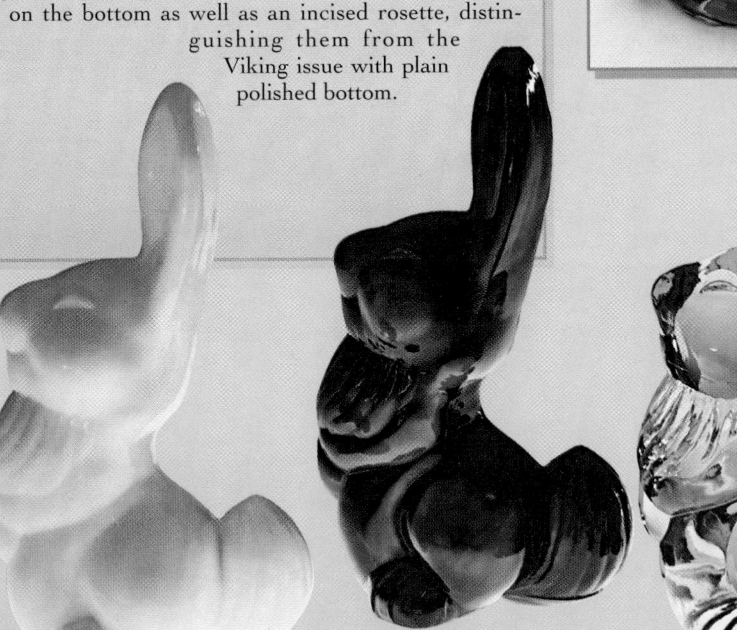

Plate 689
Viking Glass Company
#7908 Small Rabbit. 2" high, circa 1980s.
Lilac, $25.00 – 30.00
Pink, $25.00 – 30.00
Green frosted, $25.00 – 30.00

Other colors: blue frosted, pink frosted, clear lavender, and possibly other colors.

Plate 690
VIKING GLASS COMPANY
Rabbit on Scalloped Base. Amber, 2½" high, circa 1960s.
$15.00 – 20.00

Plate 691
UNKNOWN MANUFACTURER
Bunny With Ears Back. Crystal, 3½" high.
Seen at $20.00 – 25.00

This bunny is not to be confused with the Viking 6808 bunny, which is generally labeled "Viking." This bunny is labeled "Made in China."

Plate 692
UNKNOWN MANUFACTURER
Sitting Bunny With Head Up. Crystal, 2¼" high, 3" long.
Seen at $10.00 – 12.00

This bunny is labeled "Made in Taiwan." However, it has a tendency to be confused with Fenton bunnies shown in Plate 670.

Plate 693
WESTMORELAND GLASS COMPANY
#5 Rabbit on Picket Base. Milk glass, 5½" long, 4½" high, circa 1900 – 1980.
$45.00 – 55.00

Other colors: milk glass, milk glass with decorations, opaque pink top on milk base, caramel marble iridized, white carnival, and purple marble.

Mold is now owned by Phil Rosso, Port Vue, PA, and has been reissued in milk glass, milk glass with decorations, cobalt, and cobalt carnival. Some are marked PG or Key Stone "R," near original Westmoreland mark.

Plate 694
UNKNOWN MANUFACTURER
Sitting Bunny. Light blue, 5" high.
Seen at $15.00 – 20.00

Color is very similar to Paden City's blue.

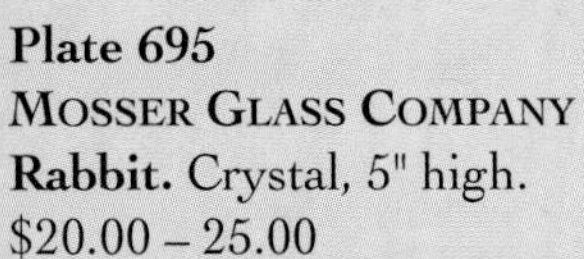

Plate 695
MOSSER GLASS COMPANY
Rabbit. Crystal, 5" high.
$20.00 – 25.00

Other colors: blue, custard, and perhaps other colors.

This rabbit was listed in the unknown section of our first edition.

Rams

Plate 696
BLENKO GLASS COMPANY
Ram's Head Solid Glass Paperweight. Cobalt, 6" high.
$30.00 – 35.00

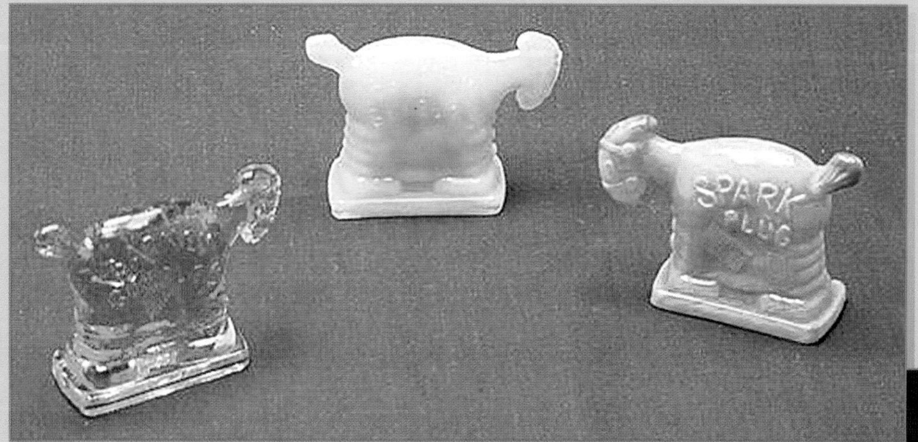

Plate 697
GUERNSEY GLASS COMPANY
Spark Plug (Horse). Blue, jade, and orange opaque, 2" high, 2¾" long, circa 1990s.
$12.00 – 15.00 each

Other colors: vaseline and possibly others.

This figure looks more like a goat than a horse. We elected to place it in this chapter for ease in identification. This is Spark Plug from the Barney Google cartoon. Marked with a "B" in a triangle.

Plate 698
HEISEY GLASS COMPANY
Ram's Head Stopper. Crystal, circa 1940s.
$300.00 – 325.00

This is a three-piece set, consisting of the shaker, glass strainer, and the stopper which fits down into the stopper. The Ram's Head and the Girl's Head stoppers are the most difficult to find and demand the highest prices.

Ram's Head Stopper. Lavender. This is *not* a Heisey stopper. It is overall larger than the Heisey stopper and will not fit down into the strainer. They are marked with a "B." They were made in colors and crystal.

Religious Figures

Plate 699
CAMBRIDGE GLASS COMPANY
Buddha. Amber, 5½", circa 1920s.
$350.00 – 375.00

Other colors: light emerald, crystal, topaz, dianthus (peach blo), bluebell, and perhaps others.

The bottom of the figurines will be seen flat or with a round threaded pedestal which was used to attach the figurine to a lamp base. See Plates 704, 705, and 706.

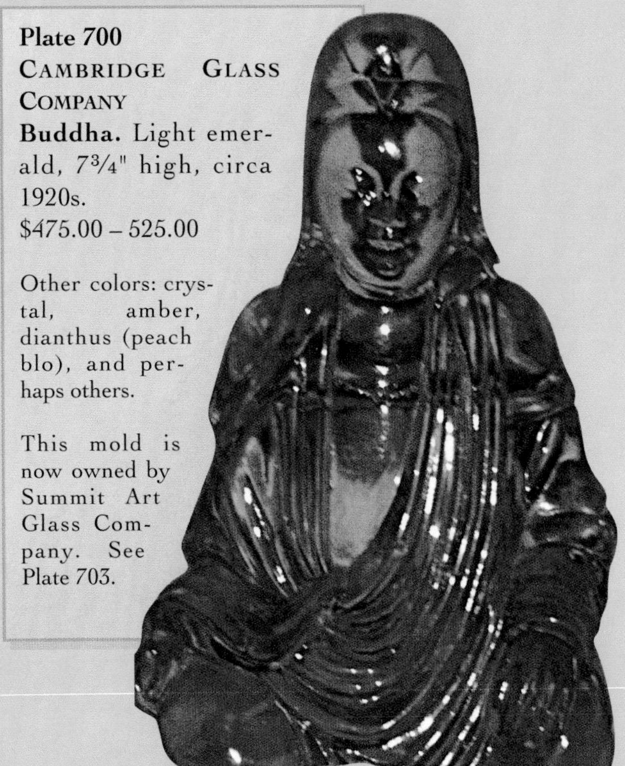

Plate 700
CAMBRIDGE GLASS COMPANY
Buddha. Light emerald, 7¾" high, circa 1920s.
$475.00 – 525.00

Other colors: crystal, amber, dianthus (peach blo), and perhaps others.

This mold is now owned by Summit Art Glass Company. See Plate 703.

Cambridge vs. Gillinder

The small Cambridge Buddha has a beaded hat with topknot and large hanging earrings, while Gillinder has neither. Gillinder Buddhas have a defined base whereas Cambridge does not.

Plate 701
GILLINDER GLASS COMPANY
Large Buddha. Flame, 6½" high, circa 1930s.
$150.00 – 175.00

Other colors: crystal, milk glass, green, vaseline, and others.

Plate 702
GILLINDER GLASS COMPANY
Small Buddha. Vaseline, 4½" high, circa 1930s.
$175.00 – 200.00

Other colors: flame, crystal, milk glass, green, and others.

Plate 703
SUMMIT ART GLASS COMPANY (original Cambridge Glass Co. mold)
Large Buddha. Teal blue, 7¼" high, contemporary.
$200.00 – 250.00

Made from the original Cambridge mold, which is now owned by Summit.

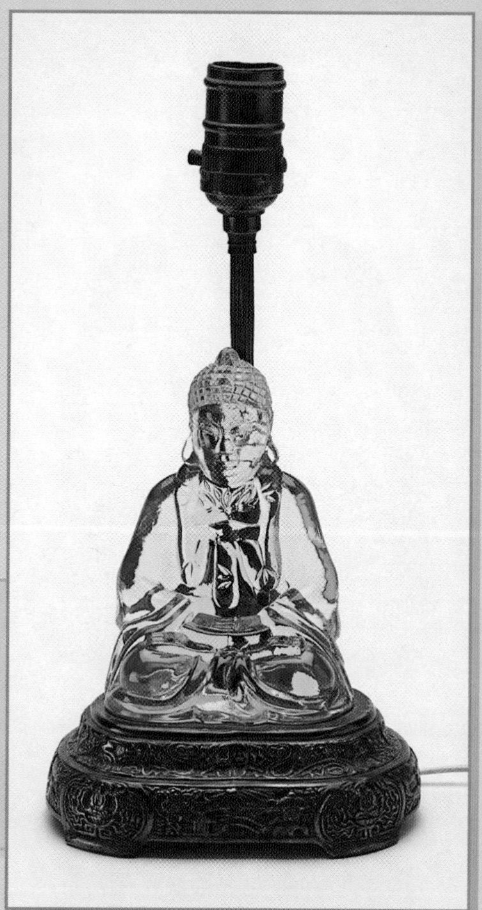

Plate 704
CAMBRIDGE GLASS COMPANY
Small Buddha Lamp. Light emerald, circa 1920s.
$475.00 – 500.00

Other colors: see Plate 699.

Plate 705
CAMBRIDGE GLASS COMPANY
Small Buddha Lamp. Amber, circa 1920s.
$425.00 – 475.00

Other colors: see Plate 699.

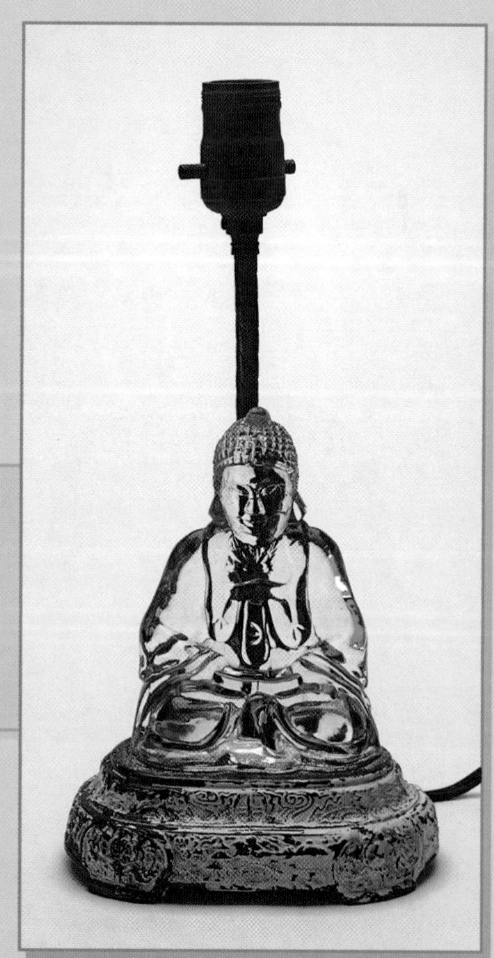

Plate 706
CAMBRIDGE GLASS COMPANY
Small Buddha Lamp. Crystal, circa 1920s.
$375.00 – 400.00

Other colors: see Plate 699.

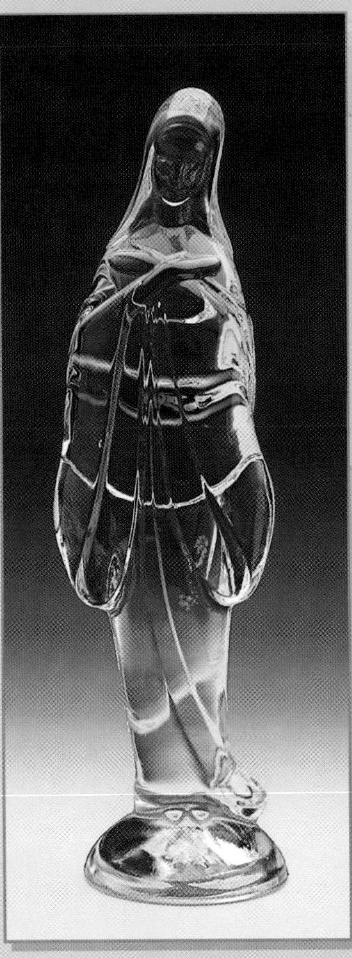

Plate 707
Fostoria Glass Company
#2635/471 Madonna. Crystal, 10" high, circa 1950s.
$75.00 – 85.00

Other colors: silver mist.

Came with optional black glass base. See Plate 708.

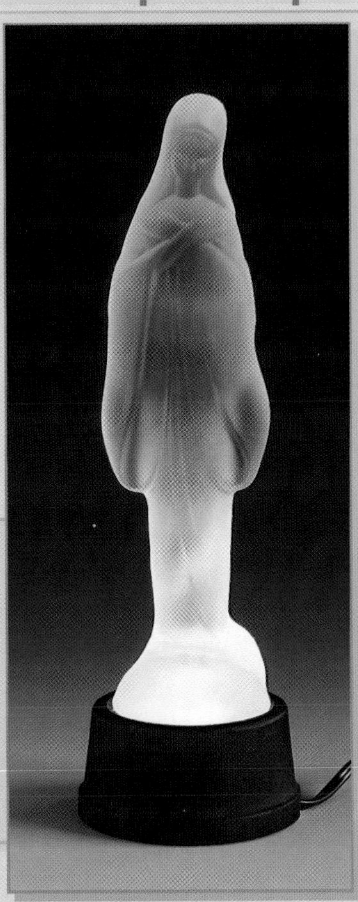

Plate 708
Fostoria Glass Company
#2635/471 Madonna and Base. Silver mist, Madonna 10" high, circa 1950s.
$125.00 – 135.00

Madonna sits on a black glass, lighted base.

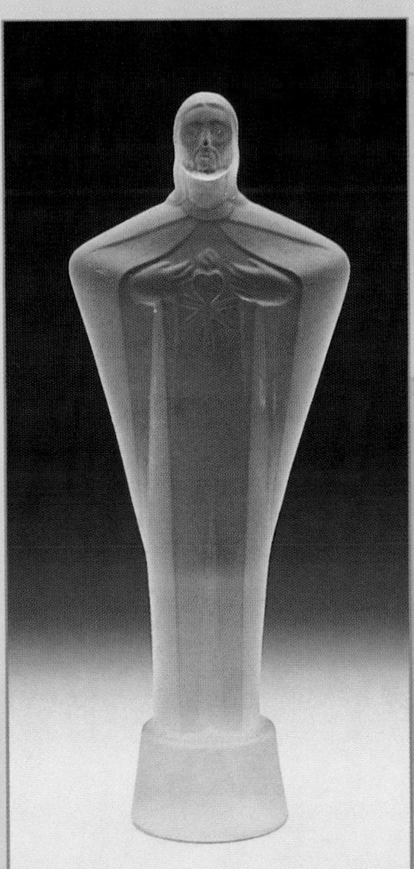

Plate 709
Fostoria Glass Company
Sacred Hearts. Silver mist, 11½" high, circa 1969 – 70s.
$400.00 – 450.00

This is a figurine of Christ and came with an optional black glass base.

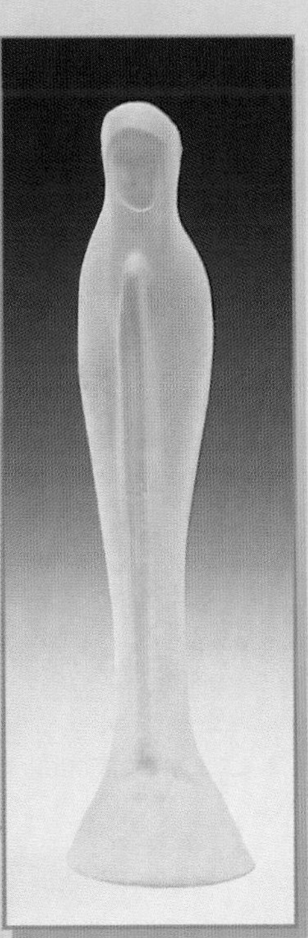

Plate 710
Fostoria Glass Company
Small Madonna. Silver mist, 4" high, circa 1978.
$25.00 – 30.00

This small Madonna was sold through the Fostoria outlet stores and also appeared in Tiara catalogs.

Plate 711
Fostoria Glass Company
#2798/472 Madonna and Child. Silver mist (black lighted base optional), 13½" high, circa 1967 – 73.
$250.00 – 300.00
#2715/469 St. Francis. Silver mist, 13½" high, circa 1957 – 73.
Original $300.00 – 350.00

The base on some of the original issue of St. Francis figurines had an irregular triangular shape, while others had a round base. St. Francis was reissued for Lancaster Colony, 1990, in silver mist (with a round base) and sold through the Fostoria outlet stores.

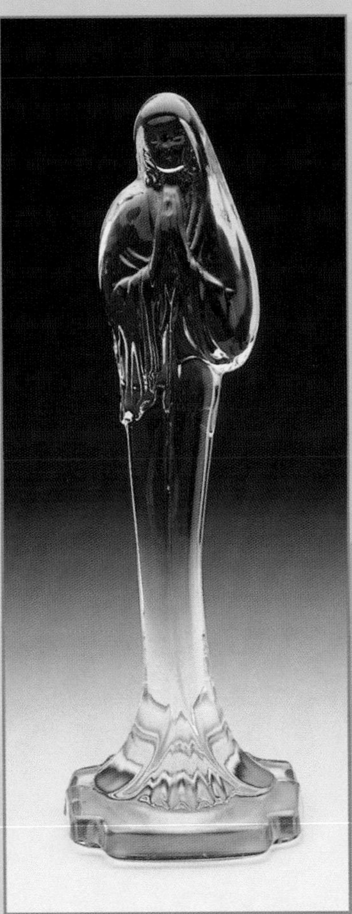

Plate 712
HEISEY GLASS COMPANY
#1 Madonna. Crystal 9" high, 3" square base, circa 1942 – 56.
$100.00 – 125.00

Other colors: crystal frosted and limelight, frosted or clear.

Reissues: Imperial Glass Company in crystal frosted with clear face, sometimes marked IG or LIG. In 1979 made in all frosted crystal but marked IG. Fenton Art Glass Company, French opalescent marked HCA 87, teal blue marked HCA 89, teal blue frosted marked HCA 89 and rosalene in 1990. Dalzell-Viking, 1991 in pink, 1993 in lavender ice, and 1995 in ice blue.

Mark appears on the back, center of base.

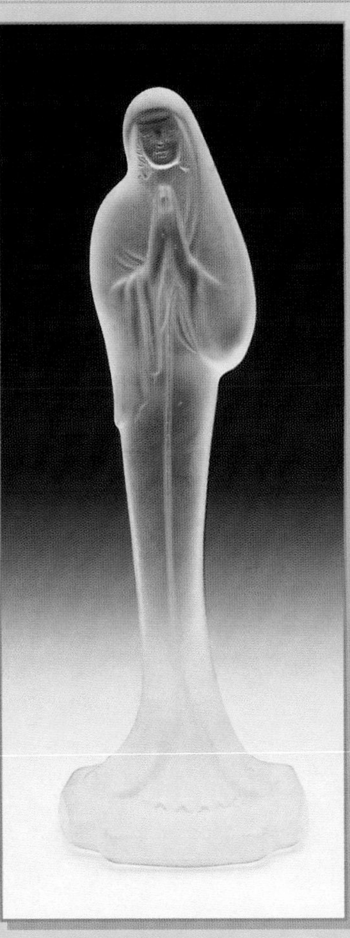

Plate 713
HEISEY GLASS COMPANY
#1 Madonna. Crystal frosted, 9" high, 3" square base, circa 1942 – 56.
$90.00 – 110.00

Heisey frosted the entire figurine and when Imperial Glass Company reissued the Madonna in crystal satin they left the face clear; however, they were generally marked IG or LIG. In 1979, Imperial started frosting the entire figurine, but these were marked "IG."

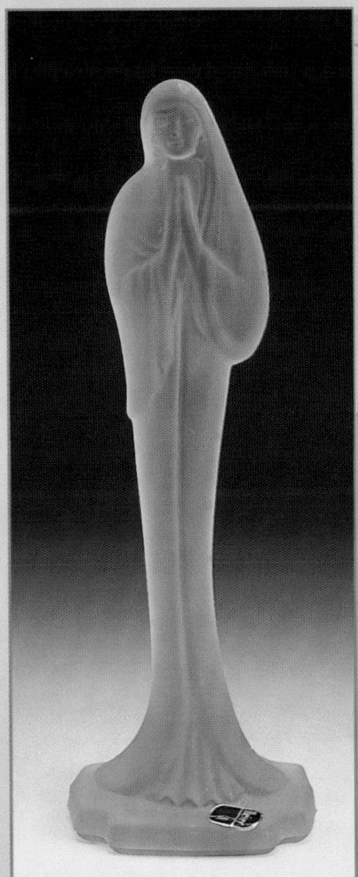

Plate 714
HEISEY GLASS COMPANY
#1 Madonna. Limelight frosted, 9" high, 3" square base.
$1,600.00 – 1,800.00

Reissues: in this color, none.

This figurine also made in limelight without frosting. This item was made in small quantities and is therefore very scarce and expensive.

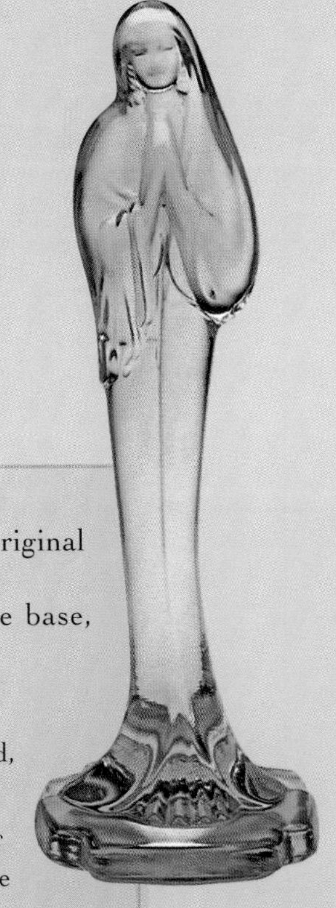

Plate 715
DALZELL-VIKING GLASS COMPANY (original Heisey Glass Company mold)
#1 Madonna. Pink, 9" high, 3" square base, circa 1991.
$35.00 – 45.00

Other colors: (Dalzell-Viking) pink frosted, ice blue clear and frosted, and lavender ice.

These were marked with a "D" on the back of the base and with HCA and the year on the front of the base.

Plate 716
FOREIGN MANUFACTURER
Madonna. Crystal frosted, 9" high, circa 1983.

This item was produced in Taiwan, and was pictured in the Spencer gift catalog in 1983 for $7.89. Base is hollow up to top of pleats in robe. The glass has many imperfections and has a yellow cast. The Heisey Madonna has a solid base. From a distance it does look like the Heisey Madonna. See Plate 713.

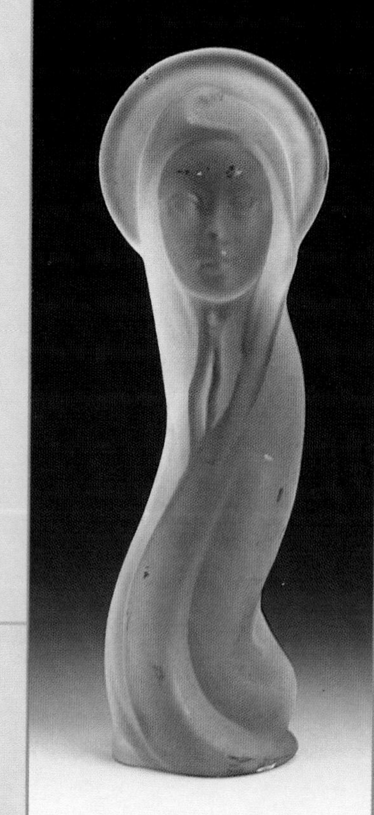

Plate 717
HEISEY GLASS COMPANY
#2 Madonna. Crystal frosted, 11" high, circa 1945 – 52.
$1,800.00 – 2,000.00

Other colors: crystal.

Reissues: Mosser Glass Company, 2003, in cobalt, for HCA.

This item was very difficult to make, which accounts for its being very scarce and expensive.

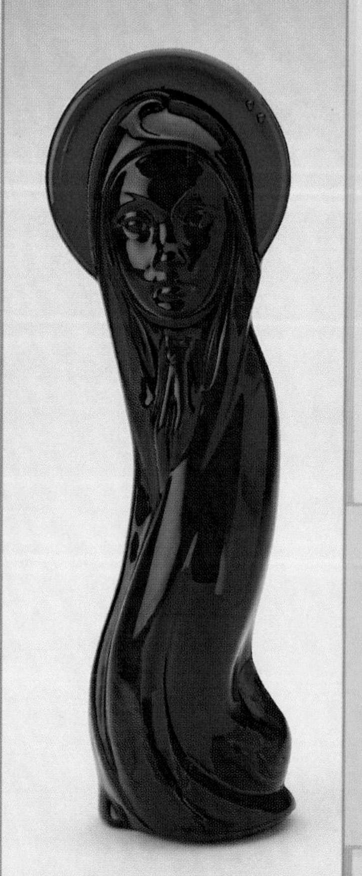

Plate 718
MOSSER GLASS COMPANY (original Heisey Glass Company mold)
#2 Madonna. Cobalt, 11" high.

This item was made in 2003 for HCA to be sold in the Heisey Museum. It is excellent quality of glass and is marked HCA, 03. Selling price in 2003 at the Museum was $65.00.

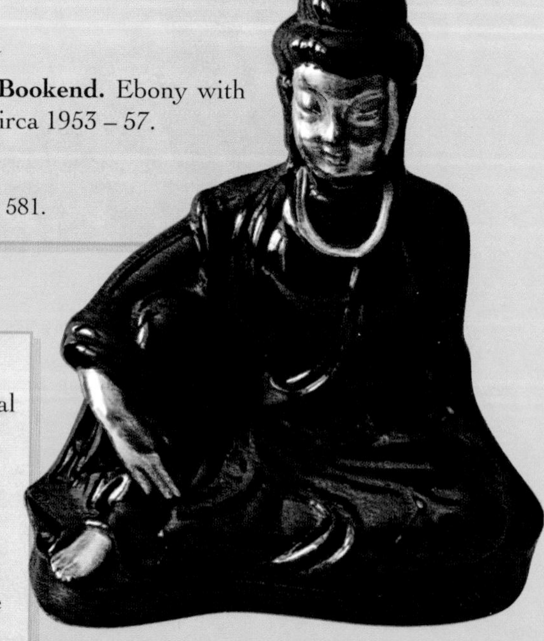

Plate 719
FOSTORIA GLASS COMPANY
#2298 Chinese "Buddha" Bookend. Ebony with gold decoration, 7½" high, circa 1953 – 57.
$500.00 – 600.00 pair

This item is also shown in Plate 581.

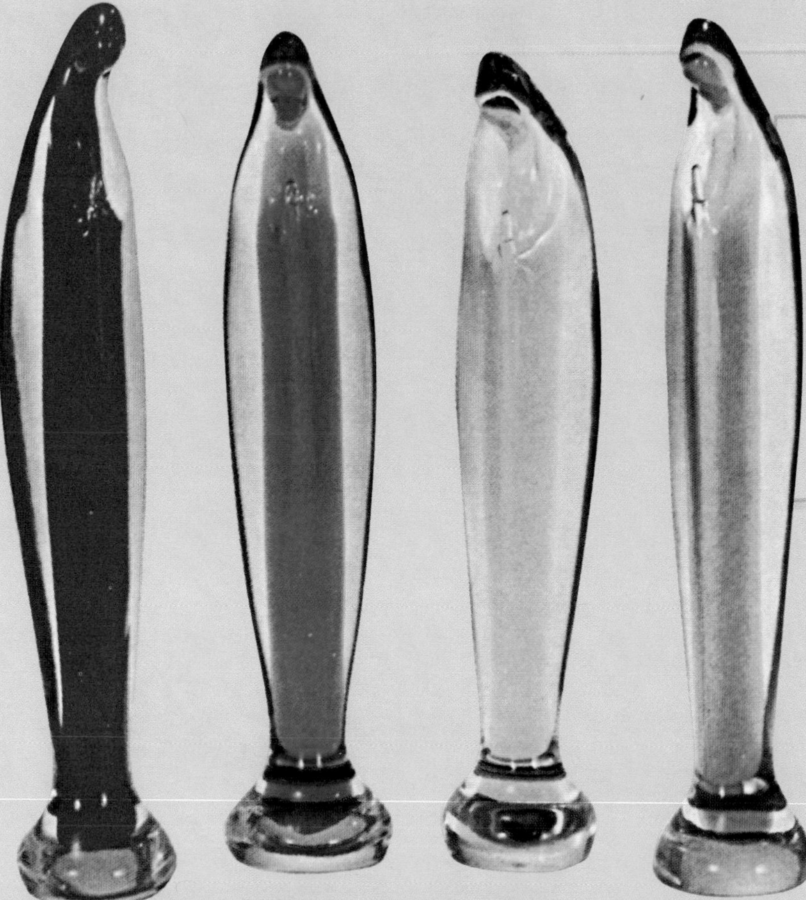

Plate 720
PILGRIM GLASS COMPANY
#999 Madonna. 13" high, circa 1976, crystal cased colors in red, blue, topaz, green, and perhaps others.
$125.00 – 150.00 each

There is an Italian version of this Madonna on the market today. This Italian Madonna has a solid halo.

Plate 721
STEUBEN GLASS WORKS
"Quan Yen" Flower Holder. Alabaster, 9¼" high, circa 1930s.
Private collection — Market

Other colors: jade and lavender.

"Quan Yen" is the Chinese equivalent of the Madonna.

Plate 722
STEUBEN GLASS WORKS
"Quan Yen" Flower Holder. Jade, 9¼" high, circa 1930s.
Private collection — Market

Other colors: lavender and alabaster (white milk).

Plate 723
Steuben Glass Works
"Quan Yen" Flower Holder. Lavender, 9¼" high, circa 1930s.
Private collection — Market

Other colors: jade and alabaster (white milk).

Plate 724
Tiffin Glass Company
Buddha Bookend. Crystal, 7½" high, circa 1949 – 52.
$250.00 – 275.00 pair.

Other colors: black, amethyst, and green.

Part of the Chinese Modern line.

Plate 725
Viking Glass Company
#7896 Madonna Bust with Crossed Hands. Crystal frosted, 6¾" high, 4¼" wide, circa 1980 – 81.
$30.00 – 35.00

Available with optional separate base with votive candleholder.

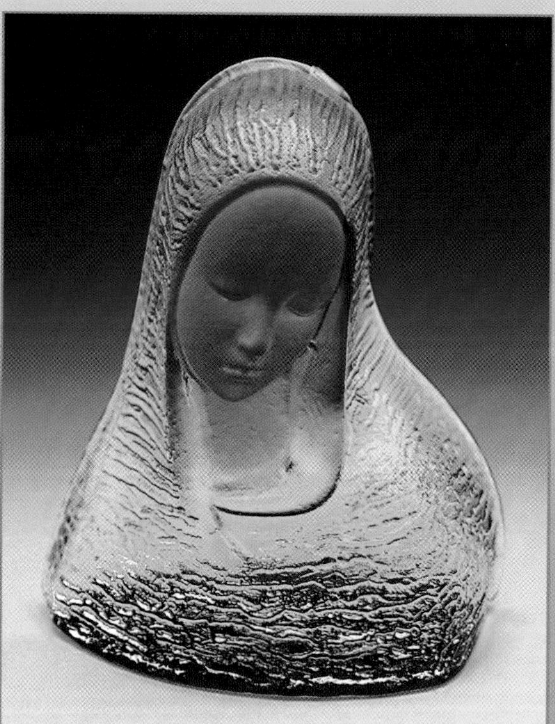

Plate 726
Viking Glass Company
#7757 Madonna Bust. Crystal, textured, 5" high, 4¼" wide, circa 1980 – 81.
$25.00 – 30.00

Available with optional separate base with votive candleholder.

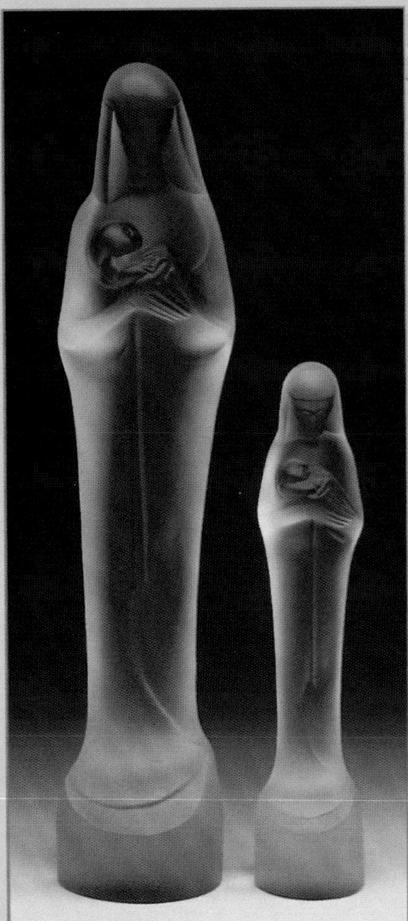

Plate 727
Foreign Manufacturer
Madonna. Crystal frosted, 15" and 9" high. Marked GUL
Seen at 15", $100.00 – 125.00; 9", $75.00 – 85.00

These Madonna figurines were thought by many to have been made by U.S. Glass because of the marks on the glass. However, they were produced by Leerdam Glass Company, Holland. They were offered with an electric lighted base. The ad shown here is from the June 1956 *China, Glass & Tablewares*.

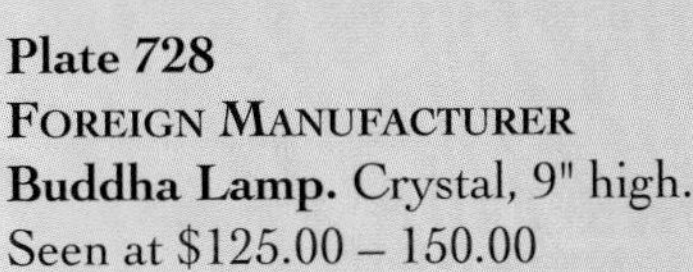

Plate 728
Foreign Manufacturer
Buddha Lamp. Crystal, 9" high.
Seen at $125.00 – 150.00

Other colors: amber and perhaps others.

There has been speculation as to the maker of these Buddha figurines, including Cambridge, U.S. Glass, and others. This Buddha has molded in the glass on the back at the bottom "Germany."

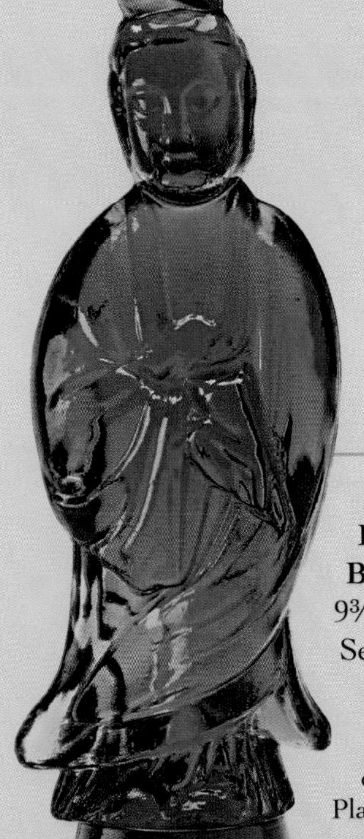

Plate 729
Foreign Manufacturer
Buddha Figure for Lamp. Amber, 9¾" high.
Seen at $200.00 – 250.00

This figurine was obviously mounted on a base for a lamp at one time. For details on the origin of this figurine, see Plate 728.

Seahorses

Plate 730
Heisey Glass Company
#5074 Seahorse Stem.
Seahorse Stem Cocktail. Amber stem, crystal bowl, 6¾" high, circa 1952.
$700.00 – 750.00

Other colors: Stem came in crystal and sultana.

#5074 Seahorse Stem Goblet. Crystal, 7½" high, circa 1952.
$750.00 – 800.00

These stems were designed by Horace King.

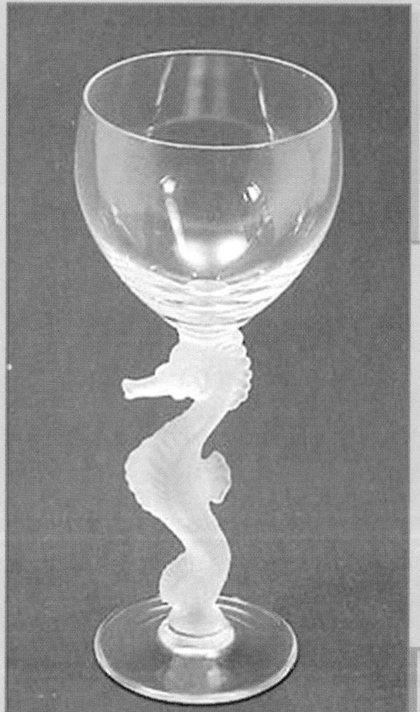

Plate 731
Foreign Manufacturer
Seahorse Stem. Crystal with frosted stem, 6⅜" high, circa pre-1980.
$40.00 – 45.00

These are often confused with American-made seahorse stems. They are Bayel Crystal, made in France. They are seen in different sizes.

Plate 732
Heisey Glass Company
Seahorse Handled Cigarette Holder. Crystal with orchid etching, 5¼" high, circa 1950.
Orchid etched, $200.00 – 225.00

This is #507 Orchid Etching on a #1519 Waverly blank. This blank also came plain and with other etchings.

Plate 733
Imperial Glass Company (original Heisey Glass Company mold)
Seahorse Handled Candy Box and Cover. Caramel slag, 5½" high, circa 1960s – 70s.
$50.00 – 70.00

Imperial did not remove the Heisey diamond-H logo before making this item, making collectors think it was produced by Heisey.

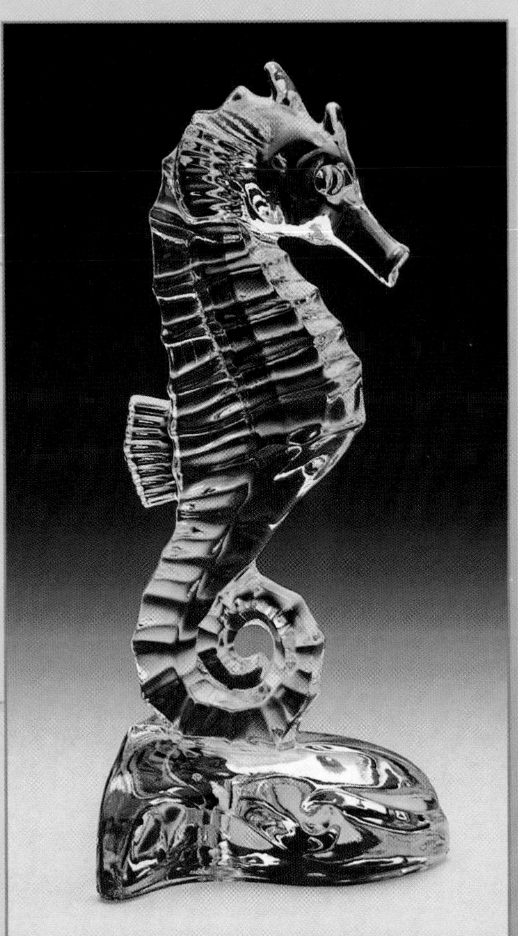

Plate 734
Fostoria Glass Company
#2641 Sea Horse Bookend. Crystal, 8" high, circa 1950 – 58.
$125.00 – 150.00

Sits on a solid base depicting waves. Sometimes confused with Sea Horse made by Paden City, see Plate 735.

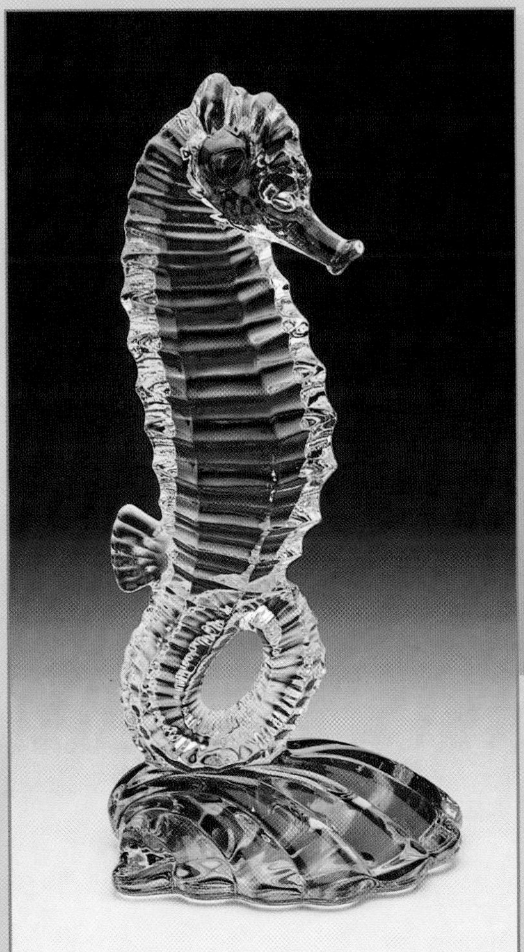

Plate 735
Paden City Glass Company
Sea Horse Book End. Crystal, 8" high.
$125.00 – 150.00

New documentation attributes this previously unknown Sea Horse to Paden City. Sometimes confused with the one produced by Fostoria. See Plate 734.

Seals

Plate 736
Fostoria Glass Company
#2531 Seal. Crystal, 3⅞" high, circa 1935 – 43.
$50.00 – 60.00

Other colors: topaz, 1935 – 36; gold tint, 1937 – 39; and silver mist 1936 – 43.

Plate 737
Fostoria Glass Company
#2531 Seal. Topaz, 3⅞" high, circa 1935 – 36.
$75.00 – 100.00

For other colors see Plate 736.

Plate 738
Viking Glass Company
Seal. Persimmon, 9¾" long.
$25.00 – 35.00

Plate 739
New Martinsville Glass Company
Seals.
#452 Seal, Large with Ball. Crystal, 7" high, circa 1938 – 51.
$65.00 – 75.00
#452 Seal, Large, with Candleholder and Janice Ivy Bowl. Crystal, 12" high, circa 1938 – 51.
Seal, $75.00 – 100.00 each
Ivy Bowl, $35.00 – 45.00
#435 Seal, Baby with Candleholder. Crystal, 4½" high.
$50.00 – 75.00 (also came with ball on nose)

Other colors: Large seals, completely frosted with clear ball, clear with ruby ball, black with ruby ivy ball. Small seal, frosted. Ivy bowl, emerald green and ruby.

Large seal (no ball or candleholder) and small seal with ball reissued by Dalzell-Viking in crystal, 1988 – 91. In the mid-1980s small seal with ball was reissued for Mirror Images in ruby plain, satin, or carnival (second in a series of five), limited edition of 500, made by Viking and marked with a "V" and "MI."

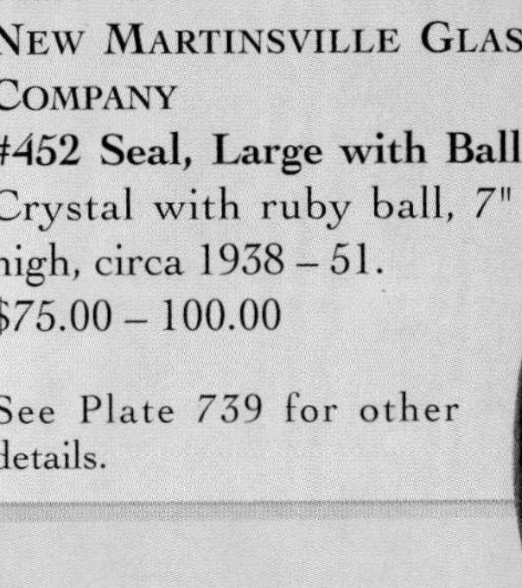

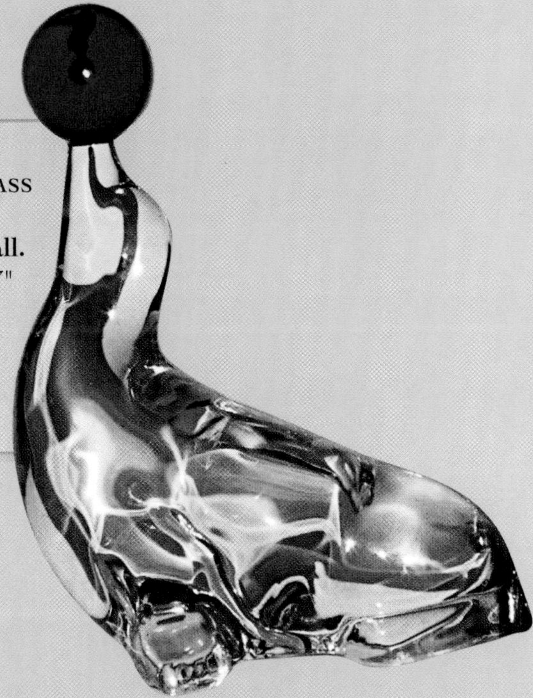

Plate 739A
New Martinsville Glass Company
#452 Seal, Large with Ball. Crystal with ruby ball, 7" high, circa 1938 – 51.
$75.00 – 100.00

See Plate 739 for other details.

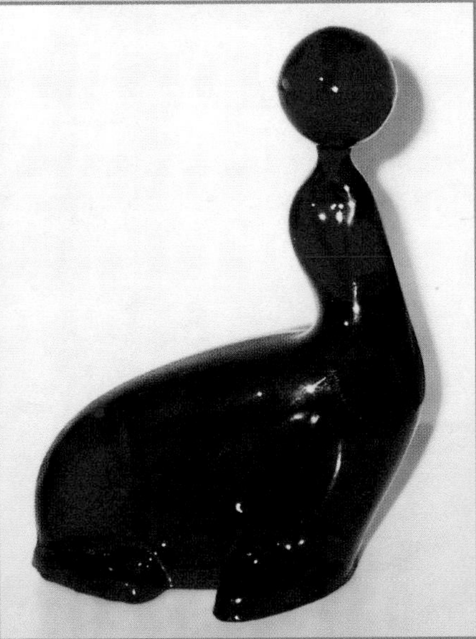

Plate 740
Viking Glass Company (original New Martinsville Glass Company mold)
Baby Seal with Ball. Ruby, 4½" high, circa mid-1980s.
$55.00 – 65.00

This was made for Mirror Images. See Plate 739.

Squirrels

Plate 741
Cambridge Glass Company
Left: **Squirrel.** Crystal, with gold tail and ruby stain body, 2" high, circa 1930 – 50.
$20.00 – 25.00

Reissues: Mosser Glass Company, in amber and green in clear and frosted colors of blue, amber, green, crystal, and cranberry.

L.E. Smith Glass Company
Right: **Squirrel.** Crystal frosted, 2" high, circa 1939 – 1980s.
$10.00 – 12.00

Reissues: In the 1980s, made for Levay Distributing Co., in purple carnival and rose pink.

The easiest way to tell the difference between the two squirrels is the base. The Cambridge base is almost round whereas the Smith base appears to be a log.

Plate 742
Fostoria Glass Company
2631/702 A and B Two-Piece Squirrel Set.
Olive green, circa 1965 – 70.
Sitting Squirrel, 3¼" high.
$25.00 – 30.00
Running Squirrel, 2½" high.
$25.00 – 30.00

Other colors: original issue crystal 1950 – 58, cobalt 1965 – 70, olive green and amber (plain or frosted), 1965 – 73.

Plate 743
Fostoria Glass Company
Two-Piece Squirrel Set. Amber, circa 1965 – 73.
Sitting Squirrel, 3¼" high.
$25.00 – 30.00
Running Squirrel, 2½" high.
$25.00 – 30.00

See Plate 742.

Plate 744
Fostoria Glass Company
Two-Piece Squirrel Set. Crystal, 1950 – 58; Cobalt, 1965 – 70.
Sitting Squirrel, 3¼" high.
$25.00 – 30.00
Running Squirrel, 2½" high.
$25.00 – 30.00

See Plate 742.

Plate 745
Kanawha Glass Company
Offhand Squirrel. Amber, 3½" high, circa 1970s.
$10.00 – 12.00

Other colors: crystal, crystal frosted, green, and probably others.

Plate 746
New Martinsville Glass Company
#674 Squirrel. Crystal, 4½" high, no base until 1953.
$65.00 – 75.00
#670 Squirrel. Crystal, 5½" high, rectangular base, until 1953.
$50.00 – 60.00

Other colors: crystal frosted on clear base and in light blue.

Plate 747
Paden City Glass Company
#677 Squirrel on Curved Log. Crystal, 5½" high.
$50.00 – 60.00

Reissues: Dalzell-Viking in crystal, 1990 – 91.

This was a Barth Art mold.

Plate 748
New Martinsville Glass Company
Comparison of **Squirrels.**
Left and right: New Martinsville Squirrel on Rectangular Base, crystal frosted, 4½" high.
$65.00 – 75.00 each
Center: Barth Art Mold Squirrel on Curved Log, crystal, 5½" high.
$50.00 – 60.00

Plate 749
L.E. Smith Glass Company
Squirrel. Crystal frosted, 4½" high, circa 1970s.
$18.00 – 22.00

Other colors: original issue in crystal.

This is the larger of the two squirrels produced by L.E. Smith. For the smaller squirrel see Plate 741.

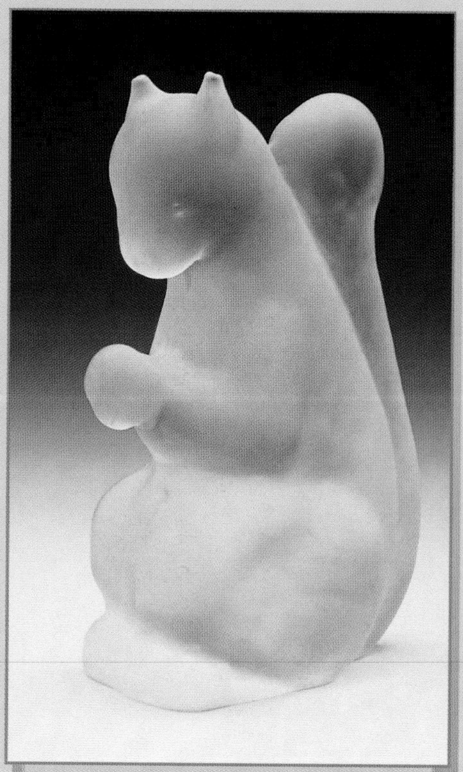

Plate 750
Unknown Manufacturer
Squirrel. Crystal frosted, 4" high.
Seen at $10.00 – 12.00

This squirrel is very similar to the L.E. Smith squirrel (Plate 749), except this squirrel has a different base and is wider and ½" shorter.

Plate 751
Viking Glass Company
Squirrel. Crystal satin, 5" high, 4¾" wide, circa 1980 – 81.
$15.00 – 20.00

Other colors: crystal.

Plate 752
Unknown Manufacturer
Squirrel. Crystal, 2" high, probably 1930s.
Seen at $8.00 – 10.00

This squirrel has some similarities to the 2" squirrel produced by L.E. Smith. When seen it is generally labeled "Smith."

Starfish

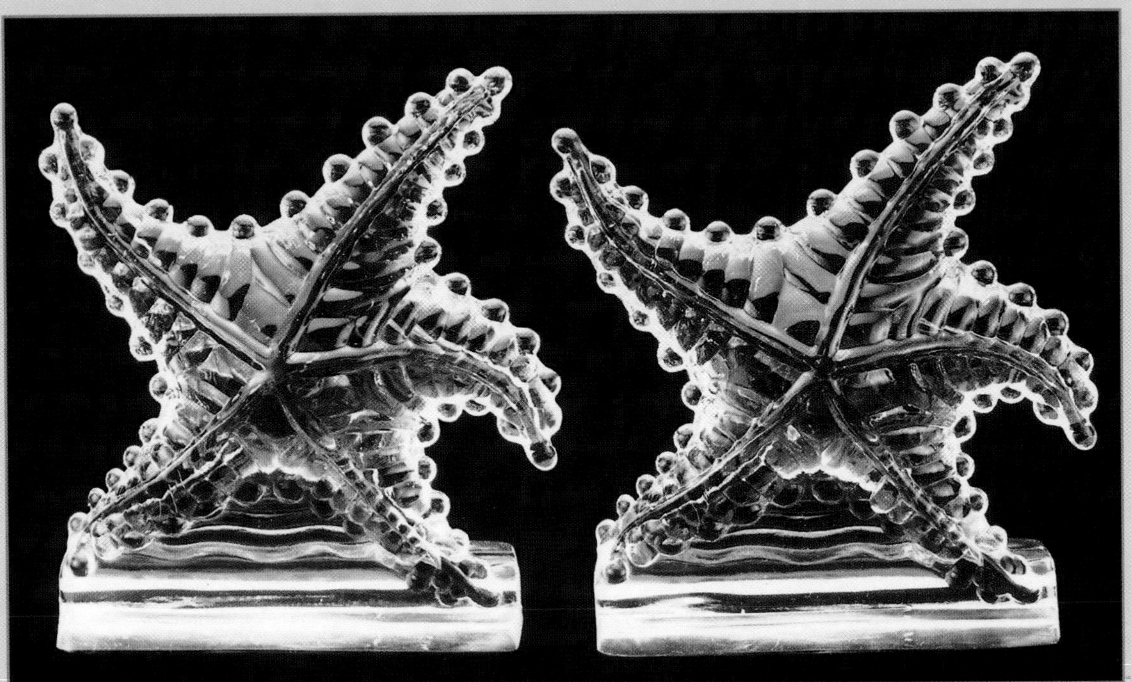

Plate 753
Paden City Glass Company
Starfish Bookends. Crystal, 7¾" high, circa 1939.
$200.00 – 225.00 pair

These were previously attributed to New Martinsville; however, documentation shows that they were originally Paden City molds.

Plate 754
Westmoreland Glass Company
#1063 Starfish Candleholders. Almond, 5" wide.
$45.00 – 55.00 pair

Other colors: crystal mist, milk glass, antique blue mist, almond, antique blue clear, and milk glass mother-of-pearl.

All colors scarce. Manufactured with the dolphin line.

Swans

Measurements reflected for the following Cambridge Swans are given in the sizes that the factory advertised as production sizes, although there are sometimes slight variations which are commonly found in handmade glassware. The following Cambridge Swans are pictured by color rather than by style.

Plate 755
Cambridge Glass Company
Swans. Crystal.
14", $450.00 – 500.00
6½", $55.00 – 65.00
4½", $35.00 – 45.00
3", $25.00 – 35.00

Plate 756
Cambridge Glass Company
Swans. Crystal.
10½", $95.00 – 115.00
6½", $55.00 – 65.00

Plate 757
Cambridge Glass Company
Swan. Sun purpled, 8½".
$45.00 – 50.00

This color is often confused with Cambridge Heatherbloom, a color which Cambridge did not use for swans.

Plate 758
CAMBRIDGE GLASS COMPANY
Swans. Crystal satin decorated.
10½", $175.00 – 200.00
3", $45.00 – 55.00 each

Plate 759
CAMBRIDGE GLASS COMPANY
Swan Candleholders. Crystal, 5".
$125.00 – 145.00 pair

Plate 760
CAMBRIDGE GLASS COMPANY
Swan, Removable Candleholders.
Crystal, 5".
$150.00 – 175.00 pair

Plate 761
IMPERIAL GLASS COMPANY (original Cambridge Glass Company mold)
Swan. Cranberry stain, 6½".
$45.00 – 55.00

Imperial reissued swans in 6½", 8½", and 10" sizes, in crystal, crystal satin, and cranberry satin.

Plate 762
Cambridge Glass Company
Swan Punch Bowl and Cups. Crystal.
Punch Bowl, 16", $1,500.00 – 1,700.00
Punch Cup, 3", $75.00 – 85.00 each

Plate 763
Cambridge Glass Company
Swan Punch Bowl, Base, and Cups. Crystal.
Punch Bowl, 16".
$1,500.00 – 1,700.00
Punch Cups, 3".
$75.00 – 85.00 each
Base, $250.00 – 300.00

Plate 764
Cambridge Glass Company
Swans. Dianthus (peach blo).
8½", $145.00 – 165.00
3, $55.00 – 65.00

Plate 765
Cambridge Glass Company
Swans. Forest green.
8½", $175.00 – 200.00
3", $55.00 – 65.00

Plate 766
Cambridge Glass Company
Swans. Light emerald.
10½", $200.00 – 225.00
4½", $125.00 – 145.00
3", $65.00 – 75.00

Plate 767
Cambridge Glass Company
Swans. Ebony.
10½", $300.00 – 325.00
8½", $250.00 – 275.00

Plate 768
Cambridge Glass Company
Swans. Carmen.
8½", $325.00 – 350.00
6½", $250.00 – 275.00

Plate 769
Cambridge Glass Company
Swans. Crown tuscan.
8½", $125.00 – 145.00
3", $35.00 – 45.00

Plate 770
Cambridge Glass Company
Swans. Milk glass.
6½", $100.00 – 125.00
4½", $65.00 – 85.00

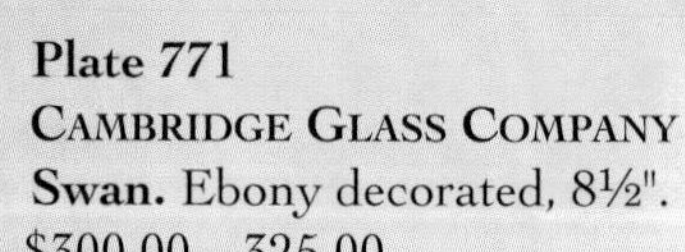

Plate 771
Cambridge Glass Company
Swan. Ebony decorated, 8½".
$300.00 – 325.00

This swan is ebony and has had a gold decoration applied.

Plate 771A
Cambridge Glass Company
Swan. Gold krystol. 8½".
$225.00 – 250.00

Plate 772
Summit Art Glass Company (original Cambridge Glass Company mold)
Swan. Chocolate glass, 8½".
$35.00 – 45.00

Plate 773
Summit Art Glass Company (original Cambridge Glass Company mold)
Swan. Amberina, 6½".
$35.00 – 45.00

Plate 774
Summit Art Glass Company (original Cambridge Glass Company mold)
Swan. Light blue, 5½".
$35.00 – 45.00

Often seen with a dealer tag stating "Cambridge."

Plate 775
DUNCAN GLASS COMPANY
Sylvan Spread-Wings Swans. Produced in blue opalescent, yellow opalescent, pink opalescent, crystal, and crystal with flashing or stains. See Plates 776, 777, 778, 779, and 780.

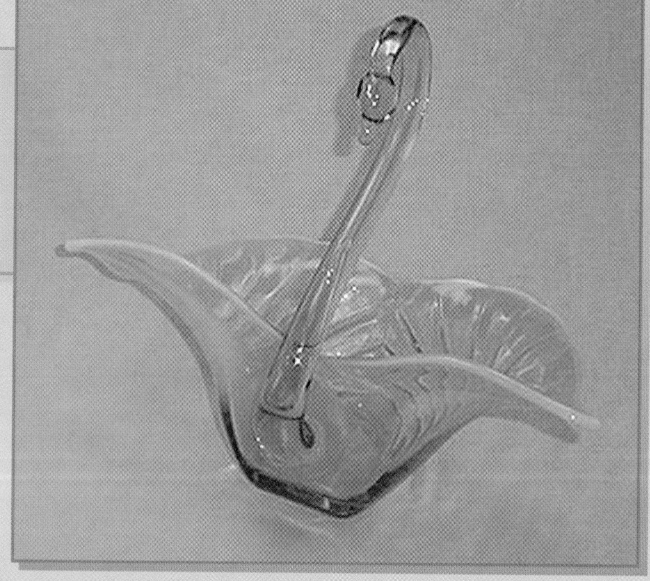

Plate 776
DUNCAN GLASS COMPANY
Sylvan Spread-Wing Swan. Blue opalescent, 12" wide, 10" high.
$265.00 – 285.00

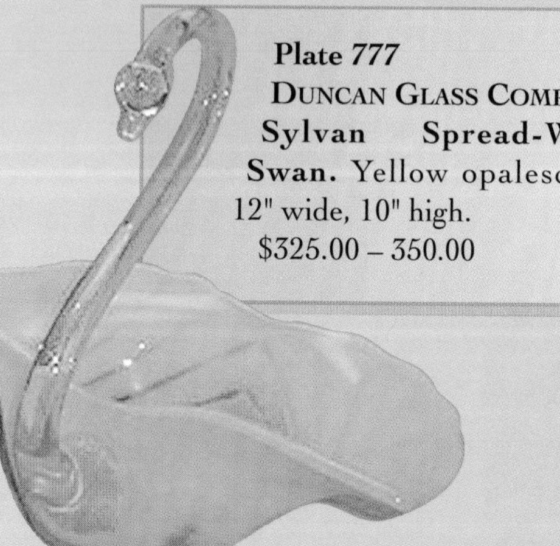

Plate 777
DUNCAN GLASS COMPANY
Sylvan Spread-Wing Swan. Yellow opalescent, 12" wide, 10" high.
$325.00 – 350.00

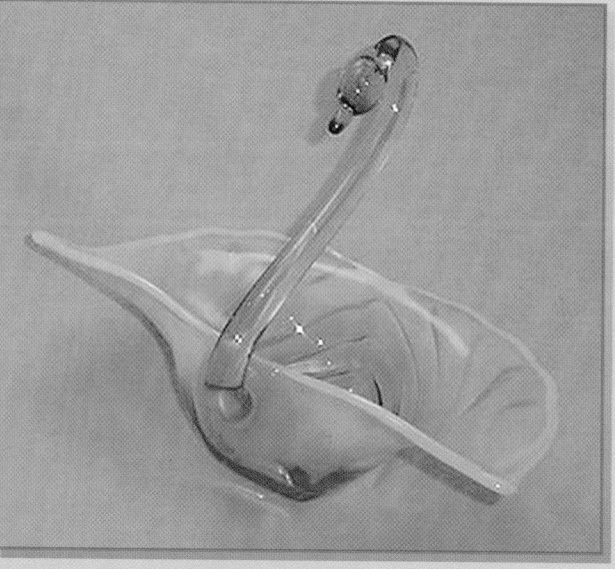

Plate 778
DUNCAN GLASS COMPANY
Sylvan Spread-Wing Swan. Pink opalescent, 12" wide, 10" high.
$265.00 – 285.00

Plate 779
DUNCAN GLASS COMPANY
Sylvan Spread-Wing Swan.
Ruby stain, 12" wide, 10" high.
$150.00 – 185.00

Plate 780
DUNCAN GLASS COMPANY
Sylvan Spread-Wing Swans.
Left: crystal, 12" wide, 10" high.
$75.00 – 95.00
Right: crystal, 8" wide, 8" high.
$75.00 – 85.00

This appears to be the mold Duncan used to create or used as a model to create the Siamese Swan shown in Plate 786.

Plate 781
Sylvan Spread-Wing Swan comparison
Left: **DUNCAN GLASS COMPANY.** Pink opalescent, 12" wide, 10" high.
$265.00 – 285.00
Right: **CZECHOSLOVAKIAN.** Has a label "Made in Czechoslovakia." Wing span will vary between 11" and 13" wide. Is generally 10" high but will vary. Note that the heads are different, wing shapes are different and the Duncan body is larger.
$65.00 – 85.00

Plate 782
Spread-Wing Swan Comparison
Left: **DUNCAN GLASS COMPANY.** Crystal, 12" wide, 10" high, $75.00 – 95.00
Right: Label "Made in Czechoslovakia." Crystal, 11" wide, 7½" high, $35.00 – 45.00

The same difference exists in the crystal swans as in color. See Plate 781.

Plate 783
FOREIGN MANUFACTURER
Spread-Wing Swan. Green opalescent, 13" wide, 9½" high.
$65.00 – 85.00

Has a label "Made in Czechoslovakia." There is no documentation that Duncan ever made spread-wing swans in this color. Most of these swans are labeled "Duncan" by vendors.

Plate 784
TIFFIN GLASS COMPANY (original Duncan Glass Company mold)
Spread-Wing Swan. Plum, 12" wide, 10" high.
$145.00 – 165.00

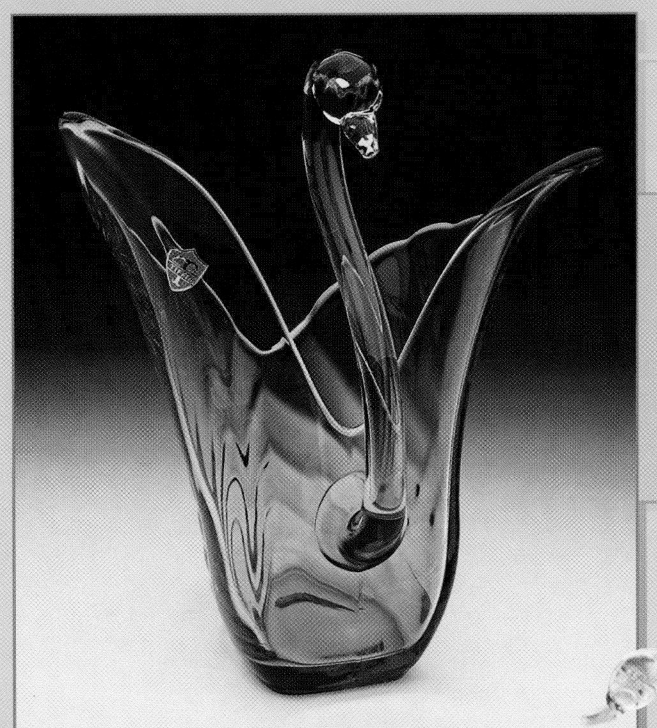

Plate 785
TIFFIN GLASS COMPANY (original Duncan Glass Company mold)
Spread-Wing Swing Vase. Wisteria, 10" high, 9" wide (wing span).
$200.00 – 225.00

After the swan came out of the mold, the wings were pulled up creating the vase.

Plate 786
DUNCAN GLASS COMPANY
Siamese Swan. Crystal, 8½" long, 8" high, 7" wide.
$500.00 – 550.00

Very scarce. Reportedly was private mold work for Weil-Freeman Company, New York.

Plate 787
DUNCAN GLASS COMPANY
Sylvan Swans. Pink opalescent.
12", $200.00 – 225.00
7½", $95.00 – 100.00
5½", $85.00 – 95.00

Plate 788
DUNCAN GLASS COMPANY
Sylvan Swans. Yellow opalescent.
12", $350.00 – 375.00
7½", $225.00 – 250.00
5½", $165.00 – 175.00

Plate 789
DUNCAN GLASS COMPANY
Sylvan Swans. Blue opalescent.
12", $200.00 – 225.00
7½", $100.00 – 125.00
5½", $75.00 – 85.00

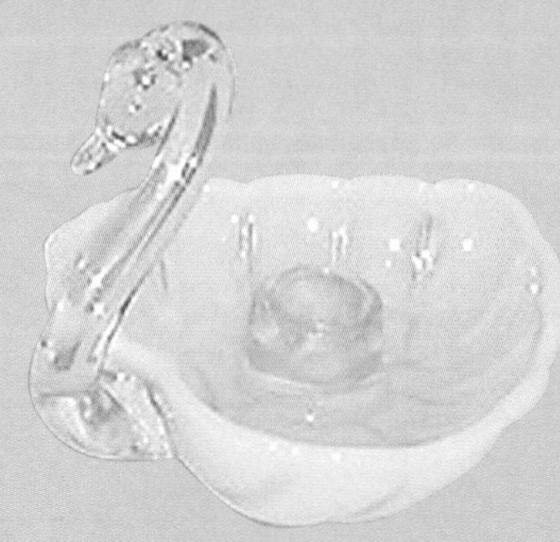

Plate 790
DUNCAN GLASS COMPANY
Sylvan Swan Candleholders. Pink opalescent, 5½".
$135.00 – 150.00 each

Plate 791
DUNCAN GLASS COMPANY
Sylvan Swan Candlehold-er. Crystal, 5½".
$75.00 – 85.00 each

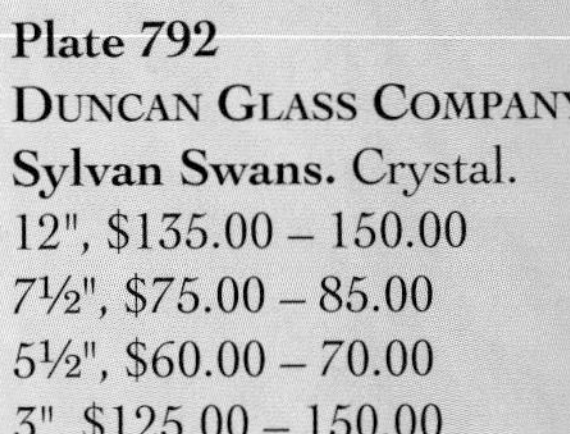

Plate 792
DUNCAN GLASS COMPANY
Sylvan Swans. Crystal.
12", $135.00 – 150.00
7½", $75.00 – 85.00
5½", $60.00 – 70.00
3", $125.00 – 150.00

Plate 793
DUNCAN GLASS COMPANY
Sylvan Swans, "Snake Head." Crystal.
12", $165.00 – 185.00
7½", $125.00 – 150.00
5½", $100.00 – 120.00
3", $150.00 – 175.00

Plate 794
Duncan Glass Company
Sylvan Swan Candy Box and Cover. Crystal, 7½".
$175.00 – 185.00

Plate 795
Duncan Glass Company
Pall Mall Swans. Crystal with frosted neck and head.
7", $85.00 – 95.00
3½", $125.00 – 135.00
Crystal with Frosted Neck and Crystal Head. 3½".
$150.00 – 175.00

Plate 796
Duncan Glass Company
Pall Mall Swan Candleholder. Crystal, 7".
$35.00 – 50.00

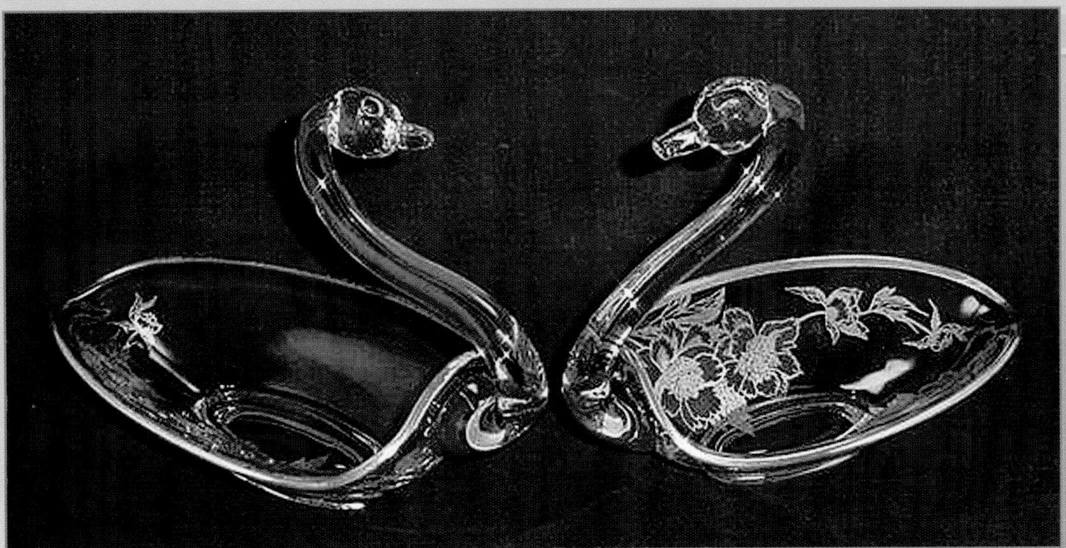

Plate 797
DUNCAN GLASS COMPANY
Pall Mall Swans. Crystal with silver overlay.
Left: Overlay one side, 7".
$85.00 – 95.00
Right: Overlay both sides, 7".
$90.00 – 100.00

Plate 798
DUNCAN GLASS COMPANY
Pall Mall Swan. Crystal with logo, 3½", rare.
$550.00 – 600.00

"Genuine Duncan" imprint on bottom.

Plate 799
DUNCAN GLASS COMPANY
Pall Mall Swans. Crystal with cuttings.
Left to right:
Star Cutting, 6", $75.00 – 85.00
Wing Feather Cutting, 7", $85.00 – 95.00
Floral Cutting, 7", $75.00 – 85.00

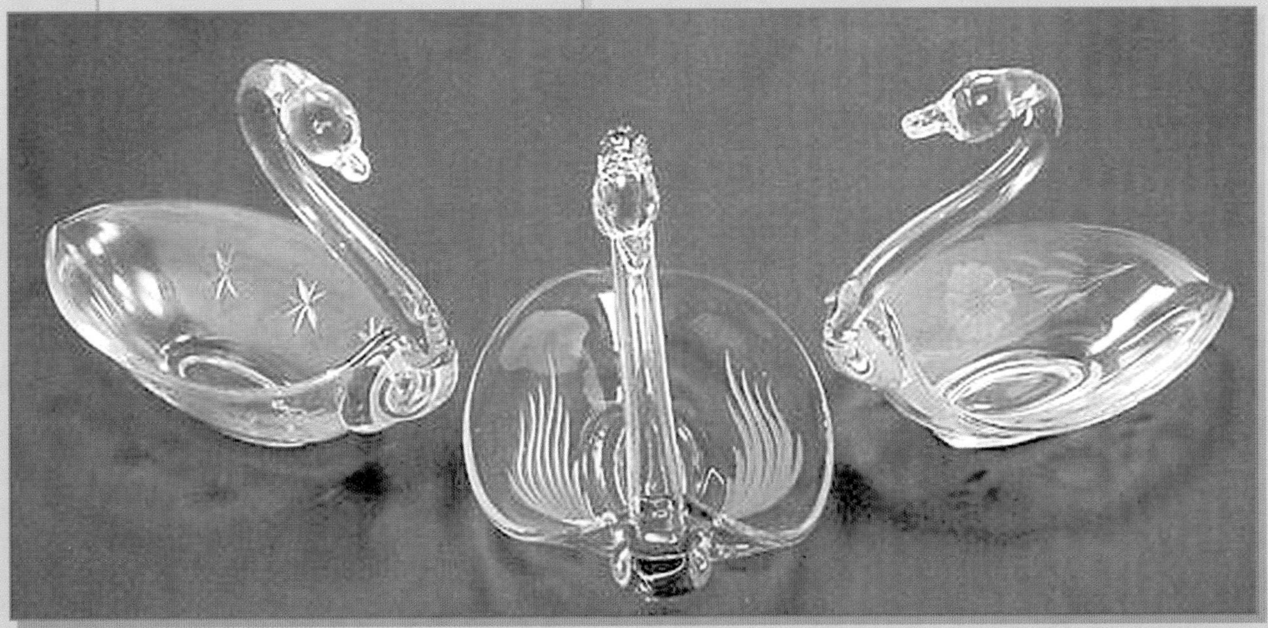

Plate 800
DUNCAN GLASS COMPANY
Pall Mall Swans. Yellow body, crystal neck and head.
10½", $185.00 – 200.00
7", $155.00 – 170.00
3½", $250.00 – 275.00

Plate 801
DUNCAN GLASS COMPANY
Pall Mall Swans. Chartreuse, total swan.
12", $150.00 – 185.00
10½", $90.00 – 100.00
7", $65.00 – 75.00
3½", $95.00 – 100.00

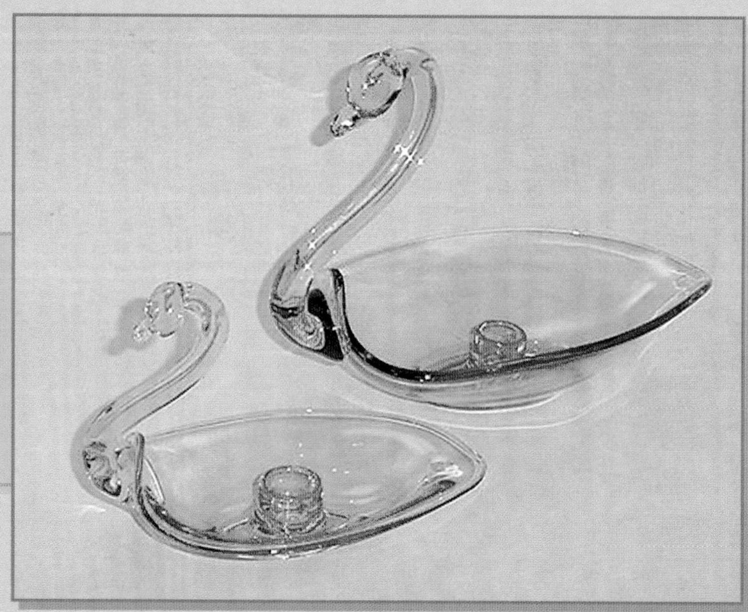

Plate 802
DUNCAN GLASS COMPANY
Pall Mall Swan Candleholders. Chartreuse, total swan.
10½", $75.00 – 85.00
7", $65.00 – 75.00

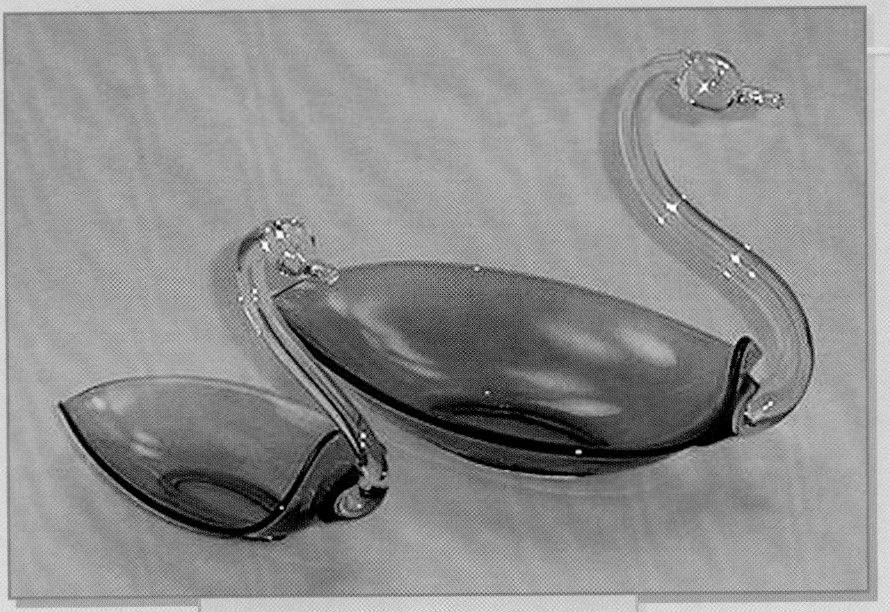

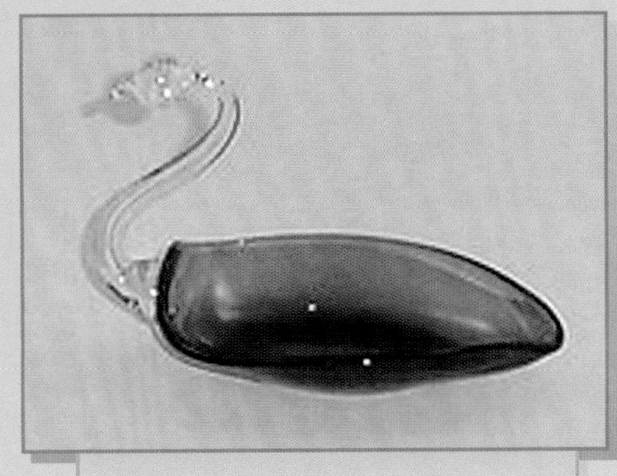

Plate 803
DUNCAN GLASS COMPANY
Pall Mall Swans. Smoky avocado body with crystal neck and head.
10½", $200.00 – 250.00
7", $85.00 – 95.00

Plate 804
DUNCAN GLASS COMPANY
Pall Mall Swan. Teakwood, 3½".
$250.00 – 300.00

Plate 805
DUNCAN GLASS COMPANY
Pall Mall Swan. Teakwood, 7".
$165.00 – 185.00

Plate 806
DUNCAN GLASS COMPANY
Pall Mall Swans. Ruby body, crystal head, and neck.
12", $150.00 – 200.00
10½", $95.00 – 100.00
7", $65.00 – 75.00
3½", $100.00 – 135.00

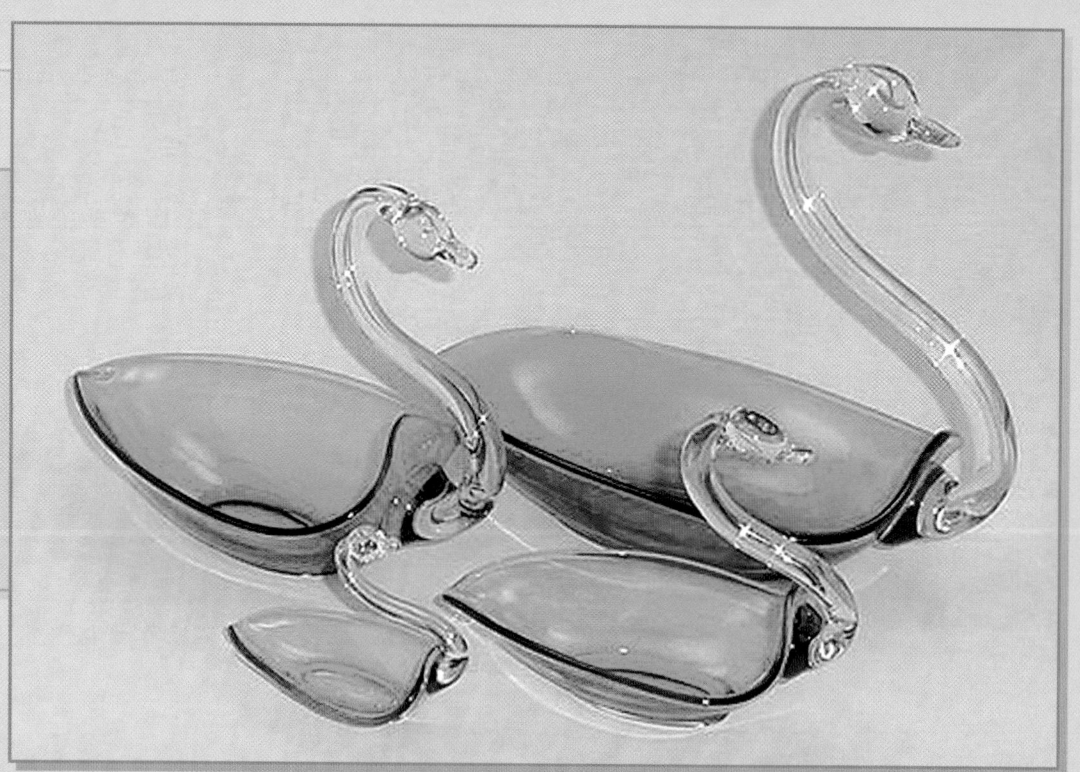

Plate 807
Duncan Glass Company
Pall Mall Swans. Emerald green body, crystal head, and neck.
12", $260.00 – 300.00
10½", $85.00 – 100.00
7", $70.00 – 90.00
3½", $250.00 – 300.00

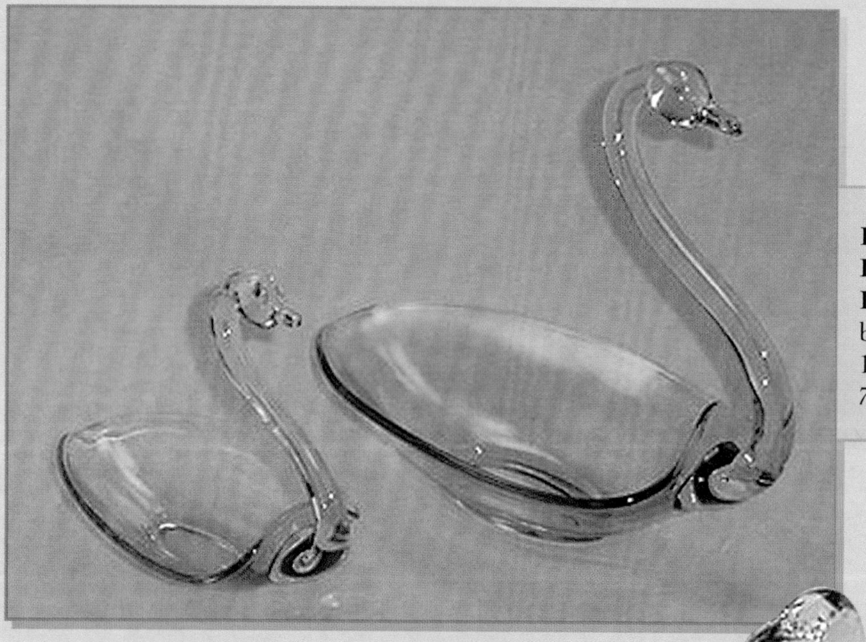

Plate 808
Duncan Glass Company
Pall Mall Swans. Ice blue body, crystal head and neck.
10½", $200.00 – 250.00
7", $165.00 – 185.00

Plate 809
Duncan Glass Company
Pall Mall Swan Candleholders. Ruby with crystal head and neck.
10½", $90.00 – 100.00
7", $75.00 – 85.00 each

Plate 810
DUNCAN GLASS COMPANY
Pall Mall Swan. Ruby body with crystal head and neck, silver overlay, 7".
$250.00 – 300.00

Plate 811
DUNCAN GLASS COMPANY
Pall Mall Swan. Ruby flashed with cutting, 6".
$135.00 – 150.00

Plate 812
DUNCAN GLASS COMPANY
Pall Mall Swans. Milk glass body with green head and neck.
10½", $350.00 – 400.00
7", $325.00 – 375.00

Plate 813
DUNCAN GLASS COMPANY
Pall Mall Swans.
Left: Milk glass body with ruby head and neck, 7".
$325.00 – 375.00
Right: Milk glass entire swan, 7".
$325.00 – 375.00

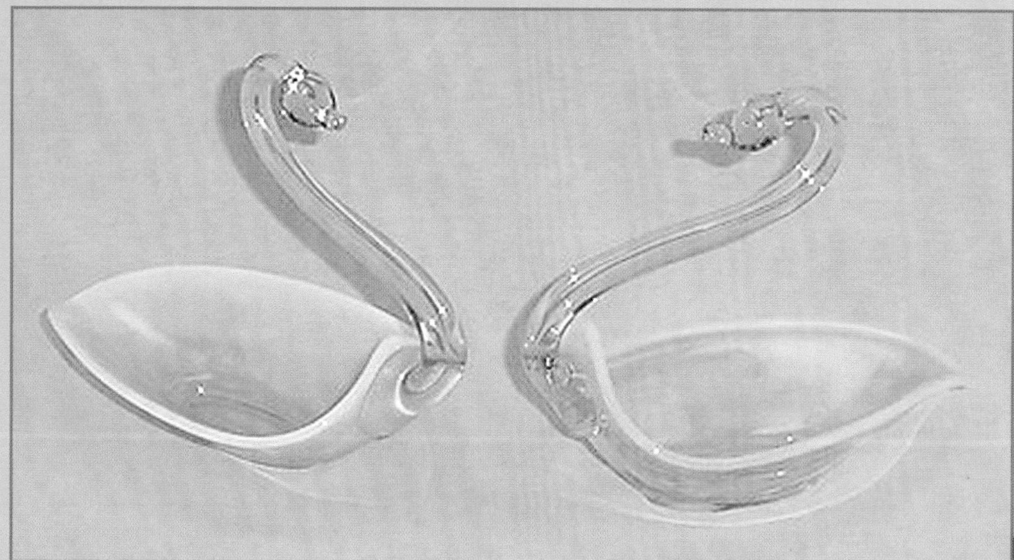

Plate 814
Duncan Glass Company
Pall Mall Swans.
Left: Blue opalescent, 7".
$250.00 – 300.00
Right: Pink opalescent, 7".
$250.00 – 300.00

Plate 815
Duncan Glass Company
Pall Mall Swan. Crystal body with red cased head and neck, 6½".
Private collection – Market

This is a very rare swan. Perhaps one of a kind.

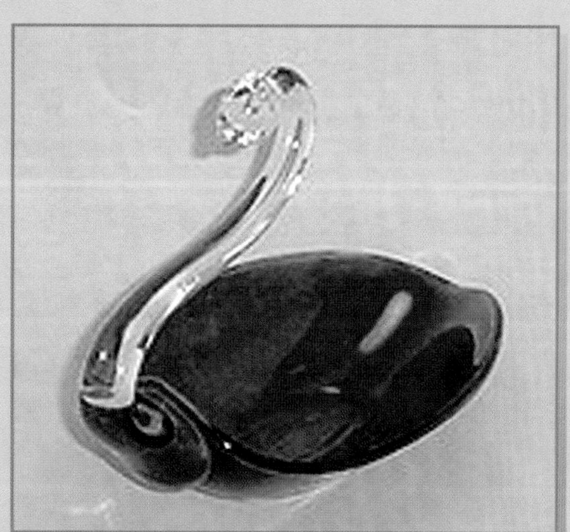

Plate 816
Duncan Glass Company
Pall Mall Swan. Ruby flashed body, crystal head and neck, 7".
$80.00 – 90.00

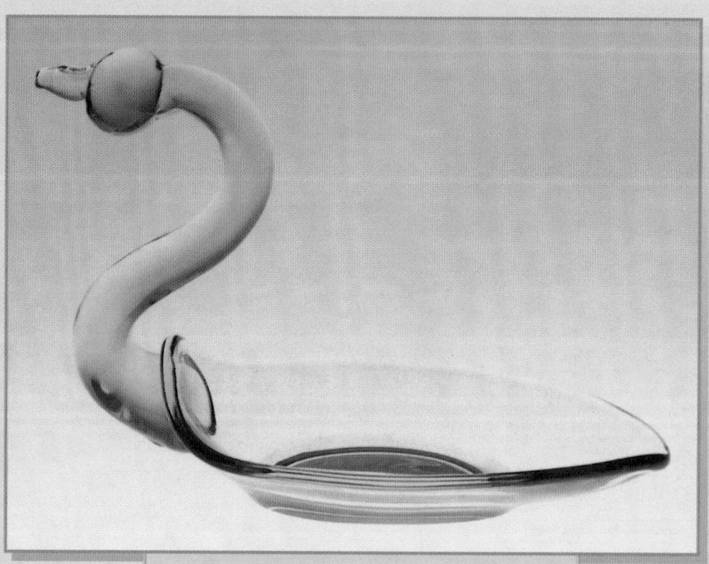

Plate 817
Tiffin Glass Company (original Duncan Glass Company mold)
Open Back Swan. Copen blue, 7".
$55.00 – 65.00

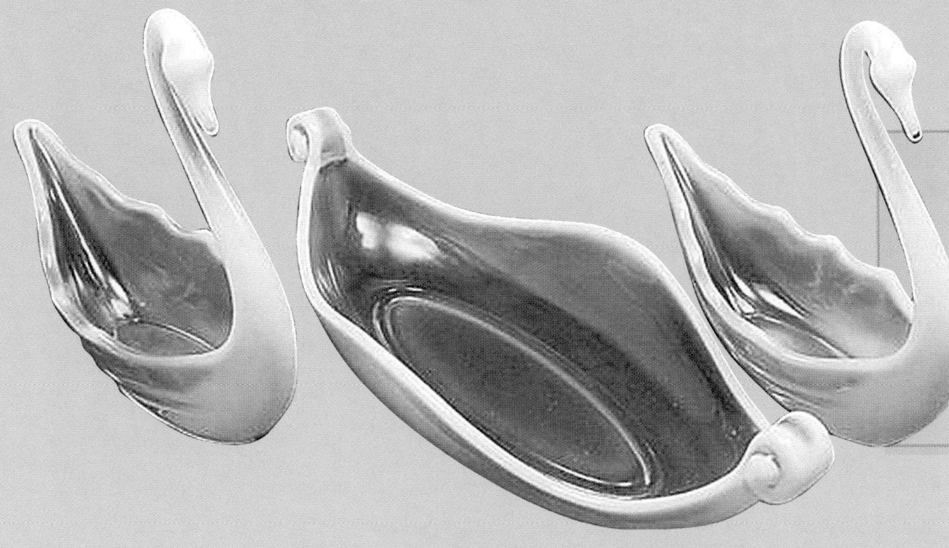

Plate 818
DUNCAN GLASS COMPANY
Viking Swan Console Set.
Blue opalescent.
Bowl: 14" long, $95.00 – 105.00
Swan: 7½" high, 8½" long, $225.00 – 250.00 each

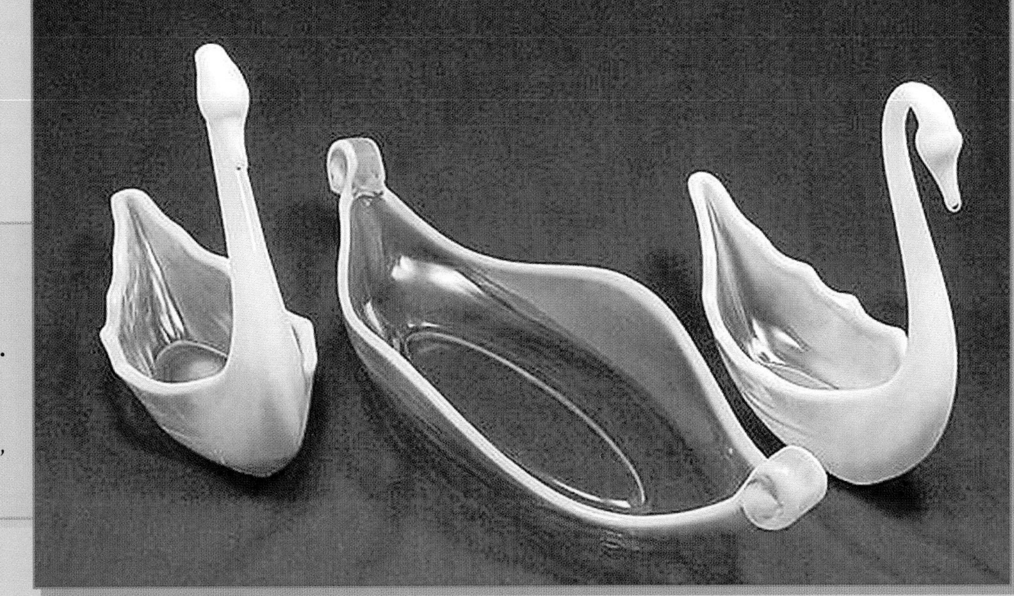

Plate 819
DUNCAN GLASS COMPANY
Viking Swan Console Set.
Pink opalescent.
Bowl: 14" long, $95.00 – 105.00
Swan: 7½" high, 8½" long, $235.00 – 255.00 each

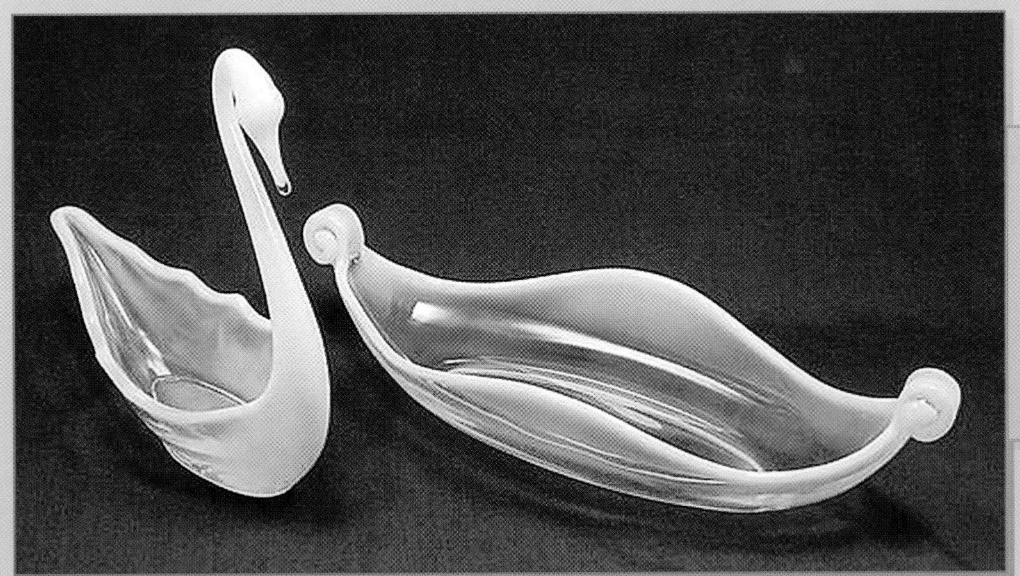

Plate 820
DUNCAN GLASS COMPANY
Viking Swan Console Set.
Yellow opalescent.
Bowl, 14" long, $125.00 – 150.00
Swan, 7½" high, 8½" long, $300.00 – 350.00 each

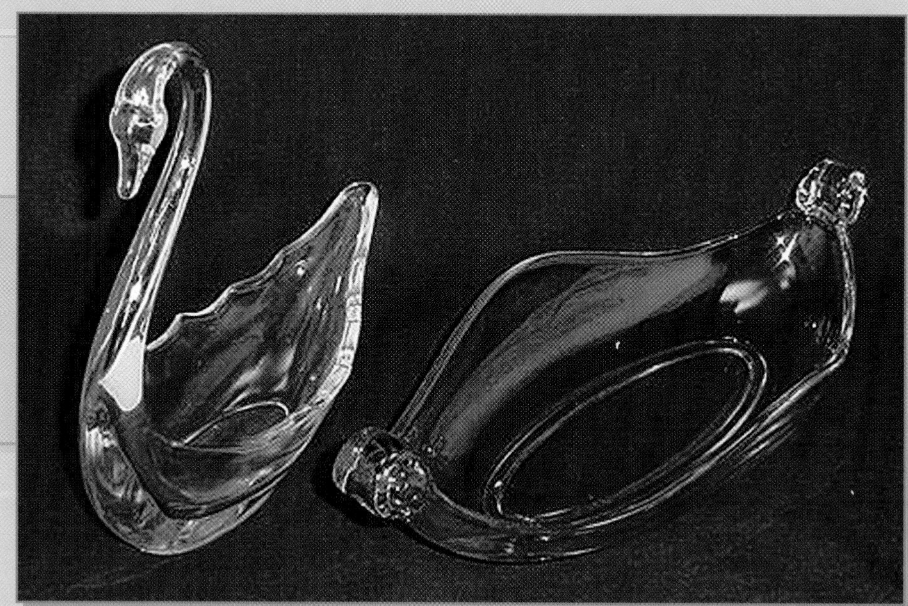

Plate 821
DUNCAN GLASS COMPANY
Viking Swan Console Set. Crystal.
Bowl, 14" long, $45.00 – 55.00
Swan, 7½" high, 8½" long, $140.00 – 150.00

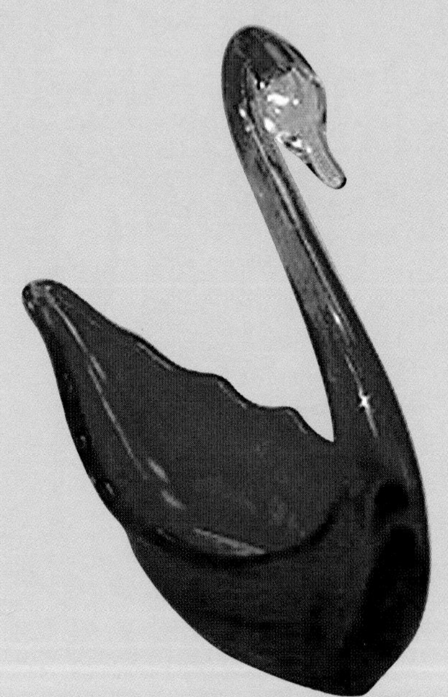

Plate 822
DUNCAN GLASS COMPANY
Viking Swans. Ruby flashed, 7½" high, 8½" long.
$265.00 – 285.00 each

Plate 823
UNKNOWN MANUFACTURER
Viking Type Swan. Light blue, 8" high, 7" long.
Seen at $40.00 – 50.00

An unconfirmed story had it that this was a private mold and was poured at the Duncan factory.

Plate 824
UNKNOWN MANUFACTURER
Swan Flower Arranger. Crystal, 10½" high.
$65.00 – 75.00

These Swan Flower Arrangers have some characteristics of the Duncan swans; however, we have found no documentation that would confirm their being Duncan. They were originally thought to be private mold work performed at the Duncan factory, but there again this cannot be confirmed.

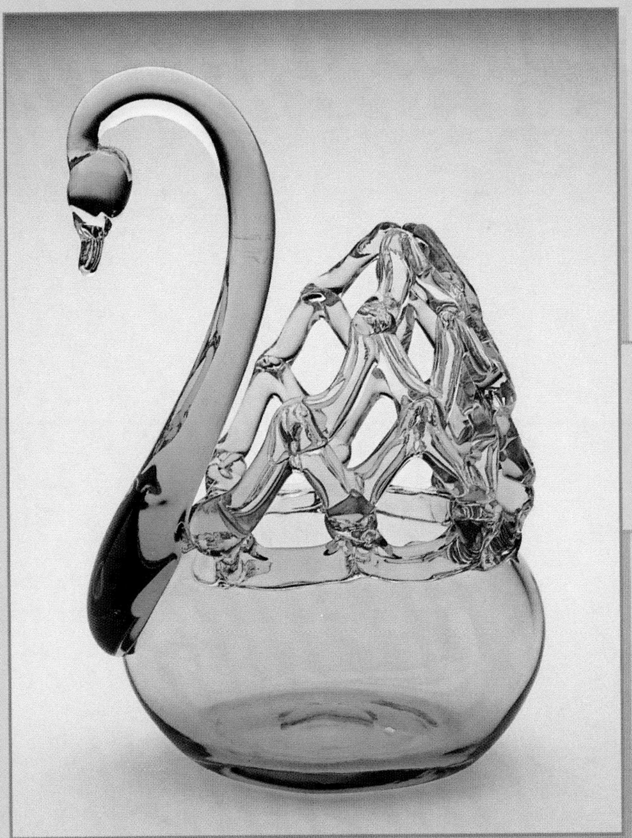

Plate 825
UNKNOWN MANUFACTURER
Swan Flower Arranger. Green, 7½" high.
$75.00 – 85.00

Plate 826
Duncan Glass Company
Pall Mall Solid Black Swans. Crystal.
3", $25.00 – 35.00
5", $45.00 – 55.00
7", $100.00 – 125.00

Solid glass, most often seen in crystal; however, they have been seen in crystal satin and have been reported with colored heads and necks.

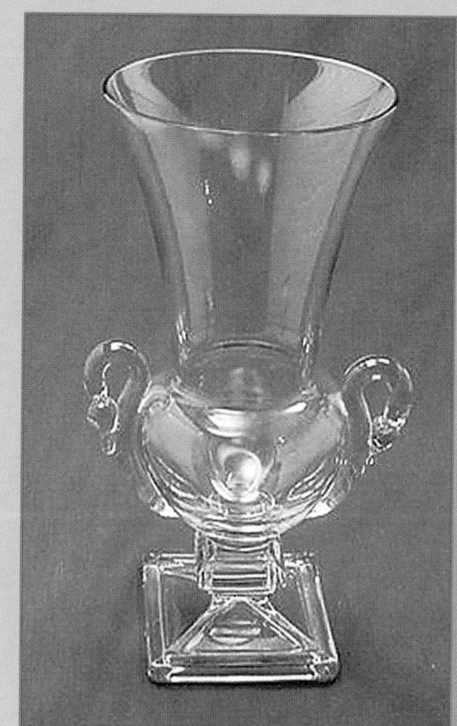

Plate 827
Duncan Glass Company
Grecian Urn with Swan Handles. Crystal, 9½" high.
$350.00 – 400.00

Plate 828
Duncan Glass Company
Three Swan Vase. Crystal, 9" high, circa 1930s.
$300.00 – 325.00

Other colors: cobalt, green, amber, and milk glass.

Reissues: Imperial Glass Company made some alterations to the mold and then produced them in iridescent colors.

Plate 829
Duncan Glass Company
Three Swan Vase. Milk glass, 9" high, circa 1930s. This item is very rare.
Private collection — Market

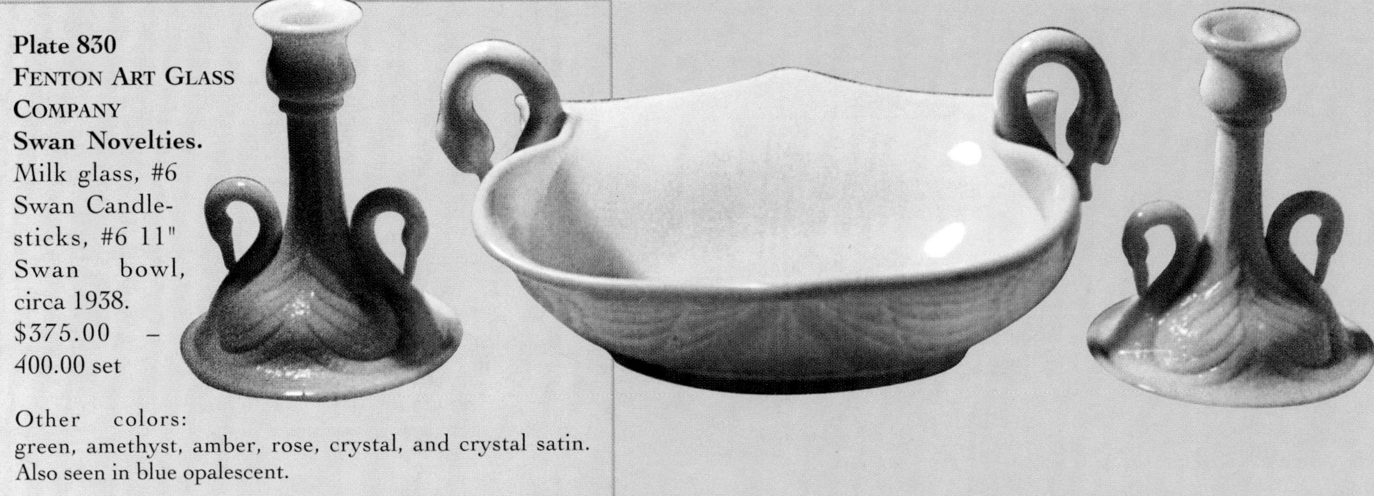

Plate 830
Fenton Art Glass Company
Swan Novelties. Milk glass, #6 Swan Candlesticks, #6 11" Swan bowl, circa 1938. $375.00 – 400.00 set

Other colors: green, amethyst, amber, rose, crystal, and crystal satin. Also seen in blue opalescent.

Plate 831
Fenton Art Glass Company
#6 Swan Bowl. Green, 7½" long, circa 1938.
$25.00 – 30.00
#6 Swan Bowl. Crystal satin, 5½" long, circa 1938.
$22.00 – 25.00

Fenton acquired these swan molds from the Dugan Glass Company.

Plate 832
Unknown Manufacturer
Swan. Crystal with Charleton decoration, 6½" high.
Seen at $40.00 – 45.00

This mold was attributed to Indiana Glass Company and reissued for Tiara.

Plate 833
Heisey Glass Company
Swan. Crystal, 7" high, 8½" long, circa 1947 – 53. $1,200.00 – 1,400.00

Other colors: crystal frosted.

Reissues: Imperial Glass Company in crystal, ultra blue, light blue, red amberina, and black.

When marked, the mark appears on the left side under the wing on the body.

Cygnet. Crystal, 2⅛" high, 2½" long, circa 1947 – 49. $225.00 – 250.00

Other colors: crystal frosted.

Reissues: Imperial Glass Company in crystal, pink satin finish, horizon blue plain and satin finish, black, and caramel slag. Dalzell-Viking in ruby. Fenton in rosalene as part of the HCA Gold Series. See Plate 126.

When marked, the mark appears on the right side under the wing, near the base.

Plate 834
Heisey Glass Company
Swan Nut Set. Large: crystal, 4" high, 7" long, unmarked, circa 1940s – 50s.
$35.00 – 40.00

Reissues: Imperial Glass Company in ultra blue. Mosser Glass Company for HCA in vaseline plain and frosted.

Individual Swan Nut. Crystal, 2¾" long, circa 1940s – 50s, not marked.
$20.00 – 25.00 each

Other colors: amber (rare).

Reissues: Boyd Glass Company (1995 – 96) in vaseline, mint julep, cobalt, black, crystal carnival, milk chocolate, and capri blue. Mosser Glass Company in vaseline plain and frosted for HCA.

Boyd Glass Company bought this mold from Imperial and used it for two years and then HCA purchased the mold.

Plate 835
Original photograph from the Heisey Factory. This photo was used for advertising in magazines and other sources. This photo shows the Heisey swan, cygnet, and a fish candleholder in the middle.

Plate 837
HEISEY GLASS COMPANY
Swan Handled Pitcher. Crystal, 9¼" high, two-quart, circa 1944.
$650.00 – 700.00

Other colors: none.

Reissues: Imperial Glass Company in teal green.

Plate 836
(original Heisey Glass Company mold)
Cygnet. 2⅛" high, 2½" long.
Ruby made by **DALZELL-VIKING GLASS COMPANY** marked D & HCA, $30.00 – 40.00
Black made by **IMPERIAL GLASS COMPANY**, marked ALIG, $45.00 – 55.00

For details including all reissues on the cygnet see Plate 833.

Plate 838
IMPERIAL GLASS COMPANY (original Heisey Glass Company mold)
Swan Handled Pitcher. Teal green, 9¼" high, circa 1980s.
$75.00 – 85.00

Plate 839
HEISEY GLASS COMPANY
#133 Swan Handled Candleholders. Moongleam, 6" high, 1929 – 36.
$150.00 – 175.00 each

Other colors:
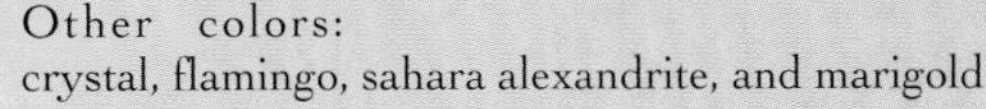
crystal, flamingo, sahara alexandrite, and marigold.

Plate 840
IMPERIAL GLASS COMPANY
Left: **Large Swan.** Caramel slag, 10" long, circa 1969.
$90.00 – 110.00

Other colors and reissues: purple slag, glossy, purple slag satin, milk glass, caramel slag satin, and jade slag. Horizon blue, pink, and meadow green iridized (sold through Levay Distributing). Reissued in 1990 in crystal for Fostoria outlets.

Right: **Small Swan.** Caramel slag, 4" high, circa 1979.
$45.00 – 55.00

Other colors; steigel green, ritz blue, amber, ruby, pink, Imperial green, and milk glass. Many iridized with a carnival-type finish. Purple and jade slags, glossy or satin finish.

Plate 841
IMPERIAL GLASS COMPANY
Large Swan. Milk glass, 10" long.
$55.00 – 65.00

Plate 842
IMPERIAL GLASS COMPANY
Small Swan. Ruby iridized, 4" high.
$30.00 – 35.00

Plate 843
IMPERIAL GLASS COMPANY
Small Swan. Blue opalescent, 4" high, circa 1930s.
$35.00 – 45.00

One of IG's many transparent blues in its Sea Foam line of opalescent colors.

Plate 844
KANAWHA GLASS COMPANY
Swan. Crystal and amber, 11" long, 8" high, circa 1970s – 80s.
$25.00 – 30.00

This swan has the appearance of cased glass. Has original label.

Plate 845
KANAWHA GLASS COMPANY
Swan. Amber, off-hand style, 10" long, 6½" high, circa 1970s – 80s.
$15.00 – 20.00

Plate 846
RAINBOW ART GLASS COMPANY
Swan. Green, off-hand style, 7" long, 6½" high, circa 1950s – 70s.
$14.00 – 18.00

Plate 847
PAIRPOINT GLASS COMPANY
Swan. Cranberry body, crystal head and neck, 12" long.
$375.00 – 450.00

This swan is very heavy and of excellent quality glass.

Plate 848
NEW MARTINSVILLE GLASS COMPANY
#974 Swan. Crystal with Prelude etching, 5".
$45.00 – 55.00

Plate 849
NEW MARTINSVILLE GLASS COMPANY
#974 Swans. Sweetheart shape, 5", collar base, circa 1940 – 60.
Light blue with crystal, $35.00 – 40.00
Ruby candleholder/crystal, $45.00 – 50.00
Ebony with crystal, $35.00 – 40.00
Amber with crystal, $30.00 – 35.00

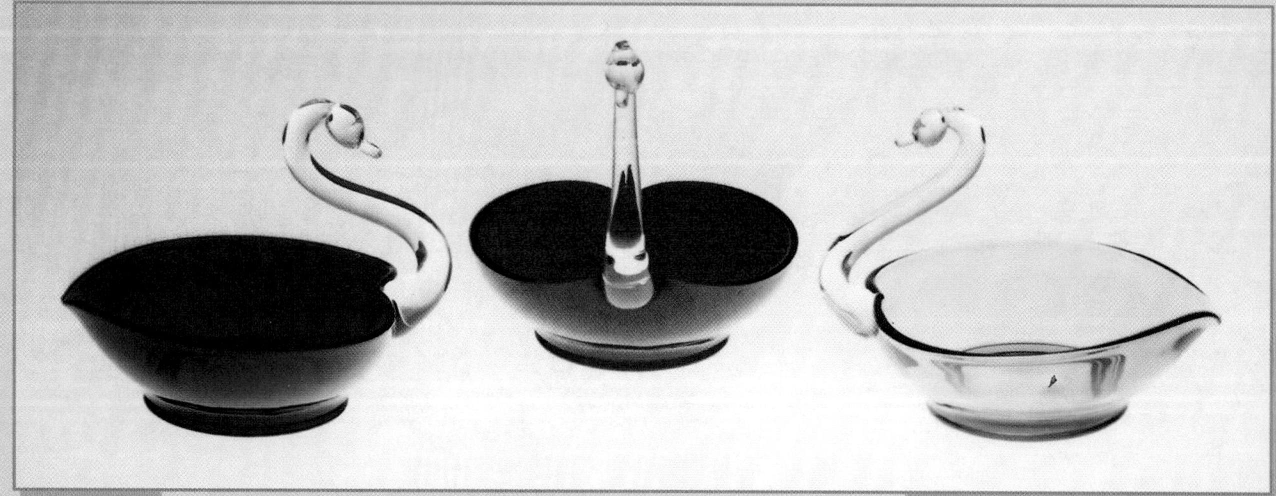

Plate 850
NEW MARTINSVILLE GLASS COMPANY
#974 Swans. Sweetheart shape, 5", collar base, circa 1940 – 60.
Cobalt with crystal, $35.00 – 40.00
Ruby with crystal, $35.00 – 40.00
Light green with crystal, $35.00 – 40.00

Plate 851
NEW MARTINSVILLE GLASS COMPANY
#974 Swan. Crystal with gold decorations, 5" collar base.
$30.00 – 35.00

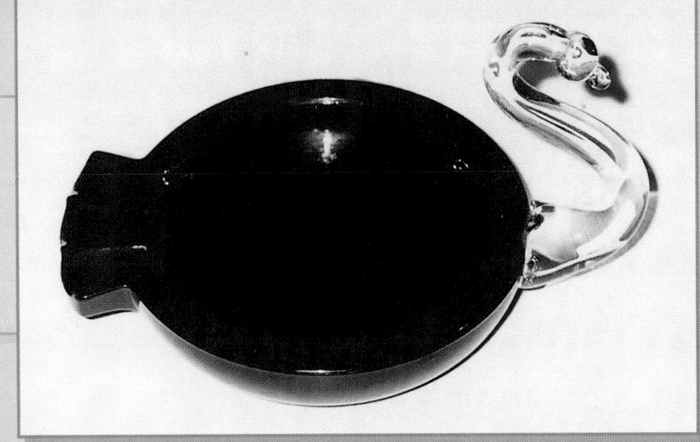

Plate 852
NEW MARTINSVILLE GLASS COMPANY
Swan Ashtray. Ebony body with crystal head and neck, indents in tail for cigarette rest.
$40.00 – 45.00

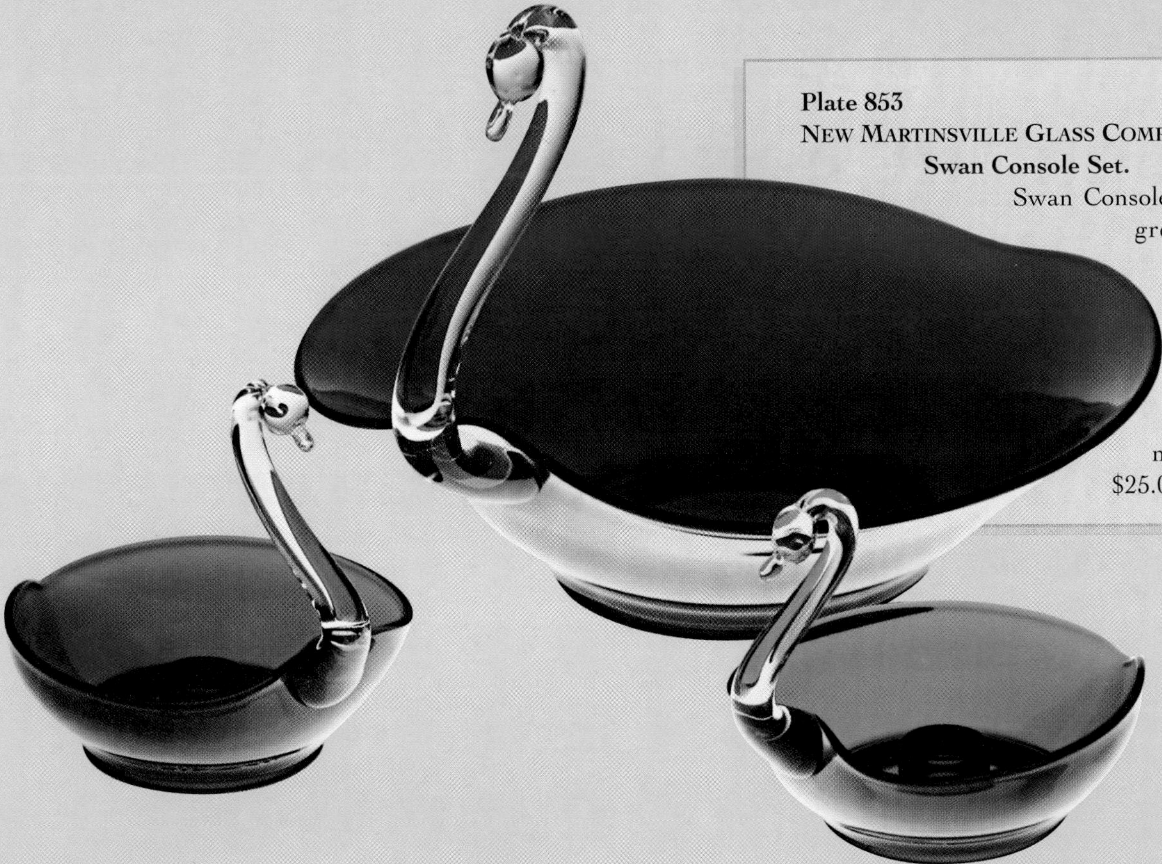

Plate 853
NEW MARTINSVILLE GLASS COMPANY
Swan Console Set.
Swan Console Bowl. Emerald green with crystal neck, 11" long.
$45.00 – 50.00
Swan Candleholders. Emerald green with crystal neck, 5" long.
$25.00 – 30.00 each

Plate 854
NEW MARTINSVILLE GLASS COMPANY
#4543 Swan Bowl Janice S Line. Ruby with crystal neck. Bowl 4¼" high, circa 1940 – 70.
$65.00 – 75.00

Plate 855
NEW MARTINSVILLE GLASS COMPANY
#4543 Swan Creamer Janice S Line. Crystal, 5" wide, 5½" high.
$35.00 – 45.00

Used with #4122 S J Sugar

Plate 856
NEW MARTINSVILLE GLASS COMPANY
#4541 Swan Bowl Janice S Line. All crystal, 6½" long, circa 1930 – 70.
$34.00 – 40.00

Plate 857
NEW MARTINSVILLE GLASS COMPANY
#4541 Swan Bowl Janice S Line. Crystal with cobalt head and neck and cutting, 6½" long, circa 1930 – 70.
$60.00 – 70.00

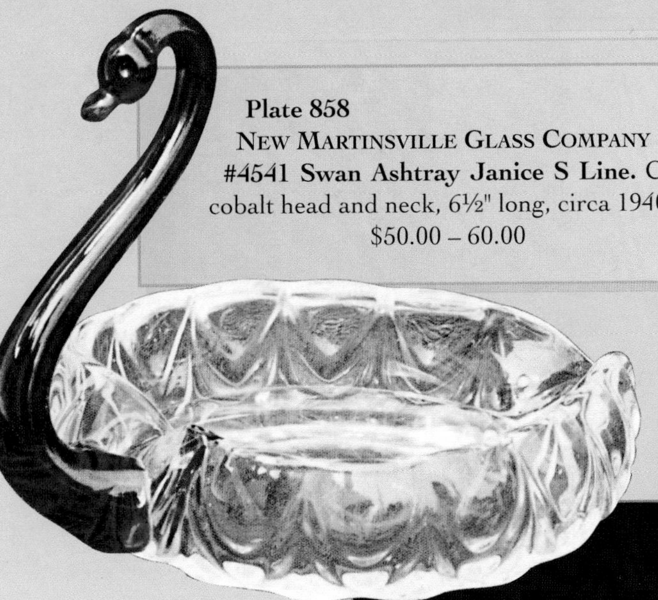

Plate 858
NEW MARTINSVILLE GLASS COMPANY
#4541 Swan Ashtray Janice S Line. Crystal with cobalt head and neck, 6½" long, circa 1940 – 70.
$50.00 – 60.00

Plate 859
NEW MARTINSVILLE GLASS COMPANY
#4551-1SJ. Swan Bowl, Janice Line. Crystal with cobalt head and neck, 11" long.
$65.00 – 75.00

Plate 860
NEW MARTINSVILLE GLASS COMPANY
#4541-1SJ Swan Covered Dish, Janice Line. Crystal with cobalt head and neck, 5½" diameter.
$75.00 – 85.00

Is sometimes used as a puff box with perfumes.

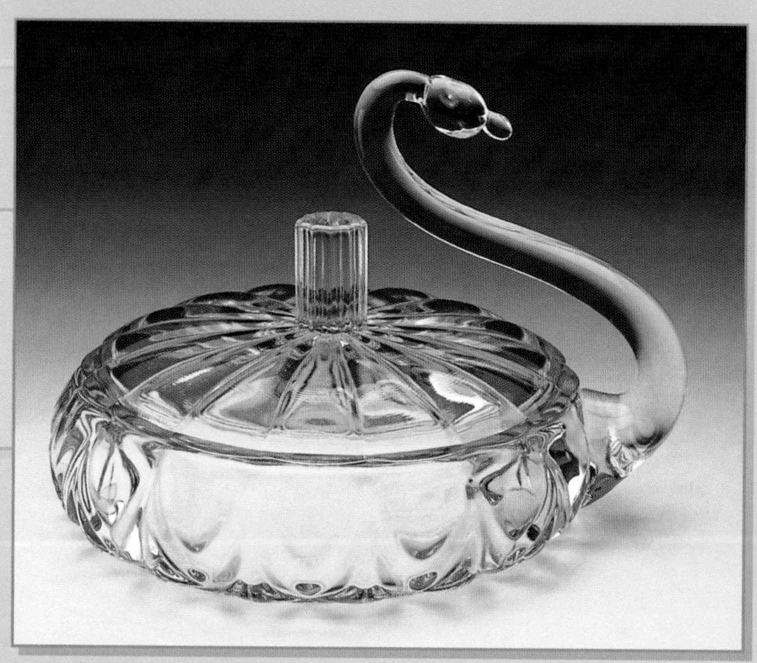

Plate 861
New Martinsville Glass Company
#4541-1SJ Swan Covered Dish, Janice Line.
All crystal, 5½" diameter.
$55.00 – 65.00

Plate 862
New Martinsville Glass Company
#4551-2SJ Bowl with Two Swan Handles, Janice Line. Crystal, 11" long.
$65.00 – 75.00

Plate 863
New Martinsville Glass Company
#4528-2SJ Plate with Two Swan Handles, Janice Line.
Crystal, 11¼" diameter.
$45.00 – 55.00

This is the plate to a Cheese and Cracker Set.

Plate 864
New Martinsville Glass Company
#4550-2SJ Vase with Two Swan Handles, Janice Line. Crystal, 7" high.
$200.00 – 225.00

Plate 865
New Martinsville Glass Company
#412-1SJ Swan Ashtray, Janice Line. Crystal, 4½" wide.
$10.00 – 15.00

Also came with cobalt necks and ruby necks.

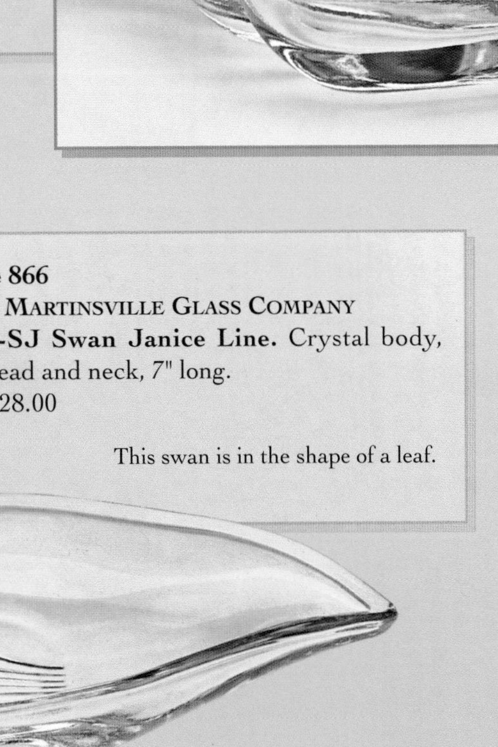

Plate 866
New Martinsville Glass Company
#443-SJ Swan Janice Line. Crystal body, ruby head and neck, 7" long.
$24.00 – 28.00

This swan is in the shape of a leaf.

Plate 867
New Martinsville Glass Company
#137-2SJ Vase, Janice Line, Two Swan Handles. Crystal, 6" high, 6" wide.
$85.00 – 95.00

Although the body of the vase does not have the Janice lines, the factory number places it in the Janice line.

Plate 868
New Martinsville Glass Company
Swan Handled Perfumes, Swan Line.
Crystal.
Large, 7" high, $100.00 – 125.00
Small, 5½" high, $75.00 – 100.00

Plate 869
New Martinsville Glass Company
Swan Handled Console Set, Swan Line. Crystal.
Bowl, 15" long, 6¾" wide, $55.00 – 65.00
Candleholders, 2½" high, 2½" diameter, $65.00 – 75.00 pair

Plate 870
NEW MARTINSVILLE GLASS COMPANY
#679-1S Swan Handled Bowl, Swan Line. Crystal, 14" long.
$45.00 – 55.00

Other colors: Came in colors in the 1940s – 60s.

Also came in a 12" bowl.

Plate 871
NEW MARTINSVILLE GLASS COMPANY
#679-1S Swan Handled Bowl, Swan Line. Green, 14" long, circa 1940s – 60s.
$75.00 – 85.00

Plate 872
NEW MARTINSVILLE GLASS COMPANY
#5203-1S Swan Handled Bowl, Princess Swan Pattern. Green, 11" long, circa 1940s – 60s.
$65.00 – 75.00

Also came in 4½" swan candlestick.

Plate 873
Paden City Glass Company
#1540 Swan Handled Server.
Crystal, 11½" diameter.
$45.00 – 55.00

Sometimes seen with a Paden City etching.

Plate 874
L.E. Smith Glass Company
#¾ Large Swan. Milk glass, 8½" long, circa 1930s.
$30.00 – 40.00

Other colors: green, blue, pink, black, and probably others.

Plate 875
L.E. Smith Glass Company
#¾ Large Swan. Green, 8½" long, circa 1930s.
$30.00 – 40.00

The beaks are generally painted orange on these swans.

Plate 876
L.E. SMITH GLASS COMPANY
#3/4 Large Swan, Flower Holder, and Matching Candleholders. Pink frosted.
Swan, 8½" long, $30.00 – 40.00
Flower Holder, $25.00 – 30.00
Candleholders, 2½" high, $35.00 – 45.00 pair

The bottoms of the candleholders have a feather detail.

Plate 877
L.E. SMITH GLASS COMPANY
#15 Small Swan. Milk glass, 4½" long, circa 1930s.
$20.00 – 25.00

Other colors: In the 1980s it was produced in crystal, purple carnival, blue frosted, almond nouveau, and probably others.

Plate 878
TIFFIN GLASS COMPANY
Blown Swan. Black, circa 1950s – 60s.
Private collection — Market

Other colors: crystal, pink, ruby, cobalt, green, smoke, and plum.

These are off-hand swans and will therefore vary in size. They were sold in outlet stores.

Plate 879
Viking Glass Company
#1324 Swan Epic Line. Amber, 7" long, circa 1960s – 70s.
$20.00 – 30.00

Other colors: blue, amberina, and other Viking colors.

Plate 880
Viking Glass Company
#1324 Swan Epic Line. Blue, 7" long, circa 1960s – 70s.
$20.00 – 30.00

Plate 881
Viking Glass Company
#1324 Swan Epic Line. Amberina, 7" long, circa 1960s – 70s.
$20.00 – 30.00

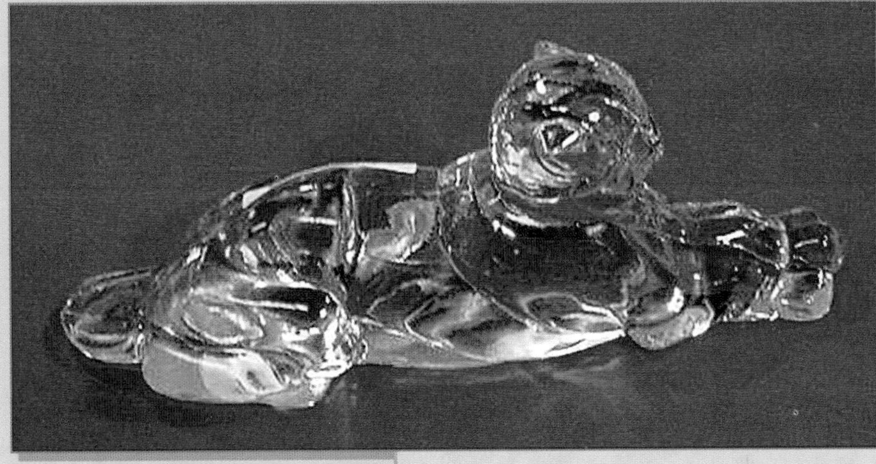

Plate 882
HEISEY GLASS COMPANY
Tiger Paperweight. Crystal, 2¾" high, 8" long, circa 1949.
$1,200.00 – 1,400.00

Other colors: crystal frosted and frosted highlighting.

Reissues: Imperial Glass Company in crystal, black, jade, amber, amber satin, ruby, nut brown, milk glass, sunshine yellow, caramel slag, ultra blue satin, and perhaps others. Dalzell-Viking in ruby, ice blue, yellow mist, and perhaps others. Fenton Art Glass Company in rosalene and rosalene satin. The rosalene was part of the HCA Gold Series, see Plate 126.

When marked, the mark appears near the base in front of the right hind leg.

Plate 883
IMPERIAL GLASS COMPANY (original Heisey Glass Company mold)
Tiger Paperweight. 8" long, 2¾" high.
Jade green: 1980, LIG.
$100.00 – 125.00
Caramel slag, 1982 – 83, ALIG.
$90.00 – 100.00

In the early 1980s when Imperial was making some of the Cathay figurines in jade, they included the tiger paperweight and it was added to the line at that time.

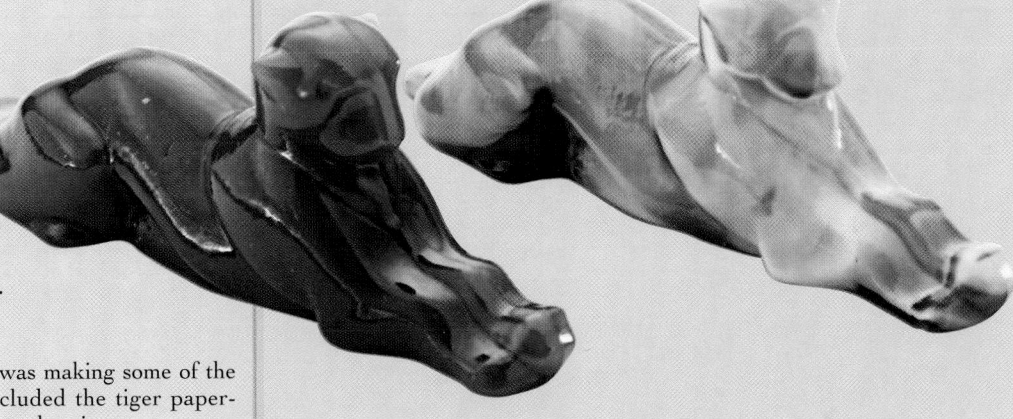

Plate 884
NEW MARTINSVILLE GLASS COMPANY
Tiger, Head Up. Crystal, 6½" high.
$200.00 – 225.00
Tiger, Head Down. Crystal satin, 7¼" high.
$200.00 – 225.00

Both tigers came in crystal and crystal satin.

Turkeys

Plate 885
Cambridge Glass Company
Turkey. Amber, $600.00 – 650.00

Cambridge produced the covered turkey container for a period of ten years from approximately 1940 until 1950. They were made in multiple colors including amber, carmen, gold krystol, royal blue, dianthus (peach blo), willow blue, emerald, and in crystal. The top of the tail is 7¼" high, while the base is 4¾" wide, and 5¾" long. The tail feathers have a simple line down the middle of each feather and no other detail. Both feet are visible, with the right foot further extended than the left and he appears to be standing on a leaf-covered mound of dirt. Cambridge turkeys are often confused with turkeys made by L.E. Smith Company, by turkeys made for L.G. Wright, and turkeys made presumably by U.S. Glass. The Cambridge turkey is much larger than the Smith turkey, almost twice the size. See Plate 887 for comparison. Turkeys made for L.G. Wright have comparable detail; however, they were made in white milk glass, amethyst carnival, carnival with milk glass head, and milk glass body with a carnival head. The turkey presumably made by U.S. Glass causes the most confusion. See Plate 886 for differences.

Plate 886
Unknown Manufacturers
Turkey. Amber, $250.00 – 300.00

The turkey pictured here is *not* Cambridge; however, it is most often confused with the Cambridge production. An 1898 U.S. Glass Company catalog shows a picture or drawing of this turkey container. There is also speculation that this mold was an import. Nonetheless there are several differences between the two even though they are comparable in size. The first difference is the base. This turkey stands on a base which has a waffle appearance. The design would remind one of the old pattern glass cut block. The other difference is the fine feather detail in the tail. The feathers are plain on the Cambridge production whereas the detail is so fine on this turkey that they appear much more like feathers. The popularity of the Cambridge turkeys have brought the price up, or perhaps it is the confusion.

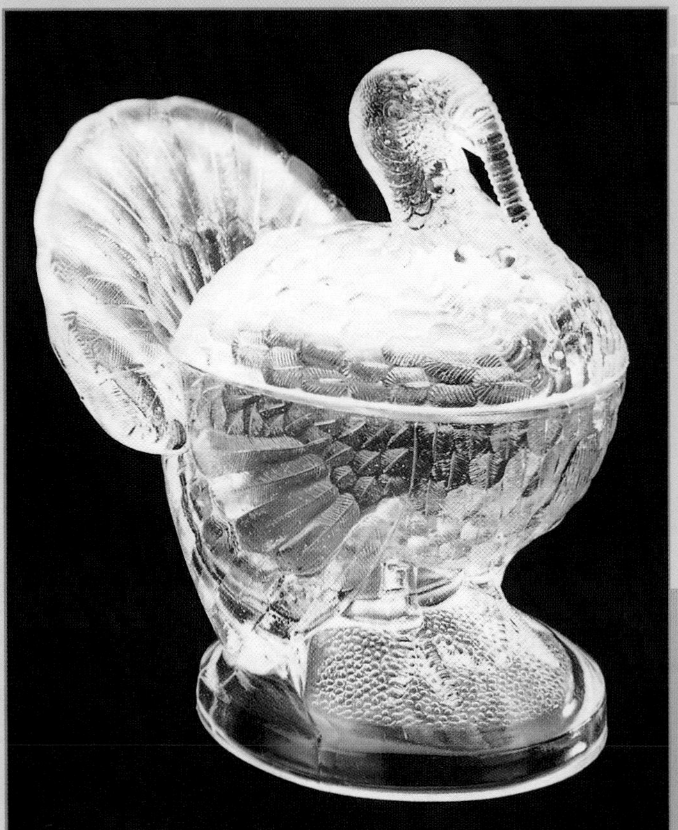

Plate 887
LE. Smith Glass Company
#207 Turkey Two-piece Candy Dish. Crystal, 7¾" high, circa 1973.
$35.00 – 45.00

Other colors: 1971, milk glass; 1973, amber, amberina, green, blue, amethyst carnival, amberina carnival, crystal, cobalt, cobalt carnival, and others; 1982, crystal and crystal frosted with red hand-painted head made for Levay Distributing. Reissued for Martha Stewart in milk glass and jadite, marked "M.S." Other reissues marked "S" on the underside.

A pink covered turkey identical to the Smith turkey is appearing on the market with raised letters on the bottom, "Made in Tiawan."

Plate 888
L.E. Smith Glass Company
#207 Turkey Two-piece Candy Dish.
Green, 7¾" high, circa 1973.
$45.00 – 55.00

The color of this turkey is much the same shade as that of the Cambridge turkey; however, the Cambridge turkey is much larger.

Plate 889
Imperial Glass Company
#42973 Turkey Covered Dish. Rubigold, 4¾" high, 5" long, circa 1973 – 74
$50.00 – 75.00

Other colors: amber carnival original issue and later in milk glass.

Plate 890
ANCHOR HOCKING GLASS COMPANY
Turtle Covered Box. Crystal, 3¾" high, circa 1940s – 50s.
$15.00 – 20.00

Marked Anchor Hocking on the bottom.

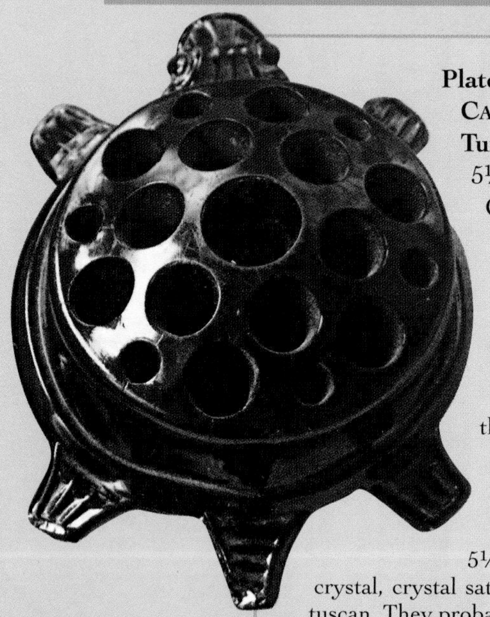

Plate 891
CAMBRIDGE GLASS COMPANY
Turtle Flower Holders. 3½" wide, 5¼" long.
Crystal satin, $150.00 – 175.00
Ebony, $200.00 – 225.00

Cambridge produced two types of turtle flower holders. The first (not pictured) was produced probably in the early 1920s and the second was produced circa 1940. Basically there is very little difference except for the top (the turtle's back). The early turtle was nearly flat whereas the later version was domed. Both had 19 holes and are 3½" wide and 5¼" long. They have been found in crystal, crystal satin, cobalt, ebony, green, and crown tuscan. They probably exist in other colors.

Plate 892
FENTON ART GLASS COMPANY
Turtle Figurine. Crystal satin, 3½" long, contemporary.
$18.00 – 22.00

The #9199 Turtle Ring Tree mold was altered to create this figurine.

Plate 893
NORTHWOOD GLASS COMPANY/FENTON ART GLASS COMPANY
#1564 Turtle Flower Block. 4" long.
Top row, left to right: Northwood. 6 holes. Crystal, coral, blue, vaseline, opaque blue. Market.
Bottom row: Fenton. Circa 1929, 8 holes, transparent green, $45.00 – 65.00, transparent amethyst, $75.00 – 85.00, transparent pink, $45.00 – 65.00, and jade, $90.00 – 100.00
Colors not shown: crystal, $45.00 – 55.00, vaseline, $65.00 – 90.00, celeste blue, $65.00 – 90.00
Early 1920s colors: mandarin red, rare; pekin blue, black, mongolian green, periwinkle blue, $105.00 – 145.00 each

When Northwood went out of business, Fenton purchased the turtle mold and added two extra holes. Northwood's colors and prices would match those of Fenton.

Plate 894
FENTON ART GLASS COMPANY
#1565 Turtle Flower Bowl/Aquarium Base.
Black, 8⅞" long, circa 1929, rare.
$200.00 – 225.00

Other colors: teal, jade green, crystal, pink, and green

This turtle was also made with a lid for a covered bonbon dish, or, in green only, to accommodate a crystal fish bowl.

Plate 895
FENTON ART GLASS COMPANY
#1565 Turtle Covered Bonbon Dish.
Green, 8⅞" long, circa 1929.
$350.00 – 400.00

Plate 896
VIKING GLASS COMPANY
#1301 Turtle. Amber, 5½" long, circa 1957.
$25.00 – 35.00

Made in other Viking colors.

Plate 897
WESTMORELAND GLASS COMPANY
1,000 Eye Turtle, Two-piece Cigarette Box. Crystal with flashed dots of ruby, lavender, and pale yellow, 7¾" long.
$45.00 – 55.00

Other colors: crystal, white milk glass, black milk glass, golden sunset, moss green, and olive green.

Reissues: After Westmoreland closed, in amberina, cobalt blue, mother-of-pearl, amethyst, light blue, white milk glass, blue milk glass, orange, and some with hand-painted decorations.

A set also included two small ashtrays, see Plates 898 and 899.

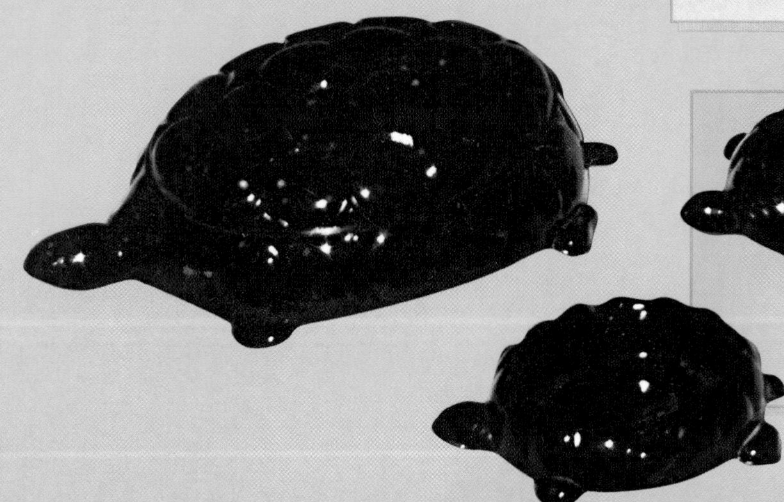

Plate 898
WESTMORELAND GLASS COMPANY
1,000 Eye Turtle Cigarette/Ashtray Set. Black.
Cigarette Box, 7¾" long, $45.00 – 50.00
Ashtray, 4¼" long, $10.00 – 15.00 each

Plate 899
WESTMORELAND GLASS COMPANY
1,000 Eye Turtle Cigarette/Ashtray Set. Crystal.
Cigarette Box, 7¾" long, $30.00 – 35.00
Ashtray, 4¼" long, $8.00 – 10.00 each

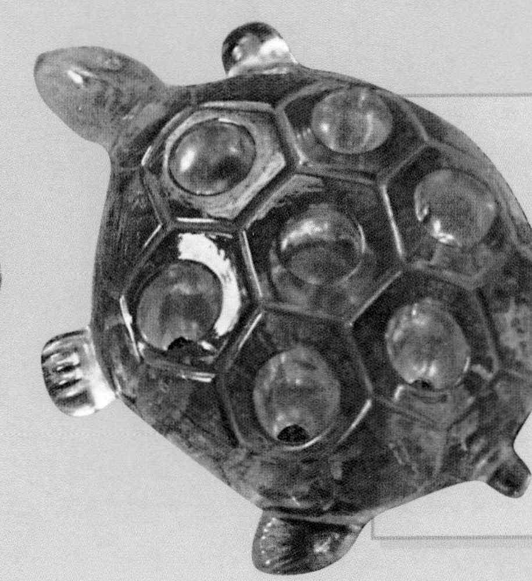

Plate 900
Westmoreland Glass Company
#1860 Turtle Flower Block. 4" long, 7 holes, circa 1924, crystal and green. $55.00 – 65.00 each

Reissues: By another company since Westmoreland closed in 1984. Cobalt, mother-of-pearl, amethyst, and milk glass.

Plate 901
Westmoreland Glass Company
#10 Paperweight. Green mist, 4" long, no holes, circa 1970. $20.00 – 25.00

Made from the #1860 turtle flower block mold. See Plate 900.

Plate 902
Pilgrim Glass Company
#931 Turtle. Amber, 4½" long, circa 1970. $18.00 – 20.00

Other colors: blue, crystal, and possibly other Pilgrim colors.

Plate 903
L.G. Wright Glass Company
Covered Turtle Dish. Amber, 10" long.
$75.00 – 85.00

Other colors: crystal, dark emerald green, chocolate, and other colors.

This turtle was referred to as the "Belfish" turtle in Weatherman's Book 2 and maker unknown. Since the publication of this book, it has been learned that the mold belonged to L.G. Wright, who had various companies make glass for him.

Plate 904
L.G. Wright Glass Company
Covered Turtle Dish. Dark emerald green, 10" long.
$85.00 – 95.00

See Plate 903.

Plate 905
Unknown Manufacturer
Covered Turtle Dish. Green, 10" long.
$125.00 – 150.00

Appears to be malachite.

Woodchucks

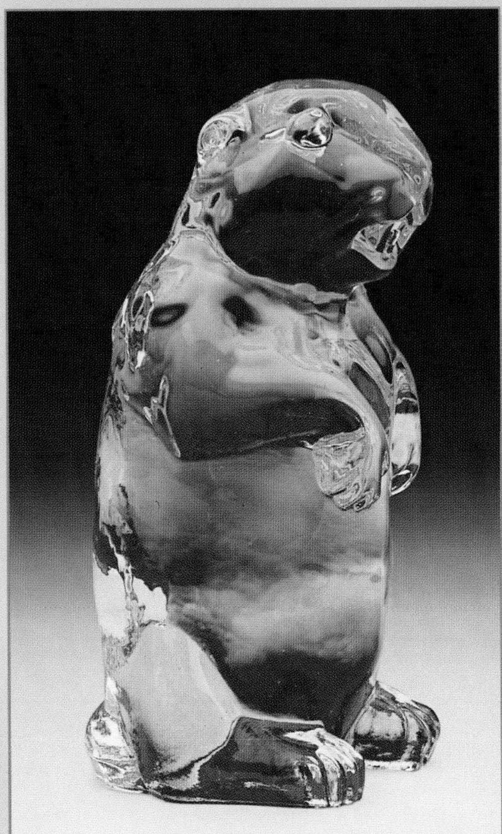

Plate 906
IMPERIAL GLASS COMPANY
Marmota Sentinel (Woodchuck). Crystal, 4½" high, original issue, circa 1969 – 76.
$30.00 – 35.00

Other colors: amber and caramel slag.

Reissues: In 1983 for Mirror Images in ultra blue.

Boyd Glass owned the mold as of 1985, and their issues were marked with the Boyd logo.

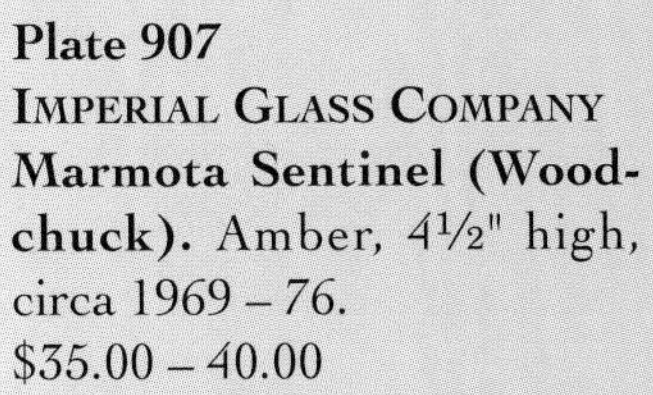

Plate 907
IMPERIAL GLASS COMPANY
Marmota Sentinel (Woodchuck). Amber, 4½" high, circa 1969 – 76.
$35.00 – 40.00

Other colors: crystal (original issue) and caramel slag.

See Plate 906.

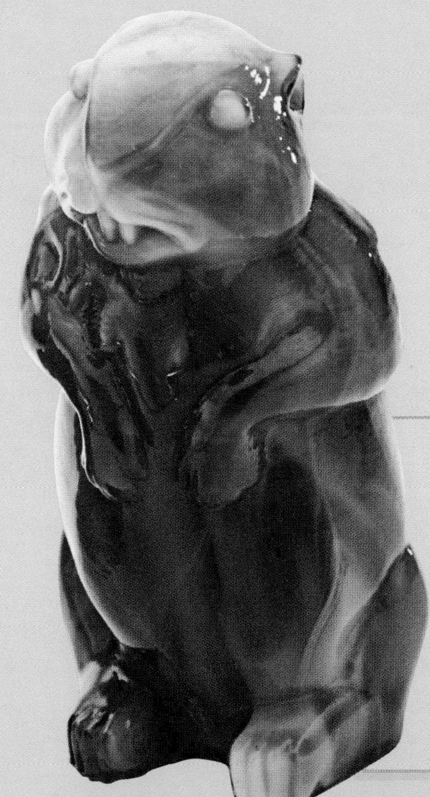

Plate 908
IMPERIAL GLASS COMPANY
Marmota Sentinel (Woodchuck). Caramel slag, 4½" high, circa 1969 – 76.
$50.00 – 60.00

Other colors: crystal (original issue) and amber.

See Plate 906.

Glass Factories

American Glass Company, Carney, Kansas, was an affiliate of General Glassware which was started by Herman Lowertiz and K.R. Haley, a glass designer. American Glass Company produced glass made from molds made from Mr. Haley's designs. The glass was then marketed by General Glassware. American Glass Company was dissolved in 1946, after the death of Mr. Lowerwitz.

Barth Art Company. Harry Barth was associated with New Martinsville Glass Company as early as 1918. He became general manager of the company in the late 1930s. He resigned in the early 1940s to form Barth Art Company, an organization of glass grinders, polishers, and decorative cutters. As different molds were completed to Barth's specifications, they were assigned to Paden City Glass Company (and a few other companies) for the manufacturing process. The glassware was then returned to the Barth Art Company for the finishing work, and sold under that company's label. In 1952, Mr. Barth sold some animal molds to the Viking Glass Company.

Blenko Glass Company, Milton, West Virginia. William Blenko established the Blenko Glass Company in 1922. Blenko has always been and continues to be a family operated business. They are still in business today producing fine hand-crafted glassware, including glass animals and figurines.

Boyd Crystal Art Glass Company, Cambridge, Ohio. Bernard F. Boyd, a long-time employee of Degenhart Glass Company, purchased the company after Mrs. Degenhart's death in 1978, and opened the plant as the Boyd Crystal Art Glass Company. They had produced animals and figurines in the Degenhart molds, a practice which continues today.

Cambridge Glass Company, Cambridge, Ohio. Cambridge, founded in 1902, produced excellent quality glass. Included in their production were a number of glass animals, a large selection of nude stems, and many etched patterns on glass, the most popular being Rose Point. Cambridge closed briefly at the end of 1954, but reopened and operated until 1958. Imperial Glass Company, Bellaire, Ohio, bought Cambridge which included a number of molds.

Co-Operative Flint Glass Company, Beaver Falls, Pennsylvania, opened in 1879 as the Beaver Falls Co-Operative Glass Co., but the name was changed to Co-Operative Flint Glass Company in 1889. This company was known for its extensive line of gift items as well as soda fountain and restaurant ware. They made a number of excellent animals and other figurines. The company closed in 1934.

Degenhart Glass Company, Cambridge, Ohio. John Degenhart founded the Degenhart Glass Company in 1947. He ran the business until his death in 1964, at which time his wife took over the business and ran it until her death in 1978. The business was then closed. During their years of operation the Degenharts produced mainly novelty items, animals, and figurines.

Dalzell-Viking Glass Company, New Martinsville, West Virginia. In 1987, Mr. Kenneth Dalzell (long associated with Fostoria Glass Company) purchased the defunct Viking Glass Company, reopening its doors under the banner of Dalzell-Viking Glass Company. Many of the New Martinsville, Viking, and Barth Art molds were put into use. Dalzell-Viking also performed a considerable amount of contract work for the Heisey Collectors of America, Inc., producing reissues from the original Heisey molds, exclusively for HCA. Dalzell-Viking closed in 1998.

Duncan Glass Company, Washington, Pennsylvania. George Duncan took over the Ripley Glass Company in Pittsburgh, Pennsylvania, in a partnership with his two sons and son-in-law, A.H. Heisey. The factory was destroyed by fire in 1892. The firm moved to Washington, Pennsylvania, and established the Duncan-Miller Glass Company, although glassware continued to be marketed as "Genuine Duncan." Duncan produced a general glassware line, including many excellent animals and figurines. They are well known for their extensive line of swans. The molds and equipment were sold to the U.S. Glass Company, in mid-1955. One year later the Duncan factory was destroyed by fire.

Federal Glass Company, Columbus, Ohio. Federal started making handmade glassware in 1900, changing to automation by the 1920s. Federal became a major supplier of restaurants, motels, etc., and pioneered the decorated tumbler. Only a few collectible animals are attributed to Federal. The company became a division of Federal Paper Board Company in 1958.

Fenton Art Glass Company, Williamstown, West Virginia. Frank and John Fenton opened a glass decorating plant in Martins Ferry, Ohio, in order to decorate glass for other companies. Shortly thereafter, in approximately 1906, the brothers moved to Williamstown, West Virginia, establishing the Fenton Art Glass Company. The company is still in full operation today. Fenton has, over the years, produced and continues to produce, a wide variety of animals and figurines. Excellent decorations are still prevalent in their present day productions.

Fostoria Glass Company, Moundsville, West Virginia. The Fostoria Glass Company was first established in Fostoria, Ohio, in 1887, moving to Moundsville, West Virginia, in 1891. Fostoria first produced many fine lamps but later migrated into a general line of glassware including the long-lived and highly marketed American pattern. Fostoria produced a wide variety of fine glass animals and figurines. In 1983, Fostoria was purchased by Lancaster-Colony, and in 1986 the plant was closed.

Gillinder & Sons Glass Company, Port Jervis, New York, was founded in 1861 by William T. Gillinder. It was known as Gillinder & Sons after James and Frederick who joined their father in 1867, in the former Franklin Flint Glass Works in Philadelphia, Pennsylvania. They produced pressed tableware at a second factory in Greensburg, Pennsylvania, in 1888. This factory was known as factory G when they joined U.S. Glass Co. in 1891. Third generation of Gillinders established a new plant at Port Jervis, New York, circa 1900. The name became Gillinder Bros. Inc. The Philadelphia plant closed in 1930. At present the plant at Port Jervis, New York, is still in operation and is known as Gillinder Glass.

K.R. Haley Glassware Company, Greensburg, Pennsylvania. K.R. Haley worked for Overmeyer Mold of Pennsylvania, becoming vice president in 1937. Two years later he and Herman Lowerwitz, president of American Glass Company, formed the General Glassware Company. Through this company they marketed glassware made by the American Glass Company from Mr. Haley's designs. The company was dissolved in 1946, after the death of Mr. Lowerwitz. Mr. Haley then opened the K.R. Haley Glassware Company, which operated until 1972. Mr. Haley was never a manufacturer of glassware, but a superb creative artist. Kemple Glass Company acquired a number of Mr. Haley's designs when his company closed.

Heisey Glass Company, Newark, Ohio. The Heisey Glass Company was founded during the mid-1890s by A.H. Heisey, the son-in-law of George Duncan, owner of the George Duncan & Sons Glass Company. The Heisey Glass Company produced a general line of excellent quality of glassware from 1896 until 1957. Heisey registered the now famous Diamond H trademark and started marking glassware with it in 1902. They made excellent quality glass animals and figurines from the late 1930s until they closed in 1957. After the factory closed, Imperial Glass Company, Bellaire, Ohio, bought the existing molds.

Hocking — Anchor Hocking Glass Company, Lancaster, Ohio. The Hocking Glass Company was established in 1905, making small wares, mainly by hand. Hocking started acquiring subsidiaries in the 1920s, and claims the first glass baby food jar. Numerous glasshouses were assumed by Hocking in the early years and in 1937, the name was changed to Anchor Hocking Corporation.

Houze Glass Corporation, Point Marion, Pennsylvania, was founded in 1902 by Leon J. Houze, Sr. They produced gear shift knobs in the 1930s, and through the years made a wide variety of glass from window glass to lamp parts, percolator handles, glass eyes, candy boxes, auto tail lights, plus many more utilitarian wares. In 1952, they became a decorating company. Today they are one of the largest specialty decorators of porcelain, ceramic, and glass items.

IMPERIAL GLASS COMPANY, Bellaire Ohio. The Imperial Glass Company was organized in 1901, and produced excellent quality general line glassware until they closed in 1984. Imperial developed and marketed the Candlewick pattern which has become very popular with today's collectors. Imperial, utilizing their own molds, combined with those acquired from Cambridge and Heisey, became the largest producer of glass animals and figurines. Imperial Glass Company closed in 1984. The Heisey Collectors of America purchased all the existing Heisey molds, except the Old Williamsburg line, which went to Lennox Glass Company. The National Cambridge Club was able to purchase some of the existing Cambridge molds and the remainder of the molds in the Imperial factory were purchased by individuals and numerous other companies.

KANAWHA GLASS COMPANY, Kanawha, West Virginia. The former Dunbar Glass Company was purchased and from that a plant was established in Kanawha, West Virginia, in 1955. They were known for their crackle glass. The company went out of business and was sold in 1988 to Raymond Dereume Glass Company, Punxsutawney, Pennsylvania.

KEMPLE GLASS COMPANY, East Palestine, Ohio. John E. Kemple Glass Works began in 1945, as a partnership between John and his wife Geraldine. They produced mainly milk glass from retired molds from 1945 to 1956, and blue milk glass from 1951 to 1956. The factory in East Palestine, Ohio, was destroyed by fire in 1956. They relocated in Kenova, West Virginia. They reproduced items from many different defunct factories, McKee Glass Co., American Glass Co., Sinclair Glass Co., Hobbs Brockunier, and Indiana Tumbler and Goblet Co. Kemple Glass Company closed in 1970.

MANTLE LAMP COMPANY OF AMERICA, Alexandria, Indiana. The Mantle Lamp Company of America began operations in 1908, with kerosene burning lamps being their main production until the 1940s (even with electric lamps in the picture). Aladdin lamps became their trade name and the collectible lamps of today were made in Alexandria, Indiana. Alacite was introduced in 1939. In 1949, they moved operations to Nashville, Tennessee.

MORGANTOWN GLASS WORKS, Morgantown, West Virginia, was founded in 1899 by Frank Bannister. They were best known for handmade, mold-blown stemware and tumblers. They also made decorative glassware baskets, bowls, candleholders, and free forms. In 1965, then known as Morgantown Glassware Guild, the company was sold to Fostoria Glass Company. Operations continued until 1971, at which time Fostoria closed the plant.

MOSSER GLASS COMPANY, Cambridge, Ohio. Mosser is noted for their variety of novelty items and their wide array of animals and figurals on today's market. They have a wide variety of colors and produce excellent quality glass. The company was built by and is operated by Tom Mosser.

New Martinsville Glass Company. New Martinsville Glass Company began operations in New Martinsville, West Virginia, in 1901. The factory was rebuilt in 1907, after being destroyed by fire. New Martinsville produced a general line of glassware as well as numerous glass animals and figurines. In 1944, there was a change in management and the company was renamed Viking Glass Company.

Paden City Glass Company, Paden City, West Virginia. Paden City began operations in 1916, and was known as the "Color Company," having made colored glass from its inception. Paden City produced a general line of glassware as well as many fine glass animals and figurines. They produced many items from Barth Art molds. The company closed in 1951, and most of their molds were sold to Canton Glass Company of Marion, Indiana.

Pilgrim Glass Company, Ceredo, West Virginia, was founded in 1949 by Alfred E. Knabler, when he bought out a glass company in Huntington, West Virginia, and renamed it Pilgrim Glass Company. In 1956 he built a factory in Ceredo, West Virginia, and moved operations to the new location. When brothers Alessandro and Roberto Moretti came from Italy to work at Pilgrim in the 1950s, they introduced a Venetian style of animals and figurines. The factory ceased operations in 2002.

Rainbow Glass Company, Huntington, West Virginia. Established in 1939, Rainbow was primarily a decorating company who purchased glassware from other companies and applied various decorations. They became a subsidiary of Viking Glass Company in 1954, and continued operations until 1972, when they closed.

L.E. Smith Glass Company, Mt. Pleasant, Pennsylvania, was founded in 1907. Lewis E. Smith, a chef in Mt. Pleasant, is credited with Smith's early beginning, operating from the old deserted Anchor Glass factory and making utilitarian glass products. The company is credited with making the first automobile headlight lens, the non-glare headlights, and "vault lights" — those translucent bricks that allow the light but not the image to shine through. They have made a number of animals and figurines throughout the years of production. In 1979, Libbey-Owens Ford became the new owner. The company remains in business today.

Steuben Glass Works, Corning, New York. Named after Steuben County in which it is located, Steuben was founded by Frederick Carder, who manufactured beautiful colored glass in Art Nouveau style. Steuben has been a division of Corning Glass Works since 1918. Since 1933, Steuben's glass production is primarily in clear lead crystal. Their operations continue today, producing superior quality lead crystal items.

Summit Art Glass Company, Ravenna, Ohio, was founded by Russell and Joann Vogelsong, in 1972. Many of the Summit-owned glass molds were purchased from defunct glass companies such as St. Clair Glass Works, Westmoreland, Imperial, Tiffin, and Cambridge. Summit produces novelty glass as well as a number of animals and figurals.

Tiffin Glass Company, Tiffin, Ohio. On January 1, 1892, A.J. Beatty & Sons joined 15 other companies to comprise U.S. Glass Company of Pittsburgh, Pennsylvania, and became known as Tiffin Glass Company (Factory "R") of The U.S. Glass Company, Tiffin, Ohio. In 1955, the Duncan & Miller Glass Company of Washington, Pennsylvania, became the Duncan & Miller Division of the U.S. Glass Company, Tiffin, Ohio. The move involved relocation of a large number of molds, as well as some of the Duncan workers. Tiffin produced general line glassware including some excellent animals and figurines until the factory closed in 1963.

Viking Glass Company, New Martinsville, West Virginia. In 1944, under new management, the New Martinsville Glass Company became the Viking Glass Company. The now famous Epic Line was introduced in many brilliant colors. Many other highly collectible animals and figurines, other than the Epic Line, were produced. The factory closed in 1986.

Westmoreland Glass Company, Grapeville, Pennsylvania. Westmoreland was originally known as Westmoreland Specialty Company, producing condiment jars and the condiments as well. In 1925 Westmoreland dropped the word "Specialty" and became known as the Westmoreland Glass Company, producing a general line of glassware. Westmoreland made a wide variety of covered animal dishes in slag and a variety of colors. They made a variety of animals and figurines during their years of operation. Westmoreland closed in 1984.

L.G. Wright Glass Company was started by Si Wright, in the mid- to late 1930s, when he started acquiring glass molds from defunct glass companies and then contracting with various glass companies to have items made. The company operated until 1999, at which time the molds were sold at public auction. The molds are now scattered around the globe.

Glass Museums

When planning to visit a museum it is always a good idea to call ahead and confirm the hours of operation.

National Cambridge Glass Museum, 136 South Ninth St., Cambridge, OH 43725, (740) 432-4245. Museum open April through October, Wednesday through Saturday, 9:00 a.m. to 4:00 p.m. and Sunday noon to 4:00 p.m., closed Easter and July 4.

Duncan and Miller Glass Museum, 525 Jefferson Avenue, Washington, PA 15301, (724) 225-9950. Museum open from April 1 to October 31, Thursday through Sunday 11:00 a.m. to 4:00 p.m.

Fenton Glass Museum, 700 Elizabeth Street, Williamstown, WV 26187, (304) 375-6122. Museum open January to March, Monday through Friday, 8:00 a.m. to 5:00 p.m. March through December, Sunday 12:00 noon to 5:00 p.m., Monday through Friday, 8:00 a.m. to 8:00 p.m. and Saturday 8:00 a.m. to 5:00 p.m. Contact for times of glass factory tours.

Fostoria Glass Museum, 6th Street and Tomlinson, Moundsville, WV 26041, (304) 845-9188. Museum open Thursday through Sunday, 1:00 p.m. to 4:00 p.m.

National Heisey Glass Museum, 169 West Church Street, Newark, OH 43055, (740) 345-9638. Museum open Tuesday through Saturday, 10:00 a.m. to 4:00 p.m. and Sunday 1:00 p.m. to 4:00 p.m.

National Imperial Glass Museum, 3210 Belmont Street, Bellaire, OH 43906, (740) 671-3971. Museum open April 1 to October 31. Wednesday through Saturday 10:00 a.m. to 4:00 p.m. Closed holidays.

Tiffin Glass Museum, 25 South Washington Street, Tiffin, OH 44883, PH (419) 448-0200. Museum open Tuesday through Saturday 1:00 p.m. to 5:00 p.m. To schedule tours, please call the museum.

Bibliography

Books

Bennett, Harold and Judy. *The Cambridge Glass Book*. Des Moines, IA: Wallace-Homestead Co., 1970.

Bickenheuser, Fred. *Tiffin Glassmasters, Book II*. Grove City, OH: Glassmaster Publications, 1981.

________. *Tiffin Glassmasters, Book III*. Grove City, OH: Glassmasters Publications, 1985.

Bredehoft, Neila. *The Collector's Encyclopedia of Heisey Glass 1925 – 1938*. Paducah, KY: Heisey Collectors of America, Inc., Collector Books, 1986.

Coe, Debbie and Randy. *Glass Animals & Figurines*. Atglen, PA: Schiffer Publishing, Ltd., 2003.

Courter, J.W. *Aladdin Electric Lamps*. Wallace-Homestead Company, 1971.

Edwards, Bill and Mike Carwile. *Standard Encyclopedia of Carnival Glass, 8th Edition*. Paducah, KY: Collector Books, 2002.

The Fenton Art Glass Collectors of America, Inc. *Caught in the Butterfly Net*, compilation of articles edited by Ferill J. Rice and LaVeria McMichael, 1991.

Ferson, Regis F. and Mary F. *Yesterday's Milk Glass Today*. published by authors, 1981.

Florence, Gene. *A Collector's Encyclopedia of Akro Agate Glassware*. Paducah, KY: Collector Books, 1975.

Gallagher, Jerry. *A Handbook of Old Morgantown Glass*. Minneapolis, MN: Merit Printing, 1995.

Garrison, Myrna and Bob. *Milk Glass Imperial Glass Corporation*. Atglen, PA: Schiffer Publishing, Ltd., 2001.

Grizel, Ruth. *American Slag Glass, Identification and Values*. Paducah, KY: Collector Books, 1998.

Heacock, William. *Fenton Glass, the First Twenty Five Years*. Marietta, OH: O-Val Advertising Corp, 1978.

________. *Fenton Glass, the Second Twenty Five Years*. Marietta, OH: O-Val Advertising Corp, 1980.

________. *Fenton Glass, the Third Twenty Five Years*. Marietta, OH: O-Val Advertising Corp, 1989.

Hotchkiss, John F. *Carders Steuben Glass Handbook and Price Guide*. Pittsford, NY: Hotchkiss House Inc., 1972.

Kikeli, Paul and Hahn, Frank L. *Collectors Guide to Heisey and Heisey by Imperial Glass Animals*. Lima, OH: Golden Era Publications, 1991.

Kovar, Lorraine. *Westmoreland Glass, 1950 – 1984*. Antique Publications, 1971.

________. *Westmoreland Glass, 1950 – 1984, Vol. II*. Antique Publications, 1991.

Krause, Gail. *The Years of Duncan 1865 – 1955*. Heyworth, IL: Heyworth Star, 1980.

Long, Milbra, and Emily Seate. *Fostoria Tableware 1944 – 1946*. Paducah, KY: Collector Books, 1999.

________. *Fostoria, Useful & Ornamental, The Crystal for America*. Paducah, KY: Collector Books, 2000.

Measell, James. *New Martinsville Glass, 1900 – 1944*. Marietta, OH: Antique Publications, 1994.

Measell, James, Editor, National Imperial Glass Collectors Society. *Imperial Glass Encyclopedia, Vol. I, A – Cane*. The Glass Press, Inc., dba, Antique Publications, 1995.

Miller, Everett and Addie R. *The New Martinsville Glass Story.* Marietta, OH: Richardson Publishing Co., 1972.

________. *The New Martinsville Glass Story, Book II, 1920 – 1950.* Manchester, MI: Rymack Printing Co., 1975.

National Cambridge Collectors, Inc. *Cambridge Glass 1930 – 1934.* Paducah, KY: Collector Books, 1978.

________. *Colors in Cambridge Glass.* Paducah, KY: Collector Books, 1984.

Newbound, Betty and Bill. *Collector's Encyclopedia of Milk Glass.* Paducah, KY: Collector Books, 1995.

O'Kane, Kelly. *Tiffin Glassmasters, the Modern Years.* Kelly O'Kane, 1998.

Over, Naomi L. *Ruby Glass of the 20th Century.* Antique Publications, 1990.

Pelt, Mary Van and Wanda Huffman. *Animal Kingdom in Treasured Glass.* Authors, 1972.

Pelt, Mary Van. *Fantastic Figurines.* Author, 1973.

________. *Figurines in Crystal.* Author, 1975.

Pina, Leslie. *Depression Era Glass by Duncan.* Schiffer Publications, Ltd., 1999.

________. *Popular '50s & '60s Glass, Color Along the River,* Atglen, PA: Schiffer Publishing Ltd., 1995.

Pina, Leslie and Jerry Gallagher. *Tiffin Glass, 1914 – 1940.* Atglen, PA: Schiffer Publishing, Ltd., 1996.

Smith, Bill and Phyllis. *Cambridge Glass 1927 – 1929.* 1986.

Stout, Sandra McPhee. *The Complete Book of McKee Glass,* N. Kansas City, MO: Trojan Press, 1972.

Toohey, Marlena. *A Collector's Guide to Black Glass.* Antique Publications, 1988.

Weatherman, Hazel Marie. *Colored Glassware of the Depression Era 2.* Springfield, MO: A Glassbook Production, 1974.

Weitman, Stan and Arlene. *Crackle Glass Identification & Value Guide.* Paducah, KY: Collector Books, 1996.

________. *Crackle Glass Identification & Value Guide, Book II.* Paducah, KY: Collector Books, 1998.

Welker, Lynn, Mary and Lyle. *Cambridge, Ohio Glass in Color, Book II.* Parkersburg, WV: Pappas Brothers, 1973.

Whitmyer, Margaret and Kenn. *Bedroom & Bathroom Glassware of the Depression Years.* Paducah, KY: Collector Books, 1990.

________. *Fenton Art Glass, 1907 – 1939, Identification & Value Guide, Second Edition.* Paducah, KY: Collector Books, 2003.

Wilson, Charles West. *Westmoreland Glass Identification and Value Guide.* Paducah, KY: Collector Books, 1996.

Wilson, Jack D. *Phoenix and Consolidated Art Glass, 1926 – 1980.* Antique Publications, 1989.

Zemel, Evelyn. *American Glass Animals A to Z.* Author.

Newsletters and Periodicals

Antique Publications. *Glass Collectors Digest.*
Fenton Art Glass Collectors, Inc. *The Butterfly Net.*
Grizel, Ruth. *The Glass Animal Bulletin.*
Heisey Collectors of America, Inc. *Heisey News.*
National Cambridge Collectors, Inc. *Cambridge Crystal Ball.*
Shaeffer, Barbara. *Glass Review.*
Steele, Teri. *The Daze, Inc.*
Tiffin Glass Collectors Club Newsletter. *Tiffin Glassmasters.*

Factory Catalogs

At Home in Any Home, Imperial Glass, by Lenox, 1979.
"Cathay Crystal" designed by Virginia B. Evans, Bellaire Glass Festival, 1981 booklet.
China Glass & Tablewares, June 1956.
Dalzell-Viking Catalog, 1990 – 91, "An American Tradition in Glass Since 1884."
Handcrafted Imperial Glass, 1975 – 76.
Imperial Glass Corporation, Bellaire, OH, 1974 – 75.
Imperial Glass by Lenox, 1978.
Imperial Glass, 1966.
Imperial Glass by Lenox 1980.
Kanawha Glass Catalog, 1976, Dunbar, WV.
Kanawha Glass Catalog, 1980 – 81.
Kanawha Glass Catalog, Supplement, 1977.
L.E. Smith, Glass 1982, for the Antique Trade.
L.E. Smith, 1980, Supplement.
Mosser Glass Inc., 1984, Cambridge, OH.
Pilgrim Glass, 1976 – 77, Kitchen Chemistry.
Steuben Glass, 1980 – 81, Catalog.
Summit Art Glass, Ravenna, OH.
Viking Catalog 1980 – 81, Handmade American Glass, Mount Pleasant, PA.

4719 Fostoria, Etched, Carved & Cut Designs, Vol. II, Kerr $24.95
5261 Fostoria Tableware, 1924 – 1943, Long/Seate....$24.95
5361 Fostoria Tableware, 1944 – 1986, Long/Seate....$24.95
5604 Fostoria, Useful & Ornamental, Long/Seate....$29.95
5899 Glass & Ceramic Baskets, White $19.95
4644 Imperial Carnival Glass, Burns....$18.95
5827 Kitchen Glassware of the Depression Years, 6th Ed., Florence $24.95
5600 Much More Early American Pattern Glass, Metz....$17.95
5915 Northwood Carnival Glass, 1908 – 1925, Burns $19.95
6136 Pocket Guide to Depression Glass, 13th Ed., Florence....$12.95
6023 Standard Encyclopedia of Carnival Glass, 8th Ed., Edwards/Carwile....$29.95
6024 Standard Carnival Glass Price Guide, 13th Ed., Edwards/Carwile....$9.95
6035 Standard Encyclopedia of Opalescent Glass, 4rd Ed., Edwards/Carwile....$24.95
4732 Very Rare Glassware of the Depression Years, 5th Series, Florence....$24.95

POTTERY

4927 ABC Plates & Mugs, Lindsay....$24.95
4929 American Art Pottery, Sigafoose $24.95
4630 American Limoges, Limoges....$24.95
1312 Blue & White Stoneware, McNerney....$9.95
1959 Blue Willow, 2nd Ed., Gaston....$14.95
4851 Collectible Cups & Saucers, Harran $18.95
1373 Collector's Encyclopedia of American Dinnerware, Cunningham $24.95
4931 Collector's Encyclopedia of Bauer Pottery, Chipman $24.95
5034 Collector's Encyclopedia of California Pottery, 2nd Ed., Chipman....$24.95
3723 Collector's Encyclopedia of Cookie Jars, Book II, Roerig....$24.95
4939 Collector's Encyclopedia of Cookie Jars, Book III, Roerig....$24.95
5748 Collector's Encyclopedia of Fiesta, 9th Ed., Huxford....$24.95
3961 Collector's Encyclopedia of Early Noritake, Alden....$24.95
3812 Collector's Encyclopedia of Flow Blue China, 2nd Ed., Gaston....$24.95
3431 Collector's Encyclopedia of Homer Laughlin China, Jasper....$24.95
1276 Collector's Encyclopedia of Hull Pottery, Roberts....$19.95
3962 Collector's Encyclopedia of Lefton China, DeLozier $19.95
4855 Collector's Encyclopedia of Lefton China, Book II, DeLozier....$19.95
5609 Collector's Encyclopedia of Limoges Porcelain, 3rd Ed., Gaston $29.95
2334 Collector's Encyclopedia of Majolica Pottery, Katz-Marks....$19.95
1358 Collector's Encyclopedia of McCoy Pottery, Huxford $19.95
5677 Collector's Encyclopedia of Niloak, 2nd Edition, Gifford $29.95
3837 Collector's Encyclopedia of Nippon Porcelain, Van Patten $24.95
1665 Collector's Ency. of Nippon Porcelain, 3rd Series, Van Patten $24.95
5053 Collector's Ency. of Nippon Porcelain, 5th Series, Van Patten....$24.95
5678 Collector's Ency. of Nippon Porcelain, 6th Series, Van Patten....$29.95
1447 Collector's Encyclopedia of Noritake, Van Patten....$19.95
5564 Collector's Encyclopedia of Pickard China, Reed....$29.95
5679 Collector's Encyclopedia of Red Wing Art Pottery, Dollen $24.95
5618 Collector's Encyclopedia of Rosemeade Pottery, Dommel $24.95
5841 Collector's Encyclopedia of Roseville Pottery, Revised, Huxford/Nickel.... $24.95
5842 Collector's Encyclopedia of Roseville Pottery, 2nd Series, Huxford/Nickel $24.95
5917 Collector's Encyclopedia of Russel Wright, 3rd Editon, Kerr $29.95
5370 Collector's Encyclopedia of Stangl Dinnerware, Runge....$24.95
5921 Collector's Encyclopedia of Stangl Artware, Lamps, and Birds, Runge $29.95
3314 Collector's Encyclopedia of Van Briggle Art Pottery, Sasicki $24.95
5680 Collector's Guide to Feather Edge Ware, McAllister....$19.95
3876 Collector's Guide to Lu-Ray Pastels, Meehan....$18.95
3814 Collector's Guide to Made in Japan Ceramics, White....$18.95
4646 Collector's Guide to Made in Japan Ceramics, Book II, White $18.95
1425 Cookie Jars, Westfall....$9.95
3440 Cookie Jars, Book II, Westfall....$19.95
5909 Dresden Porcelain Studios, Harran....$29.95
5918 Florence's Big Book of Salt & Pepper Shakers....$24.95
2379 Lehner's Ency. of U.S. Marks on Pottery, Porcelain & China....$24.95
4722 McCoy Pottery, Collector's Reference & Value Guide, Hanson/Nissen....$19.95
5913 McCoy Pottery, Volume III, Hanson & Nissen....$24.95
5691 Post86 Fiesta, Identification & Value Guide, Racheter....$19.95
1670 Red Wing Collectibles, DePasquale $9.95
1440 Red Wing Stoneware, DePasquale $9.95
6037 Rookwood Pottery, Nicholson & Thomas....$24.95
1632 Salt & Pepper Shakers, Guarnaccia $9.95
5091 Salt & Pepper Shakers II, Guarnaccia $18.95
3443 Salt & Pepper Shakers IV, Guarnaccia $18.95
3738 Shawnee Pottery, Mangus....$24.95
4629 Turn of the Century American Dinnerware, 1880s–1920s, Jasper....$24.95
3327 Watt Pottery – Identification & Value Guide, Morris $19.95
5924 Zanesville Stoneware Company, Rans, Ralston & Russell....$24.95

OTHER COLLECTIBLES

5916 Advertising Paperweights, Holiner & Kammerman....$24.95
5838 Advertising Thermometers, Merritt....$16.95
5898 Antique & Contemporary Advertising Memorabilia, Summers $24.95
5814 Antique Brass & Copper Collectibles, Gaston $24.95
1880 Antique Iron, McNerney $9.95
3872 Antique Tins, Dodge....$24.95
4845 Antique Typewriters & Office Collectibles, Rehr....$19.95
5607 Antiquing and Collecting on the Internet, Parry $12.95
1128 Bottle Pricing Guide, 3rd Ed., Cleveland....$7.95
3718 Collectible Aluminum, Grist $16.95
5060 Collectible Souvenir Spoons, Bednersh $19.95
5676 Collectible Souvenir Spoons, Book II, Bednersh $29.95
5666 Collector's Encyclopedia of Granite Ware, Book 2, Greguire $29.95
5836 Collector's Guide to Antique Radios, 5th Ed., Bunis $19.95
3966 Collector's Guide to Inkwells, Identification & Values, Badders $18.95
4947 Collector's Guide to Inkwells, Book II, Badders $19.95
5681 Collector's Guide to Lunchboxes, White....$19.95
5621 Collector's Guide to Online Auctions, Hix $12.95
4864 Collector's Guide to Wallace Nutting Pictures, Ivankovich....$18.95
5683 Fishing Lure Collectibles, Vol. 1, Murphy/Edmisten $29.95
5911 Flea Market Trader, 13th Ed., Huxford $9.95
6227 Garage Sale & Flea Market Annual, 11th Edition, Huxford $19.95
4945 G-Men and FBI Toys and Collectibles, Whitworth....$18.95
3819 General Store Collectibles, Wilson $24.95
5912 The Heddon Legacy, A Century of Classic Lures, Roberts & Pavey $29.95
2216 Kitchen Antiques, 1790–1940, McNerney....$14.95
5991 Lighting Devices & Accessories of the 17th – 19th Centuries, Hamper....$9.95
5686 Lighting Fixtures of the Depression Era, Book I, Thomas....$24.95
4950 The Lone Ranger, Collector's Reference & Value Guide, Felbinger....$18.95
6028 Modern Fishing Lure Collectibles, Vol. 1, Lewis....$24.95
6131 Modern Fishing Lure Collectibles, Vol. 2, Lewis....$24.95
2026 Railroad Collectibles, 4th Ed., Baker....$14.95
5619 Roy Rogers and Dale Evans Toys & Memorabilia, Coyle....$24.95
6137 Schroeder's Antiques Price Guide, 21st Edition $14.95
5007 Silverplated Flatware, Revised 4th Edition, Hagan $18.95
6239 Star Wars Super Collector's Wish Book, 2nd Ed., Carlton $29.95
6139 Summers' Guide to Coca-Cola, 4th Ed....$24.95
5905 Summers' Pocket Guide to Coca-Cola, 3rd Ed....$12.95
3977 Value Guide to Gas Station Memorabilia, Summers & Priddy $24.95
4877 Vintage Bar Ware, Visakay....$24.95
5925 The Vintage Era of Golf Club Collectibles, John $29.95
6010 The Vintage Era of Golf Club Collectibles Collector's Log, John $9.95
6036 Vintage Quilts, Aug, Newman & Roy....$24.95
4935 The W.F. Cody Buffalo Bill Collector's Guide with Values....$24.95

This is only a partial listing of the books on antiques that are available from Collector Books. All books are well illustrated and contain current values. Most of these books are available from your local bookseller, antique dealer, or public library. If you are unable to locate certain titles in your area, you may order by mail from COLLECTOR BOOKS, P.O. Box 3009, Paducah, KY 42002-3009. Customers with Visa, Master Card, or Discover may phone in orders from 7:00–5:00 CT, Monday–Friday, Toll Free 1-800-626-5420, or online at www.collectorbooks.com. Add $3.00 for postage for the first book ordered and 50¢ for each additional book. Include item number, title, and price when ordering. Allow 14 to 21 days for delivery.

1-800-626-5420 Fax: 1-270-898-8890

www.collectorbooks.com

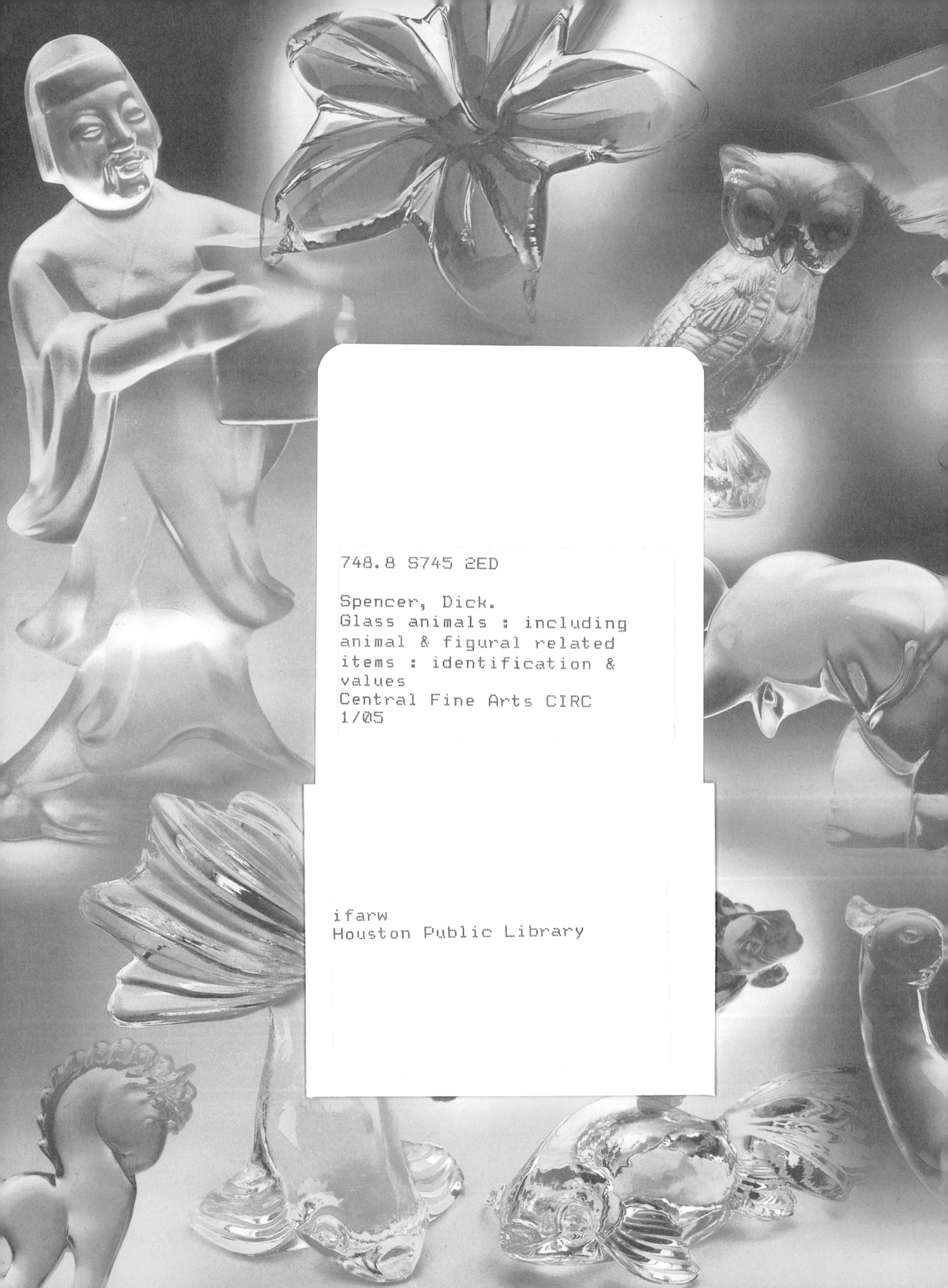